GLASS CEILINGS and IVORY TOWERS

GLASS CEILINGS

and

IVORY TOWERS

Gender Inequality in the Canadian Academy

Edited by
RACHAEL JOHNSTONE and BESSMA MOMANI

UBCPress · Vancouver

UBC Press is a Benetech Global Certified Accessible™ publisher. The epub version of this book meets stringent accessibility standards, ensuring it is available to people with diverse needs.

Printed in Canada on FSC-certified ancient-forest-free paper (100% post-consumer recycled) that is processed chlorine- and acid-free.

Library and Archives Canada Cataloguing in Publication

Title: Glass ceilings and ivory towers : gender inequality in the Canadian academy / edited by Rachael John+stone and Bessma Momani.

Names: Johnstone, Rachael, editor. | Momani, Bessma, editor.

Description: Includes bibliographical references and index.

Identifiers: Canadiana (print) 20230587348 | Canadiana (ebook) 20230587399 | ISBN 9780774869249 (hardcover) | ISBN 9780774869256 (softcover) | ISBN 9780774869263 (PDF) | ISBN 9780774869270 (EPUB)

Subjects: LCSH: Sex discrimination in higher education—Canada. | LCSH: Women in higher education—Canada. | LCSH: Glass ceiling (Employment discrimination)—Canada.

Classification: LCC LC212.863.C3 G53 2024 | DDC 378.00820971—dc23

Canada Council Conseil des arts
for the Arts du Canada

Canadä

BRITISH COLUMBIA
ARTS COUNCIL

BRITISH
COLUMBIA

UBC Press gratefully acknowledges the financial support for our publishing program of the Government of Canada, the Canada Council for the Arts, and the British Columbia Arts Council.

This book has been published with the help of a grant from the Canadian Federation for the Humanities and Social Sciences, through the Scholarly Book Awards, using funds provided by the Social Sciences and Humanities Research Council of Canada.

UBC Press is situated on the traditional, ancestral, and unceded territory of the xʷməθkʷəy̓əm (Musqueam) people. This land has always been a place of learning for the xʷməθkʷəy̓əm, who have passed on their culture, history, and traditions for millennia, from one generation to the next.

UBC Press
The University of British Columbia
www.ubcpress.ca

Table of Contents

Acknowledgments

The contributions in this book are grounded in ideas first presented at a workshop in April 2020 that was meant to be hosted at the University of Waterloo but had to shift online because of the first COVID-19 lockdown. The disproportionate impact of the lockdown on women, especially those with young children, was apparent from our first sessions, as many of us attempted to give papers while keeping our children entertained off-screen (not always successfully) long enough to discuss our work. We are grateful to our contributors for their exceptional work and commitment to the project in the face of these and other pandemic-related hurdles as this volume developed. We are also thankful to the chairs and discussants from the workshop for their insightful comments on many earlier versions of the chapters, including Veronica Kitchen, Colleen Lewis, Lori Curtis, Margaret Walton-Roberts, Alison Mountz, Anna Drake, Howard Ramos, Rachel Caplan, Lynn Arner, Ana Ferrer, and Sarah Shoker.

We are thankful to our editor, Randy Schmidt, our two anonymous reviewers, and the editorial team at UBC Press, for their feedback and guidance throughout this process.

This publication would not have been possible without the dedicated administrative work and managerial guidance of Kersty Kearney, the glue who held our whole research team together with her passion for keeping us all organized and productive, and the contributions of talented research assistants Melanie Slimming, Nawroos Shibli, Lydia Callies, Yaseen Abdulhai, and Lauren V. Judge. The joy of our work as academics often comes from the loving interaction we have with these talented individuals.

This volume, and the workshop that motivated its creation, draw on the generous support of the Social Sciences and Humanities Research Council through both a Connection Grant and a Scholarly Book Award. We are also grateful to Dalhousie University, the Balsillie School of International Affairs, and the University of Manitoba for their additional financial support in the preparation of this volume.

Finally, we do not exaggerate when we say this undertaking would not have been possible without the support of our families and colleagues. Specific thanks are in order.

Rachael would like to thank her partner, Christopher. Since the original workshop organization began, her family of two became a family of four. Christopher, you defied every trend by proving that equal parenthood really is possible. Thank you for helping me salvage enough quiet moments to make this project a reality. And to you, Beckett and Garnet, who came into the picture while this volume was underway, although the sleepless nights were not exactly helpful to the writing and editing process, you two make everything worthwhile.

Bessma would like to thank the amazing women who have supported her in her academic career. There are too many great colleagues to list, and they know who they are, but she would like to acknowledge the support of two exceptional academic women in her life. Her fantastic mother-in-law, Dr. Hoda Elmaraghy, the first woman dean of engineering in North America who has been a trailblazer in her academic field and an inspiring role model to Bessma and countless other women in STEM and beyond. Bessma would also like to thank Dr. Charmaine B. Dean, a mentor who has guided her through the wonderful journey of senior administration and a true champion of equity, diversity, and inclusion, from supporting individual academics to promoting change at an institutional level.

GLASS CEILINGS and IVORY TOWERS

Introduction
Gender Inequality in the Canadian Academy

RACHAEL JOHNSTONE and BESSMA MOMANI

Canadian academia has a serious gender problem. Although women have made up a majority of the undergraduate student body for decades, only 31 percent of faculty who self-identify as women[1] are full professors and only 44 percent are associate professors (Statistics Canada 2022a). Women only reached parity as assistant professors in 2020 and continue to be underrepresented in certain disciplines, especially the most lucrative ones (Statistics Canada 2022a). The STEM (science, technology, engineering, and math) fields have the lowest proportion of women undergraduate students, graduate students, and faculty compared to all other disciplines (Council of Canadian Academies 2012). Due to poor representation at the lower rungs of academic administration, fewer women are appointed to academic leadership positions, and those that occupy such positions face gender-specific challenges.[2] Women who are appointed deans in Canada are less likely than men to be reappointed (Lavigne 2020) and the percentage of women among university presidents in Canada has stagnated since the mid-1990s at around 20 percent (Turpin, De Decker, and Boyd 2014). The situation for racialized women is worse. A 2019 study of five major Canadian universities showed racialized women occupying 7.1 percent of associate dean roles, 2.3 percent of deanships, and 2.4 percent of senior executive roles (Johnson et al. 2020). Moreover, even when women do enter high-level leadership positions, they are more likely to be paid less than men (Momani, Dreher, and Williams 2019) and are more likely than men to quit or be fired before the end of their term (Chiose 2016). Given that 30 percent of the senior management positions in the corporate world are held by women, this poor showing in academia is especially alarming (Zippia 2022; McKinsey 2022).

The reasons for women's underrepresentation in academia are manifold. There is ample evidence that women academics face systemic disadvantages in trying to secure funding (Wenneras and Wold 1997), placing peer-reviewed publications in high-ranking journals (Bendels and Muller 2018), having their work cited by colleagues (Ferber and Brün 2011; Larivière et al. 2013), and attaining high teaching scores (MacNell, Driscoll, and Hunt 2015; Mitchell and Martin 2018), all of which inhibit their ability to land coveted tenure-track positions. Moreover, even if they secure a faculty position, academics who are women are more likely to have lower starting salaries (Perna 2001) and to be pressured to take on a disproportionate amount of service work in their departments (Mitchell and Hesli 2013), work that is undervalued in tenure and promotions.[3] As these uneven service expectations illustrate, universities are not insulated from the gendered expectations of care work experienced in Canada more generally.

For women in academia who have young children, or are considering starting a family, the need to balance work and family life is a significant barrier to entering the professorate and thriving once there. In many respects, the demands placed on early-career academics, including the need to publish, network, apply for permanent positions, and secure tenure, are especially ill-suited to accommodating family life. These demands often come at a time when women are having children or thinking about having children (Schoening 2009), leading some women to opt out of academia entirely (Canetto et al. 2017). One study of women graduate students (Mason, Wolfinger, and Goulden 2013, 43) found a high proportion of those surveyed believe a job in academia and family life are "incompatible."[4]

Concerns about balancing family and work life are justified. Research consistently shows that men often benefit professionally from fatherhood while women in academia who have children contend with "lower promotion rates, high exit patterns and personal vicissitudes such as family breakdowns and divorce" (Troeger and Epifanio 2019, 109). Research utilizing a large database of PhD recipients in the United States, for example, found that women who became mothers as graduate students were half as likely to land a tenure-track position compared to men (Mason and Goulden 2002). They also found that women who attain tenure are more likely not to have children compared to men.[5] For those who chose to remain in academia, the strain of managing care responsibilities pushes many women with PhDs to become either part-time or sessional instructors, positions that are both poorly remunerated and precarious (Canetto et al. 2017). In Canada, women and racialized people are more likely to hold these positions (see Acker and Muzin 2019).[6]

The "baby gap" in academia is both gendered and glaring (Mason and Goulden 2002). Added care responsibilities and expected norms around motherhood, coupled with a lack of support and an environment of high competition (Pedersen and Minnotte 2017), often leave women faculty stressed (Wilton and Ross 2017), prompting more women than men to leave academia.[7] The challenge of finding a work-life balance continues to exhaust women in academia (Wilton and Ross 2017), a reality aggravated by the COVID-19 pandemic, which forced many women with young children to take on more of the care responsibilities in their households. Studies are now being published that demonstrate what many women with children or eldercare in academia already knew; namely, women were less likely to publish during the pandemic lockdowns when compared to their men counterparts (King and Frederickson 2021; Davis et al. 2022).

Many of the above barriers, and the lack of progress in redressing them, are rooted in gender discrimination. As environmental historian Troy Vettese (2019) explains, sexism and misogyny are reinforced at all levels of academic institutions, from the more banal practices of men supervisors asking women researchers, but not men, to repeat their lab tests to outright sexual harassment in the workplace. The challenges faced by women who are further marginalized because of other factors, including their race, age, and ability, compound this discrimination (see, e.g., Henry et al. 2017; Guitiérrez y Muhs et al. 2012; Johnson and Howsam 2020; Lazos 2012). Sizeism, a prejudice against people based on their size, and other forms of discrimination based on people's appearance, is also part of the toxic misogyny that is prevalent against women working in intellectual pursuits (see Manthey 2017). In short, despite their reputation as some of Canada's most progressive institutions, universities continue to have gender issues at every level.[8]

While significant research on women in academia has been undertaken, particularly in the United States and Europe, the results have been siloed by disciplinary boundaries. Much of this research has also taken the form of narrative and first-hand accounts (see, e.g., Gutiérrez y Muhs et al. 2012; Shelton et al. 2018; Chilly Collective 1995). These accounts are valuable for their ability to "emphasize the personal as being both political and worthy of academic attention" (Shelton et al. 2018, 208) and to highlight the human cost of discrimination, but they often lack the hard numbers and robust science-backed figures necessary to convince some in the profession to commit to institutional change. Our book fills this significant research gap by taking an in-depth look at Canadian academia from a range of disciplinary perspectives and methodologies. The chapters that follow are primarily rooted in data-driven research focusing on the ongoing challenges women in academia face and, in so doing, lay the groundwork for substantive policy change in Canada.

This book brings together academics from different disciplines and at different stages of their careers studying gender in Canadian universities. Our goal is to explore intersections and new ways of interpreting trends in Canadian data to identify core themes and issues and proffer best practice recommendations for women, administrators, and stakeholders in academia. In the chapters that follow, our authors outline academia's gender problems, consider which women are being counted, explore the role of women as academic leaders, and reflect on strategies for positive change. Through these lines of inquiry, we focus our attention on showcasing evidence-based research. We have taken this approach for two reasons. First, it is rare for a collection on women in Canadian academia to foreground evidence-based research. While such autobiographical narratives found in many other volumes are valuable, we believe that a collection employing quantitative and qualitative data analysis is a necessary catalyst for public debate and policy action (Momani, Dreher, and Williams 2019; Shelton, Flynn, and Grosland 2018; Black and Garvis 2018; Lemon and Garvis 2014). This focus seems especially relevant as Canadian universities are currently undergoing radical changes in their consideration of equity, diversity, and inclusion (EDI), including developing best practices in how to talk about, prepare for, and address systemic discrimination on campuses. Second, there is a persistent complacency concerning the advancement of women in Canadian academia (Momani, Dreher, and Williams 2019; Acker, Webber, and Smyth 2012, 753), with many people mistakenly concluding that issues related to women's advancement have been resolved or will resolve themselves given sufficient time. A common refrain is the presentation of these challenges as a pipeline problem that will self-correct when an adequate supply of women at lower ranks of the academy is attained. Yet, despite improvements to representation at the lower rungs, the lack of representation of women in the most coveted and respected professions of the academy, including full professors, senior administrators, and Canada Research Chairs, suggests that the pipeline is broken and reflects important features of oppression within society at large. In *The Equity Myth*, which focuses on racism in Canadian universities, anthropologist Frances Henry, one of Canada's leading experts in the study of racism and anti-racism, and her colleagues assert that universities represent "a bastion of liberal democracy that enjoys a popular image of an institution free in the pursuit of knowledge, avant-garde in thinking, and fair in practice" (Henry et al. 2017, 3). The authors contend that the internalization of this myth leads to unsubstantiated acceptance of the idea that racism, and we would add sexism and misogyny, do not exist within these institutions. The myth that universities are sites of progressive policies because their faculty ostensibly hold progressive views is unsupported by the evidence we present in this volume. As such, highlighting evidence-based research adds force to our outputs by allowing us to repudiate the cultures of denial that perpetuate gender inequality.

This book is notable because it is a Canada-specific volume. Of the many titles on gender and women in the academy, there are relatively few that emphasize the struggles faced by women in Canadian universities (exceptions include Whittaker 2015; Wagner, Acker, and Mayuzumi 2008; Reimer 2004; Chilly Collective 1995). Our book focuses on gender in Canadian academia and collects Canada-specific data from multiple universities of differing sizes and types across the country. We intend for this collection to deepen scholarly understandings of how women experience academia and the factors preventing them from fully participating at all levels of academic life. Given the size and significance of the research and policy gaps that exist about women academics, this book only scratches the surface of the topic of women and gender in Canadian academia.

Our overarching goal in this volume is to launch a national and interdisciplinary conversation to better understand, and thereby more effectively address, the persistent gender imbalance among academics at Canadian universities. This imbalance is apparent in easily measurable categories, like the number of women in specific roles and their salaries, and in more elusive but equally critical metrics, like perceptions of respect and safety. By bringing together researchers for an interdisciplinary exchange, these chapters collectively portray the current gendered situation of faculty and administrators working in Canadian academia and highlight its significance, with an aim to develop strategies to increase the status, participation, and leadership of women academics.

Before laying out the plan of this book, we need to be clear about our terminology. Our book's title suggests a focus on gender in the academy, but we, and many of our contributors, often use terminology related to sex and gender interchangeably. In its simplest form, sex refers to a biological difference, which is typically treated as binary (e.g., male/female), while gender refers to the characteristics often tied to sex (e.g., masculinity and femininity). In everyday parlance, and a significant array of institutional and government documentation, these terms are treated as synonyms, and there is little room to identify outside of this binary. For example, some of the data collected in this book uses official Canadian government statistics that only allow binary male/female designations. Reducing gender to sex assigned at birth strips important statistical information about variations in gender among individuals. This is most obviously true of transgender and nonbinary people, whose assigned sex at birth is not reflective of their gender identity. This leads to consequences ranging from loss of entire analytical categories (e.g., variations of nonbinary identities) to misidentification of a portion of the population (e.g., identifying trans women as male). Loss of categories and misattributions tend to bias data findings and mask the lived realities of people who typically experience more discrimination and lower economic outcomes than cisgender people.[9] Capturing important nuances to conduct a comprehensive intersectional analysis of gender in academia is further complicated by the challenges of collecting relevant data that accounts for multiple, interlocking, and cocompounding identities, including race, class, ability, and age (see Acker and Muzin 2019; Henry et al. 2017; Kitossa and Tanyildiz 2022 for work on gender and race in universities).

The concepts of sex and gender are the subjects of a vast literature. Although a more thorough discussion of the literature problematizing these terms is beyond the scope of this collection, and the contributors to this volume were free to use and pursue their own terminology to best capture the nature of their particular studies, it is worth pointing out that the differences between these terms are highly personal, political, and contested. Even though some of our data are limited in this capacity, we are still able to draw significant conclusions about the ongoing significance of gender in the academy, while highlighting fruitful areas for future research.

In the same vein, we recognize that the terms used to describe discrimination based on gender, in particular inequality and inequity, are themselves disputed. The distinction between equality and equity is often portrayed as one of sameness of treatment (equality) versus differential treatment to help individuals achieve the same ends (equity). Like the terminology of sex and gender, these terms are political, and their ongoing use has been shaped by their past application, both in Canada and abroad. However, the use of these terms is more streamlined in Canada than in other locales. Guarantees of equality are part of Canada's constitution and have been consistently interpreted in substantive terms. That is, guarantees of equality do not require that the government must or even should treat people the same in all cases; indeed, "sometimes protecting equality means that we must adapt rules or standards to take account of people's differences" (Department of Justice 2018). Thus, there are few practical differences in the ways that equality and equity are differentiated and legally applied in Canada. Although we did not seek to impose this language on our contributors, whose varied disciplinary backgrounds bring nuances to these terms, we draw attention to the implications of this language to highlight and contextualize further the arguments of our contributors.

PLAN OF THE BOOK

This volume contains thirteen chapters divided into four parts, which move from a micro to macro perspective. Although data is crucial to compel policy change, we also recognize that an overreliance on data risks obscuring the lived experiences of the very individuals whose plight we wish to showcase. In the hopes of humanizing the data we bring to the table, each of the four sections is introduced by a brief vignette, and a final vignette closes out the volume. These vignettes are personal accounts from academics, university staff, and an academic recruiter who reflect on their individual struggles, share their observations, and remind us of the realities of the personal, professional, and intellectual struggle to achieve equality.

Part 1 examines the daily life of women academics as they balance their roles as instructors, researchers, and service providers. Here we explore issues including the gendered implications of contract teaching and teaching evaluations and the unique challenges faced by women researchers in the ethics approval process. We also delve into the gendered dynamics of service work and its implications for tenure and promotion. Part 2 examines gendered dynamics within university leadership. As is true of the business world, the data show that the "glass ceiling" and, indeed, the "glass cliff" are ongoing problems within universities. This section takes a more holistic view of leadership, which includes the role of women as primary investigators in large-scale research projects as well as middle management and senior leadership in universities – from deans to presidents – to learn about ongoing challenges to women's representation and power. Part 3 looks at the broader structural and institutional challenges faced by women academics. Here, we investigate long-standing issues of racism and wage discrimination in the academy as well as the physical and psychological difficulties women academics must contend with, including harassment. Finally, Part 4 looks at approaches that are needed to change institutions and practices to make academia more equitable or, in some cases, to dismantle entire systems by levelling the playing field or completely reinventing the game. In this section, we look at alternative pedagogical practices, allyship models, and advocacy platforms that spotlight, navigate, and help mitigate the challenges faced by women academics. In so doing, we reconsider the approaches and ideas currently valued in academia, who is responsible to change these approaches and ideas, and what should be changed.

We begin with a vignette about the gendered challenges and expectations of a newly minted tenure-track professor. Andrea M. Collins explains how universities claim to want change, yet women like her continue to face tokenism. Then, in Chapter 1, Sandra Smele and Andrea Quinlan investigate the intersection of contract teaching and student evaluations, finding serious gender inequities. Numerous studies have demonstrated that student evaluations of teaching (SETs) reflect systemic biases against women academic instructors, especially those marginalized because of race, ethnicity, age, and ability. What is missing from this body of research is a look at the impact SETs have on instructors from equity-seeking groups who are working in contract positions. The precarity of nontenure-track and sessional instructors adds another layer of complexity to how gendered classrooms are experienced by vulnerable and marginalized academics. Contract teaching positions are on the rise in Canadian postsecondary institutions and women hold a higher percentage of these positions than men (see Webber 2008). This chapter questions how contract academic teaching and SETs contribute to the perpetuation of gender inequities in the academy. To this end, it employs thirty-four interviews with women employed in contract faculty positions at an Ontario university, arguing that SETs must be critically assessed for their negative impact.

In Chapter 2, Tanya Bandula-Irwin looks at gender and bias in research ethics approval processes. Fieldwork and the research ethics review processes are highly gendered. Ensuring that research and fieldwork abide by standards of ethics and participant safety are crucial for the integrity of academic research and yet it is noteworthy and concerning that women often have a more difficult time securing research ethics approvals than men. This fact, in turn, has implications for the types of research women scholars can or choose to perform. This chapter investigates where and when women scholars can conduct their research. Drawing on data from the research ethics boards of research-intensive universities across Canada, it explores the disparities among men and women in securing ethics approval for fieldwork.

Studies have shown that women faculty members, especially racialized women, often shoulder a larger amount of service responsibilities (Harley 2008). In Chapter 3, Jude Walker, Elena Ignatovich, and Maryam Nabavi examine university service work and its value in tenure and promotion processes. Looking specifically at language in tenure and promotion policies at U15 universities – a "collective of Canada's most research-intensive universities" (U15 n.d.) – this chapter lays out how service work is reported, recognized, and rewarded in tenure and promotion decisions at U15 universities. This chapter utilizes content analysis of U15 university policies on service and interviews with senior faculty to determine how service is conceptualized, recognized, and distributed. There is often a prioritization of institutional service at the expense of community-based service. These findings are then framed in relation to tenure and promotion policies across all U15 universities and best practices for recording and addressing service workload disparities (see O'Meara et al. 2018). Prioritizing some forms of service over others has gendered implications and the authors demonstrate how this often mirrors the ways women's care work is valued within society.

In Part 2, we examine the gendered dynamics of university leadership. We begin with a vignette by Amorell Saunders N'Daw, a professional recruiter who helps universities hire senior administrators. She reviews the challenges many women, especially racialized, Black, and Indigenous women, face in attaining these coveted positions. She argues that the F-word – fit – is too often used as an excuse by institutions failing at inclusion. In Chapter 4, Anne Wagner and Sandra Acker interrogate the gender dimensions of what is often framed as leadership in higher education. Moving beyond conventional understandings of leadership based on administrative and hierarchical structures, they focus on the relatively unexplored area of the leadership activity of principal investigators heading research projects. As part of a larger study of academic research work, Wagner and Acker conducted in-depth, qualitative interviews with twenty-four women scholars in education, social work, sociology, and geography at seven Ontario universities. Participants were chosen based on their substantial records of receiving external funding and their engagement with social justice topics as a means for investigating whether these commitments result in non-traditional forms of leadership. This chapter explores how these principal investigators understand leadership in the context of their research projects. Results suggest a tension between traditional hierarchical forms of leadership that are consistent with the logistics of neoliberal individualism found in the university and the approaches pursued by these leading researchers who prioritized collaboration, community, and caring in their social-justice related projects.

In Chapter 5, Rachael Johnstone and Bessma Momani look at the ways deanships in Canada continue to reflect gendered dynamics. Using both a country-wide survey and one-on-one interviews with university deans across Canada, this chapter seeks to understand whether men and women deans perceive gender to be an influential factor in the career paths of a dean and the extent to which their perceptions are supported by external data. Johnstone and Momani find that gender, as a variable, significantly influences perception divergences for two major survey areas: 1) opportunities to take on deanships and further advance into more senior administrative roles and 2) the wage gap. In both cases, women deans perceived gender to have a significant effect on opportunities and wages, while men did not. When corroborated with existing data, the authors find decisive evidence of the existence of the wage gap for deans. Although it is more difficult to make conclusive claims about opportunity, as the concept itself is not clear-cut and many of the metrics one might use are not publicly accessible, they find indicators that opportunity is also a gendered phenomenon for deans.

Continuing the focus on gendered dynamics of university administration, in Chapter 6, Genevieve Fuji Johnson, Özlem Sensoy, and El Chenier look at five Canadian universities to see how leadership remains highly gendered and racialized. This chapter focuses on identifying the barriers that women, especially Black, Indigenous, and racialized women, face in their career paths through central and senior administration in Canadian universities. The data discussed in this chapter comes from a diversity audit of five different universities throughout Canada and reveals a sobering diversity gap, especially for racialized women. In fact, in most cases, there is no way for women to even move up to the first step of the administration ladder. In finding ways to address this gap, the authors argue that the only way to bring about meaningful change is to completely rethink the cultural and structural landscapes of universities. Current EDI mechanisms do not address the highly racialized and gendered norms underpinning the university structure.

In Part 3, we examine some of the broader structural and institutional challenges facing academics as they attempt to navigate their profession. Aisha Ahmad's vignette identifies some of the less talked about structural problems in academia; namely, gendered racism. Too often, BIPOC women face a culture that denies their experiences of sexism and racism and retaliates against them for calling it out. Like generations of academics who refused to see the sexist nature of academia, racism needs to be part of our lexicon on structural and institutional change. One way these structural challenges of discrimination manifest is in wage disparity. Moving to Chapter 7, Catherine Beaudry, Laurence Solar-Pelletier, and Carl St-Pierre assess data from a survey of more than five thousand Canadian academics and confirm not only the basic gender wage gap, but also how administrative premiums, wage market premiums, chair, performance, and other bonuses, as well as consulting income, have amplified gendered gaps in earnings. In recent years, gender disparities regarding the salary of university professors in Canada have attracted greater attention from media, scholars, governmental organizations, and unions (see Doolittle and Wang 2021). Among the numerous studies that elucidate the factors affecting salary evolution during a professor's career, none has examined in detail the premiums and bonuses that contribute to exacerbating an already nonnegligible wage gap between men and women in academia.

In Chapter 8, Melanie A. Morrison, Joshua W. Katz, Bidushy Sadika, Jessica M. McCutcheon, and Todd G. Morrison examine whether there is a bias for administrative leaders to have backgrounds in STEM. Building on leadership literature that demonstrates a broader societal bias in favour of leaders who have STEM education and training, the authors investigate whether the same preference for STEM-educated leaders exists in Canada's U15 universities. They find that while such a bias does exist in faculty-level administrative positions like deans and associate deans, there is no statistical difference to be found in senior-level administrative positions like provosts or presidents.

In Chapter 9, Jennifer Chisholm, Kasey Egan, and Kristin Burnett argue that the frequency of sexual harassment in academia has gained more and more attention in recent years, especially regarding unequal power relations. In this area, however, research into harassment in which the student is the perpetrator and the faculty member is the victim has not gained much attention. Additionally, the range of harassment linked to gender – but not constituting sexual harassment – is largely unexplored. Based on survey data collected from faculty across Canada, the authors focus on the experiences of women faculty with contrapower harassment in the classroom, its relation to teaching responsibilities, and its overarching effects for faculty members. The chapter focuses on the experiences of women who teach women's and gender studies, sexuality studies, Indigenous studies, and subjects that tend to decolonize curriculum or challenge traditional norms, often producing more class disruption and student pushback. The study in this chapter fills a gap in the knowledge concerning faculty members' experiences with contrapower harassment at Canadian institutions while providing empirical support for institutional and policy changes that will help protect faculty.

In Chapter 10, Louise Forsyth looks at the challenges of achieving equality in the highly vaunted Canada Research Chairs (CRC) program, a Tri-Council initiative that invests $295 million annually to recruit the top research talent for Canadian universities (Canada Research Chairs 2020). Launched in 2000, the CRC program had the vision of recognizing and supporting a new generation of Canadian scholars. The program had the potential to nurture the expansion of research and teaching initiatives into neglected areas and to address inequities in the academic community, but, unfortunately, it did not. In 2003, Forsyth and seven others lodged a complaint with the Canadian Human Rights Commission alleging that the program was rewarding those already in privileged positions – that is, able-bodied white men – but despite the commission's recognition of their allegations as justified in 2006, little changed. In 2018, they once again engaged in mediation on the same matter. Using an autoethnographic approach, Forsyth, a feminist scholar who has witnessed and fought for gender equality since the mid-1980s, demonstrates the value of collective action in the fight for equality.

Finally, Part 4 examines ways to alter or fundamentally rethink the ways our academic institutions are shaped and the values that underlie them. Michael F. Charles's vignette describes how institutional culture is often an impediment to enacting change and offers compelling proposals to make EDI a lived reality. In Chapter 11, Janice Niemann takes up the focus on the gendered dimensions of SETs unpacked in previous chapters to question how different pedagogical traits can be reformulated, valued, and used to address inequities. The results of Niemann's study show that most solutions are premised on the assumption that women-coded qualities are worth less than men-coded ones and must be corrected for equitable assessment to be possible. However, following the compassionate turn in pedagogy studies (see Waddington 2017; Gibbs 2017), she argues that kindness and compassion (stereotypically women-coded attributes) are traits for which we should strive, giving women in academia the power to reclaim kindness as an act of empowered pedagogy.

In Chapter 12, Audrey E. Brennan and Katherine V.R. Sullivan examine how Twitter and other social media platforms are providing an alternative space of expression and refuge for women in academia. Building on previous studies that have revealed the democratic potential of social media (see, e.g., Sullivan and Bélanger 2016), Brennan and Sullivan look at how the professional lives of women academics are shared and cultivated online. They find that women in academia have been taking to social media to voice their professional struggles and create a sense of community. This finding echoes other research, which has found that Twitter and other social media platforms have become a space for women to voice their opinions and professional struggles and create a sense of collectiveness and community (Rocheleau and Millette 2015). Their study also identifies key hashtags such as #WomenInAcademia, #WomenAlsoKnowStuff, and #AcademicTwitter that show the positive and supportive space that social media can offer women academics who find university environments alienating.

In Chapter 13, Cheryl N. Collier examines how men's allyship at Canadian universities works. Systemic gender bias and institutional path dependency are two core challenges that hinder progress on the issue of gender equality in Canadian universities. One combative strategy is to employ men's allyship models to turn institutional culture away from these gender biases and toward more acceptance of equality goals (Drury and Kaiser 2014; Sherf, Tangirala, and Weber 2017). This chapter looks at the levels of institutional engagement with this approach of allyship in working toward gender equality in universities through an exploration of EDI strategies and university mission statements. Examining U15 universities, plus a number of smaller institutions, in each province across the country, Collier uses a discourse and content analysis model to assess the public, explicitly stated commitment levels of Canadian institutions to these core equality strategies. While it is true that such statements do not necessarily signify a real commitment, an absence of such a statement is certainly telling of the institution's dedication to the issue. This approach provides a clear scan of institutional willingness to embrace gender equality and allyship models across the country.

Before we turn to our conclusion chapter, Sara Anderson's vignette provides us with a call for action to take reconciliation seriously in the research ecosystem.

As a university staff member, her engagement with faculty highlights the challenges of decolonizing research and, invariably, curriculum. In our conclusion chapter, Lorna A. Turnbull reflects on her role as a feminist legal scholar and former dean of a faculty of law and on her research on inequality flowing from gendered expectations of care work. She ruminates on the need for legal approaches to address social inequality and realize social justice while also recognizing the limitations of law in addressing entrenched inequalities in universities, particularly in the absence of "evidence." To address systemic inequalities, Turnbull notes the need for more data and considers the challenges volume contributors faced in collecting disaggregated data, especially data disaggregated by race, gender identity, sexuality, and disability. To make a change, we must prove that systemic inequality exists, a key goal of this volume.

We close out the volume with a vignette from a contract professor stuck in a pattern of sessional teaching while trying to apply for tenure-track positions and balance the needs of a young family. Melissa Finn shares her increasingly relatable experience of being unable to get into the coveted ivory tower and the personal and emotional challenges she experienced in her attempts.

NOTES

1 For the purposes of this book, the term "women" includes all individuals who self-identify as women. However, it must be noted that when statistics are cited, self-identification may not have been an option, and respondents may have been limited to gender categories that only allow for binary male/female identification.

2 In response to these challenges, groups like Senior Women Academic Administrators of Canada (SWAAC) formed to offer guidance to women in leadership positions and to promote women's leadership in the academy.

3 A 2020 study of promotions from associate to full professor in Ontario from 2010 to 2014 showed that men were "more than twice" as likely to be promoted as women (Millar and Barker 2020, 55).

4 The women surveyed also noted that their supervisors overwhelmingly discouraged them from having children, and those who did get pregnant noted that they did not get adequate support.

5 Specifically, 62 percent of women and 39 percent of men in the humanities and social sciences and 50 percent of women and 30 percent of men in the hard sciences do not have children.

6 This reality indicates that understanding and measuring intersectionality in the stratification of university appointments is necessary.

7 In a small study of Canadian psychology departments, McCutcheon and Morrison (2016) found that women, on average, spend ten more hours on childcare work each week compared to men. A single US university case study revealed similar findings (see O'Laughlin and Bischoff 2005).

8 These gendered dynamics are also apparent outside of Canada. Moreover, as *The Equity Myth* aptly points out, Canadian universities also have a serious problem with racism, equity, and indigenization (see Henry et al. 2017).

9 Although most government offices are currently limited to data rooted in the male/female binary, some are now working to give more options for gender self-identification; for example, in 2017, Ontario changed its policies to allow individuals to designate themselves as male (M), female (F), or gender neutral (X) on their driver's license (Government of Ontario 2017), and in 2021, the Canadian census added "at birth" to its sex identification question and included an additional question on gender (Statistics Canada 2022b).

WORKS CITED

Acker, Sandra, and Linda Muzzin. 2019. "Minoritized Faculty in Canada's Universities and Colleges: Gender, Power, and Academic Work." In *Working Women in Canada: An Intersectional Approach*, edited by Leslie Nichols, 177–201. Toronto: Canadian Scholars' Press.

Acker, Sandra, Michelle Webber, and Elizabeth Smyth. 2012. "Tenure Troubles and Equity Matters in Canadian Academe." *British Journal of Sociology of Education* 33 (5): 743–61.

Bendels, Michael H.K., and Ruth Muller. 2018. "Gender Disparities in High-Quality Research Revealed by Nature Index Journals." *PLoS One* 13 (1).

Black, Alison L., and Susanne Garvis. 2018. *Women Activating Agency in Academia: Metaphors, Manifestos and Memoir.* New York: Routledge.

Canada Research Chairs. 2020. "About Us." https://www.chairs-chaires.gc.ca/about_us-a_notre_sujet/index-eng.aspx.

Canetto, Silvia S., Carlie Trott, Erin Winterrowd, and Dorothy Haruyama. 2017. "Challenges to the Choice Discourse: Women's Views of Their Family and Academic-Science Career Options and Constraints." *Journal of Feminist Family Therapy* 29 (1–2): 1–24.

Chilly Collective, eds. 1995. *Breaking Anonymity: The Chilly Climate for Women Faculty.* Waterloo, ON: Wilfrid Laurier University Press.

Chiose, Simona. 2016. "More Female Leaders Needed at Canadian Universities, Presidents Say." *Globe and Mail.* April 28, 2016. https://www.theglobeandmail.com/news/national/more-female-leaders-needed-at-canadian-universities-presidents-say/article29795727/.

Council of Canadian Academies. 2012. "Strengthening Canada's Research Capacity: The Gender Dimension." https://gender-summit.com/images/Docs/cafe%201%20zena%20sharman.pdf.

Davis, Jennifer C., Eric Ping Hung Li, Mary Stewart Butterfield, Gino A. DiLabio, Nithi Santhagunam, and Barbara Marcolin. 2022. "Are We Failing Female and Racialized Academics? A Canadian National Survey Examining the Impacts of the COVID-19 Pandemic on Tenure and Tenure-Track Faculty." *Gender, Work and Organization* 29 (3): 703–22.

Department of Justice. 2018. "The Rights and Freedoms the Charter Protects." *Department of Justice*. September 13, 2018. https://www.justice.gc.ca/eng/csj-sjc/rfc-dlc/ccrf -ccdl/rfcp-cdlp.html#s5.

Doolittle, Robyn, and Chen Wang. 2021. "This Is the Power Gap: Explore the Investigative Series and Data." *Globe and Mail*, January 21, 2021. https://www.theglobeandmail. com/canada/article-power-gap/.

Drury, Benjamin J., and Cheryl R. Kaiser. 2014. "Allies against Sexism: The Role of Men in Confronting Sexism." *Journal of Social Issues* 70:637–52. doi:10.1111/josi.12083.

Ferber, Marianne A., and Michael Brün. 2011. "The Gender Gap in Citations: Does It Persist?" *Feminist Economics* 17 (1):151–58.

Gibbs, Paul, ed. 2017. *The Pedagogy of Compassion at the Heart of Higher Education.* Cham, Switzerland: Springer.

Government of Ontario. 2017. "Change the Sex Designation on Your Government IDs." *Government of Ontario*. Last modified May 6, 2019. https://www.ontario.ca/page/ change-sex-designation-your-government-ids.

Gutiérrez y Muhs, Gabrielle, Yoland Flores Niemann, Carmen G. Gonzalez, and Angela P. Harris, eds. 2012. *Presumed Incompetent: The Intersections of Race and Class for Women in Academia.* Boulder: Utah State University Press, an imprint of University Press of Colorado.

Harley, Debra A. 2008. "Maids of Academe: African American Women Faculty at Predominately White Institutions." *Journal of African American Studies* 12 (1): 19–36.

Henry, Frances, Enakshi Dua, Carl E. James, Audrey Kobayashi, Peter Li, Howard Ramos, and Malinda S. Smith. 2017. *The Equity Myth: Racialization and Indigeneity at Canadian Universities.* Vancouver: UBC Press.

Johnson, Genevieve Fuji, and Robert Howsam. 2020. "Whiteness, Power and the Politics of Demographics in the Governance of the Canadian Academy." *Canadian Journal of Political Science/Revue Canadienne De Science Politique* 53 (3): 676–94. doi:10.1017/ S0008423920000207.

Johnson, Genevieve, Robert Howsam, Malinda Smith, and Nancy Bray. 2020. "Leadership Pipelines at Five Canadian Universities (Aggregate)." Edmonton: University of Alberta.

King, Molly M., and Megan E. Frederickson. 2021. "The Pandemic Penalty: The Gendered Effects of COVID-19 on Scientific Productivity." *Socius* 7:23780231211006977.

Kitossa, Tamari, and Gökbörü Sarp Tanyildiz. 2022. "Anti-Blackness, Criminology and the University as Violence Work: Diversity as Ritual and the Professionalization of Repression in Canada." In *Diversity in Criminology and Criminal Justice Studies,* edited by Derek M.D. Silva and Mathieu Deflem, 39–61. Bingley, UK: Emerald.

Larivière, Vincent, Chaoqun Ni, Yves Gingras, Blaise Cronin, and Cassidy R. Sugimoto. 2013. "Bibliometrics: Global Gender Disparities in Science." *Nature News* 504: 211–13. https://www.nature.com/articles/504211a.

Lavigne, Eric. 2020. "The Demographics and Career Paths of Canadian University Deans: Gender, Race, Experience, and Provenance." *Studies in Higher Education* 45 (9): 1949–60.

Lazos, Sylvia R. 2012. "Are Student Teaching Evaluations Holding Back Women and Minorities? The Perils of 'Doing' Gender and Race in the Classroom." In *Presumed Incompetent: The Intersections of Race and Class for Women in Academia,* edited by Gabriella Gutiérrez y Muhs, Yolanda Flores Niemann, Carmen G. Gonzalez, and Angela P. Harris, 164–85. Boulder: Utah State University Press, an imprint of University of Colorado Press.

Lemon, Narelle, and Susanne Garvis, eds. 2014. *Being "In and Out": Providing Voice to Early Career Women in Academia.* Boston: Sense.

MacNell, Lillian, Adam Driscoll, and Andrea Hunt. 2015. "What's in a Name: Exposing Gender Bias in Student Ratings of Teaching." *Innovative Higher Education* 40 (4): 291–303.

Manthey, Katie. 2017. "Dress for Success: Dismantling Politics of Dress in Academia." In *Surviving Sexism in Academia,* 178–85. Routledge: New York.

Mason, Mary Ann, and Marc Goulden. 2002. "Do Babies Matter? The Effect of Family Formation on the Lifelong Careers of Academic Men and Women." *Academe Online* 88.

Mason, Mary Ann, Nicholas Wolfinger, and Marc Goulden. 2013. *Do Babies Matter? Gender and Family in the Ivory Tower.* New Brunswick, NJ: Rutgers University Press.

McCutcheon, Jessica M., and Melanie A. Morrison. 2016. "'Eight Days a Week': A National Snapshot of Academic Mothers' Realities in Canadian Psychology Departments." *Canadian Psychology* 57 (2): 92-100.

McKinsey. 2022. *Women in the Workplace 2022.* https://www.mckinsey.com/featured -insights/diversity-and-inclusion/women-in-the-workplace-archive.

Millar, Paul, and Jane Barker. 2020. "Gender and Academic Promotion to Full Professor in Ontario." *Canadian Journal of Sociology* 45 (1): 47–69.

Mitchell, Kristina, and Jonathan Martin. 2018. "Gender Bias in Student Evaluations." *PS: Political Science and Politics* 51 (3): 648–52.

Mitchell, Sara M., and Vicki L. Hesli. 2013. "Women Don't Ask? Women Don't Say No? Bargaining and Service in the Political Science Profession." *Political Science and Politics* 46 (2): 355–69.

Momani, Bessma, Emma Dreher, and Kira Williams. 2019. "Evaluating the Gender Pay Gap in Canadian Academia from 1996 to 2016." *Canadian Journal of Higher Education* 49 (1): 2–35.

O'Laughlin, Elizabeth M., and Lisa G. Bischoff. 2005. "Balancing Parenthood and Academia: Work/Family Stress as Influenced by Gender and Tenure Status." *Journal of Family Issues* 26 (1): 79–106.

O'Meara, KerryAnn, Audrey Jaeger, Joya Misra, Courtney Lennartz, and Alexandra Kuvaeva. 2018. "Undoing Disparities in Faculty Workloads: A Randomized Trial Experiment." *PLOS One* 13 (12): e0207316.

Pedersen, Daphne E., and Krista Lynn Minnotte. 2017. "Workplace Climate and STEM Faculty Women's Job Burnout." *Journal of Feminist Family Therapy* 29 (1–2): 45–65. doi:10.1080/08952833.2016.1230987.

Perna, Laura Walter. 2001. "Sex Differences in Faculty Salaries: A Cohort Analysis." *The Review of Higher Education* 24 (3): 283–307.

Reimer, Marilee, ed. 2004. *Inside Corporate U: Women in the Academy Speak Out.* Toronto: Sumach Press.

Rocheleau, Sylvain, and Mélanie Millette. 2015. "Meta-Hashtag and Tag Co-Occurrence: From Organization to Politics in the French Canadian Twittersphere." In *The Power and Politics of Discursive Networks*, edited by N. Rambukkana, 243–54. Toronto: Peter Lang Press.

Schoening, Anne M. 2009. "Women and Tenure: Closing the Gap." *Journal of Women in Educational Leadership* 7 (2): 77–92.

Shelton, Stephanie Anne, Jill Ewing Flynn, and Tanetha Jamay Grosland, eds. 2018. *Feminism and Intersectionality in Academia: Women's Narratives and Experiences in Higher Education.* New York: Palgrave Macmillan.

Sherf, Elad N., Subrahmaniam Tangirala, and Katy Connealy Weber. 2017. "It Is Not My Place! Psychological Standing and Men's Voice and Participation in Gender-Parity Initiatives." *Organization Science* 28:193–210.

Statistics Canada. 2022a. "Table 37-10-0077-01: Number and Median Age of Full-Time Teaching Staff at Canadian Universities, by Highest Earned Degree, Staff Functions, Rank, Gender." https://www150.statcan.gc.ca/t1/tbl1/en/tv.action?pid=3710007701.

–. 2022b. "Filling Gaps in Gender Diversity Data in Canada." https://www150.statcan.gc.ca/n1/en/daily-quotidien/220427/dq220427b-eng.pdf?st=zvC0qP16

Sullivan, Katherine V., and Pierre C. Bélanger. 2016. "La cyberdémocratie québécoise: *Twitter bashing*, #VoteCampus et *selfies*." *Politique et Sociétés* 35 (2–3): 239–58. https://doi.org/10.7202/1037017ar.

Troeger, Vera E., and Mariaelisa Epifanio. 2019. "Productivity Takes Leave? The Maternity Benefits and Career Opportunities for Women in Academia." In *Which Way Now? Economic Policy after a Decade of Upheaval: A CAGE Policy Report*, edited by Vera E. Troeger, 109–23. https://warwick.ac.uk/fac/soc/economics/research/centres/cage/manage/news/cage_report_2019_web.pdf#page=107.

Turpin, David H., Ludgard De Decker, and Brendan Boyd. 2014. "Historical Changes in the Canadian University Presidency: An Empirical Analysis of Changes in Length of Service and Experience since 1840." *Canadian Public Administration/Administration publique du Canada* 57 (4): 573–88.

U15. n.d. "About Us." Accessed March 16, 2020. http://u15.ca/about-us.

Vettese, Troy. 2019. "Sexism in the Academy." *Head Case* 34: 1–26.

Waddington, Kathryn. 2017. "Creating Conditions for Compassion." In *The Pedagogy of Compassion at the Heart of Higher Education*, edited by Paul Gibbs, 40–70. Cham, Switzerland: Springer.

Wagner, Anne, Sandra Acker, and Kimine Mayuzumi, eds. 2008. *Whose University Is It, Anyway?: Power and Privilege on Gendered Terrain.* Toronto: Canadian Scholars' Press.

Webber, Michelle. 2008. "Miss Congeniality Meets the New Managerialism: Feminism, Contingent Labour, and the New University." *Canadian Journal of Higher Education* 38 (3): 37–56.

Wenneras, Christine, and Agnes Wold. 1997. "Nepotism and Sexism in Peer-Review." *Nature* 387:341–43.

Whittaker, Elvi, ed. 2015. *Solitudes of the Workplace: Women in Universities*. Montreal: McGill-Queen's University Press.

Wilton, Shauna, and Lynda Ross. 2017. "Flexibility, Sacrifice and Insecurity: A Canadian Study Assessing the Challenges of Balancing Work and Family in Academia." *Journal of Feminist Family Therapy* 29 (1–2): 66–87. doi:10.1080/08952833.2016.1272663.

Zippia. 2022. "25 Women in Leadership Statistics [2022]: Facts on The Gender Gap in Corporate and Political Leadership." November 9, 2022. https://www.zippia.com/advice/women-in-leadership-statistics/.

PART 1

Daily Life of Women Academics

Between Tokenism and Belonging in the Academy

ANDREA M. COLLINS

When I was a master's student in the mid-2000s, my classmates referred to me as "the token feminist." The label fit and I wore it with pride. I was one of just three students that identified as a woman in my cohort and the lone student who could be relied on to ask questions about gender in our historically male-dominated field of international relations. Up to that point, the training in feminist inquiry I had received was very white, very liberal, and very naïve. I embraced the idea of being the token feminist because the classroom felt like a space in which I belonged, despite the gender gap in representation. Here, I could question everything and feel heard. In these early stages of my academic career, I expected that academia would keep its promise that I could reach the same echelons as men. I graduated that year with cautious optimism about the possible academic career that laid ahead. It would not take long for me to learn that having that seat at the table is not the same as belonging to the group.

Today, as a tenured faculty member, I bristle when I think about embracing the term "token." Complicit in that joke, I did not recognize the ways academic institutions have tokenized historically disadvantaged and underrepresented people. Many universities have hired more women since then but remain ill-equipped to address sexism, racism, heterosexism, ableism, and transphobia. The increased representation of (white, cis) women like myself has not revolutionized how the academy recognizes gendered divisions of labour within its ranks. It has not fixed the "leaky pipeline" of women, LGBTQ2SIA+, and racialized individuals from undergraduate programs into the academy and particularly its prestigious upper ranks. It has not resolved outdated sexist and heterosexist assumptions about care work, family structures, and home life. It does not challenge gendered expectations about behaviours and styles of leadership. It does not imagine alternative, inclusive cultures of learning and research. The distance between tokenism and belonging has yet to be bridged. I "belong," but I do not belong all the way.

University expectations of pretenure women are often contradictory. Despite the 40/40/20 time split that many tenure-track faculty members have for research, teaching, and service, we come to learn that the split is either artificial or that to meet such demands requires giving more than 100 percent. Many of us – regardless of gender identity – are told to prioritize research. We must apply for grants. Publish or perish. We are advised against service at our own peril. We are told not to put much stock in student course evaluations and perhaps even not to spend too much time on teaching altogether.

The gap between the tokenism of the past and actual belonging shows up in how women must navigate the contradictions between this advice and the expectations of administrators, colleagues, and students. When academic institutions introduce identity-based representation requirements for committees, there can be downward pressure on a select few women or racialized faculty to accept such service roles when these groups are underrepresented. Women are still underrepresented in the STEM fields, among others, and in the senior ranks of universities. Precariously employed or pretenure scholars may not be able to decline requests for service made by people whose support they need for contract renewal or tenure. Many universities also still rely on student course evaluations as the basis for evaluating teaching performance, despite evidence that these evaluations are rife with racism and sexism and are more often reflections of student perceptions rather than learning outcomes. These surveys typically punish groups that are underrepresented in the academy, including women who fail to meet gendered expectations of being sufficiently responsive, caring, or conventionally attractive. We also know that women, LGBTQ2SIA+, and racialized people are more likely to receive inappropriate or abusive comments through these anonymous surveys, and that this is compounded for people who experience intersecting oppressions.

If they demonstrate concern about students' experiences, women faculty may also find themselves responding to students who themselves face discrimination and distress. As a younger, woman faculty member, some see me as more approachable than other university colleagues. As a result, I have mentored or counselled students that I never taught because they did not know who else they could turn to. Please do not misunderstand me: this emotional labour is important, but it is also grounded in common gendered assumptions about who is or should be capable of delivering this work. Moreover, it is time-consuming, emotionally taxing, undervalued, and unseen. When I pointed out this emotional labour is not reflected in pay or performance reviews, I was told by a senior professor that such work is its own reward.

These expectations of research, teaching, and service are also all couched in the whispered gendered biases that shape perceptions of job performance, sometimes uttered by the same well-meaning people who support gender equality. I have heard gossip about scholars of so-called childbearing age or speculation about which colleagues have the "two body problem" of academic employment (as I do). I have heard about the implicit and explicit ways faculty members inquire about job candidates' parental or marital status, although they know such questions are prohibited. I have heard students recount how a professor in another discipline told their class that women belong in the home. I have had crude comments about my appearance anonymously written on my office door. These rumblings are the background noise in which we are asked to do the work of the university. The noise can be isolating and alienating.

Universities boast about meeting their goals for hiring women into the faculty ranks, but cultural shifts are needed to ensure lasting and inclusive change. Meaningful change requires faculty and administrators to have a better understanding of the everyday experiences of bias, discrimination, and intersectional oppression, and how members of university communities are complicit in their reproduction. Yes, there are those who make their chauvinism clear for all to see, but they may be a dying breed. It is perhaps more frustrating to see well-meaning faculty members and administrators talk about their personal and institutional commitments to equity, diversity, and inclusion while failing to reckon with the ways their own words and actions stand in the way. I say this as someone that has also failed to do this. True change means letting go of the "add women and stir" fantasy of gender representation in the academy and grappling with what gender-inclusive, antiracist, accessible institutional cultures could look like.

I know my experience as a woman in the academy today still comes from a place of privilege and is not nearly as challenging as it was for my predecessors, but I do not apologize for imagining a better future for all of us. I am inspired by the voices of mentors and colleagues who supported me along the way: the quiet words of confidence from a professor on graduation day; the whisper networks that informed me where dangers lay; the colleague who empathized with the number of service requests and promised to find someone else; the administrator showing me how to buck the expectations imposed from above; and of course, my students that refuse to tolerate sexist, homophobic, transphobic, racist, and ableist discrimination. All of these people are here, too, and their voices help to foster real inclusion and belonging, beyond just seats at the table.

1

The Precarious Work of Contract Teaching and Student Evaluations

SANDRA SMELE and ANDREA QUINLAN

While Canadian universities identify teaching evaluations as necessary for ensuring quality teaching in higher education (see, e.g., University of Toronto 2020; University of British Columbia 2007; McGill University 2014), a growing literature calls the methods of evaluation being used into question. Despite their widespread adoption in Canadian universities, student evaluations of teaching (SETs) have been shown to negatively impact equality in the academy. Existing literature demonstrates that SETs commonly reflect biases against women academic instructors, particularly those marginalized in relation to race, ethnicity, and age (Joye and Wilson 2015; Lazos 2012; Mitchell and Martin 2018; Reinsch, Goltz, and Hietapelto 2020). This literature reveals that SETs contribute to the systematic marginalization of equity-seeking groups in the academy. Missing from this literature, however, is an investigation into the impact of SETs on a growing equity-seeking group in Canadian universities: precariously employed academic women instructors.

Recent studies on neoliberal trends of employment precarity indicate that contract teaching positions are on the rise in Canadian postsecondary institutions and are negatively impacting equity in higher education (Foster and Birdsell Bauer 2018; Pasma and Shaker 2018). Both Ontario-based and nationwide research demonstrate that the majority of contract academic teaching staff are women, with estimated ratios as high as two women to every one man (Field and Jones 2016; Pasma and Shaker 2018), and with roughly a third belonging to racialized groups (Foster and Birdsell Bauer 2018). Given these known links between precarity, SETs, and inequality, it is high time to explore how precarious academic employment and SETs intersect and contribute to inequality. This chapter takes up that challenge by looking specifically at how SETs are experienced by precariously employed academic women. Working from an intersectional feminist framework that seeks to centre marginalized perspectives and attend to lived experiences, this chapter analyzes thirty-four qualitative interviews with women employed as contract faculty to investigate their experience of SETs.

This chapter analyzes precariously employed academic women's experiences of SETs in relation to the expectations of care and aesthetic labour in teaching in higher education. In so doing, this chapter reveals how these expectations and forms of labour are uniquely shaped by gender, race, and age. We identify how SETs act as a measure of instructors' conformity to expectations of how academic authority and femininity should be performed in the classroom. We explore the harmful impacts this has on precariously employed academic women, both in terms of the additional labour and the mental distress it generates. We also locate these experiences of SETs in the context of the neoliberal imperatives that are increasingly shaping higher education. While existing research has demonstrated the broader, systemic nature of gendered inequities in neoliberal universities, this chapter crucially identifies how SETs are contributing to the perpetuation of these inequities among precariously employed academic women.

CARE AND EMOTIONAL AND AESTHETIC LABOUR

Significant feminist scholarship has been dedicated to problematizing and theorizing care (see, e.g., Armstrong and Braedley 2013; Folbre and Wright 2012; Glenn 2010; Neysmith 1991; Noddings 1984; Sevenhuijsen 1998; Tronto 2013). This is perhaps most evident in works that have examined gendered divisions of paid and unpaid labour (Armstrong 1997; Bezanson and Luxton 2006; Grant et al. 2004), as well as in the work built upon sociologist Arlie Hochschild's (1983) conceptualization of emotional labour in the workplace (see, e.g., Mann and Cowburn 2005; Whitelegg 2002). Important contributions to this scholarship have been made by feminists seeking to demonstrate the multiple power relations that shape and inform care practices and experiences, including those tied to gender, race, citizenship/migration, colonization, sexuality, disability, and class (see, e.g., Arber and Ginn 1992; Cronin and King 2010; Ferguson 2008; Hall 2016; Mirchandani 2003; Thomas 2007; Yeates 2012).

Much of the scholarship on care focuses on its provision in contexts where care is commonly understood as a central activity (e.g., hospital/health care facility or home/community). Feminized service work, such as hairdressing, retail, and hospitality, has also been the focus of some of this scholarship, particularly in terms of the emotional labour performed by those working in these service sectors to meet the "needs" and desires of clients (Good and Cooper 2016; Toerien and Kitzinger 2007; Watt 2007). Some scholarly attention has also been paid to other contexts not commonly associated with care and emotional labour (see, e.g., Iszatt-White 2013; Mavin 2009; Strongman and Wright 2008). This literature attends to academic women's experiences, most often regarding teaching and service work expectations (Acker and Feuerverger 1996; Bellas 1999; Guarino and Borden 2017; Tuck 2018) and in terms of childcare and family caregiving (Bos, Sweet-Cushman, and Schneider 2017; Dickson 2018; Huppatz, Sang, and Napier 2018; Nzinga-Johnson 2013; Misra, Lundqist, and Templer 2012). However, the experiences of precariously employed academic women is missing in this literature. Further to this, the relationship between SETs and care-related expectations in contract teaching remains unexamined.

Like the care scholarship, scholarship focusing on aesthetic labour tends to be siloed in particular sectors. Aesthetic labour encompasses expectations of specific "workplace embodiments" (Lipton 2021, 768) that place value on specific stylizations and looks. This form of labour requires skill and effort and involves expending resources, such as time and money. In some cases, aesthetic labour is tied to physical discomfort and can even involve subjecting oneself to health risks. Much of the scholarship on aesthetic labour has focused on the service and professionalized business sectors, where the expectation of this form of labour is generally more explicitly expressed and often closely tied to body work (Cutcher and Achtel 2017; Karlsson 2012; Kelan 2013; Mears 2014; Petersson McIntyre 2016; Ramjattan 2019). Some research has examined the experiences of academic women in relation to expectations about their gender and academic performances (Donaghue 2017; Mählck 2013; Moore and Williams 2014), including early-career women academics' experiences of these expectations (Bono, De Craene, and Kenis 2019; Brown 2017). The relationship between SETs and the reinforcement of these aesthetic expectations of academic women has been explored in some of the literature (see, e.g., Basow and Martin 2013; Lazos 2012). However, to our knowledge, no literature has examined the impact of these expectations on precariously employed academic women's experiences of teaching.

In this chapter, we extend the literature on care and aesthetic labour to examine the impact of SETs on the experiences of precariously employed academic women. To do so, we focus on the impacts of this evaluation tool identified by our research participants and discuss the broader consequences of these impacts for equality in higher education. Crucially, we argue that increasing equality in the academy depends, in part, on examining and addressing the role of SETs in perpetuating the inequities experienced by precariously employed academic women.

METHODS

This chapter draws on thirty-four semi-structured interviews with contract faculty (n = 21) and sessional instructors (n = 13) who identify as women at a research-intensive university in Ontario. Contract faculty and sessional instructors represent two categories of workers who are precariously employed: sessional instructors are hired for individual courses and contract faculty are hired for one- to three-year terms. The study's sample included twenty-four faculty/instructors from disciplines in the social sciences and humanities and ten from STEM fields. Potential participants were identified through publicly available faculty lists on departmental websites and through snowball sampling and were recruited via email. Efforts were made to obtain as diverse a sample as possible across the categories of age, race, disciplinary background, and years of teaching experience. Ethics clearance for this study was sought and granted through the researchers' institutional ethics board.

While most of the interviews were conducted in person by one or both of us, depending on the participants' preference, a few interviews were conducted over the phone or via video conferencing. Building on existing themes in the literature, interview questions focused on experiences of job precarity in the academy; participants' perceptions of the impact of SETs on teaching experiences; the effectiveness of SETs in measuring teaching performance; how gender, race, ability, and other[1] power relations may have impacted SET responses; the use of SETs in hiring and performance appraisals; and alternative evaluation methods for teaching. All interviews were audiorecorded and transcribed verbatim. Following each interview, we met and discussed emergent themes.

Our analysis was loosely informed by Timmermans and Tavory's (2012) abductive approach to qualitative analysis, which they define as a "creative, inferential process aimed at producing new ... theories based on surprising research evidence" (167). Unlike more traditional forms of qualitative analysis, such as the inductive approach used in Grounded Theory, abductive analysis is grounded in insights from existing literature, which are used to identify patterns and theoretical themes in data. Drawing on this abductive approach, the theoretical literature on care, aesthetic labour, and gender inequality guided the construction of preliminary coding categories from the interview data. Given the study's specific focus on gender and equality, we focused on participants' expressed concerns and experiences of inequities. Following Timmermans and Tavory, we also paid particular attention to "surprising research evidence" or unexpected responses from participants, which was used to further refine the coding categories. Following the initial coding of the transcripts, we then "revisited" the codes, which Timmermans and Tavory suggest is a crucial process for "see[ing] things in new ways," and further refined our codes.

As the following findings illustrate, participants described a range of personal experiences with SETs and their impacts on equality in the academy. Crucially, what these perspectives make clear is that SETs significantly shape precariously employed instructors' experiences both in and outside of the classroom, often in detrimental ways that go largely unseen in higher education.

FINDINGS

Personal Experiences of Inequities and Their Reflection in the SET Research Literature

Given their occupation as academics, it is perhaps not surprising that many of our participants discussed the research literature on the impact of SETs on equity-seeking groups. They expressed familiarity with "research that finds that they [SETs] are biased against women or minorities or people whose first language is not English" and data that indicate that "teaching evaluations are lower for women, older people, and people of colour." Importantly, many participants not only were aware of the key findings in the research literature on SETs, but also recognized that their specific experiences were reflected in the research literature.

Several of our participants identified the impact of racism on their experiences of SETs. In some cases, this was expressed through acknowledgment that they experienced white privilege. For example, one lecturer stated that she experiences a "bit of a white girl effect," while a sessional participant similarly explained that she had not been subjected to racialized discrimination because she is "pretty white-passing." Women of colour who had experienced racism in the clarroom identified racism in the types of comments they received in their SETs and in challenges to their authority in the classroom. One participant commented that these comments originate from those "who feel that they have this power over you because they are white." In accounting for these kinds of experiences, several participants addressed the impacts of an instructor's race, as well as their gender and age, on SETs. Summarizing this succinctly, one participant said that these "characteristics which we already know from research" help to "determine how you're going to get rated."

Our participants also recognized how other forms of discrimination that have impacted their personal experiences of SETs are reaffirmed in the research literature. Many described experiences of gender- and/or age-based discrimination. In relation to her personal experiences of sexual objectification through SETs, for instance, one sessional instructor explained, "There's a moment where I become very conscious of the fact that my status as someone who is pretty young and female impacts their perception of me as an instructor." Another similarly stated, "Oh, yeah, I'm conscious of the fact that they're going to be evaluating me in a gendered way and in an ageist way." Along the same lines, a contract lecturer described her experience that students "sometimes have an idea that they don't want a certain professor. And that's ... almost always an older woman," further stating, "I know the data supports this, that the older you get, particularly if you're female, [the] less credible you seem to look."

Having their personal experiences validated in the research literature seemed to add insult to injury for several precariously employed academic women we interviewed. For example, one participant expressed great frustration with the continued use of SETs in light of the research literature, pointing out that it is understood that they are both sexist and racist: "So, why are we continuing to use them at all?" She was not alone in expressing this sentiment. Many sessional instructors and contract lecturers identified the specific impacts of the continued use of SETs on themselves as precariously employed academic women. They expressed frustration that SETs were contributing to the inequities they were experiencing in the university, and that these inequities had been demonstrated by the research literature but remained unaddressed at their institution.

Aesthetic Labour in Response to the Inequities Engendered by SETs

Our participants recognized that SETs are engendering, and to mitigate the inequities, several of them described engaging in various forms of aesthetic labour. One sessional instructor explained that, to appear attractive and professional for students, "I dress well. I'm very fit and stylish. I've found it to be very helpful in my popularity in the classroom. Like, you've gotta win them over somehow. I don't overdo it. I don't always wear a suit jacket, but I look professional, you know, I wear a bit of makeup." Several of our participants described similar work to achieve a look of feminized professionalism, which they hoped would circumvent gendered comments and notions of gender-based competency. In the face of these pressures, for some, the performance of professionalism in the classroom was the one thing they felt they could control. As one sessional put it, "I can't change my physical features, I can't change my gender, I can't change how I look, but what I can do is I can make sure that when I enter that classroom, that I'm professional, that I look professional, and that I act professionally."

These efforts were often unsuccessful in circumventing these gendered dynamics. As one participant put it, "Because I look young, I try to look older than them, even older than I am. When I teach, I'm wearing a dress and I have lipstick and makeup on." She explained that these efforts were ultimately in vain because she still received "the most gendered comments," including students sarcastically asking, "do you like my lipstick?" She also recounted students saying that "she's incompetent and she doesn't know what she's doing." One of our participants summed up the experience of being unable to circumvent or successfully mitigate against these impacts by stating, "I have a PhD. It shouldn't matter what clothes I'm wearing, but it does."

To circumvent discrimination based on their gender, age, and race, many of our participants also described engaging in aesthetic labour that involves performances of academic authority in the classroom. As one contract lecturer explained:

> I have very good credentials. I got a PhD from [an ivy league university]. So, I make a point, at the beginning of every class, of spending a lot of time telling them my background, "oh, I did this, I got a PhD, I've been to this, I've done these internships, I've been to these places." It serves a bunch of purposes. It tells them I am very qualified, so you cannot judge me by my appearance, and you cannot judge me by my gender, and you have to respect me.

Along similar lines, another participant stated: "I make a point of starting the term off like that because it establishes me as a professional, whereas if I just came in and started teaching the material, I'm not sure that they would take me seriously."

Rather than emphasizing credentials, other participants described how they intentionally draw attention to their teaching expertise. One of our participants explained this as follows: "I will signal to them why I do things, pedagogically communicating why the course is the way it is. I specifically communicate 'I did this, so you are going to be able to succeed.' But doing so entails a lot of labour." Others outlined similar approaches that were also labour intensive, involving the expenditure of significant time and energy to explain their pedagogical approaches and teaching-specific experience or training to students. Like the work of performing feminized professionalism, however, many participants acknowledged that the forms of aesthetic labour used to establish academic authority were not always successful. They explained how their SET scores and comments suggest that students continue to judge their bodies, clothing, or accents according to discriminatory assumptions about who is a "real" academic. In particular, they described how, unlike their older, white, male colleagues, who do not have to work hard to convince students of their professorial status, their gender, age, and racialized characteristics make students less likely to see their competence and skill. Thus, one participant described how she "corrects" her accent to avoid negative comments, recognizing that "if I was white, it wouldn't be as [much of] a concern." Some instructors also described instances when students made discriminatory assumptions about them and their status based on their gender and age. As one sessional instructor said:

> I'm certain that if someone who looked a lot older than me and who was male walked into the classroom, they would be treated much differently. I do look very

young for my age. I actually once walked into one of my classrooms and someone thought I was a student. I've had male students ask me if I'm single. Because I look like I'm, you know, eighteen, I get a very different response.

For many of these instructors, performing feminized professionalism was one small but often futile way to exercise agency in the face of students' inescapable discriminatory assumptions about their competence and skill.

Many participants also described how being a precariously employed instructor undermined the aesthetic labour of performing and maintaining the academic role. They recognized that the material conditions of their teaching were part of the issue, such as not having an office in which to meet students, but identified the significant role that SETs play in undermining this work. They explained the incongruence of portraying themselves as professionals and being subjected to evaluations that do not measure their teaching abilities. They emphasized the fact that these evaluations determined their future employment prospects, in terms of contract renewal, the possibility of an eventual tenure-track position, or even being pushed out of academe all together, and explained that these threats pushed them to engage in customer-service types of behaviour that detract from their credibility as academics. As one contract lecturer said, "I'm trapped, I'm stuck. I don't think people get how hamstringing that is." They further explained that "what gets me the job two years from now is going be whether or not these guys are happy and had fun? I'm not a fucking cruise director ... And that's what evaluations engender! They engender cruise directing." These are the kinds of inequities that precariously employed academic women recognized they were uniquely subjected to. The relation between their job (in)security, SETs, and broader gender-based assumptions about academic appearance compelled many to engage in this additional, and often ineffectual or demeaning, labour.

The Hidden Work of Caring

SETs impose unique pressures on precariously employed women instructors to engage in other forms of labour that are often unrelated to teaching and learning. However, in a context where positive evaluations affect continued employment, this labour can feel necessary for the precariously employed. Describing these pressures, many participants spoke about the care work and emotional labour they feel pressured to perform in the classroom. Unlike men, these women instructors said that students expect them to be emotionally sensitive, caring, and "motherly," particularly if they are older women, and evaluate their teaching accordingly. Many suggested that the work of conforming to these expectations not only adds to their workload, but also has larger impacts on their mental health and well-being. One sessional explained:

> I've had a number of courses in which the emotional labour that I had to put into them, for the students not to consider me cold or off-putting, was quite intense. They expect me to be very concerned with the things that are going on in their lives. That's not to say that I'm not, but there is a sense that they're more likely to be more personal with me because I'm female, to tell me about their troubles or specific aspects of their personal lives, which I'm then supposed to make accommodations for.

Along similar lines, another sessional said, "I feel like I have to be nurturing them as well as educating them. There's an expectation that I do these things that may not necessarily be there with male faculty." Some described these expectations as rooted not only in their gender, but also in their age. Older women, many participants said, are often expected to be mothering toward students. Describing this phenomena, one contract instructor asserted, "It's amazing how many of us, all women, most of us older, have students who will send emails saying 'I can't come to class today because I'm having menstrual cramps.' Would you say that to a man? Do you say that to women who look more like your own age, rather than *mom*?" From the perspective of these participants, women, particularly older women, work under unique pressures to "mother" students and respond to their emotional needs in the classroom and beyond.

Not living up to these gendered expectations can have consequences for precariously employed instructors. When expectations are not met, many participants explained that students often become disappointed, frustrated, or angry, which can have negative impacts on quantitative scores and qualitative comments in their SETs. Describing this, one participant said, "I've seen this, not just with me, but with other middle-aged women ... students will sometimes come to us as though we're mom, and if we're not mom, that's disappointing." Expressing a similar sentiment, another participant said, "If we fail to be mom, we're mean." Several participants described how they feel significant pressure to engage in gendered forms of emotional labour when responding to students to avoid negative comments in their SETs that they are insufficiently caring.

Participants also expressed frustration with the fact that the emotional labour they feel pressured to perform is often devalued and unrecognized by their colleagues and supervisors. One contract instructor explained that in the last two years over fifty students had disclosed their experiences of sexual and physical victimization to her, to which she worked to respond with empathy and compassion. This emotional labour, she said, not only added to her workload, but also went largely unseen and unacknowledged by her colleagues. Reflecting on this experience, she said, "That's a lot of emotional labour, and I don't think that anybody sees that. It's a lot of emotional labour on top of all of the teaching, and the service, and then the research I'm trying to do, and I don't feel like it's valued."

Students' expectations of women instructors' emotional labour, as well as the broader consequences of this labour on instructors, have far reaching impacts on equality in the academy. Under the threat of negative teaching evaluations, instructors who identify as women are pressured to do additional labour in the classroom that can be mentally, emotionally, and psychologically draining and which often goes largely unrecognized. These negative impacts are not equally felt across the academic workforce and thus fuel existing inequities in the academy.

IMPACTS ON MENTAL HEALTH AND EQUALITY IN THE ACADEMY

SETs have significant impacts on individual instructors' mental health, confidence, and well-being. For some, these impacts were most acute when they first started teaching. One contract lecturer stated, "I was scared to look at my evaluations myself. I had to ask a friend, 'Can you read my evaluations and summarize them for me?' Yeah, it was very hard on me." Another participant explained that she briefly stopped teaching because of a particularly negative experience with SETs early in her career, of which she said she still feels the effects; another described how "early on, it was really tough" because her evaluations had contributed to "a sort of spiral into depression" that led her to take antidepressants for several years. Other participants spoke of the unique challenges that new instructors face, and several suggested that the combination of employment precarity and SET pressures made these challenges more difficult to bear. One contract lecturer described living through that experience as follows: "I cried a lot the first couple of years I was here. It was a few years of a kind of hellish, non-existence."

Others described the SETs' negative effects on mental health as an ongoing struggle. One sessional explained how demoralizing it can be to read the comments and see the SET scores after a teaching term, while another called SETs "emotionally devastating." Many participants described the ongoing negative impact that SETs have on their confidence in the classroom. One said, "Negative feedback always impacts my sense of security standing in front of a room," while another explained, "[SETs] made me fearful, anxious, and changed how I teach. I think I probably do a lot more work than maybe male professors do in terms of trying to keep students satisfied." Others went further and talked about SETs in terms of abuse. Expressing this sentiment, one sessional suggested that SETs are "kind of like an abusive relationship. They twist your mind and they make you think that you are the problem." To manage these negative impacts, several participants said they avoid looking at their SETs. Putting this succinctly, one sessional explained, "I try not to read them because they're hurtful." However, others suggested that, unlike their permanently employed colleagues, they do not always have the privilege of not looking at their SETs because they are often forced to include them in job applications for new teaching positions.

The negative impacts of SETs on instructors' mental health are inequitably distributed across the academic workforce and, in many ways, are exacerbated for precariously employed instructors from equity-seeking groups. One participant described how the pressures to maintain positive SETs are amplified by her employment precarity by saying, "As a sessional instructor who's very, very aware of the precariousness of her position, formal students evaluations seem more like a ... threat is not really the word, but like they're just this thing that hangs over you." By employing SETs, university administers are relying on a tool that has potential to negatively affect the mental health of their employees, particularly those who are precariously employed and from equity-seeking groups. Given the differential impacts of SETs on precariously employed and permanent instructors, the inequitable conditions of academic work are maintained through the continued use of SETs.

DISCUSSION

An increase in mental distress among academics has been recognized in recent academic literature (Catano et al. 2010; Hall and Bowles 2016). Whereas the academy has long been a highly competitive space for privileged (white, straight, middle-class, able-bodied, and cisgender) men, sociologists Claire Polster and Janice Newson (2015) and many other scholars have demonstrated that neoliberalism, a socioeconomic philosophy and ideology characterized by free-market policies and fiscal austerity, is transforming higher education. Management of universities as corporations driven by the interests of profit is fuelling new distress through the growth of underpaid and precarious teaching positions. Neoliberalism in the academy also engenders "more profound kinds and levels of competition than existed previously in higher education, and ... there are significant qualitative transformations of the academy arising from this competition" (Berg, Huijbens, and Larsen 2016, 172). The increased experience of anxiety and mental distress, moreover, has been recognized as not simply symptomatic of neoliberalism; as sociologist Vik Loveday (2018) explains, it also perpetuates neoliberalism by inciting precariously employed academics to continuously participate in competitiveness.

More broadly, these research findings demonstrate the importance of attending to the gendered, age-related, and race-related dynamics that contribute to mental distress in the context of the competitive cultures in higher education. The participants in this study demonstrated the fundamental role that SETs play in producing these effects and the unique ways that precariously employed academic women experience them. The participants' engagement in various forms of aesthetic labour was often grounded in their recognition that SETs contribute to gender, age-based, and racial inequities. Giving this labour was an attempt to circumvent or strategically navigate these inequities in their individual lives. As many of them suggested, this work was often unsuccessful in averting these negative outcomes. Aesthetic labour was an additional, substantial form of labour that academic women felt compelled to engage.

Our findings also address the ways that SETs impact the care-related ideals and practices of precariously employed academic women. The small but growing literature on care and precariously employed academic women renders salient the current reality of care in these spaces despite the fact that care is generally ignored or taken for granted in the university context. This scholarship has outlined the challenges that academic women face engaging in caring relations. Care-free masculinized ideals of competition and neoliberal justifications and validations of precarious academic labour remain preeminent (Cardozo 2017; Ivancheva, Lynch, and Keating 2019). Despite work conducted to date, care scholarship places insufficient emphasis on how precariously employed academic women are "forced to care" (Glenn 2010) and how this imperative is experienced by them. Our participants identified SETs as a coercive instrument that forced them to engage in caring behaviours and this experience requires research attention as well.

Acknowledging the potential coerciveness of this form of care work in higher education is an essential part of addressing increasing inequities in higher education. Among those seeking to apply the broader care literature to higher education, those focusing on value care ideals and practices in universities must contend with the reality of coerced care and its impact on precariously employed academic women's mental health. Moreover, while students deserve instructors who care about teaching, and precariously employed academic women deserve to engage in care practices, those who value the ethic of care in higher education will not find it supported by SETs as a tool (for one perspective on how care might be valued in higher education, see Niemann, this volume). SETs do not produce this "vivifying ethic of care that (re)turns institutional resources toward the providers of the nurturant labor that our society so desperately needs" (Cardozo 2017, 423). Indeed, quite the opposite is true. SETs reinforce the treatment of students as "consumer-critics" and do not engender the "practices that encourage acceptance, trust, inclusion, and openness" (O'Brien 2010, 109, 114). Redress of the inequities caused by SETs is needed to transform institutions of higher education into spaces where caring is neither punished nor coerced and it can serve an ethical foundation for the conditions of education.

CONCLUSION

This study demonstrates the importance of addressing precariously employed academic women's experiences of SETs and the impact of SETs on aesthetic labour, caring labour, and mental health. Research on precariously employed academic women's experiences of SETs is crucial for developing a better understanding of the impact of SETs on inequities in higher education. Applying an intersectional feminist framework to this problem and extending scholarship on emotional labour and care to these experiences can illustrate the contributions of SETs to greater mental distress and additional labour burdens for precariously employed academic women. Our findings clearly demonstrate that this evaluation tool is creating additional labour and mental distress. Moreover, despite recognition of these inequities among precariously employed academic women, and their attempts to circumvent or strategically navigate these negative impacts at an individual level, what is needed is systemic redress of these inequities. Without this redress, these dynamics will continue to perpetuate and deepen inequities within academe.

A starting point for this is recognition of the ways that SETs are implicated in broader neoliberal trends of increased competition, anxiety, and mental distress that combine with gendered, age-related, and race-related dynamics to produce particularly fraught inequitable working and teaching conditions for precariously employed academic women. This redress must also carefully address how SETs sustain coerced forms of caring from precariously employed academic women and more equitably distribute the responsibility for caring within higher education.

NOTE

1 During the interviews, we provided our participants the opportunity to share insights about the impact of power relations beyond those we specified in our questions. This elicited some broad discussions of power relations in the context of SETs, as described below.

WORKS CITED

Acker, Sandra, and Grace Feuerverger. 1996. "Doing Good and Feeling Bad: The Work of Women University Teachers." *Cambridge Journal of Education* 26 (3): 401–22. https://doi.org/10.1080/0305764960260309.

Arber, Sara, and Jay Ginn. 1992. "Class and Caring: A Forgotten Dimension." *Sociology* 26 (4): 619–34. https://doi.org/10.1177/0038038592026004005.

Armstrong, Pat. 1997. "Restructuring Public and Private: Women's Paid and Unpaid Work." In *Challenging the Public/Private Divide: Feminism, Law and Public Policy*, edited by Susan Boyd, 37–61. Toronto: University of Toronto Press.

Armstrong, Pat, and Susan Braedley, eds. 2013. *Troubling Care: Critical Perspectives on Research and Practices.* Toronto: Canadian Scholars Press.

Basow, Susan, and Julie Martin. 2013. "Bias in Student Evaluations." In *Effective Evaluation of Teaching: A Guide for Faculty and Administrators*, edited by Mary Kite, 40–49. Washington: Society for the Teaching of Psychology.

Bellas, Marcia L. 1999. "Emotional Labor in Academia: The Case of Professors." *The ANNALS of the American Academy of Political and Social Science* 561 (1): 96–110. https://doi.org/10.1177/000271629956100107.

Berg, Lawrence D., Edward H. Huijbens, and Henrik Gutzon Larsen. 2016. "Producing Anxiety in the Neoliberal University." *Canadian Geographer/Géographe canadien* 60:168–80. https://doi.org/10.1111/cag.12261.

Bezanson, Kate, and Meg Luxton, eds. 2006. *Social Reproduction: Feminist Political Economy Challenges Neo-liberalism.* Montreal: McGill-Queen's University Press.

Bono, Federica, Valerie De Craene, and Anneleen Kenis. 2019. "My Best Geographer's Dress: Bodies, Emotions and Care in Early-Career Academia." *Geografiska Annaler: Series B, Human Geography* 101 (1): 21–32. https://doi.org/10.1080/04353684.2019.1568200.

Bos, Angela, Jennie Sweet-Cushman, and Monica Schneider. 2017. "Family-Friendly Academic Conferences: A Missing Link to Fix the 'Leaky Pipeline'?" *Politics, Groups, and Identities* 7 (3): 748–58. https://doi.org/10.1080/21565503.2017.140393.

Brown, Scarlett. 2017. "PhD Barbie Gets a Makeover! Aesthetic Labour in Academia." In *Aesthetic Labour*, edited by Ana Sofia Elias, Rosalind Gill, and Christina Scharff, 149–63. London: Palgrave Macmillan.

Cardozo, Karen M. 2017. "Academic Labor: Who Cares?" *Critical Sociology* 43 (3): 405–28. https://doi.org/10.1177/0896920516641733.

Catano, Vic, Lori Francis, Ted Haines, Haresh Kirpalani, Harry Shannon, Bernadette Stringer, and Laura Lozanzki. 2010. "Occupational Stress in Canadian Universities: A National Survey." *International Journal of Stress Management* 17 (3): 232–58. https://doi.org/10.1037/a0018582.

Cronin, Ann, and Andrew King. 2010. "A Queer Kind of Care: Some Preliminary Notes and Observations." In *LGBT Issues: Looking Beyond Categories*, edited by Rebecca Jones and Richard Ward, 69–81. Edinburgh: Dunedin.

Cutcher, Leanne, and Pamela Achtel. 2017. "'Doing the Brand': Aesthetic Labour as Situated, Relational Performance in Fashion Retail." *Work, Employment and Society* 31 (4): 675–91. https://doi.org/10.1177/0950017016688610.

Dickson, Martina. 2018. "The Joys and Challenges of Academic Motherhood." *Women's Studies International Forum* 71 (November–December): 76–84. https://doi.org/ 10.1016/j.wsif.2018.08.008.

Donaghue, Ngaire. 2017. "Seriously Stylish: Academic Femininities and the Politics of Feminism and Fashion in Academia." In *Aesthetic Labour*, edited by Ana Sofia Elias, Rosalind Gill, and Christina Scharff, 231–46. London: Palgrave Macmillan.

Ferguson, Sue. 2008. "Canadian Contributions to Social Reproduction: Feminism, Race and Embodied Labor." *Race, Gender and Class* 15 (1–2): 42–57.

Field, Cynthia C., and Glen A. Jones. 2016. *A Survey of Sessional Faculty in Ontario Publicly-Funded Universities.* Toronto: Centre for the Study of Canadian and International Higher Education, OISE-University of Toronto.

Folbre, Nancy, and Erik Olin Wright. 2012. "Defining Care." In *For Love and Money*, edited by Nancy Folbre, 1–20. New York: Russell Sage Foundation.

Foster, Karen, and Louise Birdsell Bauer. 2018. *Out of the Shadows: Experiences of Contract Academic Staff.* Canadian Association of University Teachers. https://www. caut.ca/sites/default/files/cas_report.pdf.

Glenn, Evelyn Nankano. 2010. *Forced to Care.* Cambridge, MA: Harvard University Press.

Good, Laura, and Rae Cooper. 2016. "'But It's Your Job to Be Friendly': Employees Coping with and Contesting Sexual Harassment from Customers in the Service Sector." *Gender, Work and Organization* 23 (5): 447–69. https://doi.org/10.1111/ gwao.12117.

Grant, Karen, Carol Amartunga, Pat Armstrong, Madeline Boscoe, Ann Pederson, and Kay Willson, eds. 2004. *Caring For/Caring About: Women, Home Care, and Unpaid Caregiving.* Aurora, ON: Garamond Press.

Guarino, Cassandra M., and Victor M.H. Borden. 2017. "Faculty Service Loads and Gender: Are Women Taking Care of the Academic Family?" *Research in Higher Education* 58:672–94. https://doi.org/10.1007/s11162-017-9454-2.

Hall, Rebecca. 2016. "Caring Labours as Decolonizing Resistance." *Studies in Social Justice* 10 (2): 220–37.

Hall, Richard, and Kate Bowles. 2016. "Re-Engineering Higher Education: The Subsumption of Academic Labour and the Exploitation of Anxiety." *Workplace: A Journal of Academic Labour* 28:30–47. http://ices.library.ubc.ca/index.php/workplace/article/ view/186211/185389.

Hochschild, Arlie. 1983. *The Managed Heart: Commercialization of Human Feeling.* Berkeley: University of California Press.

Huppatz, Kate, Kate Sang, and Jemina Napier. 2018. "'If You Put Pressure on Yourself to Produce Then That's Your Responsibility': Mothers' Experiences of Maternity Leave and Flexible Work in the Neoliberal University." *Gender, Work and Organization* 26 (6): 772–88.

Iszatt-White, Marian, ed. 2013. *Leadership as Emotional Labour.* London: Routledge. https://doi.org/10.4324/9780203098400.

Ivancheva, Mariya, Kathleen Lynch, and Kathryn Keating. 2019. "Precarity, Gender and Care in the Neoliberal Academy." *Gender, Work and Organization* 26:448–62.

Joye, Shauna, and Janie H. Wilson. 2015. "Professor Age and Gender Affect Student Perceptions and Grades." *Journal of the Scholarship of Teaching and Learning* 15 (4): 126–38.

Karlsson, Jan Ch. 2012. "Looking Good and Sounding Right: Aesthetic Labour." *Economic and Industrial Democracy* 33 (1): 51–64. https://doi.org/10.1177/0143831X11428838.

Kelan, Elisabeth K. 2013. "The Becoming of Business Bodies: Gender, Appearance, and Leadership Development," *Management Learning* 44 (1): 45–61. https://doi.org/10.1177/1350507612469009.

Lazos, Sylvia R. 2012. "Are Student Teaching Evaluations Holding Back Women and Minorities? The Perils of 'Doing' Gender and Race in the Classroom." In *Presumed Incompetent: The Intersections of Race and Class for Women in Academia*, edited by Gabriella Gutiérrez y Muhs, Yolanda Flores Niemann, Carmen G. González, and Angela P. Harris, 164–85. Boulder: Utah State University Press, an imprint of University of Colorado Press.

Lipton, Briony. 2021. "Academics' Dress: Gender and Aesthetic Labour in the Australian University." *Higher Education Research and Development* 40 (4): 767–80. https://doi.org/10.1080/07294360.2020.1773767.

Loveday, Vik. 2018. "The Neurotic Academic: Anxiety, Casualisation, and Governance in the Neoliberalising University." *Journal of Cultural Economy* 11 (2): 154–66. https://doi.org/10.1080/17530350.2018.1426032.

Mählck, Paula. 2013. "Academic Women with Migrant Background in the Global Knowledge Economy: Bodies, Hierarchies and Resistance." *Women's Studies International Forum* 36 (January-February): 65–74. https://doi.org/10.1016/j.wsif.2012.09.007.

Mann, Sandi, and James Cowburn. 2005. "Emotional Labour and Stress within Mental Health Nursing." *Journal of Psychiatric and Mental Health Nursing* 12 (2): 154–62. https://doi.org/10.1111/j.1365-2850.2004.00807.x.

Mavin, Sharon. 2009. "Navigating the Labyrinth: Senior Women Managing Emotion." *International Journal of Work Organisation and Emotion* 3 (1): 81–87.

McGill University. 2014. "Policy on End-of-Course Evaluations." https://www.mcgill.ca/mercury/about/policy.

Mears, Ashley. 2014. "Aesthetic Labor for the Sociologies of Work, Gender, and Beauty." *Sociology Compass* 8 (12): 1330–43.

Mirchandani, Kiran. 2003. "Challenging Racial Silences in Studies of Emotion Work: Contributions from Anti-Racist Feminist Theory." *Organization Studies* 24 (5): 721–42. https://doi.org/10.1177/0170840603024005003.

Misra, Joya, Jennifer Hickes Lundquist, and Abby Templer. 2012. "Gender, Work-Time, and Care Responsibility among Faculty." *Sociological Forum* 29 (2): 300–23. https://doi.org/10.1111/j.1573-7861.2012.01319.x.

Mitchell, Kristina, and Jonathan Martin. 2018. "Gender Bias in Student Evaluations." *PS: Political Science and Politics* 51 (3): 648–52. https://doi.org/10.1017/S104909651800001X.

Moore, Monica, and Gwyneth Williams. 2014. "No Jacket Required: Academic Women and the Problem of the Blazer." *Fashion, Style and Popular Culture* 1 (3): 359–76. https://doi.org/10.1386/fspc.1.3.359_1.

Neysmith, Sheila. 1991. "From Community Care to a Social Model of Care." In *Women's Caring: Feminist Perspectives on Social Welfare,* edited by Carol Baines, Patricia Evans, and Sheila Neysmith, 272–99. Toronto: McClelland and Stewart.

Noddings, Nel. 1984. *Caring: A Feminine Approach to Ethics and Moral Education.* Berkeley: University of California Press.

Nzinga-Johnson, Sekile. 2013. "Carefully Vetted: Black Academic Women's Negotiations of Motherhood." *Journal of the Motherhood Initiative* 4 (1): 138–54.

O'Brien, Leigh, M. 2010. "Caring in the Ivory Tower." *Teaching in Higher Education* 15 (1): 109–15.

Pasma, Chandra, and Shaker, Erika. 2018. *Contract U: Contract Faculty Appointments at Canadian Universities.* Ottawa, ON: Canadian Centre for Policy Alternatives. https://www.policyalternatives.ca/sites/default/files/uploads/publications/National%20Office/2018/11/Contract%20U.pdf.

Petersson McIntyre, Magdalena. 2016. "Looking the Part: Negotiating Work Clothes, Gender and Expertise in Retail." *Fashion Practice* 8 (1): 117–34. https://doi.org/10.1080/17569370.2016.1147698.

Polster, C., and Newson, J. 2015. *A Penny for Your Thoughts: How Corporatization Devalues Teaching, Research, and Public Service in Canada's Universities.* Ottawa, ON: Our Schools/Our Selves and the Canadian Centre for Policy Alternatives.

Ramjattan, Vijay A. 2019. "Raciolinguistics and the Aesthetic Labourer." *Journal of Industrial Relations* 61 (5): 726–38. https://doi.org/10.1177/0022185618792990.

Reinsch, Roger, Sonia Goltz, and Amy Hietapelto. 2020. "Student Evaluations and the Problem of Implicit Bias." *Journal of College and University Law* 45: 114–40.

Sevenhuijsen, Selma. 1998. *Citizenship and the Ethics of Care: Feminist Considerations on Justice, Morality, and Politics.* London: Routledge.

Strongman, Kenneth, and Sarah Wright. 2008. "The Emotional Labour of Accountancy." *Pacific Accounting Review* 20 (2): 102–6. https://doi.org/10.1108/01140580810892454.

Thomas, Carol. 2007. "Care and Dependency: A Disciplinary Clash." In *Sociologies of Disability and Illness: Contested Ideas in Disability Studies and Medical Sociology.* New York: Palgrave Macmillan.

Timmermans, Stefan, and Iddo Tavory. 2012. "Theory Construction in Qualitative Research: From Grounded Theory to Abductive Analysis." *Sociological Theory* 30: 167–86.

Toerien, Merran, and Celia Kitzinger. 2007. "Emotional Labour in Action: Navigating Multiple Involvements in the Beauty Salon." *Sociology* 41 (4): 645–62. https://doi.org/10.1177/0038038507078918.

Tronto, Joan C. 2013. *Caring Democracy: Markets, Equality, and Justice.* New York: New York University Press.

Tuck, Jackie. 2018. "I'm Nobody's Mum in This University: The Gendering of Work around Student Writing in UK Higher Education." *Journal of English for Academic Purposes* 32:32–41. https://doi.org/10.1016/j.jeap.2018.03.006.

University of British Columbia. 2007. "Policy on Student Evaluation of Teaching." https://senate.ubc.ca/vancouver/policies/student-evaluation-teaching.

University of Toronto. 2020. "The Course Evaluation Framework at the University of Toronto." https://courseevaluations.utoronto.ca.

Watt, Paul. 2007. "I Need People That Are Happy, Always Smiling": Guest Interaction and Emotional Labour in a Canadian Downtown Hotel." *Just Labour: A Canadian Journal of Work and Society* 10 (Spring): 45–59.

Whitelegg, Drew. 2002. "Cabin Pressure: The Dialectics of Emotional Labour in the Airline Industry." *The Journal of Transport History* 23 (1): 73–86. https://doi.org/10.7227/TJTH.23.1.8.

Yeates, Nicola. 2012. "Global Care Chains: A State-of-the-Art Review and Future Directions in Care Transnationalization Research." *Global Networks* 12 (2): 135–54. doi:10.1111/j.1471-0374.2012.00344.

2

Research Ethics Boards, Women Researchers, and Fieldwork

TANYA BANDULA-IRWIN

Ethical behaviour and the safety of both researchers and research participants should be a top priority for academics, especially when undertaking fieldwork in fragile and conflict-ridden regions. It has been well-documented that conducting research on the ground in insecure settings incurs heightened risks for the researcher and research participants (Mazurana, Andrews Gale, and Jacobsen 2013). Correspondingly, ensuring the safety and protection of all involved – the researcher, research teams, research participants, and anyone else implicated by the presence of the researcher – requires the anticipation and implementation of greater precautions to mitigate the increased risks of such zones (Wood 2006; Cronin-Furman and Lake 2018; Mazurana and Andrews Gale 2013). Research has highlighted, however, that existing formal ethics processes designed to protect researchers and participants are inadequate to assure the necessary protections required in conflict zones (Fujii 2012). Researchers are left to adjudicate the creation and implementation of appropriate strategies, beyond those stipulated by the formal ethics approval processes, to ensure the protection of their participants and themselves in the field. Ad hoc decision making is particularly acute when researchers face unpredictable and changing circumstances in the field and must navigate ethical obligations upon field exit (Fujii 2012; Greenwald 2019; Schmidt 2020).

As this chapter demonstrates, a gendered examination of research ethics board (REB) approvals and protocols reveals an even greater disparity between formal REB processes and the realities and practices of researchers in conflict zones when compared across genders. While field research certainly presents unique and grave ethical considerations, conducting field research as a woman, or an individual who identifies as nonbinary, poses its own set of discrete challenges. While research has started to identify some of the challenges faced by women researchers in conflict zones (Clark and Grant 2015), institutional REBs' formal approval processes and protocols for women in fragile contexts has not been investigated.

To discourage discrimination on the grounds of gender, institutional REBs remain formally gender-blind when reviewing research protocols. Gender-blind review has a number of perverse implications, including REBs being unable to consider the unique challenges faced by women while researching in the field and, when the gender of the researcher is either voluntarily admitted or uncovered, unevenly applying gender-based requirements ad hoc. This chapter problematizes the gender-blind approach currently in practice across Canadian universities and identifies the disparities and inconsistencies in addressing gender-based safety and ethics concerns for researchers in insecure and conflict-affected areas. This chapter argues that a researcher's identity and positionality affect the nature and degree of complex challenges and risks of fieldwork and should therefore be considered in formal REB protocols and informal ethical practices.

This research is important for multiple reasons. First, gendered analysis of REBs helps inform appropriate and effective REB protocols to systematically address the specific challenges faced by researchers working in fragile contexts. Gender-sensitive amendments would consider important protections for researchers in the field, the teams of individuals that support research, and the research participants under study.

Second, consideration of gender in REB decision making is necessary from an equality perspective. For example, women remain underrepresented in the field of international security. Traditionally, research related to security, conflict, and war has been dominated by the voices and perspectives of men, and while the diversity of the field has increased, women's voices remain marginalized (Sjoberg 2008; Catic and von Hlatky 2014). Political scientist Stephen Saideman (2019) found that women made up only 29 percent of international relations scholars in Canada in 2014, growing to only 34 percent in 2017. As the findings of this chapter demonstrate, ad hoc gender sensitivity in institutional REB approvals leads to an inconsistent and unequal application of protective and pre-emptive ethics protocols and generates an inadequate set of tools and supports for women seeking to account for their unique position when researching in conflict zones. By addressing these gendered dynamics in their official approaches to ethics protocols management, institutional REBs can help level the playing field for women attempting to secure approval and craft REB protocols that support the unique ethical requirements of individual research agendas.

This chapter contextualizes formal research ethics processes and approvals regarding fieldwork broadly before raising the specific gendered challenges faced by researchers. The data presented in this chapter was collected from junior and senior scholars across six Canadian universities who have conducted fieldwork in fragile contexts and navigated formal REB processes, five of which are members of the U15 Canadian universities. Interviews were also conducted with key informants from Canadian REBs that are part of the U15 Canadian universities. All interview data have been anonymized. Data from official policies and guidelines from Canadian REBs, such as the guiding policies and principles of the U15 Group of Canadian REBs, were also used to inform the analysis.

In this chapter, I first describe and outline the guiding principles of REBs for researchers conducting fieldwork. Next, I analyze these approaches through a gender-sensitive lens and by highlighting disparities between formal and informal strategies for ethical considerations in conflict zones. I conclude by recommending ways to mitigate gendered blind spots for Canadian REBs.

REB PROTOCOLS IN THE FIELD: DANGEROUS DISPARITIES

The limitations of formal REB processes and approvals have been highlighted by scholars working in conflict zones for over ten years (Fujii 2012; Brooks 2013; Skinner 2014; Sluka 2018). Applying a gender-based analysis reveals additional causes for concern. The gender-blind approach maintained by Canadian institutions has two major implications for researchers conducting fieldwork in dangerous areas: (1) it underestimates, misidentifies, or entirely overlooks the potential risks that women and nonbinary researchers face in the field, and (2) it fails to provide the tools women and nonbinary researchers need to secure safe access to field conditions and thus impedes equality and multiperspective analyses in the field of international security.

First, the natural outcome of gender-blind REB review is that the gender-specific risks to researchers are not considered, and when they are, due to the intentional or inadvertent gender reveal of the researcher, ad hoc protocols are drawn up, often inadequately informed by scientific evidence; as a consequence, risk-mitigating strategies are inconsistently and unsystematically applied. This has severe implications for the safety and protection of the researcher, their research teams, guides, interpreters, and participants, as well as their data. As a result, gender-specific risks such as sexual violence, harassment, movements between locations, and integration in masculinized and violent settings are not systematically considered. Although the risks associated with research in conflict settings vary on a case-by-case basis, a gender-blind approach is not a suitable way to unpack and address these risks.

The second major implication of the gender-blind institutional review board ethics processes concerns matters of equality and diversity. As critical race scholars have already convincingly demonstrated, blind reviews of researchers and research intersecting race, gender, ethnicity, and other categories, and of research related to identity politics and its entrenched inequalities only serves to impede the advancement of equality (Berlak 2001; Bonilla-Silva 2006;

Crenshaw et al. 1995; Katzenbach and Marshall 2000; Katznelson 2006). This research has demonstrated how "race-blind" policies implemented under the auspices of equality and race-neutrality ultimately fail to account for or address existing inequalities and actually perpetuate these inequalities in the long run. Based on these findings, it is perplexing that REBs would opt for a gender-blind approach in the name of preventing gender discrimination when this practice is known to further entrench gender-based inequalities and increase the gender-based risks faced by researchers.

In practice, REB processes are rarely gender-blind. When the gender of the researcher is apparent to the reviewer, the researcher is often required to take measures against perceived gender-based risks. As suggested by a senior REB administrator, gender is only raised as an issue in REB protocols if the gender of the researcher is made explicit in the protocol.[1] The burden of accounting for gender-based risks, however, falls largely on the shoulders of researchers who must build reflexive consideration of their positionality and identity into their protocols. In small institutions, the ability of REBs to identify a researcher's gender is easier, and thus it is more difficult at these institutions to remain anonymous throughout the process. The formal gender-blind approach is therefore superficial, and when gender is known, there is a heavy burden on the researcher themselves to anticipate and adjudicate potential harms, which subjects them to heightened requirements and greater discrimination.

In some cases, these gender-based REB requirements may alienate scholars subject to extra rigour, and even discourage fieldwork entirely. In one interview with a woman scholar who conducted fieldwork in a postconflict setting, the institutional REB discouraged fieldwork on the subject matter in its entirety.[2] The effects of such a change could have untold impacts on publications, future job opportunities, and general career trajectory. If not for the perseverance and tenacity of the researcher in question, the research may not have ensued as planned. Indeed, the equality-related implications of a gender-blind approach, when applied, are severe and concerning; this approach provides a false comfort in protecting researchers in the field and breaking down barriers of gender inequality.

RISKS TO RESEARCHERS CONDUCTING FIELDWORK

Generally, the risks to researchers, participants, and research assistants are higher in fragile and conflict-affected areas than in other areas of research (Cassell 1980; Peritore 1990; Nordstrom and Robben 1996; Campbell 2017). Plausible risks in these contexts include kidnapping (Gifford and Hall-Clifford 2008; Tomei 2014), internment (Devkota and Van Teijlingen 2019; Grieser 2016;

Roberts 2014), and death. The unpredictable nature of security conditions also make it difficult to anticipate specific challenges ahead of fieldwork. Additionally, a less obvious but still very real concern is the impact and legacy that an individual's presence and research outputs might have on the conflict itself (Schmidt 2020; Carpenter 2012).

These risks apply not only to the researcher, but also to the research assistants, "fixers," guides, and even family members, who frequently accompany principal investigators throughout their work (Jenkins 2018; Kaplan, Kuhnt, and Steinert 2020; Lunn and Moscuzza 2014). Further, as many have pointed out, if the researcher is not safe and secure, then neither are their data, and correspondingly, their teams and participants are put at risk (Mazurana, Andrews Gale, and Jacobsen 2013; Wood 2013; Campbell 2017). In conflict zones, the security of data and confidentiality require greater vigilance than in normal settings because a loss of data could result in harassment, threats, or even death for participants by political opponents, the state, or other violent groups (Jenkins 2018). In these circumstances of extreme unpredictability, conflict zones often create a permissive environment in which REB protocols are easily discarded in the name of changing contexts on the ground (Cronin-Furman and Lake 2018), a matter few are willing to discuss for fear of retribution or ostracization due to perceived negligence.

Despite the strong case for special and careful attention to fieldwork ethics in conflict settings, and some recent research into the formulation of practical guidelines to address these considerations, scant literature exists on the specific risks and challenges faced by women operating in these contexts. In the sections that follow, I make the case that, in addition to the usual risks in conflict settings, women researchers in the field face additional security and ethical considerations. At present, the institutional processes designed to help prepare for these situations are unable to account for these challenges.

THE CASE FOR A GENDER-SENSITIVE APPROACH TO ETHICAL CONSIDERATIONS

All researchers share some common risks and ethical concerns when conducting fieldwork in conflict zones, but each research agenda carries its own particularities that must be considered, including the identity and positionality of the researcher. Unfortunately, a lack of gender-disaggregated data and a dearth of disciplinary attention to gender-specific risks makes it difficult to discern exactly what, and to what extent, gender affects ethical considerations and risk. Despite these limitations, this chapter finds, through qualitative analysis, that researchers' practices and lived experiences are highly distinct and that fieldwork is indeed a gendered experience. The threats faced by women and men working in volatile regions differ in important ways and require different approaches to mitigate. The gender of the researcher must therefore be considered when crafting ethics protocols and in attempts to mitigate risks for all involved.

Anthropologists Imogen Clark and Andrea Grant (2015) argue that the lack of attention to gender-disaggregated guidelines for fieldwork has left women vulnerable and unprepared for the specific risks they will face in the field. The gender-specific risks identified in the literature include: street harassment and intimidation (Congdon 2015; Sharp and Kremer 2006), securing protection while travelling between research sites (Felbab-Brown 2014; Isidoros 2015; Rogers-Brown 2015), sexual violence (Klob 2016; Moreno 1995; Ross 2015), navigating hypermasculinized and violent contexts (Baird 2017), operating in zones with weak gender rights protections (Isidoros 2015; Romano 2006), and the possibility of sexualized and gendered expectations of reciprocity and exchange (Clark and Grant 2015; Kovacs and Bose 2014).

In addition to the unique physical risks faced by women in the field, gendered identities impact the way research is conducted. This is especially true of gendered expectations of researcher behaviour based on their observed gender, which can create dilemmas for women attempting to build relationships with respondents without entering ethically compromised situations. Sociologists Eszter Kovacs and Arshiya Bose (2014, 109) recall one instance in which a potential informant stated: "No dinner, no drink, no interview." Further, in extremely gender regressive contexts, it can sometimes be the case that men simply will not speak to women (Felbab-Brown 2014), particularly if they are unmarried (Mukherjee 2020).

Of course, even if women experience the field differently than men, it does not necessarily follow that they are at a higher level of risk. Men are certainly not excluded from sexual violence during fieldwork, and neither are they immune to the risks of operating in violent or hypermasculine contexts. Indeed, because their gendered embodiment allows for participation in these realms, they may be even more susceptible to violence than women. For example, scholars who operate in areas that are highly masculinized or exhibit a machismo culture of strong, masculine pride are often warned about the associated risks of aggression or violence in these zones. As an ethnographer working on male masculinities, Adam Baird (2017, 356) writes about his experiences working with young gang members in Colombia, leveraging his own gender identity to develop relationships, or as he describes them, "ethically opaque friendships with gang members," which fostered trust between respondents and himself. As a result, Baird was granted access to violent environments that, as he writes, he may not have been able to access without leveraging his identity as a man. This experience demonstrates the very real likelihood that, in some cases, men are at higher risk because of their ability to enter and operate within masculinized contexts.

Women's experiences in the field, especially in more masculinized or patriarchal contexts, have also resulted in differential treatment by REBs. For example, some women scholars noted that their bodily safety was prioritized and protected, a privilege that one respondent suggested would likely not have been afforded to her had she been a man. This respondent, who worked among gang members in Central and South America, revealed her sense that, as a woman excluded from machismo culture, her protection and security was important to the gang members.[3] This was echoed by respondents interviewed for this chapter who work in highly patriarchal contexts that prioritized the protection of women.[4]

There is ample evidence that women working in conflict zones are typically perceived by locals as nonthreatening or harmless (Schmidt 2020; Zalcberg 2015; Felbab-Brown 2014). Women researchers have highlighted that, in some cases, their identity as a woman provides unique access as a result of this perceived lack of threat or, in other cases, on the grounds of a shared gender-based identity, such as a mother. Men operating in similar contexts may not be afforded the same leniency and access and might, in turn, be considered threatening to whomever they are researching, such as gang members, ex-guerrillas, or insurgent organizations, and thus vulnerable to riskier situations. What these findings make apparent is that the assumption that highly masculinized contexts are particularly risky for women places undue burden on women to account for their safety while also neglecting to address the unique risks that researchers of any gender may encounter in the field.

Finally, and importantly, there are very real differences in how researchers experience the field based on their intersectional identities. Race, sexuality, class, and other identity markers intersect with gender to create unique and distinct challenges for each individual researcher (Ortbals and Rincker 2009). On the one hand, some researchers have identified the benefits of a perceived insider status on the basis of shared racial identities (Ortbals and Rincker 2009) or racial ambiguity (Fujii 2018), which can create opportunities for increased access or at least an entry way for conversation and trust building (De Andrade 2000). On the other hand, a more frequently shared experience is limited access and challenges to legitimacy on the basis of certain marginalized identity markers (e.g., race, sexuality, class) (Henderson 2009; Di Feliciantonio, Gadelha, and DasGupta 2017; Kobayashi 1994). Worse still, researchers of colour and nonbinary or queer researchers have experienced violence because of their identity markers (Crenshaw 1991; La Pastina 2006). In sum, while men and women certainly experience the field in different ways, multiple aspects of identity are always intersecting to create disparate fieldwork experiences.

FINDINGS

The literature detailed above reveals the complexity of gendered challenges and risks in the field. In the winter of 2019, I conducted interviews with Canadian researchers and supervisors of international security and conflict across six Canadian universities and held discussions with Canadian REB offices and REB experts. These interviews and conversations revealed that these gender-specific risks are not adequately or consistently accounted for during REB reviews. This investigation uncovered the gendered nature of the burdens placed on researchers to account for their safety in the field, with gender much more likely to become a salient issue when the researcher identified as a woman.

In most instances, I found that the safeguards mandated by REBs were both inapplicable to field realities and undermined researcher expertise on the contexts under study. Further, the findings revealed an inconsistent application of gender-based considerations regarding potential risks to the researcher and research teams, with some researchers experiencing significant pushback because of their identity and others experiencing little to no discussion of gender-based risks. These findings are discussed in more detail below, though some details have been omitted to protect the identities of respondents given the comparatively small security and conflict research community in Canada.

One goal of this research is to capture the degree and extent to which women were required to address gender-based considerations from REBs. The results from interviews with both researchers and those who have supervised research revealed a number of gender-specific measures women have been required to undertake as a result of their gendered identity, including: chaperoned research; daily check-ins with institutional representatives or supervisors; limits on where research could be conducted; limits on when research could be conducted (i.e., only during the daytime); constraints and changes to the types of research questions being asked; general patronizing tones that implied researcher helplessness and dismissal of a researcher's expertise on the region(s) of research; and, at the most extreme, the termination of proposed fieldwork based on concerns for a woman's safety.

The general REB approval process was, for the most part, described as lengthy, with many (particularly junior) scholars having to revise and resubmit numerous drafts to meet these requirements. One respondent with extensive supervisory experience noted that women almost always incurred extra challenges when securing REB approval in comparison to men conducting similar work. In one telling case, another researcher who mimicked her REB protocol on an example provided by a man conducting similar research in the same region received extensive feedback and had to integrate gender-specific components and safeguards for which the men did not. These interviews demonstrate a clear gendered gap between the extra expectations of women to account for their security when conducting fieldwork.

In the cases where these restrictions and limitations were put in place, tangible impacts were felt on the research project itself. Many of the REB protocols forced researchers to amend the type of research they were conducting – that is, in several cases, subject matter and questions "were sanitized to the point of futility,"[5] while in other cases some fieldwork was outright rejected. Even in cases where women researchers consistently and repeatedly attempted to highlight the measures taken to protect themselves and to provide a better understanding of the real risks they expected to face in the places about which they were experts, REBs would not budge. In one instance, a junior scholar was required to take a chaperone despite the fact that the research would be conducted in international green zones, on nongovernmental organizations' compounds, and at large multinational companies – all areas where gender rights were safeguarded and safety concerns are relatively low risk. Yet, the REB insisted on a chaperone. The respondent noted feeling "patronized" and "like my regional expertise was completely disregarded."[6] In one other instance, due to lack of access to a chaperone, one respondent had to cancel a planned trip to the field. These anecdotes are troubling when we consider the potential implications these experiences may have for the future trajectories of women researchers in these fields, particularly for early-career researchers. As one respondent noted, negative experiences with the REB process turned her away from a career in academia.

Finally, and importantly, these findings demonstrate the uneven application of the official gender-blind approach to REB approvals, which is intended to discourage discrimination on the basis of gender for researchers conducting fieldwork. While some women faced the types of burdens and repeated negative interactions highlighted above, others had little to no discussion of gender-based risks at all – in some cases, they were given only an institutional phone number to the "safety abroad" unit and no training or guidance. This is, unfortunately, one of the implications of a gender-blind approach; such blindness cannot be uniformly applied in practice, and the extent to which it can be applied at all is questionable.

Given that REB protocols do not require researchers to identify their gender, it was curious that gender issues came up at all. During interviews in which gender challenges in the REB process were highlighted, it was revealed that in these cases, researchers either voluntarily provided reflexive accounts of how their gender would impact their research or else were probed on the basis of gender cues given in their proposals. Such an uneven approach has two perverse implications: First, it fails to systematically address the unique gender-based risks faced by researchers; and second, it runs the risk of placing undue, lengthy burdens on some scholars, especially women, to account for their safety in the field.

The extent to which gender-associated risks can be discerned is bounded by limited and reluctant disciplinary engagements on the subject. Researchers perceive very real threats to their credibility if they are honest about ethical practices in the field, especially if they contradict the guidelines set out in formal REB protocols.[7] Further, due to the gender-blind nature of REB protocol adjudications, large-N analysis of REB procedures is not possible due to the absence of gender-disaggregated data. Although fieldwork is gendered, mitigating gendered risks and challenges requires a balancing act between meeting the security needs and ethical obligations of researchers without creating undue burdens or unnecessary barriers on the grounds of gender. With these concerns in mind, the following section examines the current approach of Canadian REBs in relation to identifying and accounting for these risks.

MITIGATING RISKS FOR RESEARCHERS IN THE FIELD

Institutional review boards (IRBs) are the main official channel through which researchers develop their ethics protocols for fieldwork. Most academics are familiar with the process of crafting an ethics protocol for their home institution REB. For many, board approval is required before a new research project can begin. In Canada, most universities adhere to the guidelines set out by the Canadian government in the *Tri-Council Policy Statement (TCPS) on Ethical Conduct for Research Involving Humans* (TCPS 2018) and the *Tri-Agency Framework (TAF): Responsible Conduct of Research* (TAF 2016). The TCPS covers all research with human participants for the natural, health, and social sciences and primarily focuses on procedural matters, such as the application and approval processes, the process of securing informed consent, and privacy and confidentiality as it relates to data protection.

Unfortunately, matters of procedure are not terribly useful when navigating volatile contexts. Routine and formal procedures are often not possible and, in some cases, heighten risk. For example, the TCPS (2018, 47) states that "evidence of consent shall be contained either in a signed consent form or in documentation by the researcher of another appropriate means of consent." While obtaining consent is a crucial and essential component of fieldwork involving human participants, it can be dangerous to carry a signed consent form, in the case that a researcher is compromised while moving between locations (Skinner 2014). To make matters worse, the TCPS (2018, 25) makes it clear that "risks to researchers ... are not a formal part of [REBs'] responsibilities." As many have pointed out, this is unacceptable because it is impossible to keep data protected and confidential if the researcher is compromised, which in turn compromises all of those who are implicated in the research in any way (Fujii 2012; Mazurana, Andrews Gale, and Jacobsen 2013).

The TCPS (2018, 21) conceptualizes risk as the magnitude of harm considered against the likelihood of harm, and then contrasts this measure of risk against the potential benefits of the research. The TCPS (2018, 23) accounts for these varying degrees of risk by having proportionate levels of review assessment – the higher the perceived risk, the higher the level of scrutiny applied to the ethics protocol. Despite this flexibility, the TCPS, TAF, and institutional REBs regulate and adjudicate ethics protocols without explicitly accounting for the gender of the researcher (TCPS 2018; TAF 2021).[8] So, while conflict-specific risks might be accounted for at the institutional level, there is no formal and official way to account or prepare for the gender-specific risks that researchers might face when entering in the field. There are many dangerous discrepancies between official institutional ethics protocol procedures and the realities faced by researchers in conflict zones.

CONCLUSION

Navigating the gender-based dilemmas in REB processes is a two-pronged challenge. On the one hand, it is crucial that REBs consider the gender-based risks faced by researchers, their teams, and participants. Misguided assumptions about these risks due to the failure to account for gender makes formal REB protocols unhelpful and inappropriate for mitigating many challenges field researchers face. On the other hand, accounting for gender and other identity-based factors risks creating barriers or burdens for some researchers and not for others. The impacts of these barriers could be far reaching – from placing undue constraints on some researchers' projects to discouraging researchers from conducting fieldwork entirely. Neither of these outcomes are acceptable. I, therefore, argue that institutional REBs' current gender-blind assessment must be amended. Equality cannot be achieved by ignoring difference, and, as the works of critical race scholars show, researchers and their participants cannot be adequately protected without gendered considerations. Acknowledging these challenges, I now turn to some potential ways for researchers, REBs, and disciplines as a community to move practices forward – including reflexive practices of field ethics, directly addressing gender in REBs, and having open and honest conversations about the role of gender in ethical considerations within each relevant disciplinary community.

The safety and well-being of researchers, research participants, research teams, and field guides should remain the top priority for researchers – especially those operating in contexts with heightened risks, such as conflict and postconflict settings. As a result, there are some considerations that a researcher should weigh, regardless of formal and institutional processes of ethics approvals. The inapplicability of formal REB protocols has led some scholars to take safety and ethical concerns into their own hands, with some promising examples of ingenuity in fieldwork. For example, political scientist Jaimie Bleck and colleagues (2018) highlight the promise of North-South research collaborations to capitalize on local knowledge of risky areas, and political scientist Melani Cammett (2013) uses local researchers as proxy interviewers to help mitigate risks to herself and her participants by ensuring that the identity of the interviewers remains nonthreatening.

Researchers should also be cognizant of their positionality and the ways identity factors could influence or bias their outlook and impact on the world. Political scientist Lauren M. MacLean and colleagues (2019) call this "reflexive openness," a process that involves constant reflection on the ethics of one's research practices, which are then adjusted throughout the research process to adapt to changing circumstances or to insufficient ethical practices set out in original ethics protocols. The authors encourage a "reasoned ethical justification" for their research methods and actions, "especially when seeking to publish their analysis" (1). Likewise, political scientists Jenny Pearce and Nicholas Loubere (2017) suggest a "relational framework" for analyzing one's positionality vis-à-vis their research participants, teams, and the setting of their research to identify the risks precipitated by one's identity. Incorporating these reflexive insights into research design could help mitigate risks from the outset by ensuring that researchers are aware of the identity-based risks they face – risks that are, at present, omitted in the formal REB process.

It is useful for researchers to be proactive about their ethical considerations, but their institutional counterparts must also be reconfigured to support these efforts. At minimum, institutional REBs should account for gender in their ethics protocols assessments to address equality and discrimination as well as gender-specific risks related to research. The gender-blind stance of REBs is unacceptable because blindness to identity factors has been proven to inhibit equality, and, moreover, as discussed above, REB approval processes are unable to ensure gender-blindness to begin with. Further, the lack of gender-disaggregated data related to ethics protocol processes and approvals make it impossible to begin evaluating equality at the institutional level. Gender must be considered universally, consistently, and explicitly so that burdens and constraints are not disproportionately placed on some researchers and not others. Requiring REB applicants to explicitly consider their positionality in their research projects would ensure that REB approval processes account for the particular risks that a research project may entail, for both researcher and research participants.

In so doing, REBs could also begin collecting gendered data on their processes to enable gender-based analysis of best practices for fieldwork in various contexts.

At the same time, to explicitly identify and address researcher-specific risks, gender must be treated as an important issue for the ethics review process. This is necessary not only to protect and better prepare researchers as they enter the field, but also to protect their respondents and research teams. To account for these specific risks, REBs should encourage diversity on their approval boards, including a gender-balanced review team and subject-matter experts. These actions would help develop risk assessment and management protocols that are appropriate for the particular context in which the researcher is operating and relevant to the specific risks faced by the researcher's identity. Some promising examples of this approach have recently emerged at the institutional level. For example, in one case, a major Canadian research university invited an expert on conflict and postconflict research from a different university to sit on their REB board to advise on future cases involving fieldwork in dangerous regions.[9] Other institutions have allowed researchers to consult with in-house risk and security offices before, during, and after the research process. Unfortunately, these practices are not widespread and, where they are in place, still require service and support fine-tuning and accessible and standardized requirements for researcher-office engagement.[10] Including subject matter or methodology experts related to the proposed research would better enable REBs to provide meaningful and relevant guidelines for researchers as they embark on their fieldwork.

Finally, each discipline needs to engage in open and honest conversations regarding the discrepancies between formal REB protocols and the realities faced by researchers in the field. Although more rigorous work has been done on fieldwork ethics in the last decade, candid conversations about gendered challenges and practices while conducting fieldwork remain stifled due to researcher concerns about disclosing REB violations. These conversations remain, for the most part, private among trusted colleagues. Until researchers feel empowered to discuss these challenges openly and without repercussions, researchers will continue to face grave and perilous discrepancies between official training, protocols, and preparations for fieldwork and the realities on the ground – risking the safety of researchers, their teams, and research participants.

NOTES

1 Author interview with REB administrator, October 2019.
2 Author interview with researcher, March 2020.

3   Author interview, February 2020.
4   Author interviews, Winter and Spring 2020.
5   Author interview with researcher, February 2020.
6   Author interview with researcher, March 2020.
7   Author interviews with researchers, January and February 2019.
8   Based on an interview with a senior expert on Canadian REB practices, February 2019.
9   Author interview with researcher, March 2020.
10   In an interview conducted by the author in February 2020, one respondent indicated they were obliged to report to their appointed contact at their risk and security office – adding an additional task for the researcher that, they noted, was not required of others doing similar research in the field.

WORKS CITED

Baird, Adam. 2017. "Dancing with Danger: Ethnographic Safety, Male Bravado, and Gang Research in Colombia." *Qualitative Research* 18 (3): 342–60.

Berlak, Harold. 2001. "Race and the Achievement Gap." *Rethinking Schools* 15 (4): 10–11.

Bleck, Jaimie, Chipo Dendere, and Boukary Sangare. 2018. "Making North-South Research Collaborations Work." *PS: Political Science and Politics* 51 (3): 554–58.

Bonilla-Silva, Eduardo. 2006. *Racism without Racists: Color-Blind Racism and the Persistence of Racial Inequality in the United States.* Lanham, MD: Rowman and Littlefield.

Brooks, Sarah M. 2013. "The Ethical Treatment of Human Subjects and the Institutional Review Board Process." In *Interview Research in Political Science*, edited by Layna Mosley, 45–66. Ithaca, NY: Cornell University Press.

Cammett, Melani. 2013. "Using Proxy Interviewing to Address Sensitive Topics." In *Interview Research in Political Science*, edited by Layna Mosley, 125–43. Ithaca, NY: Cornell University Press.

Campbell, Susanna P. 2017. "Ethics of Research in Conflict Environments." *Journal of Global Security Studies* 2 (1): 89–101.

Carpenter, Charli. 2012. "'You Talk of Terrible Things So Matter-of-Factly in this Language of Science': Constructing Human Rights in the Academy." *PS: Political Science and Politics* 39 (3): 363–83.

Cassell, Joan. 1980. "Ethical Principles for Conducting Fieldwork." *American Anthropologist* 82 (1): 28–41.

Catic, Maja, and Stefanie von Hlatky. 2014. "Women, Gender, and International Security." *International Journal* 69 (4): 570–73.

Clark, Imogen, and Andrea Grant. 2015. "Sexuality and Danger in the Field: Starting an Uncomfortable Conversation." *Journal of the Anthropological Society of Oxford* 7 (1): 1–14.

Congdon, Venetia. 2015. "The 'Lone Female Researcher': Isolation and Safety upon Arrival in the Field." *Journal of the Anthropological Society of Oxford* 7 (1): 15–24.

Crenshaw, Kimberle. 1991. "Mapping the Margins: Intersectionality, Identity Politics, and Violence against Women of Color." *Stanford Law Review* 43 (6): 1241–1300.

Crenshaw, Kimberle, Neil T. Gotanda, Gary Peller, and Kendall Thomas. 1995. *Critical Race Theory: The Key Writings That Formed the Movement.* New York: The New Press.

Cronin-Furman, Kate, and Milli Lake. 2018. "Ethics Abroad: Fieldwork in Fragile and Violent Contexts." *PS: Political Science and Politics* 51 (3): 607–14.

De Andrade, Lelia Lomba. 2000. "Negotiating from the Inside: Constructing Racial and Ethnic Identity in Qualitative Research." *Journal of Contemporary Ethnography* 29 (3): 268–90.

Devkota, Bhimsen, and Edwin Van Teijlingen. 2019. "Challenges and Dilemmas in Conducting Conflict Research during Armed Violence: Lessons Learnt from Fieldwork in Nepal." Paper presented at the Nepal Research Conference on Peace, Justice and Inclusive Society, Lalitpur, Nepal, June 27–29, 2019.

Di Feliciantonio, Cesare, Kaciano B. Gadelha, and Debanuj DasGupta. 2017. "'Queer(y)Ing Methodologies: Doing Fieldwork and Becoming Queer' – Guest Editorial." *Gender, Place and Culture* 24 (3): 403–12. https://doi.org/10.1080/09663 69X.2017.1314950.

Felbab-Brown, Vanda. 2014. "Security Considerations for Conducting Fieldwork in Highly Dangerous Places or on Highly Dangerous Subjects." Working Paper No. 3. Washington: The Brookings Institution.

Fujii, Lee Ann. 2012. "Research Ethics 101: Dilemmas and Responsibilities." *PS: Political Science and Politics* 45 (4): 717–23.

–. 2018. *Interviewing in Social Science Research: A Relational Approach.* 1st ed. Routledge Series on Interpretive Methods. New York: Routledge.

Gifford, Lindsay, and Rachel Hall-Clifford. 2008. "From Catcalls to Kidnapping: Towards an Open Dialogue on the Fieldwork Experience of Graduate Women." *Anthropology News* 49 (6): 26–27.

Greenwald, Diana B. 2019. "Political Science Research in Settings of Intractable Conflict." *PS: Political Science and Politics* 52 (3): 1–5.

Grieser, Anna. 2016. "When the Power Relationship Is Not in Favour of the Anthropologist: Reflections on Fieldwork in Gilgit-Baltistan." *Zeitschrift Fur Ethnologie* 141 (2): 177–95.

Henderson, Frances B. 2009. "'We Thought You Would Be White': Race and Gender in Fieldwork." *PS: Political Science and Politics* 42 (2): 291–94.

Isidoros, Konstantina. 2015. "Between Purity and Danger: Fieldwork Approaches to Movement, Protection and Legitimacy for a Female Ethnographer in the Sahara Desert." *Journal of the Anthropological Society of Oxford* 7 (1): 39–54.

Jenkins, Sarah Ann. 2018. "Assistants, Guides, Collaborators, Friends: The Concealed Figures of Conflict Research." *Journal of Contemporary Ethnography* 47 (2): 143–70.

Kaplan, Lennart, Jana Kuhnt, and Janina I. Steinert. 2020. "Do No Harm? Field Research in the Global South: Ethical Challenges Faced by Research Staff." *World Development* 127.

Katzenbach, Nicholas deB., and Burke Marshall. 2000. "Not Color Blind: Just Blind." In *Sex, Race, and Merit: Debating Affirmative Action in Education and Employment*, edited by Faye J. Crosby and Cheryl VanDeVeers, 48–55. Ann Arbor: University of Michigan Press.

Katznelson, Ira. 2006. *When Affirmative Action Was White: An Untold History of Racial Inequality in Twentieth-Century America.* New York: W.W. Norton.

Klob, Sinah Theres. 2016. "Sexual(ized) Harassment and Ethnographic Fieldwork: A Silenced Aspect of Social Research." *Ethnography* 18 (3): 396–414.

Kobayashi, Audrey. 1994. "Coloring the Field: Gender, 'Race,' and the Politics of Fieldwork." *The Professional Geographer* 46 (1): 73–80. https://doi.org/10.1111/j.0033-0124.1994.00073.x.

Kovacs, Eszter, and Arshiya Bose. 2014. "Flirting with Boundaries: Ethical Dilemmas of Performing Gender and Sexuality in the Field." In *Fieldwork in the Global South: Ethical Challenges and Dilemmas*, edited by Jenny Lunn, 109–19. New York: Routledge.

La Pastina, Antonio C. 2006. "The Implications of an Ethnographer's Sexuality." *Qualitative Inquiry* 12 (4): 724–35.

Lunn, Jenny, and Alessandro Moscuzza. 2014. "Doing It Together: Ethical Dimensions of Accompanied Fieldwork." In *Fieldwork in the Global South: Ethical Challenges and Dilemmas*, 69–82. New York: Routeledge.

MacLean, Lauren Morris, Elliot Posner, Susan Thomson, and Elisabeth Jean Wood. 2019. "Research Ethics and Human Subjects: A Reflexive Openness Approach." American Political Science Association Organized Section for Qualitative and Multi-Method Research, Qualitative Transparency Deliberations, Working Group Final Reports, Report I.2. http://dx.doi.org/10.2139/ssrn.3332887.

Mazurana, Dyan, and Lacey Andrews Gale. 2013. "Preparing for Research in Active Conflict Zones: Practical Considerations for Personal Safety." In *Research Methods in Conflict Settings: A View from Below*, edited by Dyan Mazurana, Karen Jacobsen, and Lacey Andrews Gale, 277–92. Cambridge: Cambridge University Press.

Mazurana, Dyan, Lacey Andrews Gale, and Karen Jacobsen. 2013. "A View from Below: Conducting Research in Conflict Zones." In *Research Methods in Conflict Settings: A View from Below*, 3–26. Cambridge: Cambridge University Press.

Moreno, E. 1995. "Rape in the Field: Reflections from a Survivor." In *Taboo: Sex, Identity, and Erotic Subjectivity in Anthropological Fieldwork*, edited by Don Kulick and Margaret Willson, 219–50. London: Routeledge.

Mukherjee, Shruti. 2020. "Gendered Embodiment of the Ethnographer during Fieldwork in a Conflict Region of India." *Social Epistemology* 34 (1): 43–54.

Nordstrom, Carolyn, and Antonius C.G.M. Robben. 1996. *Fieldwork under Fire: Contemporary Studies of Violence and Culture*. Berkeley: University of California Press.

Ortbals, Candice D., and Meg E. Rincker. 2009. "Fieldwork, Identities, and Intersectionality: Negotiating Gender, Race, Class, Religion, Nationality, and Age in the Research Field Abroad: Editors' Introduction." *PS: Political Science and Politics* 42 (2): 287–90. https://doi.org/10.1017/S104909650909057X.

Pearce, Jenny, and Nicholas Loubere. 2017. "Under Threat: Working in Dangerous Environments." In *Understanding Global Development Research: Fieldwork Issues, Experiences and Reflections*, edited by Gordon Crawford, Lena J. Krukenberg, Nicholas Loubere, and Rosemary Morgan, 155–76. London: Sage Publications.

Peritore, Patrick. 1990. "Reflections on Dangerous Fieldwork." *The American Sociologist* (Winter): 359–72.

Roberts, Jennifer. 2014. "U of T Student's Detention Abroad Raises Issue of Schools' Responsibilities." *The Globe and Mail*, June 25, 2014.

Rogers-Brown, Jennifer B. 2015. "More Than a War Story: A Feminist Analysis of Doing Dangerous Fieldwork." *At the Center: Feminism, Social Science and Knowledge Advances in Gender Research* 20:111–31. https://doi.org/10.1108/S1529-212620150 000020006.

Romano, David. 2006. "Conducting Research in the Middle East's Conflict Zones." *PS: Political Science and Politics* 39 (3): 439–41.

Ross, Karen. 2015. "'Nor Sir, She Was Not a Fool in the Field': Gendered Risks and Sexual Violence in Immersed Cross-Cultural Fieldwork." *The Professional Geographer* 67 (2): 180–86.

Saideman, Stephen. 2019. "The State of International Relations Studies in Canada." Ottawa: Open Canada. https://www.opencanada.org/features/state-international -relations-studies-canada/.

Schmidt, Rachel. 2020. "When Fieldwork Ends: Navigating Ongoing Contact with Former Insurgents." *Terrorism and Political Violence* 33 (2): 312–23.

Sharp, Gwen, and Emily Kremer. 2006. "The Safety Dance: Confronting Harassment, Intimidation, and Violence in the Field." *Sociological Methodology* 36:317–27.

Sjoberg, Laura. 2008. "The Norm of Tradition: Gender Subordination and Women's Exclusion in International Relations." *Politics and Gender* 4 (1): 173–80.

Skinner, Chloe. 2014. "'You Can Be Jailed Here by Even Me Talking to You': Dilemmas and Difficulties Relating to Informed Consent, Confidentiality and Anonymity." In *Fieldwork in the Global South*, edited by Jenny Lunn, 183–91. New York: Routeledge.

Sluka, Jeffrey. 2018. "Too Dangerous for Fieldwork? The Challenge of Institutional Risk-Management in Primary Research on Conflict, Violence and 'Terrorism.'" *Contemporary Social Science* 15 (2): 241–57.

Tomei, Julia. 2014. "'I Always Carried a Machete When Travelling on the Bus': Ethical Considerations When Conducting Fieldwork in Dangerous Places." In *Fieldwork in the Global South*, edited by Jenny Lunn, 25–33. New York: Routledge.

Tri-Agency Framework (TAF). 2016. *Responsible Conduct of Research*. Ottawa: Secretariat on Responsible Conduct of Research. https://rcr.ethics.gc.ca/eng/documents/ Framework2016-CadreReference2016_eng.pdf.

–. 2021. *Responsible Conduct of Research*. Ottawa: Secretariat on Responsible Conduct of Research. https://rcr.ethics.gc.ca/eng/documents/framework-cadre-2021-en.pdf.

Tri-Council Policy Statement (TCPS). 2018. "Ethical Conduct for Research Involving Humans." Ottawa: Government of Canada.

Wood, Elisabeth Jean. 2006. "The Ethical Challenges of Field Research in Conflict Zones." *Qualitative Sociology* 29 (3): 373–86.

–. 2013. "Reflections on the Challenges, Dilemmas, and Rewards of Research in Conflict Zones." In *Research Methods in Conflict Settings: A View from Below*, edited by Dyan Mazurana, Karen Jacobsen, and Lacey Andrews Gale, 298–308. Cambridge: Cambridge University Press.

Zalcberg, Sara. 2015. "They Won't Speak to Me, but They Will Talk to You": On the Challenges Facing a Woman Researcher Doing Fieldwork among Male Ultra Orthodox Victims of Sexual Abuse. *Nashim: A Journal of Jewish Women's Studies and Gender Issues* 29:108–32.

3

Women and Service
Valuing Service in Tenure and Promotion

JUDE WALKER, ELENA IGNATOVICH, and MARYAM NABAVI

As women working in the academy, the topic of service is particularly close to our hearts. Many recent studies show that women faculty,[1] especially those who are racialized, tend to shoulder a comparably large amount of service responsibility, at times acting as the "maids of academe" (Harley 2008). We are aware of our privilege working in Canadian academia, which retains a tenure system in which the vast majority of assistant professors receive tenure. Even those of us who are pretenure or working as staff are particularly appreciative of our relatively secure employment. Yet, in Canada, as elsewhere, women bear a double service burden, acting as the chief operating officers at our homes (Bennett 2020; Moyer and Burlock 2018) and at the university (Acker, Weber, and Smyth 2016).

Women are often asked, or simply expected, to do more service work, which is generally unrewarded and lacking in prestige (see also Domingo et al. 2022; Hanasono et al. 2019). This dynamic has led to women experiencing increased incidences of burnout and higher rates of departure from the academy, as well as more general negative impacts on their mental and physical health, which were especially evident during the pandemic (Docka-Filipek and Stone 2021). This imbalance in labour thus reinforces gender inequality in our institutions and presents a key explanatory factor for the continuing persistence of a glass ceiling in academe, especially for minoritized women. Whereas the numbers and percentage of women in tenured positions at Canadian universities may have increased over the past decades, the "silent service economy" (Hogan 2005, 97) continues.

Service at Canadian universities is often considered the "third pillar" of faculty work, generally weighted (at least in theory) at around 20 percent of one's contributions, along with (ostensibly) 40 percent research and 40 percent teaching. However, as a category, service is often poorly articulated and can bleed into both research, for example, in community-based partnerships, and teaching, such as in community-service learning or meetings with students. Indeed, service is arguably the most obscure part of a faculty member's job. At work, as at home, women faculty appear to be performing more service on average. Women now constitute around 40 percent of full-time academic faculty in Canada (Statistics Canada 2017). Yet the institution, as with many workplaces, was designed by men for men (King 2020). Asking women to "stand up for themselves" or "just say no" to certain requests places the burden on women instead of considering what it would mean to make our institutions more equitable for women, particularly women who are members of other equity-deserving groups.

In this chapter, we reflect on the relationship between service and gender as it relates to a faculty member's job. To this end, we consider the presentation of service in tenure and promotion guidelines at U15 universities and their gendered implications.[2] In addition to a robust literature review of the relationship between gender and service, we specifically examined collective agreements and guidelines on tenure and promotion published between 2011 and 2019. We focus on U15 universities because there is a certain level of uniformity to them in the tripartite model of research, teaching, and service constituting the core activities of a faculty member's job, and in traditionally apportioning 20 percent of one's work to service. Our aim is to unpack what service means and how it is factored into tenure and promotion decisions in the context of research-intensive universities in Canada, as well as how the construction of faculty service can both allow for greater gender equity and hinder it.

Arguably, the central purpose of a university is to serve both students and society. A better understanding of *who* is serving, in what capacity, and how they are being rewarded for such service is a question of central importance in Canadian higher education. As our chapter shows, service can take a variety of different forms, some of which confer symbolic and actual capital to the faculty member and are considered directly in tenure and promotion decisions. We find that, in the collective agreements studied, there are two distinct notions of service: one that relates to the idea of the university-as-state, requiring good citizenship and adherence to the norms of the institution; and the other to the idea of university-community where a community of scholars and a connection to the outside community are emphasized. We suggest that both ideas of service are aspirational. We also believe that these distinct notions can tell us a great deal about what U15 universities consider to be the core elements of a good faculty member. Ultimately, we connect these constructions of service among the U15 universities to gendered assumptions of service, showing their direct affects on women faculty.

WHAT DO WE MEAN BY SERVICE FOR FACULTY MEMBERS IN THE ACADEMY?

Service is a catchall term that can be interpreted in a variety of ways. The main activity of an educational institution is service; teaching is service; research is service. The shift to conceiving of the university as a private economic good rather than a public asset has led us to consider students as "consumers" and faculty members as providing service delivery to enhance the brand of the university (see, e.g., Cohan 2018; Waring 2013). At the same time, we have seen increasing calls for the academy to serve the wider community; impressed upon faculty is the moral responsibility to serve beyond the confines of the institution (Walker 2008). Service, as it pertains to a faculty member's job, is therefore confusing. It has been referred to as "everything that is neither teaching, research, nor scholarship" (Blackburn and Lawrence 1995, 222). Yet, as we know, it also incorporates community-based research, community-service learning, and work-integrated learning (Alperin et al. 2019; Banerjee and Hausafus 2007; Bates 2011). It encompasses professional service (see, e.g., Boyer 1990; Rice 1995; Ward 2003) and includes sharing expertise with outside communities (O'Meara 2002), as well as providing informal mentorship, facilitating workshops, and giving advice to groups within the academy. Service relates to institutional and disciplinary citizenship (Hammer et al. 2019; Lynton 1995): doing what is expected in one's own department, institution, and discipline by serving on committees and stepping up for leadership roles in professional associations.

For faculty members, the university operates as a prestige economy (Blackmore and Kandiko 2011), where different activities and achievements allow us to accrue different amounts of symbolic capital. Certain capital is necessary for career advancement – either to take us to the next level (e.g., to attain tenure) or to help us rise above our peers as leaders in our field. We have attempted to categorize the different types of university service below.

The above categorizations and assessments may differ across universities and departments. As we note later in the chapter, the University of Toronto collective agreement makes it clear that service is not really counted in decisions for tenure and promotion. For other universities, it appears that service is counted at least nominally. What we do know is that different types of service are more likely to be counted and recognized than others. If anything, traditional research metrics have gained more importance in the tenure and promotion system, and while public and community service are increasingly expected, they are not generally rewarded (see, e.g., Alperin et al. 2019). Institutions are expanding their mission statements and goals, and university leaders are tending to place a high value on all kinds of institutional, professional, and community service (Jaeger and Thornton 2006), adding to the workloads (or at least the expected

TABLE 3.1
Faculty service: Type, prestige, and account in tenure and promotion

Type	Prestige	Counted	Benefits to tenure and promotion
University assigned (e.g., serving on departmental committees)	*Minimal or none* Depends on unit (e.g., university level more prestigious than departmental)	Often	If done well, seen as good departmental citizenship (colleagues supportive)
University invited (e.g., serving on university taskforces, senior appointments committees, etc.)	*Moderate* Depends on type of committee	Often	Can be considered as partial evidence of possessing certain expertise (folded into assessment of person as scholar)
Professionally invited or elected (e.g., grant reviewing, journal editorship, conference, association chairing, etc.)	*Moderate* Depends on prestige of committee/ journal/board, etc.	Often	Can be considered as partial evidence of scholarly expertise and leadership in the field
Community invited or elected (e.g., serving on board of directors, as adviser, engagement with community work, media interviews, etc.)	*Minimal to moderate* Depends on prestige of organization and relevance to discipline	Sometimes	Depending on community organization, could be considered as evidence of scholarly leadership
Service in teaching (e.g., student mentorship, community-service learning and partnerships, workshops, etc.)	*Minimal or none*	Sometimes	Can be considered toward assessment of teaching but much of the work is often hidden
Service in research (e.g., community-based research, research group meetings, engaging partners, etc.)	*Minimal or none*	Rarely	Outcomes and funding of research considered (grants, publications, talks) but much of the work is hidden

workloads) of faculty members. At the same time, much service is seen as minimally or completely unimportant with regards to tenure and promotion (Alperin et al. 2019; Jaeger and Thornton 2006; Woolston 2018). Further, service and administrative tasks, while often invisible or minimally rewarded, can take up a large percentage of a faculty member's time (Bacci et al. 2016; Fitzpatrick, Millette-Snodgrass, and Atef 2016; Ziker 2014). We see this as a gender-equity issue because not only are women, on average, appearing to do "more" service (cf. Figure 3.1), but they may be accruing little benefit from doing so (cf. Table 3.1). Women engage more in community-based research and teaching (Wade and Demb 2009) and also tend to be the ones to do the lowly "housework" of the department (Harley 2008).

WHAT IS THE RELATIONSHIP AMONG WOMEN FACULTY, SERVICE, AND TENURE AND PROMOTION?

We do not have a good sense of how many people who start as assistant professors in Canadian U15 universities receive tenure. Off-the-record conversations with senior administrators at Canadian universities suggest to us that official tenure denials at U15 institutions are in the single digits (see also Acker, Webber, and Smyth 2012). Our own experiences and conversations with colleagues also suggest that there are many faculty members who are encouraged to leave before they would come up for tenure or discouraged from submitting their file. Numbers, therefore, are difficult to gauge. There is, however, good evidence that women experience more "tenure troubles" than men in Canada, although this, again, is not recorded in the official statistics (Acker, Webber, and Smyth 2012).[3]

Women are less likely to receive promotion to full professor, most often for reasons of having a less traditionally strong (read: male) publication record. This can stem from several causes. Women in certain subject areas may be given more time-consuming teaching assignments (e.g., in high enrolment undergraduate courses not in their research area) or student advising roles (see, e.g., Domingo et al. 2022; Waymer 2014; Winslow and Davis 2016). Women may also choose to focus more on their teaching, perhaps due in part to lower student evaluations: a recent study (Chatman et al. 2022) grimly reports how middle-aged women instructors (i.e., those most likely to be in the associate professor rank) are most likely to receive lower student evaluations; the same women who may have received favourable assessments as young beginning professors pay a price as they age and become seen as more agentic and less warm and are thus viewed as deviating from gender norms (in contrast, men's performance as assessed by students tended to increase as they gained more experience and were viewed, on average, as more warm). Women are also more likely to engage in time-intensive, community-based research and teaching (Guarino and Borden 2017). In addition, women faculty may be less likely to submit their articles to top journals or be first author on "enough" publications. Furthermore, the predominance of male journal editors can disproportionately affect women because some men editors may be "more likely to assign manuscripts to male reviewers [who] are more likely to recommend rejection [of women authors]" (Benderly 2016). And, as claimed by English and women studies scholar Katie Hogan (2005), in reference to the *Modern Language Association's Committee on the Status of Women in the Profession* report in 2000, the increased service expectations for women at the associate professor level may be (still) be "the greatest hindrance to women's progressing to full professor" (100). More recent institutional approaches to supporting diversity on committees can disproportionately affect women associate professors, especially racialized women faculty and particularly in the STEM fields (Winslow and Davis 2016). Whereas assistant professors are often protected in their service time (and, indeed, not even allowed to perform certain service and leadership roles at the university), associate professors are not.

Additional reasons for the clogged associate professor pipeline for women (Winslow and Davis 2016) include the fact that women may be less likely to be mentored, sponsored, or supported in applying for promotion, even when they do have a strong case. Many academics, like ourselves, were gobsmacked to learn that 2018 Nobel Prize winner and Canadian physicist Donna Strickland was still an associate professor upon receiving the prize despite having held a tenure-track faculty position for over twenty years ("The Nobel Prize" n.d.). She explained that she had decided it was not worth the effort to apply – though one wonders whether this would have been different had she been encouraged and supported by her department head.

There is good evidence that women faculty, on average, perform much more university service than men (Guarino and Borden 2017; Misra et al. 2011). For instance, KerryAnn O'Meara, Alexandra Kuvaeva, and Gudrun Nyunt's (2017) two-year-long study showed that women faculty reported not only performing more total campus service than men but also engaged in a higher number of service activities at the department and university compared to men. Other studies have revealed that women are not necessarily volunteering to perform more service, but rather are being asked more frequently than men to serve in positions that hold little to no prestige (O'Meara, Kuvaeva, and Nyunt 2017; Pyke 2011). Women also disproportionately engage in research and teaching that involves large amounts of community or public service (i.e., community-service learning and community-based research) (see, e.g., Wade and Demb 2009). Women tend to spend more time on teaching and the kinds of service that is part-and-parcel of the teaching experience (Myers 2008; Winslow 2010).

However, in considering service roles that offer larger amounts of symbolic capital – that is, external professional service, such as occupying an editorial position of a top journal – there appears to be no real gender difference (Guarino and Borden 2017). Pressures on minority faculty members – whether women in science and engineering disciplines or racialized individuals in general – result in them putting in more invisible or poorly rewarded service, for example, serving on additional committees for diversity and representation reasons and unofficial mentorship of similarly racialized students (Harley 2008; Henry et al. 2017; Kelly and McCann 2014).

Women faculty, like women in other sectors, also tend to perform more service at home in caregiving and housework (Moyer and Burlock 2018; Schiebinger and Gilmartin 2010). Many more women than men are putting in a "double shift" (Hochschild 1989). They are not only (still) doing about twice the amount of housework and childcare as men (Bianchi et al. 2012; Moyer and Burlock 2018), but they are putting in much more emotional labour, carrying higher mental loads, and performing invisible and largely unrecognized levels of domestic management and clerical work that goes along with managing a household (Hochschild 1989). As sociologist Arlie Hochschild argues (in Schulte 2014), there has been a "stalled revolution" in that, while there was a revolution in professional engagement for women, "the workplace and the men they come home to have changed more slowly." Despite continuing prejudices, there is often insufficient evidence that motherhood is a "distraction" for women faculty members that is impeding "academic excellence" (Stockdell-Giesler and Ingalls 2007). Rather, institutional policies and practices can particularly negatively impact faculty members who are mothers (e.g., scheduling evening classes and service duties that may be particularly difficult to execute while caring for small children or because of the constricting schedules of K-12 schools, etc.). For example, upon studying the effect of policies that allow faculty members to stop the tenure clock in the case of parental leave, researchers found that for economics faculty in the US, men were 17 percent more likely to get tenure in their first job and women 19 percent less likely. It appeared that men were using the extra allotted time strategically to send their research to top journals and were hiring nannies while on leave; and evaluators were not always discounting the "stopped" time, thus compounding women's disadvantage (Antecol, Bedard, and Stearns 2018). Institutional policies matter as they help determine what happens and what is valued. Although we do not have the added burden of US women faculty who have little to no paid family leave, maternity leave, or medical leave, Canada still suffers from insufficient availability of affordable childcare (and even, sometimes, of decent and reliable childcare at any price).

FIGURE 3.1
Faculty service during the pandemic

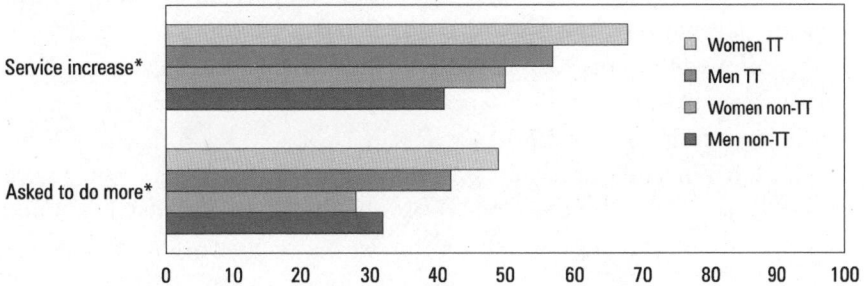

* Statistically higher for tenure-track (TT) women
Source: Reproduced with permission from Moura Quayle, *UBC-Vancouver Faculty Survey on The Effects of COVID-19: Tenure Track and Non-Tenure Track Faculty, Gender Analysis,* University of British Columbia, 13.

The most recent case of the COVID-19 pandemic further demonstrated that in new, and therefore less policy regulated, situations, inequalities between men and women embedded in society tend to get reinforced. The closure of campuses and the shift to online teaching and working from home confirmed the disproportionate amount of service women perform, on average, as compared to men (Bennett 2020). For example, a survey of faculty members at our university, the University of British Columbia (UBC), conducted in 2020 showed that service workloads among tenure-track (TT) women faculty significantly increased during the pandemic, and that women were being asked to perform service more often than their male counterparts (see Figure 3.1) (Quayle 2020, 13).

Increased workloads during the pandemic were further punctuated by the racial and colonial reckonings in Canada and abroad, resulting in changes at every level of the university to shift colonial legacies and meet the needs of a growing body of diverse students. The labour involved in this level of change often falls on the shoulders of equity-deserving groups and it is women faculty that disproportionately serve on committees struck in service of institutional-level changes.

It is important to recognize the intersectionality of struggle in faculty work: being a woman along with being a mother, an immigrant, racialized, or having a disability is more likely to result in someone having tenure troubles or being less successful in their academic careers, and service can play a key role in this (Haskins et al. 2016; Vescera 2019). A study by Penka Skachkova (2007) highlighted how immigrant women faculty members might perform more community service than other groups as a compensatory factor in lacking access to administrative and leadership positions. In the absence of opportunities for leadership at their institutions, the women faculty they researched instead directed their energy toward serving communities where their efforts and contributions would be recognized and appreciated.

Overall, women in academia can be discriminated against because they engage more in service and are seen to be more collaborative and caring. For example, a study by Juan Madera, Michelle Hebl, and Randi Martin (2009) revealed that in letters of recommendation for faculty positions, women were described as more communal and less agentic than men, and that communal characteristics had a negative relationship with hiring decisions in academia that are based on letters of recommendation. Women also tend to be earmarked for relational types of service that are largely unrecognized. Jennifer Dengate, Tracey Peter, and Annemieke Farenhorst (2019, 104) showed that women took up a large percentage of care work for students in science and engineering departments where "faculty members' responses to students' problems were informed by gendered cultural care expectations that require women to be more supportive than men." (For more on gendered expectations of care by instructors, see Smele and Quinlan, this volume). And, as Lisa Hanasono et al. (2019) found, task-oriented forms of service tend to be more visible and valued than relationally oriented service.

HOW CANADIAN INSTITUTIONS ARE DEFINING AND REWARDING SERVICE WITH GENDERED IMPLICATIONS

As many studies above have identified, women faculty are heavily engaged in service, in many cases performing more service than their male counterparts. In the section below, we explore how U15 universities construct and acknowledge service in their collective agreements and other related policies with the main focus on how such construction can explicitly and implicitly impact women faculty.

Our examination of university collective agreements across U15 universities indicates that there are a variety of expectations and interpretations of service at different institutions. There are cases, such as the University of Toronto (2016), where the concept of service is simplified and narrowed to collegial and administrative activities that are mostly associated with committee work. In others, like the University of Saskatchewan (2019), service is constructed as a multidimensional concept that includes administrative work, outreach activities, public service, and contributions to academic and professional bodies as different aspects of faculty workload. The University of Ottawa (2018) identifies eleven specific activities that are recognized as academic service. These multiple approaches are evidence of the growing complexity of faculty service and of the contradictions that policies are aimed at regulating, potentially including gender inequalities.

Collectively, these policy documents show that the initial purpose of faculty service to support the "effective functioning of university" (University of Waterloo 2011, sec. 2) can be expanded to include making a difference within academic communities (McGill 2019), benefiting "university units, and for professional organizations and the community at large" (University of British Columbia 2016, 66) and disseminating knowledge to the general public (University of Alberta 2019). Some of these definitions, and especially the one provided by McGill (2019), consider service as making a difference within academic communities to help change the perception of service to include certain aspects previously unrecognized or hidden.

Most university policy documents construct their concept of service by drawing a line between internal and external activities – that is, between the university and the communities and public outside of the university. This distinction is well captured in Dalhousie University's (2017, 68) categorization of service as academic administration within the university and "professional responsibilities outside the university." In what follows, we expand on three different types of service: 1) internal; 2) academic, professional, and community; and 3) mandatory versus optional, moving toward an expanded conversation on the relationship between service, research, and teaching, with an emphasis on tenure and promotion and the possible gendered implications.

Internal Service

There is one component that all universities seem to agree on, which can be broadly defined as institutional citizenship. This concept appears under multiple names, including administrative responsibilities (Western University 2018; Queen's University 2019), university service (University of Waterloo 2019), academic governance and development (University of Calgary 2019), academic administration (Dalhousie University 2017), collegial and administrative activities (University of Toronto 2016), and university responsibilities (McMaster University 2012). Institutional citizenship is mostly associated with serving on various collegial bodies at the unit, faculty, or university level. As Western University (2018, 10) defines it, service is "[the] share of administrative responsibilities by participation in the work of the University through membership on [various level] committees." This statement indicates the expectation that every faculty member contributes to the running of the university, though it is unclear from this sentence how such participation through serving on committees is considered in tenure and promotion decisions. Whereas the concept of institutional citizenship seems fair and politically neutral, it does contain some grounds for gender inequality. Being a reflection of society with the still-existing distinction between women's and men's roles, the application of the concept of "citizenship" in academia can reinforce gender roles and constructions of gender, pressuring women faculty to take on more service to fit the expectation of being "a good woman," "a helpful woman," or "a selfless woman."

Academic, Professional, and Community Service

Most U15 collective agreements associate service with a broader list of activities and consider not only the university citizenship component but also academic, professional, and community service (University of Alberta 2019; University of Ottawa 2018; University of Waterloo 2019; University of British Columbia 2016; University of Calgary 2019). With studies showing that women faculty are involved in more community service than men (Guarino and Borden 2017; Misra et al. 2011), the recognition of community service is a positive trend. However, the differences among these three are not distinctive, and in many cases, academic, professional, and community service appear to mean the same type of faculty activities in different settings. Along these lines, some universities include detailed lists of activities that might be considered as service, while others leave it to units and departments to decide. Among the most frequently referred to activities are: service on editorial boards, journals, or granting agencies (University of Calgary 2019, 5; University of Ottawa 2018, 145); work with professional associations, governments, serving on boards (UBC 2016, 66); counselling or advising students; contributing to university-related community projects (University of Ottawa 2018, 145–46); and engaging in continuing education activities in the community (UBC 2016, 66). These lists are broad, yet incomplete, just contouring the lines of what might be considered service rather than providing clear guidelines for assessment for tenure and promotion.

Mandatory Versus Optional Service

As the policy documents indicate, service continues to be a mandatory component of faculty workload; however, our analysis reveals that not all types of service are worded as compulsory. In fact, institutional citizenship is positioned as a faculty *responsibility*, whereas other types of service, such as professional and community service, might be viewed as a faculty *right and responsibility* (University of Manitoba 2018) or just a *right*, evidenced also in this statement: "Members ... have the *responsibility* to meet administrative service responsibilities ... Members have the *right* to engage in professional service to learned societies, associations, agencies, and organizations or to the community" (Queen's University 2019, 34).

There are also overlaps between committee service and all other types of service in university collective agreements. The policy documents emphasize institutional citizenship above all else. Even those universities that recognize a variety of types of service beyond traditional institutional citizenship use language that clearly indicates their optionality. For instance, the University of Calgary (2019) uses the modal verb "shall" with a strong assertion of the requirement that faculty participate in academic governance actively, which it changes to "may" when referring to professional and community service. Similarly, the University of Saskatchewan (2019) states that academic units *may* consider professional and community service activities. In contrast, the University of Waterloo (2011, sec. 2) underlines that "community service related to a faculty member's scholarly activities *is normally considered* as service to the university."

The optionality of professional and community service is emphasized in some policy documents in seeking to ensure that their fulfillment by faculty members does not conflict with the realization of their academic responsibilities within the university (Western University 2018, 10). Another regulatory requirement to professional and community service is formulated as conducting activities that are in line with university goals (Western University 2018), bring distinction to the university (University of Calgary 2019), and are "related to and appropriate to their discipline and field of expertise" (University of Manitoba 2018, 54). Indeed, not all "optional" service is seen as equal. As we indicate in Table 3.1, what is expected (or framed as a responsibility) may be counted but not especially rewarded, and some of what is considered a "right" or "option" can be more highly rewarded but may be completely ignored.

Different types of service, as we have noted, may: 1) allow faculty members to accrue capital (e.g., serving on a prestigious board or as chair of an important professional association), 2) be revenue neutral (e.g., undertake departmental committee responsibilities), or 3) impose opportunity costs if the service detracts from their research productivity in any way (e.g., developing and teaching a community-service learning course). Furthermore, far from promoting collaboration, some types of service can promote competition. Some policy documents specify that the most credit is given to service on prestigious bodies, including "prestigious journals, on grant selection committees and adjudication panels of national agencies" (University of Calgary 2019, 5), using the language of competition and not collaboration regarding service. We note that women and men faculty alike are still engaging in what the university would consider irrelevant, low, or negative value service, with women likely to be more engaged (see O'Meara, Kuvaeva, and Nyunt 2017; Pyke 2011). When discussing issues of faculty service with our colleagues at UBC, a senior administrator noted that a significant part of the service they did was never counted outside of their primary field of expertise, but that they had developed a passion for it and became an advocate, nonetheless. Similarly, some Indigenous faculty members we spoke to mentioned that the type of community service they engage in may not be in line with the university goals. Still, they felt obliged to their Indigenous communities to keep doing what they are doing no matter what.

How collective agreement documents are operationalized is devolved to university units and departments. For example, the University of Saskatchewan (2019, 10) states that "each academic unit shall be responsible for identifying the activities under the criteria," including administrative work, outreach activities, practice of professional skills, and public service and contributions to academic and professional bodies. Even though most of the university's policies acknowledge that service portfolios cannot be universal and will vary from one faculty member to the next and within and across units and disciplines, the language of the university-level policies is not yet supportive enough of this diversity. It does not provide clear guidelines for how to address the variety of service profiles in the appointment, tenure, and promotion processes. This sets a potential precedent of inequality.

With the rise of community-based research and learning, along with the growing demand from a diversifying body of students for mentoring, counselling, and advising services (Bates 2011; Jaschik 2015; Vescera 2019), the boundaries between teaching, research, and service are blurring. Some universities indicate such shifts by acknowledging a service component in research and teaching (University of Toronto 2016; University of Alberta 2019); others include service activities related to teaching and research in the service portfolio: counselling or advising students (University of Waterloo 2019; University of Manitoba 2018; University of Ottawa 2018), supervision of examinations (University of Manitoba 2018), and dissemination of knowledge to the general public (University of Alberta 2019). While we welcome such changes, we want to be mindful that women may be more involved in teaching than men and the inclusion of teaching-related activities under "service" might weaken their tenure and promotion profile (see Brommesson et al. 2021) – especially if faculty are still governed by the 40/40/20 formula.

The majority of U15 universities do require within their collective agreements and guidelines that service be considered in tenure and promotion decisions. The exception is the University of Toronto, which, at least on paper, treats service as an optional component that *might* be counted "as a fourth factor in the tenure decision but should not, in general, receive a particularly significant weighting" (University of Toronto Governing Council 2015, 8). The first three factors comprise: "achievement in research and creative professional work, effectiveness in teaching, and clear promise of future intellectual and professional development" (8). As is stated in its policy and procedures on academic appointments: "Only outstanding performance with respect to University service should be given any significant weight and, even then, only if there are no substantial reservations relating to the research, teaching and future promise criteria" (9). In other words, service will only be given weight if it is stellar and if all other aspects of a candidate's file are satisfying. With that said, service is considered part of faculty workload at the University of Toronto, opening space for unrewarded work.

Other research universities use a binary system of "satisfactory/unsatisfactory" to assess service. For example, McMaster University (2012, 17) states that the meritorious performance of service "shall not substitute for either effective teaching or scholarly achievement in the consideration for reappointment, tenure, permanence, and/or promotion; however, unsatisfactory performance in the discharging of these duties may be an important factor in the delaying or denial of tenure, permanence and/or promotion." Whereas the criterion satisfactory/unsatisfactory might be relevant in the assessment of active engagement in committee service, it seems much less applicable to professional and community service.

Overall, questions of equity regarding workload and its consideration in tenure and promotion decisions were sometimes mentioned but not substantially expanded on in the collective agreements we examined. Queen's University (2019), Western University (2018), and University of Toronto (2016), for example, included general statements regarding the necessity to ensure an equitable share of service responsibilities and to avoid discrimination and infringement of academic freedom; University of Manitoba (2018) and University of Ottawa (2018) were the only institutions whose statements related to service and tenure and promotion addressed gender equity. University of Manitoba (2018) included a statement regarding fulfilling gender-balance requirements on committees and implementing a reasonable workload adjustment; however, no guidelines are provided. University of Ottawa's (2018) collective agreement contains some guidelines regarding equity, diversity, and inclusion in employment, including clarifications on units on the underrepresentation of women or men that might be related to appointment, tenure and promotion, and workload allocation.

DISCUSSION

In our examination of tenure and promotion guidelines at U15 universities, we found that service is not defined in approximately one-third of institutions, and for many universities, service is often not a determining factor in whether one receives tenure. For example, at UBC, while competence is "required" in "scholarly activities and teaching," service is said to be "also important" but not able to "compensate for a deficiency" in the other two categories (University of British Columbia 2018, 15). In contrast, Dalhousie's collective agreement (2017, 43) states that no member will be reappointed if performance in any category, including service, is "less than satisfactory." As the above attests, service is defined heterogeneously across different institutions. Where certain service work is folded into considerations of scholarship and teaching, it can potentially receive recognition and thus be rewarded.

Our analysis also shows that university-level policies prioritize institutional/departmental committee service-related work over other types of service, though even these forms of service carry little to no prestige (see Table 3.1). Serving on committees is an essential part of the university operation that "needs to be done." Yet, the allocation of committee work, recognition of its weight, and fair distribution of committee service seem to result in ongoing problems that are well-documented in the literature and borne out by our current review of our own institution. Further, we are hearing more and more stories of faculty members, primarily Indigenous, racialized, or women members, who are engaging more and more in (largely unrewarded) community service who then seek out opportunities to serve on "prestigious" committees (such as at the university level or for a professional association) to boost their record for tenure and promotion, clearly adding more stress and additional tasks to an already full workload. Ironically, this too may ultimately devalue their file if they cannot then show "adequate" achievements and output in research.

Our analysis of the language of university policies also indicates that there are two distinguishable discursive ways institutions are conceiving of faculty service and workload. In one model, faculty members are called "citizens," with the universities, therefore, imagined as states. In the other, the university is described as "a community of scholars" in which "every scholar is expected to contribute" (University of Calgary 2019, 4). We suggest that these two models imply different behaviour patterns and allot different weight and value to various types of faculty service. As policy documents indicate, a university-state is more associated with prioritizing academic freedom, collegiality, and structure; committee work and administration are more visible than other types of service, and individual service is emphasized over collective input. The position/rank in which the faculty member contributes their service also matters, such that chairing key committees is given more consideration than serving on a less prestigious departmental committee. One of the concepts that represents this type of university is institutional citizenship. Citizenship as a concept is not neutral; it does not imply an equal egalitarian society and, as mentioned, can reinforce problematic gender roles pressuring women faculty to take on more service to fit gendered expectations. A university-community, in contrast, connotes the prioritization of well-being, sharing, supporting, stepping in, volunteering, engaging, and interacting. Of prime value here is the scope of work and the benefit that it brings to the community, making the university a better place to work and study in; every input and collaborative engagement is (potentially) appreciated. There is also a focus here on connecting the university-community to outside communities. Serving the university-community and enhancing university-community relations are considered crucial, especially by many Indigenous faculty, faculty of colour, and women faculty, who can often be intent on engaging in community service "no matter what." We would argue that a university-state is a more traditionally masculine construction whereas the model of university-community more associated with the feminine, though we know all people, regardless of gender, can be equally collaborative or competitive. In their mission and vision statements, most of the U15 universities indicate signs of moving toward a university-community model; however, the language of service is mostly related to the university-state construction, allowing us to point out a gap to address in further discussions of faculty service.

Unfortunately, the data necessary to better understand where tenure troubles are occurring across gendered and other identity lines is not being collected. As our literature review clearly reveals, the biggest issue likely lies – in Canadian U15 at least – in the associate to professor pipeline. How many women versus men are being stalled? How are departments and faculties reading these tenure and promotion guidelines when deciding to forward files? How are women and BIPOC associate professors informed of the relative time commitments and potential capital of serving on various committees in varying capacities? How are concerns for diversity and inclusion in representation affecting women – especially in the context of departments, associations, and units increasingly being asked to make sure, for example, to "have a woman on the committee"? And how are women faculty being compensated in other areas when they do agree to these commitments?

CONCLUSION

Our goal with this chapter is not to value or devalue certain kinds of service, and neither is it to suggest that women faculty should necessarily do less service – although this is indeed recommended in some instances. Rather, in undertaking this study, our hope was to make the invisible more visible and to better align faculty workloads with what is rewarded and recognized. As KerryAnn O'Meara and colleagues (2018, 1) suggest, we need to pay greater attention to "equity in how work is taken up, assigned and rewarded in academic departments." We call for greater thoughtfulness in institutional policies: in supporting mothers especially; in actively offering mentorship and support for all women at all stages; and in greater education of our chairs, deans, and university administrators of what supports do exist, along the lines of what is recommended by Ward and Wolf-Wendel (2012). Their recommendations include: modifying policies that concern assigned service, creating flexible tenure clocks, revising leave policies, offering mentoring and support for faculty members, and educating deans about the policies and options faculty can avail themselves of. An overall consideration of the intersectional identities women hold and how they carry a form of labour is also needed in all of this.

In the past two years, and after the publication of many of the documents we examined, universities have started adopting policies reinforcing equity, diversity, and inclusion issues, especially in light of addressing racism in academia. The recent collective agreement at our own institution, UBC, is also a welcome shift, at least discursively, with regard to considerations of equity in service:

> The Collective Agreement now explicitly acknowledges the extra service burden often shouldered by faculty from historically marginalized groups ... UBC has agreed to a joint committee to work on defining scholarly activity in diverse forms. Workload language now explicitly acknowledges the importance of having to do all the parts of one's job ... direct[ing] departments to consider the various factors affecting teaching workload, including class-size, marking support, etc. (University of British Columbia Faculty Association 2020, 2)

As many U15 institutions are starting to acknowledge, the traditional 40/40/20 formula (with service constituting 20 percent of one's job) does not work particularly well in considering a faculty member's workload or as a way of assessing performance for tenure and promotion. From a feminist perspective, we need to reimagine what faculty service is and how it is rewarded. Finding answers might start from asking crucial, and more general, questions such as: How has university and faculty service changed since women were included, first as students and later as faculty members? What have women brought into academia, and what are we advocating for now? How should an institution founded on white, European, male principles look and operate today with the inclusion of women and people of an array of cultures, ethnicities, gender identities, and sexual orientations? And how might this vision take into consideration faculty workload and overall parity?

Similarly, we want to think more carefully and creatively about supporting leadership and more prestigious service opportunities for women. It is fair to say that, up until now, the notion of service has been constructed from the perspective of men, and the research/teaching/service formula was created by men to fit the male intellectual lifestyle. Canadian universities need some rethinking and reconstruction of the concept of service, especially in its relation to teaching and research, as well as to administrative responsibilities and community work. The exploration of who serves whom in academia, and what it actually means "to serve," is a good place to start.

NOTES

1 In our use of the terms "women" and "women faculty" throughout this chapter, we are inclusive of transwomen and transwomen faculty.
2 U15 universities comprise fifteen of the top research-intensive institutions across Canada, which "undertake 80% of all competitive university research in Canada." See http://u15.ca/about-us.
3 While women are likely equally successful in obtaining tenure in Canada as men, the process and experience is, on average, more difficult for women (e.g., questioning of files, having to get additional letter writers, pushback on CV, etc.). This concurs with our own anecdotal evidence and with the findings of Acker, Webber, and Smyth's 2012 study.

WORKS CITED

Acker, Sandra, Michelle Webber, and Elizabeth Smyth. 2012. "Tenure Troubles and Equity Matters in Canadian Academe." *British Journal of Sociology of Education* 33 (5): 743–61.
–. 2016. "Continuity or Change? Gender, Family, and Academic Work for Junior Faculty in Ontario Universities." *NASPA Journal about Women in Higher Education* 9 (1): 1–20.
Alperin, Juan P., Carol Muñoz Nieves, Lesley A. Schimanski, Gustavo E. Fischman, Meredith T. Niles, and Erin C. McKiernan. 2019. "How Significant Are the Public Dimensions of Faculty Work in Review, Promotion and Tenure Documents?" *Elife* 8.
Antecol, Heather, Kelly Bedard, and Jenna Stearns. 2018. "Equal but Inequitable: Who Benefits from Gender-Neutral Tenure Clock Stopping Policies?" *The American Economic Review* 108 (9): 2420–41.
Bacci, Jennifer L., Tolu P. Akinwale, Alex J. Adams, and Melissa Somma McGivney. 2016. "An Analysis of Community Pharmacy Shared Faculty Members' Contributions to Teaching, Service, and Scholarship." *American Journal of Pharmaceutical Education* 80 (7): 115.
Banerjee, Madhumita, and Cheryl O. Hausafus. 2007. "Faculty Use of Service-Learning: Perceptions, Motivations, and Impediments for the Human Sciences." *Michigan Journal of Community Service Learning* 14 (1): 32.
Bates, Merrelyn. 2011. "Work-Integrated Learning Workloads: The Realities and Responsibilities." *Asia-Pacific Journal of Cooperative Education* 12 (2): 111.
Benderly, Beryl. 2016. "After Years of Growth, Female First Authorship in Top Medical Journals Has Stalled." *Science,* March 16, 2016. https://www.sciencemag.org/

careers/2016/03/after-years-growth-female-first-authorship-top-medical-journals
-has-stalled.

Bennett, Jessica. 2020. "'I Feel like I Have 5 Jobs": Moms Navigate the Pandemic." *New York Times*, March 20, 2020. https://www.nytimes.com/2020/03/20/parenting/childcare-coronavirus-moms.html.

Bianchi, Suzanne M., Liana C. Sayer, Melissa A. Milkie, and John P. Robinson. 2012. "Housework: Who Did, Does or Will Do It, and How Much Does It Matter?" *Social Forces* 91 (1): 55–63.

Blackburn, Robert T., and Janet H. Lawrence. 1995. *Faculty at Work: Motivation, Expectation, Satisfaction*. Baltimore: Johns Hopkins University Press.

Blackmore, Paul, and Camille B. Kandiko. 2011. "Motivation in Academic Life: A Prestige Economy." *Research in Post-Compulsory Education* 16 (4): 399–411.

Boyer, Ernest L. 1990. *Scholarship Reconsidered: Priorities of the Professoriate*. Princeton, NJ: Princeton University Press.

Brommesson, Douglas, Gissur Ó. Erlingsson, Jörgen Ödalen, and Mattias Fogelgren. 2021. "'Teach More, but Do Not Expect Any Applause': Are Women Doubly Discriminated against in Universities' Recruitment Processes?" *Journal of Academic Ethics* 20:437–50. https://doi.org/10.1007/s10805-021-09421-5.

Chatman, Jennifer, Daron Sharps, Sonya Mishra, Laura Kraya, and Michael North. 2022. "Agentic but Not Warm: Age-Gender Interactions and the Consequences of Stereotype Incongruity Perceptions for Middle-Aged Professional Women." *Organizational Behavior and Human Decision Processes* 173:104190.

Cohan, Deborah J. 2018. "Why Faculty Members Should Not Help with Move-In Day." *Inside Higher Ed*, August 8, 2018. https://www.insidehighered.com/advice/2017/08/08/downside-faculty-members-helping-students-move-essay.

Dalhousie University. 2017. *A Collective Agreement between the Board of Governors of Dalhousie University and The Dalhousie Faculty Association, 2017–2020*. https://cdn.dal.ca/content/dam/dalhousie/pdf/dept/hr/Academic-Staff-Relations/DFA-2017-20-Collective- Agreement.pdf.

Dengate, Jennifer, Tracey Peter, and Annemieke Farenhorst. 2019. "Gender and the Faculty Care Gap: 'The Obvious Go-to Person' for Canadian University Students' Personal Problems." *Canadian Journal of Higher Education* 49 (3): 104–14.

Docka-Filipek, Danielle, and Lindsey Stone. 2021. "Twice a 'Housewife': On Academic Precarity, 'Hysterical' Women, Faculty Mental Health, and Service as Gendered Care Work for the 'University Family' in Pandemic Times." *Gender, Work and Organization* 28 (6): 2158–79.

Domingo, Carmen, Nancy Counts Gerber, Diane Harris, Laura Mamo, Sally Pasion, R. David Rebanal, and Sue Rosser. 2022. "More Service or More Advancement: Institutional Barriers to Academic Success for Women and Women of Color Faculty at a Large Public Comprehensive Minority-Serving State University." *Journal of Diversity in Higher Education* 15 (3): 365–79.

Fitzpatrick, Leo R., Carol Millette-Snodgrass, and Eman Atef. 2016. "A Novel Mathematical Model for Determining Faculty Workload." *American Journal of Pharmaceutical Education* 80 (9): 152.

Guarino, Cassandra M., and Victor M.H. Borden. 2017. "Faculty Service Loads and Gender: Are Women Taking Care of the Academic Family?" *Research in Higher Education* 58 (6): 672–94.

Hammer, Dana P., Leigh Ann Bynum, Jean Carter, Nicholas E. Hagemeier, Daniel R. Kennedy, Parto Khansari, Pamela Stamm, and Brian Crabtree. 2019. "Revisiting Faculty Citizenship." *American Journal of Pharmaceutical Education* 83 (4): 7378–473.

Hanasono, Lisa K., Ellen M. Broido, Margaret M. Yacobucci, Karen V. Root, Susana Peña, and Deborah A. O'Neil. 2019. "Secret Service: Revealing Gender Biases in the Visibility and Value of Faculty Service." *Journal of Diversity in Higher Education* 12 (1): 85–98.

Harley, Debra A. 2008. "Maids of Academe: African American Women Faculty at Predominately White Institutions." *Journal of African American Studies* 12 (1): 19–36.

Haskins, Natoya H., Jolie Ziomek-Daigle, Cheryl Sewell, Lonika Crumb, Brandee Appling, and Heather Trepal. 2016. "The Intersectionality of African American Mothers in Counselor Education: A Phenomenological Examination." *Counselor Education and Supervision* 55 (1): 60–75.

Henry, Frances, Enakshi Dua, Audrey Kobayashi, Carl James, Peter Li, Howard Ramos, and Malinda S. Smith. 2017. "Race, Racialization and Indigeneity in Canadian Universities." *Race Ethnicity and Education* 20 (3): 300–14.

Hochschild, Arlie Russell. 1989. *The Second Shift: Working Parents and the Revolution at Home*. New York: Viking.

Hogan, Katie. 2005. "Superserviceable Feminism." *Minnesota Review* 63–64: 95–111.

Jaeger, Audrey J., and Courtney H. Thornton. 2006. "Neither Honor nor Compensation: Faculty and Public Service." *Educational Policy* 20 (2): 345–66.

Jaschik, Scott. 2015. "Mentoring as Tenure Criterion." *Inside Higher Ed*, July 20, 2015. https://www.insidehighered.com/news/2015/07/20/purdue-moves-make-mentoring -undergraduates-criterion-tenure.

Kelly, Bridget Turner, and Kristin I. McCann. 2014. "Women Faculty of Color: Stories Behind the Statistics." *The Urban Review* 46 (4): 681–702.

King, Michelle P. 2020. *The Fix: Overcome the Invisible Barriers That Are Holding Women Back at Work*. New York: Atria Books.

Lynton, Ernest A. 1995. *Making the Case for Professional Service. Forum on Faculty Roles and Rewards*. Washington, DC: American Association for Higher Education.

Madera, Juan M., Michelle R. Hebl, and Randi C. Martin. 2009. "Gender and Letters of Recommendation for Academia: Agentic and Communal Differences." *Journal of Applied Psychology* 94 (6): 1591–99.

McGill University Office of the Provost and Vice-Principal (Academic). 2019. *Tenure-Track Academic Staff: Professors and Librarians: Ranks, Descriptors, and Designations*. https://mcgill.ca/apo/academic-life-cycle/tenure-track-academic-staff-professors -and-librarians/ranks-descriptors-and-designations.

McMaster University. 2012. *Revised Policy and Regulations with Respect to Academic Appointment, Tenure and Promotion*. https://secretariat.mcmaster.ca/app/uploads/ 2019/05/Tenure_and_Promotion_Revised-July2017.pdf.

Misra, Joya, Jennifer Hickes Lundquist, Elissa Holmes, and Stephanie Agiomavritis. 2011. "The Ivory Ceiling of Service Work." *Academe* 97 (1): 22–26.

Moyer, Melissa, and Amanda Burlock. 2018. *Time Use: Total Work Burden, Unpaid Work and Leisure. Women in Canada: A Gender-Based Statistical Report.* 7th ed. Ottawa: Statistics Canada, July 30, 2018. https://www150.statcan.gc.ca/n1/pub/89-503-x/2015001/article/54931-eng.htm.

Myers, Carrie B. 2008. "College Faculty and the Scholarship of Teaching: Gender Differences across Four Key Activities." *Journal of the Scholarship of Teaching and Learning* 8 (2): 38–51.

"The Nobel Prize: Women Who Changed Science: Donna Strickland." n.d. The Official Website of the Nobel Prize – NobelPrize.org. Accessed April 5, 2020. https://www.nobelprize.org/womenwhochangedscience/stories/donna-strickland.

O'Meara, KerryAnn. 2002. "Scholarship Unbound: Assessing Service as Scholarship for Promotion and Tenure." In *Studies in Higher Education Dissertation Series*, edited by Phillip G. Altbach. New York: Routledge.

O'Meara, KerryAnn, Audrey Jaeger, Joya Misra, Courtney Lennartz, and Alexandra Kuvaeva. 2018. "Undoing Disparities in Faculty Workloads: A Randomized Trial Experiment." *PloS One* 13 (12): e0207316.

O'Meara, KerryAnn, Alexandra Kuvaeva, and Gudrun Nyunt. 2017. "Constrained Choices: A View of Campus Service Inequality from Annual Faculty Reports." *The Journal of Higher Education* 88 (5): 672–700.

Pyke, Karen. 2011. "Service and Gender Inequity among Faculty." *PS: Political Science and Politics* 44 (1): 85–87.

Quayle, Moura. 2020. *UBC-Vancouver Faculty Survey on the Effects of COVID-19: Tenure Track and Non-Tenure Track Faculty, Gender Analysis.* November 2, 2020. https://academic.ubc.ca/sites/vpa.ubc.ca/files/documents/BoG%20Final%20UBCV%20COVID%20Faculty%20Survey%20results%20by%20Gender%20Nov%202020.pdf.

Queen's University at Kingston. 2019. *The Collective Agreement between Queen's University Faculty Association and Queen's University at Kingston, May 1, 2019 to 2022.* https://www.qufa.ca/wp-content/uploads/2023/01/QUFA-CA-2019-22-January-23-2023-for-web.pdf.

Rice, R. Eugene. 1995. "The New American Scholar: Scholarship and the Purposes of the University." In *Metropolitan Universities: An Emerging Model in American Higher Education*, edited by Daniel M. Johnson and David A. Bell, 135–46. Denton: University of North Texas Press.

Schiebinger, Londa, and Shannon K. Gilmartin. 2010. "Housework Is an Academic Issue." *Academe* 96 (1): 39–44.

Schulte, Bridgit. 2014. "'The Second Shift' at 25: Q & A with Arlie Hochschild." *Washington Post*, August 6, 2014. https://www.washingtonpost.com/blogs/she-the-people/wp/2014/08/06/the-second-shift-at-25-q-a-with-arlie-hochschild/.

Skachkova, Penka. 2007. "Academic Careers of Immigrant Women Professors in the U.S." *Higher Education* 53 (6): 697–738.

Statistics Canada. 2017. "Numbers and Salaries of Full-Time Teaching Staff at Canadian Universities, 2016/2017." *The Daily: Statistics Canada*, April 25, 2017. https://www150.statcan.gc.ca/n1/daily-quotidien/170425/dq170425b-eng.htm.

Stockdell-Giesler, Anne, and Rebecca Ingalls. 2007. "Faculty Mothers." *Academe* 93 (4).

University of Alberta. 2019. *A Collective Agreement between the Governors of the University of Alberta and the Association of the Academic Staff of the University of Alberta, July 1, 2018 to June 30, 2020.* https://cloudfront.ualberta.ca/-/media/hrs/my-employment/agreements/university-aasua-2018-2020-collective- agreement.pdf.

University of British Columbia. 2016. *The Collective Agreement between UBC and the UBC Faculty Association 7/2016–6/2019.* https://www.facultyassociation.ubc.ca/assets/media/Faculty-CA-2016-to-2019_V_6July2018.pdf.

–. 2018. *Guide to Reappointment, Promotion, and Tenure Procedures at UBC.* http://www.hr.ubc.ca/faculty-relations/files/SAC-Guide.pdf.

University of British Columbia Faculty Association. 2020. *Highlights of the New Agreement.* https://www.facultyassociation.ubc.ca/assets/media/UBCFA-Ratification-Package-2020_web_Jan2020.pdf.

University of Calgary. 2019. *GFC Academic Staff Criteria and Processes Handbooks Approved by the General Faculties Council.* https://www.ucalgary.ca/hr/sites/default/files/teams/239/gfc-academic-staff-criteria-and-processes-handbook_final.pdf.

University of Manitoba. 2018. *Collective Agreement between the University of Manitoba and University of Manitoba Faculty Association 2017–2021.* http://www.umfa.ca/images/UMFA-CA-2017-2021.pdf.

University of Ottawa. 2018. *Collective Agreement between the University of Ottawa and the Association of Professors of the University of Ottawa (APUO) May 1, 2018 to April 30, 2021.* https://www.uottawa.ca/human-resources/sites/www.uottawa.ca.human-resources/files/apuo_convention_collective_agreement_2018-2021.pdf.

University of Saskatchewan. 2019. *The Collective Agreement between the University and USFA.* http://www.usaskfaculty.ca/wp-content/uploads/2019/11/2017-2022-Collective-Agreement-True-Copy-for-initial-posting.pdf.

University of Toronto. 2016. *Memorandum of Agreement between the Governing Council of the University of Toronto and the University of Toronto Faculty Association.* https://governingcouncil.utoronto.ca/sites/default/files/import-files/memoagree6594.pdf.

University of Toronto Governing Council. 2015. *Policy and Procedures on Academic Appointments.* Toronto, ON. http://www.governingcouncil.utoronto.ca/Assets/Governing+Council+Digital+Assets/Policies/PDF/ppoct302003.pdf.

University of Waterloo. 2019. *Memorandum of Agreement between University of Waterloo and The Faculty Association of the University of Waterloo.* https://uwaterloo.ca/secretariat/documents-potential-interest/memorandum-agreement-uw-fauw.

University of Waterloo Secretariat. 2011. *Policy 77: Tenure and Promotion of Faculty Members.* https://uwaterloo.ca/secretariat/policies-procedures-guidelines/policy-77.

University of Western Ontario. 2018. *Faculty Collective Agreement between The University of Western Ontario and The University of Western Ontario Faculty Association, July 1, 2018 – June 30, 2022.* https://www.uwo.ca/facultyrelations/pdf/collective_agreements/faculty.pdf.

Vescera, Zak. 2019. "The Unseen Labour of Racialised Faculty." *Ubyssey Magazine,* February 2019. https://www.ubyssey.ca/magazine/unseen-labour/#reclaim.

Wade, Amy, and Ada Demb. 2009. "A Conceptual Model to Explore Faculty Community Engagement." *Michigan Journal of Community Service Learning* 15 (2): 5.

Walker, Judith. 2008. "Social/Corporate Accountability: A University's 'Trek' Towards Excellence." *The Canadian Journal of Higher Education* 38 (2): 45.

Ward, Kelly. 2003. *Faculty Service Roles and the Scholarship of Engagement. ASHE-ERIC Higher Education Report*. Jossey-Bass Higher and Adult Education Series. ERIC Clearinghouse on Higher Education, Washington, DC, Association for the Study of Higher Education, and George Washington Univ., Washington, DC. Graduate School of Education and Human Development.

Ward, Kelly, and Lisa Wolf-Wendel. 2012. *Academic Motherhood: How Faculty Manage Work and Family*. New Brunswick, NJ: Rutgers University Press.

Waring, Matthew. 2013. "All in This Together? HRM and the Individualisation of the Academic Worker." *Higher Education Policy* 26 (3): 397–419.

Waymer, Damion. 2014. "Shouldering the Load: An Analysis of Gender-Based Differences in the Undergraduate PR Writing Classes and Advising Undergraduate PRSSA Chapters." *Journalism and Mass Communication Educator* 69 (4): 404–14.

Winslow, Sarah. 2010. "Gender Inequality and Time Allocations among Academic Faculty." *Gender and Society* 24 (6): 769–93.

Winslow, Sarah, and Shannon Davis. 2016. "Gender Inequality across the Academic Life Course." *Sociology Compass* 10 (5): 404–16.

Woolston, Chris. 2018. "University Tenure Decisions Still Gloss Over Scientists' Public Outreach." *Nature* 10.

Ziker, John. 2014. The Long, Lonely Job of Homo Academicus. *The Blue Review*, March 31, 2014. https://www.boisestate.edu/bluereview/2014/03/31/faculty-time -allocation/.

PART 2

Gendered Dynamics of University Leadership

Witnessing Academic Recruitment Weighed Down by the F-word

AMORELL SAUNDERS N'DAW

President. Vice-president. Provost. Dean. Chair. Full professor. These are impressive and much sought-after roles within the academy; they are also roles that were once primarily the domain of highly credentialed white men. Recently, a focus on addressing diversity within institutions of higher education has helped pave the way for more women to enter these positions. As a search consultant and recruiter within the postsecondary education sector at both the academic and administrative levels, I have first-hand experience with the approaches taken by universities in pursuit of more diverse representation in their leadership. Through this work, I have seen that the worthy goal of realizing gender equality in leadership positions is not as simple as outsourcing candidate selection to search firms. Real change cannot be achieved without dismantling the systems of power that cause women-identified faculty to question their credentials, doubt their worth, and sometimes leave their academic roles altogether.

Research shows that women are more likely to pass on job opportunities if they do not feel that they meet 100 percent of the advertised criteria. Consider the heavy emotional toll of doubting your qualifications before you even get on a short list for an interview. I have had many conversations with women candidates with extensive experience who questioned whether they were qualified for a given role based on the long list of criteria approved by the search committee. I often counsel women candidates about the importance of bragging about their accomplishments in their cover letter and asserting their value and worth during the interview process. This comes easier for some than others and, depending on who is serving on the search and selection committee, a woman's confidence can be misinterpreted as arrogant and egotistical, while men do not usually suffer from the same level of scrutiny.

Addressing gender bias in recruitment should be a conscious effort by those involved in the recruitment process. Are unfair standards being applied to qualifications, competencies, and experience that make it difficult to attract women candidates? Academic institutions need to be mindful of the policies that create artificial barriers of entry into the academy. I have seen committee members question the credibility of the institutions where women candidates have studied, doubt the value of their scholarship, or snicker at the dollar value of the research funding they have received. If institutions are serious about gender equality, flexibility is required. There is much to be said for differently qualified candidates – those whose career paths and experience may not conform to traditional expectations. Many women, for example, have had to take breaks in their career trajectory because they have primary responsibility for child and family care. Women often do not have the same flexibility to relocate as men, often because of familial obligations. As a result, their commitment to their work is sometimes questioned by search committee members with a laser focus on an idealized depiction of a perfect candidate.

As a recruiter, I attempt to have conversations with the search committee about how to address issues of equity, diversity, and inclusion in the hiring process, as well as strategies to address biases and microaggressions. As part of this process, I try to impress on them the importance of considering who gets to serve on the search committee. If there is homogeneity in the look of the committee, this can reinforce perceptions of a potentially biased and discriminatory process for candidates who do not move along in the process. However, I also caution committees not to select someone from a diverse background for appearances sake, since tokenism is a form of microaggression.

I have witnessed many institutions voice a desire for gender parity without showing any willingness to effect real change, instead hoping to devolve the responsibility of finding highly qualified women to recruiters and the search committee. From a recruitment perspective, it is important to acknowledge that dismantling these barriers takes collective effort. For recruiters to help address barriers like bias and microaggressions, individuals need to be open and willing to listen as well as accept and act on advice. At the same time, recruiters should consider it their duty to ensure that processes are fair and equitable and not just an opportunity to find someone who fits in order to tick a box.

In fact, I believe that the reliance on the notion of "fit" is one of the main barriers to gender equality in the academy. I call it the other F-word. Relying on the idea of fit indicates a desire to maintain the status quo; to stick with what is comfortable and easy. When committees say they are looking for fit, they often mean that they want someone who looks and behaves like them – it is a form of othering that is compounded when one considers the intersectionality of gender, race, sexual orientation, nationality, and the multiplicity of other identities women bring to the academic space. Imagine being interviewed by an all-male panel and then being told that you were not selected because of fit. Recruiting for fit requires no effort to make meaningful change for women-identified candidates to feel a sense of belonging.

Rather than fit, academic institutions should be aiming for alignment. That is, they should question whether the candidate's values and goals are aligned with theirs and how they can adjust the working environment to be supportive and inclusive. They should also consider what changes they need to make to ensure their women-identified colleagues do not suffer from exclusionary and isolationist practices. When hiring managers and selection committees make this pivot to alignment instead of fit, I believe that recruitment efforts can be more positive and rewarding for both candidates and institutions. We all want candidates who will thrive and flourish in their roles, which means ensuring that they feel supported to be their authentic selves and to do their best work.

While the recruitment and retention of diverse university leadership absolutely requires a commitment from universities to rethink aspects of the hiring process, hiring is only part of the problem. Nonetheless, it can be a significant hurdle. There are still many barriers to entry and advancement that signal to women that they do not belong. Creating an inclusive recruitment process requires intentionality and collective effort. If committees want more women to apply, they need to consider who serves on the committee, the wording of material advertising the position, the types of interview questions that are asked, their approach to reference checking, and how robust their orientation and onboarding process is. For meaningful advances in gender equality in the academy to occur, we must first examine the policies and practices that may be unintentionally creating barriers for women to gain entry and to thrive when they do take on leadership roles. Part of this examination requires an honest assessment of whether the work environment is ready for a woman to lead, particularly in traditionally male-dominated disciplines. Candidates will ask about the work environment, and if the search committee is not honest, a woman leader's experience may be short-lived and the hiring cycle will continue, at financial cost to the institution and potentially significant emotional cost to the exiting leader.

4

Women's Research Leadership
in the Academy

ANNE WAGNER and SANDRA ACKER

Although it is broadly reported that women are underrepresented in positions of academic leadership, these findings tend to be grounded in narrow conceptualizations of leadership that primarily consider managerial hierarchies. In this chapter, we question these conventional approaches and put forward a more expansive definition that includes research leadership, a largely unexplored topic (Evans 2014, 47–48). Our study is premised on an original dataset consisting of qualitative interviews with twenty-four women academics working in Ontario universities in the fields of education, social work, sociology, and geography, all with track records of successfully securing external research grants and scholarship in social justice. Our interest is in the extent to which these highly accomplished researchers consider themselves to be leaders. Further, we consider whether research based on a social justice agenda produces leadership that differs from conventional understandings. Our overall research question is thus: How do accomplished women researchers conceptualize their research leadership?

The designation "research leaders" is not without complications and is used in at least four ways: "manager-academics" with responsibilities for institutional oversight of research (Deem 2003); senior academics who are expected to provide help and inspiration to others (Evans 2014); heads of research groups, where researchers and students work on a range of projects, usually in the sciences or medicine (Kyvik and Reymert 2017); and principal investigators (PIs) of individual projects.

The fourth category refers to an individual academic, normally also holding teaching and service obligations, who fulfills the institution's research expectations by undertaking research projects, some (but not necessarily all) funded through grants. Although the PI in this category resembles the research group leader, the continuity between projects is less marked and each project may involve different colleagues and students. As this mode is common in the social sciences and allied professional fields like education and social work, it is the focus of our research.

RESEARCH LEADERSHIP

The literature on leadership has changed over time from featuring a search for effective leadership types vested in a solo leader, to an understanding of leadership as shared among organizational actors, to a view of leadership as a practice or process rather than an individual attribute (Crawford 2012; Raelin 2016). Various authors have tried to expand the meaning of academic leadership to include nontraditional forms, including leadership designated as nonpositional (Juntrasook et al. 2013), ivory basement (Eveline 2004), lower-middle (Acker 2014), and grassroots (Teelken 2012). These alternative conceptualizations open up the idea of leadership and potentially allow more women and people from marginalized groups to see themselves as legitimate leaders. In our view, considering PIs as research leaders has the same potential.

In Norway, Svein Kyvik (2013, 530) found that the "tasks of a research group leader" included applying for funding, supervising group members, overseeing timetables and budgets, connecting with other researchers, exercising quality control, and ensuring results are published. In a study of the science, technical, and engineering sector in Ireland, James Cunningham and colleagues (2014) identified "inhibiting factors" that impact upon publicly funded projects and their PIs, categorized as political and economic, institutional, and project based. Leadership responsibilities are also discussed in several case studies of social science research projects (Armstrong and Lowndes 2018; Mailhot et al. 2016).

Many such responsibilities are "invisible" (Willcoxson, Kavanagh, and Cheung 2011) although time consuming. Planning the project, recruiting team members, and applying for funding all happen prior to the actual start date (McGinn et al. 2019). Securing ethics approval may take months (Karram Stephenson et al. 2020) and requires periodic updates and renewals. Neoliberal trends in many countries have put an emphasis on producing research, obtaining external funds, and extending collaborations, even in institutions not traditionally oriented toward research (Torres-Olave et al. 2020), all of which pose challenges for PIs (Acker and McGinn 2021; Mauthner and Doucet 2008).

Team research is increasingly common, even in fields where the lone scholar has previously been the norm (Sumsion 2014). While in some countries, research teams include paid, full-time research staff, Canadian social science teams usually consist of a PI, other academic colleagues, and master's or doctoral students working part-time. The Social Sciences and Humanities Research Council (SSHRC), the primary funding body for social science research in

Canada, expects student assistance and training to feature in successful research proposals. We have explored the consequences of this model elsewhere (Acker, Wagner, and McGinn 2018).

Team research may be fraught. The common practice of assigning data collection to junior investigators, who are students or contract workers, while senior academics do the analysis and writing, raises questions about how authentic this "divided knowledge" can be (Mauthner and Doucet 2008). For a PI, coordinating research teams that cross disciplinary, institutional, or national boundaries presents potential problems, among them communication, power differences, and incompatible funding regimes (Baguley et al. 2021; Liinason 2013; Sumsion 2014). If team members are overloaded with other work, a project that starts with good intentions may never reach completion.

Nevertheless, many teams and their PIs find strategies with which to overcome these difficulties (Armstrong and Lowndes 2018; Willcoxson et al. 2011). In previous Canadian research, we reported that project leaders with social justice commitments made extensive efforts to help, mentor, and teach their graduate student research assistants (Acker, Wagner, and McGinn 2018). Sarah R. Davies and Maja Horst (2015) coined the phrase "caring craftwork" to describe the PI's role in science research groups in Denmark, the UK, and the US. In their view, the research group is to be crafted and then nurtured. While the authors note that "both men and women used the language of care, nurture and family" (384), they do not make other connections to gender or to the feminist literature on caring.

WOMEN AND ACADEMIC LEADERSHIP

Although there is a large international body of work on women and academic leadership (Blackmore and Sachs 2007; Fitzgerald 2013; Read and Kehm 2016; and many others), it is generally unintegrated into mainstream leadership literature and rarely includes a consideration of research leadership. The "recurrent theme" is "women's absence from senior leadership" (Morley 2013, 121). Canadian studies report similar trends.[1] However, in tandem with increasing awareness of discriminatory treatment of Indigenous communities and the pervasiveness of anti-Black racism, the federal government and research funding agencies have issued mandates related to equity, diversity, and inclusion (EDI). Consequently, many universities now have policies in place around EDI (Collier, this volume; Cukier et al. 2021; Tamtik and Guenter 2019). Analyses by researchers have revealed some progress over time for white women but typically find that racialized and Indigenous academics, especially women, are extremely scarce at senior levels of university leadership (Cukier et al. 2021; Fuji Johnson, Chenier, and Sensoy, this volume; F. Henry et al. 2017).

Deeply sedimented within the historically male-centred university is what Camille Kandiko Howson, Kelly Coate, and Tania de St Croix (2018, 534) describe as "the hyper-individualistic reward and recognition processes through which men gain easier access to the indicators of esteem ... that advance their careers." The neoliberal turn in higher education has reinforced aspects of university work often thought to be masculinist, such as competitiveness, hierarchy, and individualism (Morley 2013) while leaders are expected to be strong, resilient, inspirational, and innovative (Drake 2015) rather than relationship-centred and committed to social justice (Thompson 2019).

For some academic women, the leadership experience is alien or even damaging (Morley and Crossouard 2016). The departmental or institutional culture may be at odds with their efforts to be authentic, as noted by several racialized women leaders (Faircloth 2017; A. Henry 2015). In the interests of EDI, Indigenous faculty may be encouraged to take up specialized leadership positions with extensive responsibilities that are not well-understood by others and may not lead to further promotions (Cukier et al. 2021; Trudgett, Page, and Coates 2022).

Various feminist theories have informed studies of women academics and women's academic leadership (Acker 1994, 2012). In the 1970s and 1980s, liberal, socialist, and radical feminist theory competed for ascendance, but by the 1990s, the influence of poststructuralism led to grand theories being seen as competing discourses rather than versions of truth and claims about "women's ways" as essentialist. Feminist scholars now generally understand the category "women" to be intersected by multiple and fluid identities such as age, race, class, and Indigeneity.

In the more practical and activist writing on leadership, feminist approaches advocate mentoring (Breeze and Taylor 2020), collaboration (Mountz et al. 2003), and caring for others and oneself (Mountz et al. 2015). Jane O'Dea (2020), a Canadian dean, sees feminist leadership as a blend of transformative leadership and feminism, drawing upon the feminist "ethics of care" (Niemann, this volume; Noddings 2013). Feminist research leadership, less explored, means enabling equality and democracy and "working productively with differences among team members" (Mountz et al. 2003, 41). Natasha S. Mauthner and Rosalind Edwards (2010, 494) assert that research managers who attempt feminist praxis encounter contradictions, "find[ing] themselves ricocheting between different management styles—collaborative one moment and directive the next."

METHODS

Twenty-four women academics from seven Ontario universities were recruited based on a record of securing significant external research funding as well as a

TABLE 4.1
Number and distribution of faculty interviews

Number of institutions	Institution type	Social work	Education	Social sciences[a]	Total
2	Research-intensive	3	2	4	9
3	Comprehensive	3	4	4	11
2	Undergraduate	2	1	1	4
Total		8	7	9	24

a Includes geography and sociology.

focus on social justice within their research. Participants were from four disciplinary areas and from institutions with varying levels of research intensity (Table 4.1).

Appropriate researchers were identified through university websites, supplemented by Google searches and the SSHRC Awards Search Engine. After receiving ethics approval from the relevant institutions, we approached potential participants via email, asking for a sixty- to ninety-minute interview. Purposeful sampling was used to ensure participants were distributed fairly equally across subject fields and university types. Not surprisingly, it proved more difficult to find candidates in the primarily undergraduate universities. Recruiting men was another challenge as they were less well represented in some of the departments and only three responded to our email invitations; thus, our focus here is on women only.

Interviews were conducted between May 2019 and March 2020, either in person or online over Skype or Zoom.[2] Our selection included thirteen full professors, eight associate professors, and three assistant professors. Many held additional leadership positions such as directorships of centres or research institutes or various types of honorary chairs; these positions were rarely at the top of the managerial hierarchy, leading us to speculate that distinct career patterns were in evidence. Ages ranged from late thirties to early seventies; given the time required for building up a research record, most (sixteen) were in their fifties and sixties. The majority of the women (twenty of twenty-four) had children. While most were no longer raising young children, three had children under ten and five had teenagers.

An advantage of including a social justice focus was that nearly half of our participants were racialized or Indigenous women, beyond what would be expected in Canadian academe (F. Henry et al. 2017), which takes the conventional work on research leadership in an unusual direction.[3] Those who did not identify as white named various heritages, including Black, Indigenous, Middle

Eastern, East Asian, and South Asian, with further variations within these broad categories. Similarly, social class origins appeared to encompass an unusually wide range, as ten of the twenty-four described their backgrounds as working class or poor (another two did not answer the question, which was optional). Only three indicated some type of disability. Given anonymity concerns, we do not specify racial or ethnic affiliation or other demographic characteristics. As well, pseudonyms are common Canadian "English" names, deliberately not associated with particular ethnicities.

Questions covered research history, experiences with funding bodies, institutional supports, and perceptions related to leadership. The semi-structured nature of the interview guide enabled participants to elaborate on issues that were significant to them. Interviews were recorded, transcribed, and coded based on our research question.

RESEARCH PROJECT LEADERSHIP

We asked: "When managing a project, do you consider yourself a leader?" Answers fell into four groups. Nine, like Ruth, responded positively: "Yes, I do. Yes, absolutely," while five, like Mary, were clearly negative: "I don't. I don't." Two of the three assistant professors were unsure, given their relatively brief experience in the role. The remaining eight participants responded "yes" but immediately qualified their response. For example: "Yeah, I do. But leadership to me is not telling people what to do. It's actually supporting what people want to do" (Wendy); "Yes, but a kind of a collaborative leader" (Cheryl); "Yes, amongst other leaders" (Christine).

What we came to call the "Yes but" group most often alluded to a shared or distributive leadership practice (Crawford 2012). Even among those who said "No," we find this theme again. Brenda, for example, acknowledged that she might have a leadership role in giving a presentation but "after that everything is open to discussion. So that's not leadership anymore, because everyone has a piece." Others appeared to have an aversion to the word "leader," preferring alternative terminology: "I see myself as a facilitator ... as a coach ... as an organizer who is bringing a group of people together to start thinking about the gaps in our society" (Mary); "I see myself as the most responsible [person] ... teaching other responsible people ... coaching other people to grow" (Crystal).

While responding "yes" to the question, Jacqueline was a reluctant leader: "It sounds like a really great thing, but it just means doing all the work, I find. Leading is just another word for working hard." Lori concurred: "I have to say something – I'm tired of being the leader." Others who were reluctant attributed their response to early socialization. Rosemary, despite a stellar record of publications and grants, nevertheless responded, "I will feel an imposter before I feel I am a leader," adding, "I think genuinely it goes back to being in the [country name] education system as somebody who came from a working class background and that has stayed with me all these years. It just doesn't go away."[4] Although there is evidence that a working class background can hamper an academic career (Haney 2015; Waterfield, Beagan, and Mohamed 2019), it may be that pursuing a social justice line of research sustains motivation or builds on critical background knowledge.

For Emily, whose background was middle class but who was first in her family to obtain a higher education, it was gender socialization that made her uncomfortable with the leader terminology: "Leadership within research for me is not a comfortable position ... I had a loving family, but nobody said you're a born leader." Finally, among the ten racialized or Indigenous scholars in the study, only one said an unequivocal "yes" to the leadership question, in contrast with eight of fourteen nonracialized participants. Later in the chapter, we return to this question of why a leadership identity is so hesitantly embraced by these highly accomplished women researchers.

When asked about how they enact leadership (or whatever term they preferred), participants often described managerial responsibilities, such as overseeing finances and contractual issues, setting meeting agendas, and keeping track of deadlines. Responsibility and accountability were frequently mentioned. Denise used an interesting maternal metaphor:

> If I'm the PI, I try to say "I'm responsible for noticing things." It's sort of how the mother's the one that always notices whether you need milk. Everyone else just is upset that there's no milk but didn't notice that you were getting down on the milk. I always think that the PI is the one who notices that we're getting low on milk.

Another theme that emerged was the provision of intellectual or conceptual leadership. Ruth asked questions such as, "So what are we about? Where are we headed? In trying to get this information, what's the best way to do it? What are we missing?" Nancy's leadership involved educating team members from other disciplines about "[the way] a social practitioner might think about it," while Kathy described how she provided "theoretical leadership" through informal teaching of colleagues.

Even when the intent was to prioritize intellectual leadership, it was evident that many PIs found themselves mired in detailed administration (Mauthner and Doucet 2008). Those with sufficient funds to hire project management staff felt relief, while others lamented the absence of assistance: "Having a great project manager will really help ... So somebody I've worked with for six years and love and trust ... will join and so I feel very fortunate" (Cheryl); "The [big] grant is the only one that came with a requirement to have an administrator and I've complained a lot about the failure to have administrative assistance on other things" (Sheila).

The next section identifies three themes that go beyond logistical concerns and characterize the participants' leadership approaches: collaboration, community, and caring. Whether or not claimed as such, these principles signify a feminist approach to leadership (O'Dea 2020) and also parallel Sarah R. Davies and Maja Horst's (2015) discussion of research leadership as "caring craft."

FORGING A NEW LEADERSHIP APPROACH

Collaboration

As our selection criteria included having a significant research record, all participants had been PIs and/or coresearchers on funded projects. When asked if they preferred collaboration or solo research, the majority opted for collaboration or "both," with only two expressing a preference for solo work. With few exceptions, having a grant equated to working with a team. A team might be anything from the PI and one or two students to a large-scale international, interdisciplinary collaboration including other academics, community members, students, and paid researchers. Despite evidence in the literature that academics, including social scientists, are currently under pressure to work in large teams (Torres-Olave et al. 2020), this expectation was not the experience of our participants (although some did do so), suggesting a difference between Canada and some other countries.

Both Margaret Baguley and colleagues (2021) and Blanca Torres-Olave and colleagues (2020) remark upon the ambiguity of the term "collaboration" in describing research. While the literature often identifies drawbacks, our participants usually presented collaboration as a desirable ideal, involving fostering good working relations and mutual learning, encouraging diversity, and countering isolation. Strategies included checking with team members to ensure they had the support they needed (Julie) and consciously building confidence and capacity within the group (Debra). Sharon described how she encourages collaboration: "In the end, I'm responsible, but in terms of how I tend to manage, I try to keep it as a collaborative kind of atmosphere, not as a hierarchical atmosphere ... it's about creating a space in which everybody can throw out their ideas."

Collaboration meant mutual learning: "[The team] was non-Native and Native and the collaboration was really good, because again, the non-Native PI was a senior researcher and she'd been doing this for a long time. She's gotten tons of grants ... and she learned so much about how to work better with Indigenous people" (Debra).

For some, establishing diverse teams was fundamental and the very composition of the team reflected their social justice commitments. Mary elaborated on her preference for diversity: "Like the team that is working with me right now, I've had a white student, South Asian student, and a Black student, because I think their perceptions are different and they help each other to understand ... when they start talking, they educate each other."

Rosemary described her team as international and intergenerational, while Cheryl's intersectional approach pointed to the importance of including collaborators with lived experience related to race, age, sexuality, ethnicity, and class: "I've been really keen to work with more diverse scholars because I think it isn't just an issue of representation, but it's also what they bring conceptually ... they have the conceptual and the experiential background." Even PIs with largely homogeneous teams acknowledged the value of diversity. Denise recalled having many discussions about how to diversify a particular research group without partaking in tokenism.

Despite dedication to collaborations, participants acknowledged difficulties. For example, Barbara said, "I'm trying to include [coresearchers] more, but generally I find it happens ... that they're busy with other things. They have full teaching loads and so they don't necessarily have the time to commit to the work that needs to be done. So I do it." Yet pleasure and intellectual satisfaction could outweigh the problems. Sharon stated that "the collaborative stuff has been a true joy because of the people I've worked with."

Community

Due to the research focus on social justice, it was unsurprising that including "community" in projects was a predominant theme. Community included organizations such as NGOs, representatives of a specific agency, individuals or in/formal groups affiliated with the topic of research, or people identified as having relevant lived experience.

Community needs were paramount to some of our participants. As Brenda reflected, "So I have my own notion of what research is and what it means for me in this context, the academic context, but what does that mean for [the community]? It might look different." Community partners also had unique understandings that were critical for ensuring that researchers understood the local context (Fertaly and Fluri 2019). Kathy explained, "We developed strong relationships with a couple of community partners there and ... we made adjustments in the project as the context changed ... and we also took the lead from the community partners."

Community collaborators were also valued as agents able to theorize their own experiences and as key members of a research team. Debra recruited team members "who don't work in universities, don't have degrees like us, but they have a wealth of knowledge in terms of working with the communities and [community] protocols." Crystal framed her research in a way "that allows us to pay attention to complexity, allows us to do work that positions participants as experts in their own lives and asks them to cotheorize with us."

However, this collaborative way of working was labour intensive and posed difficulties not apparent in more traditional approaches. For example, extra time might be required to overcome historic distrust: "First of all, we have to create a safe language, a safe space for everybody to come together" (Christine). As noted by Chantale Mailhot and colleagues (2016), meaningful inclusion of communities could require researchers to take on the role of a translator, sometimes preparing two sets of findings, one tailored to academic and funders' requirements and the other more relevant to the community participants. Pamela referred to the often unrecognized labour of developing strategies to ensure that the research matters to the community as the "hidden work of caring."

Universities and funding bodies sometimes presented institutional "inhibiting factors" (Cunningham et al. 2014). For instance, costs associated with preparing feasts or providing honorariums to community members were sometimes questioned, despite the necessity of such supports (Debra). Wendy identified a large gap between university expectations and community needs: "I think the university is very behind ... a lot of those traditional research grants are not what's actually happening in the community."

Overall, researchers' social justice commitments enabled them to reconcile this disparity. As Brenda concluded, "I think I've learned how to balance the expectations of the academy and community expectations. It's a lot of work, but it has to be done."

Caring

Academia is based on a system of practices and rewards that imagines faculty members and senior administrators unencumbered by caregiving responsibilities (Grummell, Devine, and Lynch 2009), thus impeding many women's chances for a leadership career. Research suggests that women academics do disproportionate caring and service work both at home and in the university (Acker, Webber, and Smyth 2016; Heijstra, Steinthorsdóttir, and Einarsdóttir 2017; Walker, Ignatovich, and Nabavi, this volume). Faculty from underrepresented groups frequently experience what is called "cultural taxation" or "identity taxation," finding themselves with an extra workload as they counsel and mentor racialized students and serve on diversity committees (Hirshfield and Joseph 2012).

Participants whose children were still young noted implications for their work. Emily shared that doing fieldwork abroad was constrained by the needs of her partner and children, while Crystal described setting boundaries: "My children are young and they really fill my attention when I'm with them and so, when I am not working, I am not working." Mothers of older children spontaneously mentioned pregnancies or childbirth as a marker of a career transition; for example: "and then I had our [number] child in the middle of the pretenure process and we had our [next] just after I got tenure" (Julie). Michelle commented on what Hirshfield and Joseph (2012) call gendered identity taxation:

> The institutions, they work very smoothly for a white man of a certain class and all that sort of thing, but the rest of us who get pulled on to every committee they have about diversity, have every student coming to them that feels like they don't belong in this space, who cares deeply about these issues, so says okay, sure, I'll do it.

Our main concern was caring within research leadership practice. In this context, caring could be operationalized at many levels. At the personal level, it was demonstrated in stories of being mentored and mentoring others (Breeze and Taylor 2020). At the institutional, team-based, or community level, it involved consciously providing opportunities for others. At the broader societal level, it was using one's research efforts to make a difference in the world.

Many participants spontaneously talked about their own histories of being mentored. For example, Danielle said, "[I've had] so much mentorship and really wonderful guidance from people who have been through this, they've been around much longer than me. And so I wouldn't have sought out these opportunities had it not been for their support and input." In several cases, participants believed the mentoring had been absolutely crucial to their careers. Tina commented, "Having [Name] pick me up, even though I had no record, was a big plus ... that was super, because he mentored me ... in so many ways."

The prevalence of such deeply held gratitude to mentors suggests that the kind of research success we are encountering is intertwined with networks of informal support. Not only did participants spontaneously acknowledge help from others; they paid it forward by adopting mentoring practices of their own. Acknowledging the power differences that can emerge in teams (Liinason 2013), Sheila emphasized the importance of consciously including student assistants in all phases of the work. Others mentored junior team members by making them first authors on papers (Cheryl), coauthoring (Judith, Julie), or introducing them to people who could help them in other ways (Pamela). Reflecting her social justice commitments, Emily's "mentorship philosophy is to do everything I can to mentor and advance the careers of [people from] equity seeking groups."

Caring was also manifested through concern for the communities that were involved in the research. Pamela considered these priorities integral to her role as a "caring ethical scholar." Social justice commitments also attuned participants to a broader form of caring at a societal or global level. Sometimes, such an agenda required de-emphasizing traditionally valued academic practices:

> Public sociology is sociology that actually tries to do something productive in social justice ... how to do work that was not just for the academy, how to take it beyond and actually make it meaningful. And that's been something that has been really important to me my whole career ... just working on journal articles that nobody ever read wasn't doing it for me. (Jacqueline)

When invited to identify her research interests, Rosemary gave a response that serves as an exemplar of the impressive efforts made by so many of the women in the study: "It is about fighting for issues that need fighting for. So, for me, those are issues around gender, around race, around class, sexuality. So all of those have been foci in my research."

DISCUSSION AND CONCLUSION

The degree of ambivalence toward identifying as a leader among such an accomplished group of researchers was a surprise. How are we to understand this paradox? What emerged was a prevailing sense that nonhierarchical and collaborative approaches are not considered to be aligned with "leadership" as commonly conceptualized in the neoliberal and male-dominated context of academia. Notably, many participants preferred terms such as facilitator, coach, organizer, or "the most responsible person." Some participants attributed their reluctance to identify as leaders to their early gender or social class socialization. It was also evident that racialized women researchers were most likely either to express ambivalence about their status as leaders or to completely reject the label. These findings merit further research attention.

The contemporary context is significant, as the collaborative approaches embraced by most of our interviewees are in tension with the audit and performativity cultures increasingly embedded in academia. Here we can apply James Cunningham and colleagues' (2014) "inhibiting factors" framework to single out institutional and funding body practices. Universities reward individual productivity in promotion and "merit" exercises for work actually done by research teams. Many research council grants are configured to recognize only a single project leader, eschewing the possibility of establishing a non-hierarchical team (Mountz et al. 2003) in favour of locating responsibility and accountability in a named person. Hence, it is understandable how the label "leader" may appear dissonant to those who value collaboration.

Working within a social justice framework influenced the priorities of our participants. Cunningham and colleagues' (2014) other two categories of inhibiting factors are project-based and political and economic. The project-based workload reported by PIs includes the unrecognized labour identified in the literature, such as the preparatory work required before launching a project and the administrative and communication issues that arise throughout the research. What is also not captured within audit frameworks is what Pamela termed the "hidden work of caring." While research leaders in our study broadened their focus to global issues, that is, political and economic considerations, PIs also made efforts to ensure that their research would be accessible and useful to communities. Rather than being invested in accruing individual recognition, participants were driven by a will to improve conditions for others in the world, motivated by their awareness of injustice or community needs. These commitments not only resulted in an increased workload but often created tensions with funders and academic institutions.

The tension between neoliberal individualism and the priorities of these researchers was also evident in the energy they committed to mentoring and creating opportunities for others on their teams, often deliberately structured to include colleagues from traditionally marginalized backgrounds. There was a strong sense among many of the participants that their success had been enhanced through the mentorship they had received early in their career and they were now in a position to give back.

We discovered that despite the apparent reluctance to embrace the language of leadership, researchers in our study consistently identified myriad ways they lead their research teams. It may be that they are enacting leadership in forms that are not overtly recognized in hierarchical organizational structures. Hence, they can hone their leadership skills without having to climb the administrative career ladder and while retaining some flexibility around parenting and familial responsibilities. Further research on career patterns of different types of leaders might tell us more, as might a study that focused more closely on how social class or racial backgrounds influenced later leadership orientations and social justice motivations.

We conclude that these women researchers are actively engaging in leadership, albeit in forms that are less likely to be recognized and valued within the logistics of neoliberal individualism that inform recognition within academe or within conventional leadership literature. It appears that truly collaborative approaches and the accompanying caring work that is often undertaken by women and feminist PIs are frequently uncredited and marginalized, consequently reinforcing the prevalent perception of the lack of women leaders in academia. What is required at this point is a radical reconceptualization of how academic leadership is understood.

ACKNOWLEDGMENTS

Our thanks to the Social Sciences and Humanities Research Council for supporting the research on which this chapter is based (#435–2017–0104) and to the participants who generously gave us their time. We also acknowledge our research team and others who have assisted us: Margaret Brennan, Caitlin Campisi, Pushpa Hamal, Victoria Kannen, Michelle K. McGinn, and Marie Vander Kloet. We also thank Bessma Momani, Rachael Johnstone, Kersty Kearney, and the anonymous reviewers.

NOTES

1 Reviews of scholarship on Canadian women academics can be found in Acker and Muzzin (2019) and Wagner, Acker, and Mayuzumi (2008).
2 The interviews were completed just as universities were closing due to the COVID-19 pandemic. Consequently, participants' responses did not reflect any consequent disruptions or changes in their research work that may have occurred.
3 In Canada, women as a group are about 42 percent percent of full-time university faculty (Statistics Canada 2022). According to the 2016 census, racialized men and women account for 21 percent of university faculty and Indigenous faculty represent another 1.4 percent (CAUT 2018). Many higher education researchers have noted the difficulty of finding official Canadian statistics that go beyond superficial indicators. The lengths to which chapter authors in this volume have gone to compile intersectional data on Canadian academics and administrators, often combing through masses of web sites, testify to this dilemma, as noted by Lorna Turnbull in the conclusion of this volume.
4 Social class background was not a straightforward matter as some participants were raised outside Canada and some had families who were upwardly mobile. However, there were hints that a background described as poor or working class may have influenced participants' choice of subject field and research topic.

WORKS CITED

Acker, Sandra. 1994. *Gendered Education: Sociological Reflections on Women, Teaching and Feminism.* Buckingham, UK: Open University Press.
–. 2012. "Chairing and Caring: Gendered Dimensions of Leadership in Academe." *Gender and Education* 24 (4): 411–28. https://doi.org/10.1080/09540253.2011.628927.

–. 2014. "A Foot in the Revolving Door? Women Academics in Lower-Middle Management." *Higher Education Research and Development* 33 (1): 73–85. https://doi.org/10.1080/07294360.2013.864615.

Acker, Sandra, and Michelle K. McGinn. 2021. "Fast Professors, Research Funding, and the Figured Worlds of Mid-Career Ontario Academics." *Brock Education Journal* 30 (2): 79–98. https://doi.org/10.26522/brocked.v30i2.864.

Acker, Sandra, and Linda Muzzin. 2019. "Minoritized Faculty in Canada's Universities and Colleges: Gender, Power, and Academic Work." In *Working Women in Canada: An Intersectional Approach*, edited by Leslie Nichols, 177–201. Toronto: Women's Press.

Acker, Sandra, Anne Wagner, and Michelle K. McGinn. 2018. "Research Leaders and Student Collaborators: Insights from Canada." In *Exploring Consensual Leadership in Higher Education: Co-Operation, Collaboration and Partnership*, edited by Lynne Gornall, Brychan Thomas, and Lucy Sweetman, 113–28. London: Bloomsbury.

Acker, Sandra, Michelle Webber, and Elizabeth Smyth. 2016. "Continuity or Change? Gender, Family, and Academic Work for Junior Faculty in Ontario Universities." *NASPA Journal about Women in Higher Education* 9 (1): 1–20. https://doi.org/10.1080/19407882.2015.1114954.

Armstrong, Pat, and Ruth Lowndes, eds. 2018. *Creative Teamwork: Developing Rapid, Site-Switching Ethnography*. New York: Oxford University Press. https://doi.org/10.1093/oso/9780190862268.001.0001.

Baguley, Margaret, Martin Kerby, Abbey MacDonald, and Vaughan Cruickshank. 2021. "Strangers on a Train: The Politics of Collaboration." *Australian Educational Researcher* 48:183–208. https://doi.org/10.1007/s13384-020-00386-9.

Blackmore, Jill, and Judyth Sachs. 2007. *Performing and Reforming Leaders: Gender, Educational Restructuring, and Organizational Change*. Albany: State University of New York Press.

Breeze, Maddie, and Yvette Taylor. 2020. "Feminist Collaborations in Higher Education: Stretched across Career Stages." *Gender and Education* 32 (3): 412–28. https://doi.org/10.1080/09540253.2018.1471197.

Canadian Association of University Teachers (CAUT). 2018. *Underrepresented and Underpaid: Diversity and Equity among Canada's Post-Secondary Education Teachers*. Ottawa, ON: CAUT. https://www.caut.ca/sites/default/files/caut_equity_report_2018-04final.pdf.

Crawford, Megan. 2012. "Solo and Distributed Leadership: Definitions and Dilemmas." *Educational Management Administration and Leadership* 40 (5): 610–20. http://journals.sagepub.com/doi/10.1177/1741143212451175.

Cukier, Wendy, Patience Adamu, Charlie Wall-Andrews, and Mohamed Elmi. 2021. "Racialized Leaders Leading Canadian Universities." *Educational Management Administration and Leadership* 49 (4): 565–83. https://doi.org/10.1177/1741143221 1001363.

Cunningham, James, Paul O'Reilly, Conor O'Kane, and Vincent Mangematin. 2014. "The Inhibiting Factors That Principal Investigators Experience in Leading Publicly Funded Research." *Journal of Technology Transfer* 39 (1): 93–110. https://doi.org/10.1007/s10961-012-9269-4.

Davies, Sarah R., and Maja Horst. 2015. "Crafting the Group: Care in Research Management." *Social Studies of Science* 45 (3): 371–91. https://doi.org/10.1177/0306312715585820.

Deem, Rosemary. 2003. "Gender, Organizational Cultures and the Practices of Manager-Academics in UK Universities." *Gender, Work and Organization* 10 (2): 239–59. https://doi.org/10.1111/1468-0432.t01-1-00013.

Drake, Pat. 2015. "Becoming Known through Email: A Case of Woman, Leadership, and an Awfully Familiar Strange Land." *Gender and Education* 27 (2): 148–63. https://doi.org/10.1080/09540253.2014.993936.

Evans, Linda. 2014. "What Is Effective Research Leadership? A Research-Informed Perspective." *Higher Education Research and Development* 33 (1): 46–58. https://doi.org/10.1080/07294360.2013.864617.

Eveline, Joan. 2004. *Ivory Basement Leadership: Power and Invisibility in the Changing University*. Crawley: University of Western Australia Press.

Faircloth, Susan C. 2017. "Reflections on the Concept of Authentic Leadership: From an Indigenous Scholar/Leader Perspective." *Advances in Developing Human Resources* 19 (4): 407–19. https://doi.org/10.1177/1523422317728935.

Fertaly, Kaitlin, and Jennifer L. Fluri. 2019. "Research Associates and the Production of Knowledge in the Field." *Professional Geographer* 71 (1): 75–82. https://doi.org/10.1080/00330124.2018.1455519.

Fitzgerald, Tanya. 2013. *Women Leaders in Higher Education: Shattering the Myths*. London: Routledge.

Grummell, Bernie, Dympna Devine, and Kathleen Lynch. 2009. "The Care-less Manager: Gender, Care and New Managerialism in Higher Education." *Gender and Education* 21 (2): 191–208. http://dx.doi.org/10.1080/09540250802392273.

Haney, Timothy J. 2015. "Factory to Faculty: Socioeconomic Difference and the Educational Experiences of University Professors." *Canadian Review of Sociology* 52 (2): 160–86. https://doi.org/10.1111/cars.12069.

Heijstra, Thamar Melanie, Finnborg Salome Steinthorsdóttir, and Thorgerdur Einarsdóttir. 2017. "Academic Career Making and the Double-Edged Role of Academic Housework." *Gender and Education* 29 (6): 764–80. https://doi.org/10.1080/09540253.2016.1171825.

Henry, Annette. 2015. "'We Especially Welcome Applications from Members of Visible Minority Groups': Reflections on Race, Gender and Life at Three Universities." *Race Ethnicity and Education* 18 (5): 589–610. https://doi.org/10.1080/13613324.2015.1023787.

Henry, Frances, Carl James, Peter S. Li, Audrey Lynn Kobayashi, Malinda Smith, Howard Ramos, and Enakshi Dua. 2017. *The Equity Myth: Racialization and Indigeneity at Canadian Universities*. Vancouver: UBC Press.

Hirshfield, Laura E., and Tiffany D. Joseph. 2012. "'We Need a Woman, We Need a Black Woman': Gender, Race, and Identity Taxation in the Academy." *Gender and Education* 24 (2): 213–27. https://doi.org/10.1080/09540253.2011.606208.

Juntrasook, Adisorn, Karen Nairn, Carol Bond, and Rachel Spronken-Smith. 2013. "Unpacking the Narrative of Non-Positional Leadership in Academia: Hero and/or

Victim?" *Higher Education Research and Development* 32 (2): 201–13. https://doi. org/10.1080/07294360.2011.643858.

Kandiko Howson, Camille, Kelly Coate, and Tania de St Croix. 2018. "Mid-Career Academic Women and the Prestige Economy." *Higher Education Research and Development* 37 (3): 533–48. https://doi.org/10.1080/07294360.2017.1411337.

Karram Stephenson, Grace, Glen A. Jones, Emmanuelle Fick, Olivier Bégin-Caouette, Aamir Taiyeb, and Amy Metcalfe. 2020. "What's the Protocol? Canadian University Research Ethics Boards and Variations in Implementing Tri-Council Policy." *Canadian Journal of Higher Education* 50 (1): 68–81. https://journals.sfu.ca/cjhe/index.php/ cjhe/article/view/188743/186387.

Kyvik, Svein. 2013. "The Academic Researcher Role: Enhancing Expectations and Improved Performance." *Higher Education* 65 (4): 525–38. https://www.jstor.org/ stable/23470836.

Kyvik, Svein, and Ingvild Reymert. 2017. "Research Collaboration in Groups and Networks: Differences across Academic Fields." *Scientometrics* 113 (2): 951–67. https:// doi.org/10.1007/s11192-017-2497-5.

Liinason, Mia. 2013. "Young Blood: The Social Politics of Research Collaboration from the Perspective of a Young Scholar." In *The Social Politics of Research Collaboration*, edited by Gabriele Griffin, Katarina Hamberg, and Britta Lundgren, 105–18. London: Routledge.

Mailhot, Chantale, Stéphanie Gagnon, Ann Langley, and Louis-Félix Binette. 2016. "Distributing Leadership across People and Objects in a Collaborative Research Project." *Leadership* 12 (1): 53–85. https://doi.org/10.1177/1742715014543578.

Mauthner, Natasha S., and Andrea Doucet. 2008. "'Knowledge Once Divided Can Be Hard to Put Together Again': An Epistemological Critique of Collaborative and Team-Based Research Practices." *Sociology* 42 (5): 971–85. https://doi.org/10.1177/ 0038038508094574.

Mauthner, Natasha S., and Rosalind Edwards. 2010. "Feminist Research Management in Higher Education in Britain: Possibilities and Practices." *Gender, Work and Organization* 17 (5): 481–502. https://doi.org/10.1111/j.1468-0432.2010.00522.x.

McGinn, Michelle K., Sandra Acker, Marie Vander Kloet, and Anne Wagner. 2019. "Dear SSHRC, What Do You Want? An Epistolary Narrative of Expertise, Identity, and Time in Grant Writing." *Forum: Qualitative Social Research* 20 (1): Article 8. https://doi. org/10.17169/fqs-20.1.3128.

Morley, Louise. 2013. "The Rules of the Game: Women and the Leaderist Turn in Higher Education." *Gender and Education* 25 (1): 116–31. https://doi.org/10.1080/ 09540253.2012.740888.

Morley, Louise, and Barbara Crossouard. 2016. "Gender in the Neoliberalised Global Academy: The Affective Economy of Women and Leadership in South Asia." *British Journal of Sociology of Education* 37 (1): 149–68. https://doi.org/10.1080/01425692. 2015.1100529.

Mountz, Alison, Anne Bonds, Becky Mansfield, Jenna Loyd, Jennifer Hyndman, Margaret Walton-Roberts, Ranu Basu, Risa Whitson, Roberta Hawkins, Trina Hamilton, and Winifred Curran. 2015. "For Slow Scholarship: A Feminist Politics of Resistance through Collective Action in the Neoliberal University." *ACME: An International Journal for Critical Geographies* 14 (4): 1235–59. https://acme-journal.org/index.php/acme/article/view/1058.

Mountz, Alison, Ines M. Miyares, Richard Wright, and Adrian J. Bailey. 2003. "Methodologically Becoming: Power, Knowledge, and Team Research." *Gender, Place and Culture* 10 (1): 29–46. https://doi.org/10.1080/0966369032000052649.

Noddings, Nel. 2013. *Caring: A Relational Approach to Ethics and Moral Education.* Berkeley: University of California Press.

O'Dea, Jane. 2020. "Hazardous Manoeuvres: Thoughts on Being a Female University Dean." *Irish Educational Studies* 39 (2): 205–19. https://doi.org/10.1080/03323315.2019.1698444.

Raelin, Joseph A. 2016. "Imagine There Are No Leaders: Reframing Leadership as Collaborative Agency." *Leadership* 12 (2): 131–58. http://journals.sagepub.com/doi/10.1177/1742715014558076.

Read, Barbara, and Barbara M. Kehm. 2016. "Women as Leaders of Higher Education Institutions: A British–German Comparison." *Studies in Higher Education* 41 (5): 815–27. https://doi.org/10.1080/03075079.2016.1147727.

Statistics Canada. 2022. "Statistics on Full-Time Academic Teaching Staff at Canadian Universities: Interactive Tool." https://www150.statcan.gc.ca/n1/pub/71-607-x/71-607-x2019027-eng.htm.

Sumsion, Jennifer. 2014. "Opening Up Possibilities through Team Research: An Investigation of Infants' Lives in Early Childhood Education Settings." *Qualitative Research* 14 (2): 149–65. http://journals.sagepub.com/doi/10.1177/1468794112468471.

Tamtik, Merli, and Melissa Guenter. 2019. "Policy Analysis of Equity, Diversity and Inclusion Strategies in Canadian Universities – How Far Have We Come?" *Canadian Journal of Higher Education* 49 (3): 41–56. https://doi.org/10.7202/1066634ar.

Teelken, Christine. 2012. "Academic Leadership and Its Effects on Professional Autonomy." In *Leadership in the Public Sector: Promises and Pitfalls*, edited by Christine Teelken, Ewan Ferlie, and Mike Dent, 174–94. London: Routledge.

Thompson, Barbara Marcia. 2019. "Shifting Feminisms: Collaborative or Individualized Managers? An Exploratory Study in Three UK Universities." *Gender in Management: An International Journal* 34 (4): 287–305. https://doi.org/10.1108/GM-12-2017-0179.

Torres-Olave, Blanca, Ashley M. Brown, Lillianna Franco Carrera, and Carlos Ballinas. 2020. "Not Waving but Striving: Research Collaboration in the Context of Stratification, Segmentation, and the Quest for Prestige." *Journal of Higher Education* 91 (2): 275–99. https://doi.org/10.1080/00221546.2019.1631074.

Trudgett, Michelle, Susan Page, and Stacey Kim Coates. 2022. "Great Expectations: Senior Indigenous Leadership Positions in Higher Education." *Journal of Higher Education Policy and Management* 44 (1): 90–106. https://doi.org/10.1080/1360080X.2021.2003013.

Wagner, Anne, Sandra Acker, and Kimine Mayuzumi. 2008. "Introduction." In *Whose University Is It, Anyway? Power and Privilege on Gendered Terrain*, edited by Anne Wagner, Sandra Acker, and Kimine Mayuzumi, 11–24. Toronto: Sumach Press.

Waterfield, Bea, Brenda L. Beagan, and Tameera Mohamed. 2019. "'You Always Remain Slightly an Outsider': Workplace Experiences of Academics from Working-Class or Impoverished Backgrounds." *Canadian Review of Sociology* 56 (3): 368–88. https://doi.org/10.1111/cars.12257.

Willcoxson, Lesley, Marie Kavanagh, and Lily Cheung. 2011. "Leading, Managing and Participating in Inter-University Teaching Grant Collaborations." *Higher Education Research and Development* 30 (4): 533–48. https://doi.org/10.1080/07294360.2010.526095.

5

Wage Equality and Opportunity for Women Deans

RACHAEL JOHNSTONE and BESSMA MOMANI

The specific role of a dean within the Canadian academy is surprisingly difficult to define, dependent as it is on the culture of a given faculty and the size and standing of the institution (de Boer and Goedegebuure 2009, 352). Deans are the heads of faculties, but they are also middle managers, responsible for both the academic and administrative workings of their faculties (de Boer and Goedegebuure 2009, 349) and liaising with department heads (chairs) and higher administration (e.g., provosts, vice-presidents, and presidents). The shifting relationship between Canadian universities and federal and provincial governments in recent years, especially changes to the university funding model that emphasize tuition revenue over public funding, have also created new role expectations. For instance, universities are expected to increase public outreach and play a larger role in "regional and national economic development," as well as navigate greater reliance on the private sector for financial support. Nevertheless, the specific responsibilities of deans continue to vary significantly (Boyko and Jones 2010, 83).

In this evolving neoliberal academic climate, in which success is influenced by the perception of both internal and external stakeholders, the power of deans is substantially dictated by "social norms and [the] expectations" of faculty and senior administration (Bray 2008, 692). Although gender is known to shape both social norms and expectations in Canadian universities, the specific connection of gender identity and deanships has received scant attention in Canada.[1] Our research begins to fill this gap. This chapter shares findings from a high-level investigation into the role that gender plays in the perceptions of deans in Canada.

In 2019, we conducted a Canada-wide survey of university deans to learn more about how their gender shapes their perceptions of the role. The analysis of our findings showed perceptions of gender had statistically significant effects on 1) opportunities, both to secure deanships and to advance into more senior administrative roles, and 2) wages. We found that men participants overwhelmingly perceived no inequality of opportunity to becoming a dean or any gendered pay gap for these roles, while women participants perceived both opportunities and wages to be gendered. To learn more about how these data points translated into the perceptions of deans, we undertook a series of thirty-four one-on-one interviews of current and former deans across Canada in which we asked them to elaborate on the two core findings to add depth to our survey results. We draw from our findings, in combination with existing literature and quantitative data, to demonstrate that the pay gap perceived by the women deans does, in fact, exist. While it is harder to definitively show a gender gap in opportunity, our findings suggest that such a gap exists. Notably, both securing jobs (opportunity) and salary (wage gap) are metrics of success that are normally taken as indicators of merit, which gives us some insight into the persistence of gendered divides.

Recognizing and understanding gendered perceptions is important because whether obstacles to securing equality of opportunity and salary are addressed, and how they are addressed, is influenced by beliefs of their continued existence. Who, after all, would craft a policy to address an issue they perceive to be non-existent or exaggerated? Which gendered dynamics are visible and acknowledged and which are invisible or potentially framed as individual rather than systemic problems shape the experiences of men and women holding deanships in meaningful ways and influence the gendered dimensions of these roles.

DEANSHIP IN THE ACADEMY

The systemic barriers facing women attempting to advance in the labour market are well-documented. Women are often said to hit an invisible barrier or "glass ceiling" in their attempts to rise through the ranks, a pattern borne out in both business and politics literatures (Ryan and Haslam 2005; Jalalzai 2013; Bell, McLaughlin, and Sequeira 2002). When women do ascend to higher ranks, they are more likely than men to face scrutiny (for example, women fare worse on both formal and informal measurements of their leadership and overall effectiveness) (Ryan and Haslam 2005, 88). More recently, it has also been shown that women in the corporate world are most likely to occupy and be offered precarious leadership positions, a phenomenon psychologists Michelle Ryan and Alexander Haslam (2005, 83) coined the "glass cliff," which may make them more susceptible to perceived failure within these roles.

The existing literature on gender in academia suggests that, while formal gendered barriers to progressing in academia, from undergraduate programs through to senior administration, have been largely eliminated, informal barriers continue to create potentially significant obstacles for women-identified academics. For example, women who secure tenure are less likely than men to pursue higher-ranking positions and those who do typically earn less than men – a trend that cannot be explained using "pipeline" arguments that suggest the system simply needs time to self-correct now that more women are in academia and can move to the top (Momani, Dreher, and Williams 2019). Moreover, when women do take on senior administrative positions, they are more likely to quit or be let go before the end of their term (Chiose 2016). Research reveals the significance of gender for the creation and attainment of opportunities for advancement in academia. Research also suggests the existence of stark contrasts between individual perceptions of success in particular roles and the way this success is evaluated by others. In this chapter, we contribute to this literature on gender in academia with an in-depth study of deanships in Canada.

Gendered expectations are a major social cleavage. This is particularly the case for individuals in positions of power. Gendered expectations have long been known to influence opportunities for and experiences of leadership. Although universities are governed by some strict policies, academics, including administrators, have significant autonomy in how they operate. The behaviour of academics within these administrative roles is also guided by social and institutional norms, which dictate what individuals are expected and not expected to do. In this chapter, we build on sociologist Nathaniel Bray's (2008) work on the role of norms and their influence on the power held by academic deans. Bray explores both the nature of the expectations and the role of proscriptive norms used by faculty to regulate deans, especially as they concern undesirable behaviours. Bray and others (see Bensimon 1991) stress the significance of perception in the evaluation of deans, noting that "an important element of their work and success in dealing with various interests across campus is the manner in which the deans' work is viewed by those groups" (Bray 2008, 692).

In our research, we focus on the perceptions of deans as they evaluate their own career paths and those of their peers, asking how ingrained expectations and perceptions influence both opportunities to pursue deanships, and more advanced positions, and the gender wage gap. We question how a full range of norms, both proscriptive and prescriptive, are perceived by deans.

METHODS

Assessing gendered perceptions is difficult because experiences in a given role are often deeply personal and may not be representative of wider trends. To address these challenges, we employed a mixed methods approach, which included a detailed survey and a series of in-depth one-on-one interviews. In so doing, our aim was to capture trends in the perceptions of Canadian deans while also having the opportunity to add depth to our findings through the inclusion of qualitative data.

To assess the role of gender and deanship, we compiled a list of both current and previous deans across Canada. This proved to be an arduous task. Although there are many associations representing deans in specific academic fields, such as the Canadian Council of Deans of Science and the Canadian Association of Fine Arts Deans, no one group covers the whole of deans in Canada. Moreover, membership in these groups is voluntary and typically not made public. Without a central repository of individual deans, we set about compiling our own list, focusing on current deans. To this end, we utilized the Universities Canada membership list as our sampling frame. We then explored each university website and created a list of existing deans by faculty in the fall of 2018, including their contact information. In total, we gathered contact information for 431 deans.[2]

In January 2019, we emailed all 431 deans and asked them to partake in our study. We explained that we were conducting research aimed at understanding the impact of gender on faculty deans in Canadian universities and asked if they would be willing to complete a short, ten-minute survey using Qualtrics software. We also asked these deans to feel free to forward our call for participants to any past deans who might be interested and may not have appeared on our list.

Our online survey was active for four months and we received a total of 141 responses (a response rate of 32.7 percent).[3] The survey contained demographic questions on gender identity, age, marital status, gender identity of partner (if relevant), highest degree earned, academic rank at the time of first dean appointment, and the length of their appointment. Our responses were almost evenly split between men (50.4 percent) and women (49.6 percent)[4] and the average age of participants was fifty-seven years old, with the overwhelming majority of participants holding doctoral degrees (93.2 percent). Most deans held their posts for an average of twelve years and were full professors (76.2 percent) before taking on their posts. The next section of the survey contained multiple choice questions (using Likert scales), pairwise comparisons, and open-ended questions.[5] Survey questions covered topics ranging from perceptions of gendered issues in academia (e.g., equal pay and opportunities for advancement), mentorship, work/life balance (e.g., challenges associated with care work and its distribution), and the personal qualities associated with successful deanships. The results of the survey were then coded using two modelling approaches: linear regression and analysis of variance. For each approach, we explored responses based on three demographic characteristics: gender identity, age, and length of tenure as a dean. Our survey revealed several trends among responses. While there was little difference between participants based on age or length of tenure in their position, a number of statistically significant differences were apparent based on gender identity. Specifically, deans' perceptions about wages and opportunities were statistically differentiated by participants' gender identities.

In our original invitation email to participate in our survey, we asked deans interested in participating in a one-on-one interview to reply to our message. In February of 2019, we conducted thirty-four, thirty-minute one-on-one phone interviews with deans. In total, twenty-five interviewees identified as women and nine as men. All of the women who responded identified as white. The demographics of our respondents are consistent with Genevieve Fuiji Johnson and colleagues' findings in this volume (see Chapter 6 in this volume) that racialized women are underrepresented in deanships. To ensure anonymity, we did not correspond survey responses to personal interviews. To ensure candour, the identity of these interviewees, as well as other identifying information, such as their place of employment, are anonymized. They were asked a standardized list of questions, developed with reference to the literature and to complement the survey findings. Questions focused on the process they went through to become deans, the challenges they faced as deans, the reasons they believe they were more or less successful, and their rationale for pursuing higher levels of academic administration. We also asked them to reflect on the reasons for women's relatively lower representation in senior administration at U15 universities and in STEM and gave them an opportunity to add any additional feedback they wished on the topic of study. In this chapter, we focus on the results concerning two related areas: job opportunities and the wage gap.

GENDER AND THE WAGE GAP

When we asked survey participants to rate their agreement with the statement "There is a pay gap between men and women deans at my institution," women were significantly more likely ($p < 0.001$) to report the existence of a gender pay gap than men.[6] Since we analyzed categorical variables comparing samples, a multisample chi-squared test was also used, and results remained consistent.[7] The mean response of men participants was 2.3 (between disagree and neither agree nor disagree), while the women participants was 3.17 (between neither agree nor disagree and agree). Interestingly, none of the men participants strongly agreed and only three agreed, while sixteen of our women participants agreed and nine strongly agreed. Indeed, this difference was so wide that the average man denied the existence of a pay gap while the average woman affirmed it. This finding shows a dramatic variation in the perception of wage equality.

Unlike many other issues faced by the study of women in academia, wage gaps are an especially helpful metric to study inequality because they are relatively easy to measure when the data are made available. In Canada, a series of university-wide studies have shown the existence of a gender wage gap (Brown and Troutt 2017). A 2018–19 Statistics Canada report on the Canada-Wide University and College Academic Staff System census showed that wage gaps between men and women deans have been closing since they started collecting data in 1970–71. Nevertheless, as of 2018, women deans have a 2.7 percent wage gap below men, and women assistant deans have a 5.6 percent wage gap (Statistics Canada 2019). Another study, this one focusing specifically on Ontario and using the Public Sector Salary Disclosure Data, points out that this gender wage gap is higher for university deans (5.26 percent in Ontario) than university teaching staff (2.14 percent in Ontario) (Momani, Dreher, and Williams 2019, 3).[8] Even with the ongoing wage gap, women do have better representation in deanships and other higher administrative roles than they once did, though there are proportionally fewer women in the highest-paying positions such as provost and president (Bichsel and McChesney 2017, 15).

As psychologist Phyllis Tharenou (2013, 199) aptly puts it: "A great deal is already known about the magnitude of the gender wage gap, a modest amount about why it occurs, and very little about how it occurs." There are several theories that emerge from the literature on women and work, which in part explain the gender wage gap in academia. These theories suggest a range of issues impacting women's salaries including: wage transparency (Baker et al. 2019; Bennedsen et al. 2019); an unwillingness or failure to negotiate (Babcock and Laschever 2003; Greig 2008); presumed or actual gendered division of labour, especially relating to childcare (Budig and England 2001); and discrimination against women in general (Blau and Kahn 2017) and mothers in particular (Correll, Benard, and Paik 2007).

A prevailing hypothesis for the tenacity of the gender wage gap is a lack of transparency in earnings. A recent study by Statistics Canada tested this claim by studying the impact of transparency policies for university teaching salaries on this gap. Transparency policies have been instituted by most provinces (Ontario, Manitoba, and British Columbia were first in 1996 and later joined by Nova Scotia, Alberta, and Newfoundland and Labrador) (Baker et al. 2019). Institutions are required to report annual salaries over a specific threshold, which varies by province from $50,000 to $125,000. Economist Michael Baker and colleagues (2019) found that transparency policies helped to reduce the gender wage gap by approximately 30 percent but that these effects were more prevalent in institutions where professors are unionized. They also show that transparency policies tend to reduce salaries across the board by 1 to 3 percent on average, meaning that the gains women saw often reflected a "slowing in men's wage growth" (Baker et al. 2019).[9] While this study demonstrates that transparency can help to reduce the wage gap, it can only theorize about why this gap has narrowed or why it has failed to close entirely.

One of the most cited explanations for gender wage gaps concerns negotiation, specifically, that women are less likely than men to negotiate their salaries (Babcock and Laschever 2003; Greig 2008). Since higher profile positions like deanships often come with "greater discretion and negotiation for hiring," these negotiations are especially crucial at the dean level (Momani, Dreher, and Williams 2019, 6). A number of women deans we interviewed noted that they were either unaware or unpracticed at negotiating for salaries, especially earlier in their careers. One interviewee said that "as a naïve, young assistant professor, I didn't even conceive that gender would matter as much as it has mattered. I didn't know to negotiate the salary that they offered me; I had no idea that you could do that." Another interviewee said that her salary was not really discussed when she became a dean: "I was told it would be the same salary I had with an additional stipend." She only became aware that this was abnormal after a discussion with a colleague, acknowledging that it was likely because she was a woman that she did not think to negotiate her salary. Other deans also expressed the view that transparency played a role in shaping their salaries. Even though she was not the catalyst for renegotiating her contract, one interviewee noted that

> when the sunshine list [Ontario's list of public sector salaries over $100,000] came out and it became apparent that I was being paid so much less than other deans, the vice-provost told me they were worried about my salary, told me to ask to have my salary reassessed, but then turned around and berated me for asking for more money in a formal context.

Another dean discussed challenging her superiors directly when she learned how little she was making compared to her peers who are men:

> My pay is inequitable. I'm the lowest paid dean and the most senior dean. So, I went to the provost with a spreadsheet and asked him to tell me how he decided their salaries, and I kind of backed him into a corner, and he admitted that there's no real criteria. And I pointed out that the women made less than the men and he said, "I can't do anything about it until you get another offer."

In this woman's case, unequal pay combined with the administration's refusal to correct it was one of the main reasons she decided to step down from her deanship.[10] In a similar case, in which a woman dean raised the issue of her inequitable salary with other deans in the context of a labour dispute, suggesting to her colleagues that compensation needed to be rooted in principles, she recalled: "One of the deans actually leaned over and patted me on the back." She commented that change is especially difficult when women are patronized in the workplace. Thus, even when salaries are made more transparent, change is still often met with strong resistance.

On average, men continue to hold the most lucrative academic posts (e.g., full professors, provosts, and presidents) in a university, a reality "that hasn't changed in more than four decades" (Samson and Shen 2018). This may be explained in part because men are more likely to hold higher academic ranks, like full professorships, a factor that helps to explain the gender wage gap in academia (Samson and Shen 2018). Research also shows that women academics are more likely than men to hold professorships in the humanities and about as likely to hold professorships in the social sciences, which are both lower paid than STEM professorships, in which women are poorly represented (see Bellas 1997; Kulis, Sicotte, and Collins 2002). Some research suggests women academics are also in liberal arts colleges, where pay is lower than research-intensive universities (see Jacobs 1996). US studies have demonstrated that women are underrepresented in research-intensive, doctoral granting institutions – elite universities that tend to pay higher salaries (see AAUP 2022; Colby and Fowler 2020, 8). Economist Melissa Binder and colleagues (2010) used a single case study, at the University of New Mexico, to tease out whether gender wage gaps at the professorial level can be explained. Their findings affirm that department affiliation does have an impact on wages, prompting the question of whether women are more concentrated in departments and academic fields that are undervalued. But, they note that the significant difference in starting salaries between men and women "suggests that the negotiating styles may be at least part of the story" (131). They point out that even in departments where there is a low number of women, the gender wage gaps remain very high and the gap has not improved over thirty-five years. That said, other studies have found wage discrepancies despite holding for experience and department (Chen and Crown 2019). Binder et al. (2010) claim that gender discrimination in wages may in fact originate at the department level, affirming that decentralized salary determination is a source of discrimination. Sociologist Linda Renzulli and colleagues (2013) also looked at the impact of institution, discipline, and rank simultaneously to the gender wage gap and concur that location matters significantly. What these studies do not tell us is why men are more likely to hold these positions. Common explanations are rooted in women's reproductive abilities, including increased reproductive and domestic responsibilities, such as care of dependents (Budig and England 2001), which often lead women to take more precarious and part-time work and accept reduced salaries in exchange for flexibility (Momani, Dreher, and Williams 2019).

It is also true that men tend to be overrepresented in the most lucrative academic fields. When it comes to deanships, this continues to be a problem. Women deans are underrepresented in STEM fields and health. These are also fields in which dean salaries tend to be higher. Such inequities in dean salaries between fields, especially when these were not seen to be reflective of their workloads, was an issue a number of our interviewees raised. For example, one interviewee explained that she was told that the dean of social sciences and humanities does not make as much as other deans, and when she asked if this had to do with the specifics of their work, she was told no: "They said that the dean of pharmacy is next above you, and if he made less than you his head would explode, which I didn't think was my problem." Another dean recounted a discussion with her supervisor in which she said, "I'm not okay with the dean of law making $60,000 more than me because he had a much smaller faculty. He said they couldn't fix it, so that catapulted me out of my dream job – I didn't want to stay." She went on to say that she considers "my salary an important metric of my value."

Perhaps the most common justification for the wage gap centres on women's reproductive capacities and the unequal distribution of labour that still tends to accompany them. Despite improvements to sharing the work of childrearing, this responsibility is still "borne disproportionately by mothers" (Budig and England 2001, 204). Sociologists Michelle Budig and Paula England (2001, 204) offer four common explanations for the effect of motherhood on women's wages: a loss of experience, a loss of productivity while at work, willingness to change to "mother-friendly" jobs, and discrimination by employers. When they test the actual effect of the "motherhood penalty," they, and others (Momani, Dreger, and Williams 2019, 15), find that, when other factors are controlled, discrimination accounts for much of the gendered pay gap.[11] Tharenou (2013, 203) contends that at least some of this discrimination is reflective of a desire to "ensure that the traditional gender-influenced hierarchical power structure is maintained" by limiting women's salaries and thereby limiting their independence and options.

GENDERED IMPACT ON OPPORTUNITY FOR ADVANCEMENT

When survey participants were asked to rate the statement, "There is inequality in the opportunities provided to men and women to become deans at my institution," women were more likely (p < 0.05) to report the existence of disparity of opportunity.[12] The mean response of men participants was 1.98 (between strongly disagree and disagree), while the women participants was 2.3 (between disagree and neither agree nor disagree). In this case, we saw men's responses clustered between strongly disagree and neither agree nor disagree while women's responses were much more evenly spread. Still, only one of our men participants strongly agreed and only three agreed, while ten women agreed and seven strongly agreed. However, when chi-squared tests were applied, findings were inconsistent and no longer significant.[13]

Although women deans reported gender wage inequalities at a considerably different level than men in the survey, they did not report such inequalities with respect to opportunity for advancement. Men, however, tended to report inequalities in opportunities to become deans at high levels. From this, we can assess that while men who are deans are generally more likely to admit there are observed inequalities in opportunities to become dean by gender, they tend to disagree that there is a wage gap by gender.

Unlike wages, differences in the opportunities afforded to different groups are difficult to demonstrate. This is because the concept of equal opportunity is itself quite nebulous. Does it simply mean that everyone has the right to apply for a given position? Does it mean candidates can be certain their applications will be taken as seriously as any other applicants? Or maybe it implies that all interested candidates will have an opportunity to be coached for deanships? Even when these concepts are specified more precisely, the existence of different opportunities for different individuals or groups is difficult to measure. One way of gauging opportunity is to look at current levels of representation in a given field, under the assumption that significant discrepancies in opportunity will lead to unequal representation. Of course, as evidenced by the challenges we faced in assembling a list of current deans to contact for this research project, a major issue in assessing current levels of representation is that no centralized list of deans exists. There are, however, a number of helpful statistics that offer a clearer picture of the employment landscape for Canadian deans.

A 2018–19 Statistics Canada report shows an increase in the representation of women in deanships. In 2018–19, women made up 38 percent of deans and 44 percent of assistant deans, an increase of 33 percent and 40 percent respectively from 1971–72 figures (Statistics Canada 2019). While these numbers do not include a breakdown by discipline, a 2019 Universities Canada survey, launched as part of its work to improve Equity, Diversity, and Inclusion (EDI) policies, attempted to fill this gap. The survey included a self-identification form for senior leadership positions, which they identify as "deans to presidents," and had a response rate of 46 percent (10). Participants were split evenly along gendered lines (49 percent women to 51 percent men), but there were differences in the types of positions they held. For example, in Arts, Social Sciences, and

Humanities, there was gender parity in holding deanship positions, but this was not the case for deans in health (34.4 percent women) and STEM (28.6 percent women) (15). Moreover, there were fewer women in the most prestigious roles, including vice-presidents of research (33.3 percent), provosts/vice-presidents academic (38.5 percent), and presidents (31.7 percent) (15). Since prestigious senior administrative roles are often the highest paying and women in these and similar roles are also likely to be paid less than men counterparts (Momani, Dreher, and Williams 2019), some might argue that they are not actually getting the same kind of opportunities when they take on these roles.[14]

With these figures in mind, we asked interviewees about their own experiences pursuing deanships to assess whether they had different motivations or supports in pursuing the role, and why they thought they were successful. When we asked our survey participants whether they were encouraged to pursue deanships by a mentor or had to self-advocate to be considered for new opportunities or career advancements, responses did not fall along gendered lines. Similarly, responses showed no gender differentiation when we asked interviewees about their motivations in pursuing a deanship. Both women and men interviewees overwhelming spoke either about a sense of duty and obligation to take on the role or about being convinced by colleagues/mentors to take on the position. Another common theme was that many deans were foisted into the role because there were no qualified candidates. Virtually no one spoke about their own ambition, financial stability, or prestige. No other clear patterns emerged about the most common pathways to deanships.

When asked why they were successful in securing a deanship, most deans responded that they were unsure why they were successful. Since the discussions of hiring committees are almost always closed, the rationale for a specific hire is rarely shared. As such, individuals are left to theorize about the reasons for their success. Many noted their work experience, shared vision with the department/ hiring committee (fit), and fortuitous timing (including whether the school was looking for an internal or external candidate and the reception of the last dean) as key factors. A willingness to move was also important for many deans in securing their roles and was later framed by many as an asset to anyone looking for these positions. Notably, although not stressed by interviewees, relocating has a strong gendered dimension because men still tend to "determine the geographic location of the family ... even among highly educated couples" (Blau and Kahn 2017, 854). This raises another question raised pursuant to our research – do external candidates, who are more likely to be men, have more opportunities and success in securing higher wages than women, who are more likely to be internal candidates?

Even though the experiences of our interviewees did not suggest a gendered divide in motivation or support in pursuing a deanship, the existing distribution of deans along gendered lines suggests there may be ongoing issues with equality of opportunity in the hiring process. Interestingly, it was only when we asked deans whether or not they had aspirations to pursue senior administration (e.g., vice-president, provost, president) that we noted some gendered responses. While the desire to pursue higher levels of academic administration did not differ by gender – decisions seemed to be based largely on the enjoyment and understanding deans felt in their current roles and whether or not taking on a new position would necessitate moving – some of the women deans we spoke to who had been involved in higher level searches did talk about disillusionment with the search processes, which they felt were likely still sexist (see Amorell Saunders N'Daw's vignette, this volume). Women were also more likely to talk about aging out of their positions, often because they were caring for dependents, while men discussed moving up the ladder.

DISCUSSION AND CONCLUSION

This chapter presents a high-level investigation into the role that gender plays in the perceptions of job opportunities and the wage gap for deans. Further research needs to be undertaken, but we offer an initial identification of two issues that clearly impact differences in perception between men and women deans: opportunity and salary. After identifying these issues in a Canada-wide survey, we conducted a series of one-on-one interviews to add detail and dimension to our initial findings. Finally, we scrutinized the data by asking if it has a basis in reality. We find that it does.

By triangulating our survey results, interview findings, and existing literature and data, we find perceptions to be a valuable factor in shaping the experience of working in these roles. Our survey findings showed only two questions with a statistically significant gendered split: those concerning salaries and job opportunities. Men responded that they assumed there was no pay gap and that they had the same opportunities as women, while women believed it was the opposite. We know that the pay gap is real and that the reasons for it are multiple. There is also reason to argue that there are continued discrepancies in the opportunities of women to secure deanships and higher administrative positions, but the concept of opportunity is more nebulous, and even when narrowed, it is more difficult to measure, since many of the metrics we might use (e.g., criteria and decision making by selection committees) are not publicly available.

There continue to be pervasive gendered dimensions to deanships that many men deans are largely unaware of or assume are not significant. Put differently, women show a greater awareness of the gendered nature of the deanship role. The areas of deanships where we saw this gendered divide were also notable: merit was seen to determine success in securing a job and salary rate. This finding suggests that there is a continued unwillingness by those in positions of privilege to acknowledge systemic issues that they see as potentially undermining their own successes. Meritocracies are founded on perceptions of gender wage parity and equal opportunity; these perceptions are challenged by the fact that gender and other factors shape social hierarchies, limit opportunities, and distort remuneration. If these patterns remain invisible, are denied, or are undermined by those in positions of power, they are less likely to change. Moreover, those who are disadvantaged by these norms are likely to internalize their challenges rather than associate them with larger institutional or societal patterns.

ACKNOWLEDGMENT

This chapter draws on research support from the University of Waterloo HeForShe initiative.

NOTES

1 A notable exception is Johnson and Howsam (2020).
2 With thanks to Emma Dreher for compiling this list.
3 Without knowing how many past deans were forwarded our study, we cannot be sure of our response rate. We have estimated the response rate based on the total number of current deans who were sent the survey.
4 Participants were also given the option to classify their gender identity as "nonbinary" or "prefer not to answer." None of the participants identified as nonbinary and only two chose not to answer the question.
5 Because categorical data, such as Likert scales, have no clear intervals, it can be challenging to interpret their meanings (e.g., what, precisely, is the difference between agree and strongly agree), so nonparametric tests were used instead. These tests require fewer mathematical expectations on the shapes of the curves used in test comparisons (e.g., comparing p-values). Chi-squared tests are specifically used to compare observed frequencies of categorical variable values in a sample (e.g., Likert scales) to what would be expected due to random chance alone.
6 The *gender wage gap* is not synonymous with calls for *equal pay*. Calls for equal pay suggest that individuals doing the same work should be remunerated at the same level. So, in the case of deanships, a man and a woman dean holding the same position with virtually the same responsibilities should expect to be paid the same amount. The gender wage gap, in contrast, refers to the average earnings of men and women in a given company or field, regardless of the roles they play (for data on the wage gap in Canadian universities, see Statistics Canada 2019). Expressing concerns about the gender wage gap may encompass issues with equal pay, but also points to problems with the share

of women and men in specific roles. A commonly cited concern in the gender wage gap literature is the lower number of women in prestigious, high-paying positions, which extends the gender wage gap in any organizations.

7 This test's null hypothesis, or H0, is that gender and perception of a gender wage gap are independent variables; the alternative, H1, is that they are dependent upon each other. Let the critical value for this test be set at $\alpha = 0.05$. A multisample chi-squared test rejected the null hypothesis ($X2 = 28.679$; $p < 0.001$) that gender and perception of a gender wage gap among deans were independent of each other. This means that these variables, in fact, may be dependent upon each other. As indicated, the direction of this difference is a perception of a larger gap among women than men.

8 A greater gender wage gap at the top of the gender wage distribution, or what some might refer to as the "glass ceiling," has also been observed outside of academia (for more, see Blau and Kahn 2017).

9 A similar study in Denmark (Bennedsen et al. 2019) revealed transparency of the gender pay gap tended to reduce the gap but most significantly by slowing wage growth for men.

10 Notably, there have been some examples of universities intervening to address pay inequities. For example, McMaster University (Flaherty 2015) and the University of Waterloo (Loriggio 2016) both bumped up the salaries of women faculty after finding significant wage gaps.

11 Budig and England (2001) also suggest that a loss of productivity because of a greater parenting burden also accounts for some of the gap.

12 Like the previous question, a multisample chi-squared test was used to assess the independence of two variables: gender and intensity of perception of inequality of opportunities provided to deans at their institutions.

13 While results are not significant using the 5 percent criteria, they are when we use a 10 percent criteria, which is increasingly applied in the social sciences.

14 Notably, one US study finds that women may actually be paid more than their men counterparts in high-level positions in fields where they are "drastically underrepresented" in an attempt to attract more women (Bichsel and McChesney 2017, 15).

WORKS CITED

American Association of University Professors (AAUP). 2022. *The Annual Report on the Economic Status of the Profession, 2021–22*, June, 2022. https://www.aaup.org/sites/default/files/AAUP_ARES_2021%E2%80%932022.pdf.

Babcock, Linda, and Sara Laschever. 2003. *Women Don't Ask: Negotiation and the Gender Divide*. Princeton, NJ: Princeton University Press.

Baker, Michael, Yosh Halberstam, Kory Kroft, Alexandre Mas, and Derek Messacar. 2019. "Pay Transparency and the Gender Gap." Analytical Studies Branch Research Paper Series. Statistics Canada.

Bell, Myrtle, Mary McLaughlin, and Jennifer Sequeira. 2002. "Discrimination, Harassment, and the Glass Ceiling: Women Executives as Change Agents." *Journal of Business Ethics* 37 (1): 65–76.

Bellas, Marcia L. 1997. "Disciplinary Differences in Faculty Salaries: Does Gender Bias Play a Role?" *Journal of Higher Education* 68 (3): 299–321.

Bennedsen, Morton, Elena Simintzi, Margarita Tsoutsoura, and Daniel Wolfenzon. 2019. "Do Firms Respond to Gender Pay Gap Transparency?" *National Bureau of Economic Research Working Paper* (No. 25435).

Bensimon, Estela. 1991. "The Social Processes through Which Faculty Shape the Image of a New President." *The Journal of Higher Education* 62 (6): 637–60.

Bichsel, Jacqueline, and Jasper McChesney. 2017. "Gender Pay Gap and the Representation of Women in Higher Education Administrative Positions: This Century So Far." College and University Professional Association for Human Resources (CUPA-HR). https://www.cupahr.org/wp-content/uploads/cupahr_research_brief_1.pdf.

Binder, Melissa, Kate Krause, Janie Chermak, Jennifer Thacher, and Julia Gilroy. 2010. "Same Work, Different Pay? Evidence from a US Public University." *Feminist Economics* 16 (4): 105–35.

Blau, Francine, and Lawrence Kahn. 2017. "The Gender Wage Gap: Content, Trends, and Explanations." *Journal of Economic Literature* 55 (3): 789–865.

Boyko, Lydia, and Glen Jones. 2010. "The Roles and Responsibilities of Middle Management (Chairs and Deans) in Canadian Universities." In *The Changing Dynamics of Higher Education Middle Management,* edited by V. Lynn Meek, Leo Goedegebuure, Rui Santiago, and Teresa Carvalho, 83–102. Netherlands: Springer.

Bray, Nathaniel. 2008. "Proscriptive Norms for Academic Deans: Comparing Faculty Expectations across Institutional and Disciplinary Boundaries." *The Journal of Higher Education* 79 (6): 692–721.

Brown, Laura K., and Elizabeth Troutt. 2017. "Sex and Salaries at a Canadian University: The Song Remains the Same or the Times They Are a Changin'?" *Canadian Public Policy* 43 (3): 246–60.

Budig, Michelle, and Paula England. 2001. "The Wage Penalty for Motherhood." *American Sociological Review* 66 (2): 204–25.

Chen, Joyce J., and Daniel Crown. 2019. "The Gender Pay Gap in Academia: Evidence from the Ohio State University." *American Journal of Agricultural Economics* 101 (5): 1337–52.

Chiose, Simona. 2016. "More Female Leaders Needed at Canadian Universities, Presidents Say." *Globe and Mail.* April 28, 2016. https://www.theglobeandmail.com/news/national/more-female-leaders-needed-at-canadian-universities-presidents-say/article29795727/.

Colby, Glenn, and Chelsea Fowler. 2020. "Data Snapshot: IPEDS Data on Full-Time Women Faculty and Faculty of Color: An In-Depth Look at the Makeup and Salaries of Full-Time Faculty Members in US Higher Education" American Association of University Professors. https://www.aaup.org/sites/default/files/Dec-2020_Data_Snapshot_Women_and_Faculty_of_Color.pdf.

Correll, Shelley, Stephen Benard, and In Paik. 2007. "Getting a Job: Is There a Motherhood Penalty?" *American Journal of Sociology* 112 (5): 1297–1339.

de Boer, Harry, and Leo Goedegebuure. 2009. "The Changing Nature of the Academic Deanship." *Leadership* 5 (3): 347–64.

Flaherty, Colleen. 2015. "Leveling the Field." *Inside Higher Ed,* April 30. https://www.insidehighered.com/news/2015/04/30/mcmaster-u-addresses-gender-pay-gap-3500-raises-female-faculty-members.

Greig, Fiona. 2008. "Propensity to Negotiate and Career Advancement: Evidence from an Investment Bank That Women Are on a 'Slow Elevator.'" *Negotiation Journal* 24 (4): 495–508.

Jacobs, Jerry A. 1996. "Gender Inequality and Higher Education." *Annual Review of Sociology* 22 (1): 153–85.

Jalalzai, Farida. 2013. *Shattered, Cracked, or Firmly Intact?: Women and the Executive Glass Ceiling Worldwide.* New York: Oxford University Press.

Johnson, Genevieve Fuji, and Robert Howsam. 2020. "Whiteness, Power and the Politics of Demographics in the Governance of the Canadian Academy." *Canadian Journal of Political Science* 53 (3): 676–94.

Kulis, Stephen, Diane Sicotte, and Shawn Collins. 2002. "More than a Pipeline Problem: Labor Supply Constraints and Gender Stratification across Academic Science Disciplines." *Research in Higher Education* 43 (6): 657–91.

Loriggio, Paola. 2016. "University of Waterloo Boosts Female Faculty Pay after Wage Gap Uncovered." *Globe and Mail,* August 4, 2016. https://www.theglobeandmail.com/ news/national/university-of-waterloo-boosts-female-faculty-salaries-after-gender -pay-gap-found/article31272503/.

Momani, Bessma, Emma Dreher, and Kira Williams. 2019. "Evaluating the Gender Pay Gap in Canadian Academia from 1996 to 2016." *Canadian Journal of Higher Education* 49 (1): 2–35.

Renzulli, Linda, Jeremy Reynolds, Kimberly Kelly, and Linda Grant. 2013. Pathways to Gender Inequality in Faculty Pay: The Impact of Institution, Academic Division, and Rank. *Research in Social Stratification and Mobility* 34:58–72.

Ryan, Michelle, and Alexander Haslam. 2005. "The Glass Cliff: Evidence That Women Are Over-Represented in Precarious Leadership Positions." *British Journal of Management* 16:81–90.

Samson, Natalie, and Anqi Shen. 2018. "A History of Canada's Full-Time Faculty in Six Charts: A Look at Some UCASS Data from 1970 to 2016." *University Affairs.* https:// www.universityaffairs.ca/features/feature-article/history-canadas-full-time-faculty -six-charts/.

Statistics Canada. 2019. "Number and Salaries of Full-Time Teaching Staff at Canadian Universities (final), 2018/2019." https://www150.statcan.gc.ca/n1/daily-quotidien/ 191125/dq191125b-eng.htm.

Tharenou, Phyllis. 2013. "The Work of Feminists Is Not Yet Done: The Gender Pay Gap – A Stubborn Anachronism." *Sex Roles* 68: 198–206.

Universities Canada. 2019. "Equity, Diversity and Inclusion at Canadian Universities: Report on the 2019 National Survey." https://www.univcan.ca/wp-content/uploads/ 2019/11/Equity-diversity-and-inclusion-at-Canadian-universities-report-on-the -2019-national-survey-Nov-2019.pdf.

6

EDI and the University Leadership Ladder

GENEVIEVE FUJI JOHNSON, ÖZLEM SENSOY, and EL CHENIER

Efforts to advance equity, diversity, and inclusion (EDI) within Canadian universities are paradoxical in at least two interrelated ways. First, while they are presented with an increased urgency and are gaining institutional traction, such initiatives neither fully acknowledge nor fully respond to the discriminatory norms, practices, and policies experienced by students, faculty, and staff. Second, while EDI initiatives are driven by those in positions of leadership within universities, they tend to lack grounding in robust scholarly knowledge such as peer-reviewed academic materials on equity and diversity and established findings from research tools such as interviews, focus groups, and surveys. Because of these weaknesses, most EDI efforts are insufficient to making real and lasting change. To the extent that EDI initiatives remain characterized by these limitations, they are bound to fail.

This chapter recaps and builds on a study by one of the authors (Johnson) of central and senior university leadership demographics, which demonstrated that racialized women and men faculty members face persistent barriers in their career progress through the administrative ranks of Canadian universities (Johnson and Howsam 2020). Johnson and her research team conducted a diversity audit of five universities and found that the career progress ceiling for racialized women is lower than it is for white women, who appear overrepresented in the ranks of senior administrators relative to Statistics Canada data about professors and lecturers. These research findings indicate that racialized women – Black, Indigenous, and women of colour (BIWOC) – are dramatically underrpresented in these ranks.[1] Both racism and sexism appear to determine who advances through leadership ranks and what kind of leadership they provide.

Building on these findings, in this chapter, we briefly theorize the role of norms related to white supremacy, masculinity, and dis/ableism. We then offer a set of relatively easy as well as more difficult strategies that universities can put into place to align their practices for more meaningful EDI outcomes for everyone. Ultimately, we propose that universities adopt "radical inclusion" as their model. Originally proposed by Wendy Harbour (2019), an expert on disability in educational institutions, radical inclusion pushes us beyond conventional notions of inclusion. Conventional inclusion seeks to assist people who are traditionally excluded from or marginalized within existing systems by providing them with accommodations that will permit their fuller participation. This approach leaves intact the existing system, which is built on ways of knowing, seeing, and doing that reproduce the very exclusion and marginalization EDI seeks to dismantle. In contrast, radical inclusion calls for a transformation of the structure itself.

DIVERSITY AUDIT DATA

Using a methodology similar to that developed by political scientist Malinda S. Smith (see, e.g., 2016, 2017, and 2019), Johnson led an intersectional diversity audit of academic administrators at five Canadian universities: Simon Fraser University (SFU), the University of British Columbia (UBC), the University of Victoria (UVic), the University of Toronto (UofT), and York University (York) (Johnson and Howsam, 2020). The analysis included 1,299 administrators from departmental program chairs to senior leadership and involved the independent team coding of publicly available headshots and biographical statements as posted and published directly on official and easily found university websites.[2] This broad scope enabled Johnson's research team to determine if administrators are hitting ceilings and if these ceilings are at different heights for different people. A percentage comparison with Statistics Canada data (Statistics Canada 2017, 2018a, 2018b, 2018c) on professor and lecturer income recipients shows that white men and women appear overrepresented in the senior administrative ranks, suggesting that while white men have ready access to all administrative ranks and white women appear to be making it through to senior administrative ranks, racialized women and men are held back at the middle ranks.[3]

In the most recent census data, racialized and Indigenous university professor and lecturer income recipients comprise about one-fifth of all university professor and lecturer income recipients (Statistics Canada 2017, 2018a, 2018b, 2018c). Racialized women constitute 7.2 percent and racialized men 12 percent of this population. Indigenous people make up 1.4 percent of this population, with Indigenous women representing 0.86 percent and Indigenous men representing 0.55 percent. White women represent 36 percent and white men represent 43 percent of professor and lecturer income recipients.

Both racialized women and men are hitting a ceiling at the level of associate dean (see Table 6.1). Racialized men are represented among departmental program chairs and directors, departmental chairs and directors, and associate

TABLE 6.1
Percentages of administrative positions by racialized and gender identities at five Canadian universities

		Senior executives	Deans	Associate deans	Department chairs and directors	Program chairs and directors
Indigenous	Man	0.0	0.0	0.0	1.1	0.1
	Woman	1.2	0.0	0.7	1.9	0.3
Visible minority	Man	7.2	4.6	11	10	11
	Woman	2.4	2.3	7.1	4.8	6.8
White	Man	46	59	38	51	49
	Nonbinary	0.0	0.0	0.7	0.0	0.0
	Woman	43	34	43	31	33

Source: Johnson and Howsam 2020, 685.
Note: The five universities are Simon Fraser University, the University of British Columbia, the University of Toronto, the University of Victoria, and York University.

deans just under their representation in the census data; they are more clearly underrepresented within the ranks of deans and senior executives (4.6 percent and 7.2 percent, respectively). Racialized women appear underrepresented in the ranks of senior executives, deans, and departmental chairs and directors, relative to the census data. They appear most clearly underrepresented among senior executives and deans (2.4 percent and 2.3 percent, respectively).

In contrast, white women and men are found at every administrative rank, with white women appearing to be overrepresented among associate deans (43 percent) and senior executives (43 percent), and represented among deans about on par with their representation in the census data (34 percent) (for more on gender and deanships, see Johnstone and Momani, this volume). As Table 6.1 notes, they are somewhat underrepresented among departmental chairs and directors and departmental program chairs and directors. Generally, white men persist in their significant overrepresentation in the central and senior leadership of universities (see Table 6.2) relative to their representation in the data on professor and lecturer income recipients and in the data on earned doctorate degree holders. In total, these findings indicate that about 90 percent of senior executives and deans are white (see Table 6.1), which is a significant contrast with data reported by Statistics Canada.

White men dominate the administrative structures of Canadian universities (Smith 2019). If only in terms of securing positions, we find that white women have succeeded in pushing through gender barriers and that racialized women

TABLE 6.2
Count of administrative positions by racialized and gender identities at five Canadian universities

		Senior executives	Deans	Associate deans	Department chairs and directors	Program chairs and directors	Total No.	Total %
Indigenous	Man	0	0	0	3	1	4	0.3
	Woman	1	0	1	5	2	9	0.7
Visible minority	Man	6	2	16	27	81	132	10
	Woman	2	1	10	13	52	78	6.1
White	Man	38	26	53	137	375	629	48
	Nonbinary	0	0	1	0	0	1	.08
	Woman	36	15	60	84	251	446	34
Grand total		83	44	141	269	762	1,299	100

Source: Johnson and Howsam 2020, 685.
Note: The five universities are Simon Fraser University, the University of British Columbia, the University of Toronto, the University of Victoria, and York University.

and men continue to face formidable obstacles in the pipeline to senior administration.

Racialized barriers are problematic for a range of reasons. As stated by the Ontario Human Rights Commission (2005, 32), "Numerical data showing an under-representation of qualified racialized persons in management may be evidence of employment systems that have the effect of discriminating and/or of decision-makers having an overt bias toward promoting White candidates into supervisory roles." Underlying these patterns may be various forms of discrimination (see Stewart and Valian 2018, 42; see also Hames-García 2010; and Zambrana 2018). Overt discrimination plays a role but, perhaps more seriously, systemic discrimination likely results in unfair experiential burdens placed on racialized faculty members – racialized women faculty members, in particular – all of which are well-documented (see, e.g., Ahmed 2012; Chan, Dhamoon, and Moy 2014; Harris and Gonzáles 2012; Hirshfield and Joseph 2012; James, with Chapman-Neyaho 2017; Mahtani 2006; Monforti 2012; Padilla 1994; Settles, Buchanan, and Dotson 2019; Smith 2017; Turner 2002).

CONSTRUCTIVE STRATEGIES

In this section, we outline specific strategies – some relatively easy and some more difficult – that university administrators can take to make advances toward realizing meaningful equity, diversity, and inclusion, which necessarily involves disrupting colonialism (Gutiérrez y Muhs et al. 2012; Henry et al. 2017; Sensoy and DiAngelo 2017). We argue that racialized and gendered barriers are part of the structural landscape of universities and that equitable treatment and meaningful inclusion of racialized faculty – racialized women faculty, in particular – requires significant ideological change on the part of white faculty, who remain overrepresented in senior administrative levels. As a starting point, we recommend the following three key changes to institutional thinking about EDI strategy: shifting norms, not just bodies; rewriting the book, not simply going by the book; and hiring cohorts, not merely tokens.

These changes can orient institutions toward Wendy Harbour's (2019) notion of radical inclusion. Inclusion in its current form is insufficient to create true equality. It seeks to accommodate and not to empower. For people with physical disabilities, for example, it usually means retrofitting institutions to make them accessible to people who use mobility devices. As rhetorician and disabilities scholar Jay Dolmage (2017) argues, retrofitting and other forms of accommodation seek only a temporary levelling of the playing field. They do not empower people to achieve *with* disability, but rather to "achieve around disability, or against it, or in spite of it" (70). Ableism within the university is structural in that it repeatedly rewards bodies, minds, and "forms of communication and sociality" that are "the right shape." Disablism, on the other hand, "denigrates specific bodies, minds, forms of communication, and modes of social interaction" (70). Radical inclusion seeks to empower those who are or have been excluded or marginalized by addressing the practices, policies, and structures that effectively celebrate norms related to the status of white, able-bodied men while denigrating those who "deviate" from these norms.[4]

What Harbour calls radical inclusion, legal scholar Colleen Sheppard (2010) calls "inclusive equality." Inclusive equality combines substantive equality and systemic discrimination, which occurs when "apparently neutral rules, standards, practices, or policies have disparate effects on different communities and groups in society" (147). Sheppard argues that it is "sustained (both ideologically and materially) by the cyclical and continued realities of exclusion and inequitable access to society's resources, benefits, and opportunities" (147). Inclusive equality

> highlights the ways in which inequality is linked to both the substantive effects of discrimination (including social, psychological, physical, and economic harms) and the systemic and institutional practices and processes that reproduce it. These include procedural inequities such as failure to consult or investigate the possibilities of accommodation, exclusion of historically disadvantaged groups from decision making, lack of democracy, and absence of relationships of care. (147)

Like Harbour, Sheppard (2010, 148) argues that real inclusion "requires a restructuring of the historical, structural, and systemic relations that produce, reproduce, and justify social, political, legal, and economic exclusion and inequality." It requires a deep examination of the actual realities and conditions of inequality, as well as the social, political, and institutional processes that account for its reproduction. It "incorporates attentiveness to both substance and process," and "is necessarily systemic and relational" (9). In other words, to be truly inclusive, we must rebuild the structure so that everyone can move easily through it, always, with dignity and with the fullness of their humanity.

The following strategic shifts can serve this kind of rebuilding. For each strategy, we offer relatively easy actions that can be undertaken given the current distribution of resources and more difficult actions that require a more radical redistribution of resources and reorganization of structures.

Shifting Norms, Not Just Bodies

Universities typically measure success in the integration of minoritized peoples by counting bodies. Numbers – especially with respect to decision-making positions – do indeed matter. However, moving bodies from lower teaching ranks to upper administrative ranks is not enough to achieve radical inclusion. In addition to shifting bodies, universities need to shift the norms informing evaluative processes and procedures. In addition to robust data collection, analysis, and sharing, and the establishment of numeric goals for hiring and promotion, university leaders should engage in a practice of ongoing critical self-reflection and informed dialogue specifically to identify and dismantle patriarchy, racism/white supremacy, colonialism, and ableism that appear in diverse overt and covert forms, often so deeply internalized and normalized they are regarded as common-sensical (Ahmed 2004; Academic Women 2020; Henry 2015).

One way that oppression operates at the structural level is through normalcy (Ferber 2012; Kimmel and Ferber 2017; Johnson 2018). Those who determine what practices (behaviours, beliefs, attitudes) count as "normal" are those who hold positions of privilege. However, because those in privileged positions are deemed normal, those who fall outside of the norm are viewed as either being the problem or as having a problem. Their problem is perceived to be internal to their group, even a condition of their being (for example, women may be perceived as too emotional, Black people as too angry, and people with disabilities as less intelligent), and because the unnamed normative group in relation to these groups sets the desired expressions (degrees and forms) of emotion, anger, intelligence status, EDI typically means aiding those who are perceived as nonnormative to become as much like the normative group as possible.

Oftentimes, those who advance to and survive at the top do so by upholding and – consciously or unconsciously – further entrenching privileged-group (white, heteropatriarchal) norms. For example, their leadership style may be informed by masculinist and patriarchal norms that emphasize the individual over the collective, competition over collaboration, and success-at-all costs over a work-life balance. In addition to norms concerning behaviour, career advancement often requires being acceptable in physical presentation, including *acting* – when not *being* – white and being *presentable* according to Western, patriachal, and ableist conventions of body, dress, and grooming. Challenging these norms requires time to create trust and build relationships and to name and redesign systems and procedures that are more equitable and truly inclusive. But this is a process that can create friction and conflict and increase the emotional and psychic burden already placed on people from marginalized groups. Recognition of this fact must be accompanied by the provision of appropriate supports and a thoughtful distribution of labour.

Easier Actions: Name the Hidden

We often name race and Indigeneity but not whiteness. In much the same way, we name the nonnormative, for example, *women's* soccer, but not men's soccer. We say *Special* Olympics and *Paralympics*, but not *Able-Bodied* Olympics. In this way, the norms of whiteness, patriarchy, and ablebodiness are invisiblized while they simultaneously masquerade as neutral, normal, and universal. This characteristic of power contributes to the common perception of accommodation programs that seek to remedy the existing imbalances (in hiring quotas, for example) as being "extra" and "special" opportunities and pathways that are not available to everyone (i.e., not available to white, ablebodied, cisgender men) and are therefore perceived as unfair and sometimes described as "reverse" discrimination.

Stripping away the shroud of neutrality around these norms is a necessary step toward radical inclusion. Doing so shifts attention away from historically marginalized people as needing help to, for example, acquire a leadership position and instead focuses attention on how those who hold power define and maintain cultures of normalcy that uphold – and benefit from – sexist, racist, and ableist values, structures, and epistemologies. Because of this, identifying normalcy by naming the hidden and exposing privilege can be a powerful step in dismantling systems of power.

Land acknowledgments and pronoun identifiers are two common examples that individuals in university systems have begun to name. By naming, they make visible the invisible cultures of power that shape the institution. While naming the invisible cultures of power are relatively easy to implement and can hold significance in signalling institutional goals and values, this kind of action is limited in that it is mostly external signalling. In other words, naming is often intended for outsider audiences and often takes the form of boilerplate language. The embedded issues of power are rarely taken up beyond the naming. Despite these limitations, practices to name the invisible, normative structures of power in an institution are relatively easy to implement actions that can have a remediating impact.

Harder Actions: Redistribute Power

We take the above example to show how more difficult actions – actions that require a restructuring – can be cultivated. Land acknowledgments have become normalized at many institutions. They typically occur at the start of an event held on a campus that is sitting on traditional Indigenous lands, and often they appear in email signatures. The impact of these small acts has been cumulative. They are now standard practices for university presidents, vice-presidents, and leaders. A cynical view would see these acts as ways the powerful co-opt a practice of resistance and, by doing so, dilute it of any transformative force. The signals of resistance are instead co-opted in ways that merely mimic progressive politics without the risk inherent in any real and substantive challenge to, much less displacement of, existing power relations and structures. The harder changes, in contrast, do just that. They rebalance power and redistribute resources and decision-making authority within institutions.

Canada has a unique history of denying its racist past and present (Bannerji et al. 2000; Thobani 2007). Being a "good" person – well-meaning, caring, understanding – is not sufficient for understanding matters of equity. Yet because so much equity work implicates us, our values, and experiences, we often put effort into positioning ourselves as good, caring, and understanding people. Because of this, equity education (such as a workplace diversity workshop) is often devoted to personal transformation, understanding the other, and empathy building (e.g., "putting yourself in their shoes"). For people resistant to engaging in such workshops, equity work is regarded as a particular disciplinary view at best, and political correctness at worst. Thus, equity work is positioned as just one among a host of ideas worthy of exploration, discussion, and integration into the functioning of the institution.

Developing practices of radical inclusion require us to address two forms of resistance: challenging the overdependence on personal transformation narratives and workshops associated with them, and the discursive use of political correctness that positions EDI initiatives as special accommodations made by weak leaders bowing to the pressure of activist faculty, staff, and students. Leadership can respond to these forms of resistance in a multitude of ways.

With respect to the first, administrators do not need to "believe in" the value of equity to implement practices that advance equity goals through the rebalancing of power, redistributing resources, and sharing of decision-making authority. The important step is to ensure that experts – those who have both lived experience and scholarly expertise – have a seat at the decision-making table. This is a different strategy than what is commonly taken up when administrators put out calls for special committees on EDI that are focused on a "balanced" representation of racialized and gender identities, ability, and job status. University leaders need to draw from a network of scholarly experts on EDI and to empower them within decision-making processes to develop, implement, and evaluate strategies for meaningful inclusion and equity.

Rewriting the Book, Not Just Following the Book

How do we work *within* the constraints of existing policies that have resulted in entrenched inequities, while also working to change those very policies? It is well established that even when racialized and minoritized peoples are in positions of leadership, they cannot govern outside the structure established by white people who dominate that space and who set up the very policies that need to be problematized (Ahmed 2004; Henry 2015). We could appoint BIPOC women as presidents of all universities tomorrow, for example, but they would not be able to begin their work outside entrenched rules organizing the institution. Within institutions such as universities, substantive change could take generations to implement and would likely be resisted along the way as bowing to "special interest" or "woke culture," and thus being fundamentally unfair.

Yet we know that the forms of knowledge valued in the university (e.g., knowledge over wisdom, history over memory, and written over oral) were constructed with the witting or unwitting perspectives and values of those who created (and have thus far overseen) the working rules of that institution. In this way, universities have normalized, validated, and elevated positivistic, white Eurocentric knowledge over nonwhite, Indigenous, and non-European knowledges (Battiste, Bell, and Findlay 2002; Grosfoguel, Hernández, and Velásquez 2016; Mignolo 2002; Carvalho and Flórez-Flórez 2014). These knowledge forms "inscribed a conceptualization of knowledge to a geopolitical space (Western Europe) and erased the possibility of even thinking about a conceptualization and distribution of knowledge 'emanating' from other local histories (China, India, Islam, etc.)" (Mignolo 2002, 59). Processes for knowledge development and transfer were established with particular notions of "knowledge of worth" (and worth funding) that were then institutionalized in the rules governing the institution, including career advancement. Thus, to decentre whiteness, university leaders need to interrogate not only the norms within disciplinary fields, but also the norms that are taken as "common sense" of the institution itself. For any institution's EDI initiative to truly address equity, diversity, and inclusion, it must come to terms with the rules of the game within the governance structure. This necessitates the development of new policies that not only articulate values and commitments but allocate resources and reimagine practices and the rules that we play by to begin with.

Easy Actions: Create Budget Lines

Budgets signal what institutions value. Without needing to make any fundamental revisions to the rules of the game, university leaders can ensure that discursive support of EDI is backed up by material support. Allocating sufficient funding to EDI initiatives is an easy step, but it does require that administrators grapple with the logic of whiteness that is the very foundation of the university.

As sociologist Eduardo Bonilla-Silva (2015) explains, historically white institutions reproduce whiteness and white supremacy through all aspects of the institution but present themselves as neutral spaces free of racial coding. If there are no persons of colour in the space, the space is perceived by white folks as being race-free. This is related to what Indigenous scholar Susan Dion (2009) describes as the stance of "perfect strangers," where white educators claim a racial innocence about Indigenous peoples despite a lifetime of explicit and implicit pedagogy about Indigenous peoples via stereotypes and via their invisibility in many structures of leadership. As Sara Ahmed (2012), Bryan Brayboy (2003), Eduardo Bonilla-Silva (2012), Frances Henry and Audrey Kobayashi, with Andrea Choi (2017), and others have explained, the implementation of university-wide diversity initiatives and policies are problematic because their underlying logic of whiteness often remains invisible, thus further normalizing everyday discourses that racialize only faculty of colour. In these ways, the everyday "grammar of whiteness" (Bonilla-Silva 2012) remains unaddressed. Moreover, efforts to provide adequate funds to shift institutions away from the logic of whiteness are seen as unfairly privileging nonwhite people.

An administrative commitment to EDI requires a surfacing of this logic. It requires making contextual and situational assessments to allocate funding toward balancing a seesaw that has always tilted white. When our university leaders say "we are committed to EDI," are they merely prioritizing the discourse of EDI, or are they making material commitments via explicit budget lines and budget allocations to ensure that EDI experts have appropriate resources to do their work?

Harder Actions: Restructure Decision Making

Harder actions demand that we dismantle the seesaw. Universities often lean toward high visibility and low-risk EDI initiatives. Examples of this include special messages on Rosh Hashanah and Ramadan, spaces during convocation for drumming and singing, and showcasing faculty who "hold their hands high" or "name their pronouns" as evidence of their progressive politics. But as Sarah Ahmed writes, "even 'admitting' to one's own racism, when the declaration is assumed to be 'evidence' of an anti-racist commitment, does not do what it says" (2004, para 12). In other words, such declarations are not, in and of themselves, antiracist, and they do not "necessarily commit a state, institution or person to a form of action that we could describe as anti-racist" (para 12). Thus, any declarative statements about antiracist position or critique (e.g., "We are a faculty committed to diversity") remain meaningless without a fundamental restricting of decision making that serves as the authoritative basis on which antiracist policies and practices can be developed and implemented.

University administrators can take leadership cues from activism and scholarship that show how racialization impacts and shapes the worlds of Black, Indigenous, and other people of colour, as well as white people. Central and senior administrators can begin by responding to the following questions: How has whiteness shaped prevailing norms, practices, and policies? How do these norms, practices, and policies differently impact the experiences of white faculty and those of BIPOC faculty? How do they uphold white supremacy within the institution? By reflecting on these questions, administrators can become better positioned to dismantle white-supremacist processes and structures and to restructure decision-making apparatuses so that, in addition to those with diverse forms of expertise, those with diverse bodies are active participants with real authority in decision-making processes at every level, and this becomes the institutional norm.

Hire Cohorts, Not Just Tokens

One of the central principles of equity work within institutions is that the work take place in solidarity rather than in isolation. The work of EDI and decolonizing the institution is emotionally taxing and takes a serious toll on those doing it, especially if they embody the marginalized identities in question. In considering the emotional labour involved, Black feminists identify self-care as a necessary political act (Lorde 1984; hooks 1984; Nash 2011); it requires people working alongside one another who understand that it is not just scholarly and intellectual work, but that it is also emotional and even spiritual work. There needs to be a shared understanding that people's (and entire communities') dignities and livelihoods are impacted by the work to move the institution toward meaningful equity and inclusion for all.

A well-known parable from the 1970s called "Lessons from the Geese," focusing on how these birds fly in formation (McNeish 1972), captures the importance of solidarity, which in turn highlights the potential of cohort hires for such solidarity-building.

The lessons of this parable include the following:

Like the geese, people who share a common direction and sense of community can get where they are going quicker and easier because they are traveling on the thrust of one another;

It helps to take turns doing the hard tasks and sharing in leadership as we all run out of steam from time to time;

Encouraging "honks" from behind can positively impact the momentum and stamina of those up front.

The story of the geese offers central and senior administrators a novel way to think about leadership as well as a possible remedy for some of the most common challenges facing those who do EDI and decolonizing work, such as isolation and burnout. For those doing this work – especially those who are gendered, racialized, and minoritized – these challenges result from working in the context of and against white supremacy, racism, sexism, and ableism/disablism. For example, while the norm at most institutions is to consider hiring practices one position at a time, especially related to EDI (e.g., a VP equity or an associate dean of Indigenous education), the strategy of cohort-based hiring can help move us forward on EDI and decolonizing initiatives further and faster, together.

Easy Action: Pay Attention to Hiring

An institution committed to EDI must approach every hire as an opportunity to become inclusive, in terms of racialization, but also ability and gender. All Canadian universities now include employment equity statements that encourage applications from historically marginalized communities (Henry 2015). When white able-bodied people are hired, they are often able to seamlessly enter a predominately white culture that is familiar, if not altogether welcoming. However, racialized and minoritized peoples rarely enjoy such a seamless entry. In fact, they must expend a great deal of effort finding and establishing a supportive network. Moreover, although racism is often invisible to white folks, ableism is often invisible to the able-bodied, and sexism is often invisible to cis-men, these forms of oppression are ever-present in our universities. They create what a previous generation of scholars described as a "chilly climate" (Backhouse et al. 1995). One way to counteract these social conditions and improve the social support available to marginalized peoples is to undertake cohort hires.

Most hires are "one offs," that is, for a single position specifically defined. For administrators, a productive step to developing their own collaborative network of EDI experts that support each other in work together for EDI and decoloniz-ation would be to develop a team that represents a diversity of people and, more importantly, has EDI and decolonization expertise. Hiring based on symbolic inclusion is important, but it ultimately serves to reinforce existing patterns of exclusion if substantive EDI expertise is not also included and empowered. Empowering this substantive expertise is the only way to develop evidence-based recommendations and strategies and to realize them.

Senior administrators need to commit to hiring and resourcing EDI experts, allowing them to develop their own leadership structures, accountability frame-works, and administrative support systems. This EDI network – or flock, to invoke the above metaphor – needs to have the autonomy to deploy resources toward the strategies they develop. Should administrators be nervous about making these kinds of hires and granting this autonomy, they need to remind themselves that academic fields that draw on feminist, Indigenous, and antiracist principles have robust discussions about community accountability, rigour, and benchmarks for measuring success (Kirkness and Barnhardt 1991; Fuller and Russo 2016; Palacios 2016; Villenas 2019). Developing and empowering these teams means not simply releasing them from other teaching or service responsibilities but giving them the autonomy needed to be effective to achieve the stated ideals of EDI and decolonization.

If a university or an academic unit within it does not have a critical mass of EDI experts to constitute such teams, they need to reach out to other units or universities. Sustained change and momentum toward realizing EDI can only be achieved with the development of expert teams at all levels of the institution – teams that are organized within and among the various academic units and working collectively toward the common goals of decolonizing and creating equitable learning and working spaces in the institution.

Harder Actions: Resist the Pushback

EDI advocates – both administrators as well as rank-and-file faculty members – must be prepared for resistance to hiring reorientations toward expertise, autonomy, and empowerment, all of which are necessary for the foundational and structural change needed to prioritize EDI and decolonization. Preparing means being proactive: anticipating pushback, preparing responses, and providing hard (e.g., contractual guarantees of protection from discrimination) and soft (e.g., private and public verbal and other forms of regular affirmation for the value of their work) support for those doing the work.

The following are common expressions of pushback that advocates should anticipate and to which they should develop responses in discussions around both hiring and promotion.

Won't putting EDI and decolonization ahead of subject-matter expertise bring down the quality of our applicant pool, as well as the candidates' and the institution's research profile? EDI and decolonization literacy and subject-matter expertise are not mutually exclusive; central and senior administers need to understand this fact. Moreover, they need to actively challenge the claim that they are mutually exclusive. If we continue to determine "subject-matter expertise" solely on factors such as the tier of publication and other impact factors, then due to the institutional and cultural supports that exist for mainstream work, white, men, middle-class, and otherwise privileged scholars will continue to excel by these measures. Research that does not further the cause of EDI and decolonization will continue to be elevated. Instead, central and senior administrators need to recognize that research *not* situating the subject matter and methodology within the logic of whiteness and the implications of colonialism may in fact be less sophisticated than research that does.

We are all for diversity, but isn't privileging racialized minority applicants over white applicants or women over men just reverse racism and reverse sexism? Preparing for this expression of pushback requires understanding two key points. First, racism is different from racial bias. While all people have racial biases, racism refers to the collective impact of that bias over the course of lengthy histories and with the backing of legal authority and institutional controls. In this context, racial bias is transformed into racism. From this definition, racism is structural, not fluid, and does not flip back and forth. And while anyone might wield racial discrimination against anyone else, it is only the racial discrimination of whiteness that converts that discrimination into racism (Sensoy and DiAngelo 2017). Second, there is an abundance of empirical evidence that people of colour are discriminated against in hiring and promotion and have been for generations (Cheung et al. 2016; Derous et al. 2016; Hasford 2016; Rivera 2015). Unfounded beliefs that diversity goals require unqualified people of colour to be hired over white people are deeply problematic as they are based on the assumption that any person of colour could not possibly be the most qualified. Where there are two equally qualified candidates, but one is BIPOC and the other is white, it is important to consider that the BIPOC candidate may actually be more qualified because they likely bring a perspective to the institution that is currently missing.

The job description was approved by senior administration, and it cannot be changed. Besides, if we ask them for change, we risk losing the position altogether. Central and senior administrators often argue that many of the components of a search have already been approved and thus cannot be changed. While this may sound reasonable, consider what is actually being said: "We developed these practices without a lens on equity. Now that we have begun to profess valuing equity, we won't change them." Of course, this is not true; institutions can and do change policies all the time. But we must have the will. Centuries of exclusionary policies will not shift without commitment and the courage to name, challenge, and provide alternatives that counter narratives of resistance. If we cannot demonstrate this commitment through our actions and their outcomes, in good conscience we should stop making the claim that we are campus communities that promote diversity, respect, and inclusion.

CONCLUSION

In 2019, the Canadian federal government created the Dimensions program, which, through grants and other mechanisms, aims to normalize EDI within universities. It is not funding alone that is needed, however. It is a willingness to critically interrogate the foundational norms, logic, and ideologies that leave intact the structures that sustain oppression and marginalization. Radical inclusion is a model that allows the university to thrive through and, indeed, as a result of, its transformation into a self-reflective institution whose intellectual and organizational cultures are equitable and diverse in the deepest sense of those words. We can begin this work with small, relatively easy actions as we move toward bigger, more difficult commitments.

Institutions of higher learning remain stubbornly resistant to doing the challenging work of confronting and addressing pervasive whiteness. But universities are also places where radical thinking emerges and can flourish. The opportunity to undertake this change stands right before us, but whether or not it happens rests entirely on those who hold decision-making power recognizing how systems benefit some and disenfranchise others and committing to transforming our institutions. University efforts on equity, diversity, inclusion, and decolonization can be sustained by pressure applied from all sides: from those at the top (e.g., administrators who wield power in decision-making circles), from those at the bottom (e.g., students who are among the most vulnerable but who can bring the weight, energy, and insights of their numbers to make change), and from those around the university (e.g., communities served by the university).

Intellectuals, faculty, and administrators alike are trained to regard knowledge acquisition as a process of internalizing something outside of us. With regard to the exclusion of racialized people from the central and senior administration, there is no shortage of excellent scholarly and nonscholarly materials from which we can learn about ideological and structural forms of oppression, but radical inclusion requires that we also critically examine ourselves. All of this work is uncomfortable, but how could it be otherwise? By working together, we can make the necessary normative and structural changes to more fully realize equity and inclusion for all.

NOTES

1 We recognize that there are other forms of exclusion, namely those related to ability, sexual orientation, and gender expression. In our analysis of the data on gender and racialized identity, and in our proposals of solutions, we draw on the literature from experts in these areas, including, particularly, disability studies scholars.

2 In the absence of data provided by universities, scholars interested in studying equity, diversity, and inclusion in university settings employ this methodological strategy. As Frances Henry and Audrey Kobayashi (2017, 320n2) explain, "We acknowledge that our method is a very gross measure of racialization and that we have probably missed a number of persons who would self-identify as racialized while including others who would not ... but in the absence of university data, and despite its limitations, we feel that it has some use for our study" (see also Johnson and Howsam 2020).

3 For the purposes of their analysis, Johnson's team used racialized categories derived from Statistics Canada (e.g., visible minority, aboriginal, not-visible minority). While imperfect, we have chosen to use the scholarly language of "racialized" and "BIPOC" peoples throughout the chapter but have deferred to Statistics Canada language when drawing from the data they collect.

4 Disablism negatively constructs disability and treats disabled people unfairly as a result of these values; ableism positively values able-bodiedness (Dolmage 2017, 6–7).

WORKS CITED

Academic Women. 2020. *Radical Inclusion: Equity and Diversity among Female Faculty at Simon Fraser University*. Burnaby: Academic Women. https://www.sfu.ca/academic women.html.

Ahmed, Sara. 2004. "Declarations of Whiteness: The Non-Performativity of Anti-Racism." *Borderlands E-Journal: New Spaces in the Humanities* 3 (2). http://search.proquest. com/docview/60503808/.

–. 2012. *On Being Included: Racism and Diversity in Institutional Life*. Raleigh, NC: Duke University Press. doi:10.1215/9780822395324.

Backhouse, Constance, Roma Harris, Gillian Michell, and Alison Wylie. 1995. "The Chilly Climate for Faculty Women at Western: Postscript to the Backhouse Report." In *Breaking Anonymity: The Chilly Climate for Women Faculty*, edited by The Chilly Collective, 97–132. Waterloo, ON: Wilfrid Laurier University Press.

Bannerji, Himani, Canadian Electronic Library, and Gibson Library Connections. 2000. *The Dark Side of the Nation: Essays on Multiculturalism, Nationalism and Gender.* Toronto: Canadian Scholars' Press.

Battiste, Marie, Lynne Bell, and L.M. Findlay. 2002. "Decolonizing Education in Canadian Universities: An Interdisciplinary, International, Indigenous Research Project." *Canadian Journal of Native Education* 26 (2): 82.

Bonilla-Silva, Eduardo. 2012. "The Invisible Weight of Whiteness: The Racial Grammar of Everyday Life in Contemporary America." *Ethnic and Racial Studies* 35 (2): 173–94. doi:10.1080/01419870.2011.613997.

–. 2015. "The White Racial Innocence Game." *Racism Review: Scholarship and Activism towards Racial Justice.* November 12, 2015. http://www.rac-ismreview.com/blog/2015/11/12/white-racial-innocence-game/.

Brayboy, Bryan McKinley Jones. 2003. "The Implementation of Diversity in Predominantly White Colleges and Universities." *Journal of Black Studies* 34 (1): 72–86. doi:10.1177/0021934703253679.

Carvalho, José Jorge De, and Juliana Flórez-Flórez. 2014. "The Meeting of Knowledges: A Project for the Decolonization of Universities in Latin America." *Postcolonial Studies* 17 (2): 122–39.

Chan, Adrienne S., Rita Kaur Dhamoon, and Lisa Moy. 2014. "Metaphoric Representations of Women of Colour in the Academy: Teaching Race, Disrupting Power." *Borderlands* 13 (2): 1–26.

Cheung, Ho Kwan, Eden King, Alex Lindsey, Ashley Membere, Hannah M. Markell, and Molly Kilcullen. 2016. "Understanding and Reducing Workplace Discrimination." In *Research in Personnel and Human Resources Management*, edited by M.R. Buckley, J.R.B. Halbesleben, and A.R. Wheeler, 101–52. Bingley, UK: Emerald Group. doi: 10.1108/S0742-730120160000034010.

Derous, Eva, Alexander Buijsrogge, Nicholas Roulin, and Wouter Duyck. 2016. "Why Your Stigma Isn't Hired: A Dual-Process Framework of Interview Bias." *Human Resource Management Review* 26 (2): 90–111. doi.org/10.1016/j.hrmr.2015.09.006.

Dion, Susan D. 2009. *Braiding Histories: Learning from Aboriginal Peoples' Experiences and Perspectives.* Vancouver: UBC Press.

Dolmage, Jay. 2017. *Academic Ableism.* Ann Arbor: University of Michigan Press.

Ferber, Abby L. 2012. "The Culture of Privilege: Color-Blindness, Postfeminism, and Christonormativity." *The Journal of Social Issues* 68 (1): 63–77.

Fuller, Laurie, and Ann Russo. 2016. "Feminist Pedagogy: Building Community Accountability." *Feminist Teacher* 26 (2–3): 179–97. doi:10.5406/femteacher.26.2-3.0179.

Grosfoguel, Ramon, Roberto Hernández, and Ernesto Rosen Velásquez, eds. 2016. *Decolonizing the Westernized University: Interventions in Philosophy of Education from Within and Without.* New York: Lexington Books.

Gutiérrez y Muhs, Gabriella, Yolanda Flores Niemann, Carmen G. González, and Angela P. Harris. 2012. *Presumed Incompetent: The Intersections of Race and Class for Women in Academia.* Boulder: Utah State University Press, an imprint of University Press of Colorado.

Hames-García, Michael. 2010. "Is Diversity without Social Justice Enough?" In *The Future of Diversity: Academic Leaders Reflect on American Higher Education*, edited by Daniel Little and Satya P. Mohanty, 51–67. The Future of Minority Studies series. New York: Palgrave Macmillan US. https://doi.org/10.1057/9780230107885_4.

Harbour, Wendy. 2019. "Ableism and Disability in Higher Education: Possibilities for Radical Inclusion." Lecture given at Simon Fraser University, Burnaby, BC, April 3, 2019.

Harris, Angela P., and Carmen G. González. 2012. "Introduction." In *Presumed Incompetent: The Intersections of Race and Class for Women in Academia*, edited by Gabriella Gutiérrez y Muhs, Yolanda Flores Niemann, Carmen G. González, and Angela P. Harris, 1–14. Boulder: Utah State University Press, an imprint of University Press of Colorado.

Hasford, J. 2016. "Dominant Cultural Narratives, Racism, and Resistance in the Workplace: A Study of the Experiences of Young Black Canadians." *American Journal of Community Psychology* 57 (12): 158–70. doi:10.1002/ajcp.12024.

Henry, Annette. 2015. "'We Especially Welcome Applications from Members of Visible Minority Groups': Reflections on Race, Gender and Life at Three Universities." *Race Ethnicity and Education* 18 (5): 589–610.

Henry, Frances, Enakshi Dua, Carl E. James, Audrey Kobayashi, Peter Li, Howard Ramos, and Malinda S. Smith, eds. 2017. *The Equity Myth: Racialization and Indigeneity at Canadian Universities*. Vancouver: UBC Press.

Henry, Frances, and Audrey Kobayashi, with Andrea Choi. 2017. "Representational Analysis: Comparing Canada, the United States, the United Kingdom, and Australia." In *The Equity Myth: Racialization and Indigeneity at Canadian Universities*, edited by Frances Henry, Enakshi Dua, Carl James, Audrey Kobayashi, Peter S. Li, Howard Ramos, and Malinda S. Smith, 24–45. Vancouver: UBC Press.

Hirshfield, Laura E., and Tiffany D. Joseph. 2012. "'We Need a Woman, We Need a Black Woman': Gender, Race, and Identity Taxation in the Academy." *Gender and Education*, 24 (2): 213–27.

hooks, bell. 1984. *Feminist Theory from Margin to Centre*. Boston: South End Press.

James, Carl E., with Selom Chapman-Neyaho. 2017. "'Would Never Be Hired These Days': The Precarious Work Situation of Racialized and Indigenous Faculty Members." In *The Equity Myth: Racialization and Indigeneity at Canadian Universities*, edited by Frances Henry, Enakshi Dua, Carl James, Audrey Kobayashi, Peter S. Li, Howard Ramos, and Malinda S. Smith, 84–114. Vancouver: UBC Press.

Johnson, Allan G. 2018. *Privilege, Power, and Difference*, 3rd ed. New York: McGraw-Hill Education.

Johnson, Genevieve Fuji, and Robert Howsam. 2020. "Whiteness, Power, and the Politics of Demographics in the Governance of the Canadian Academy." *Canadian Journal of Political Science* 53 (3): 676–94.

Kimmel, Michael S., and Abby L. Ferber, eds. 2017. *Privilege: A Reader*, 4th ed. Boulder, CO: Westview Press.

Kirkness, Verna J., and Ray Barnhardt. 1991. "First Nations and Higher Education: The Four R's – Respect, Relevance, Reciprocity, Responsibility." *Journal of American Indian Education* 30 (3): 1–15.

Lorde, Audre. 1984. *Sister Outsider: Essays and Speeches*. Trumansburg, NY: The Crossing Press.

Mahtani, Minelle. 2004. "Mapping Race and Gender in the Academy: The Experiences of Women of Colour Faculty and Graduate Students in Britain, the US and Canada." *Journal of Geography in Higher Education* 28 (1): 91–99. https://doi.org/10.1080/0309826042000198666.

–. 2006. "Challenging the Ivory Tower: Proposing Anti-racist Geographies within the Academy." *Gender, Place and Culture* 13 (1): 21–25. https://doi.org/10.1080/09663690500530909.

McNeish Robert. 1972. "Lessons from the Geese." Unpublished manuscript.

Mignolo, Walter D. 2002. "The Geopolitics of Knowledge and the Colonial Difference." *The South Atlantic Quarterly* 101 (1): 57–96.

Monforti, Jessica Lavariega. 2012. "*La Lucha*: Latinas Surviving Political Science." In *Presumed Incompetent: The Intersections of Race and Class for Women in Academia*, edited by Gabriella Gutiérrez y Muhs, Yolanda Flores Niemann, Carmen G. González, and Angela P. Harris, 393–407. Boulder: Utah State University Press, an imprint of University Press of Colorado.

Nash, Jennifer C. 2011. "Practicing Love: Black Feminism, Love-Politics, and Post-Intersectionality." *Meridians* 11 (2).

Ontario Human Rights Commission. 2005. *Policy and Guidelines on Racism and Racial Discrimination*. https://www3.ohrc.on.ca/sites/default/files/attachments/Policy_and_guidelines_on_racism_and_racial_discrimination.pdf.

Padilla, Amado M. 1994. "Ethnic Minority Scholars, Research, and Mentoring: Current and Future Issues." *Educational Researcher* 23 (4): 24–27.

Palacios, Lena. 2016. "Challenging Convictions: Indigenous and Black Race-Radical Feminists Theorizing the Carceral State and Abolitionist Praxis in the United States and Canada." *Meridians* 15 (1): 137–65. https://doi.org/10.2979/meridians.15.1.08.

Rivera, Lauren A. 2015. *Pedigree: How Elite Students Get Elite Jobs*. Princeton, NJ: Princeton University Press. doi:10.1515/9781400865895.

Sensoy, Özlem, and Robin DiAngelo. 2017. "'We Are All for Diversity, but ...': How Faculty Hiring Committees Reproduce Whiteness and Practical Suggestions for How They Can Change." *Harvard Educational Review* 87 (4): 557–80. https://doi.org/10.17763/1943-5045-87.4.557.

Settles, Isis H., Nicole T. Buchanan, and Kristie Dotson. 2019. "Scrutinized but Not Recognized: (In)visibility and Hypervisibility Experiences of Faculty of Color." *Journal of Vocational Behaviour* 113: 62–74. https://doi.org/10.1016/j.jvb.2018.06.003.

Smith, Malinda S. 2016. "The Diversity Gap in University Leadership." Academic Women's Association, University of Alberta. August 18, 2016. https://uofaawa.wordpress.com/awa-diversity-gap-campaign/the-diversity-gap-in-university-leadership/.

–. 2017. "Action Needed to Close the Leadership Diversity Gap at Canadian Universities." Academic Women's Association, University of Alberta. April 27, 2017. https://uofaawa.

wordpress.com/awa-diversity-gap-campaign/the-diversity-gap-in-university
-leadership-2017/.

–. 2019. "U15 Leadership Remains Largely White and Male Despite 33 Years of Equity Initiatives." Academic Women's Association, University of Alberta. June 20, 2019. https://uofaawa.wordpress.com/2019/06/20/u15-leadership-remains-largely-white
-and-male-despite-33-years-of-equity-initiatives/.

Sheppard, Colleen. 2010. *Inclusive Equality: The Relational Dimensions of Systemic Discrimination in Canada*. Montreal: McGill-Queen's University Press. ProQuest Ebook Central.

Statistics Canada. 2017. "Table 98-400-X2016287: Labour Force Status (8), Highest Certificate, Diploma or Degree (15), Aboriginal Identity (9), Age (13A) and Sex (3) for the Population Aged 15 Years and Over in Private Households of Canada, Provinces and Territories, Census Metropolitan Areas and Census Agglomerations, 2016 Census – 25% Sample Data." https://www150.statcan.gc.ca/n1/en/catalogue/98-400
-X2016287.

–. 2018a. "Table 98-400-X2016192: Visible Minority (15), Age (15A), Sex (3) and Selected Demographic, Cultural, Labour Force, Educational and Income Characteristics (900) for the Population in Private Households of Canada, Provinces and Territories, Census Metropolitan Areas and Census Agglomerations, 2016 Census – 25% Sample Data." https://www150.statcan.gc.ca/n1/en/catalogue/98-400-X2016192.

–. 2018b. "Table 98-400-X2016356: Occupation – National Occupational Classification (NOC) 2016 (691), Employment Income Statistics (3), Highest Certificate, Diploma or Degree (7), Visible Minority (15), Work Activity During the Reference Year (4), Age (4D) and Sex (3) for the Population Aged 15 Years and Over Who Worked in 2015 ..." https://www150.statcan.gc.ca/n1/en/catalogue/98-400-X2016356.

–. 2018c. "Table 98-400-X2016357: Occupation – National Occupational Classification (NOC) 2016 (691), Employment Income Statistics (3), Highest Certificate, Diploma or Degree (7), Aboriginal Identity (9), Work Activity During the Reference Year (4), Age (4D) and Sex (3) for the Population Aged 15 Years and Over Who Worked in 2015 ..." https://www150.statcan.gc.ca/n1/en/catalogue/98-400-X2016357.

Stewart, Abigail J., and Virginia Valian. 2018. *An Inclusive Academy: Achieving Diversity and Excellence*. Cambridge, MA: MIT Press.

Thobani, Sunera. 2007. *Exalted Subjects: Studies in the Making of Race and Nation in Canada*. Toronto: University of Toronto Press.

Turner, Caroline Sotello Viernes. 2002. *Diversifying the Faculty: A Guidebook for Search Committees*. Washington, DC: Association of American Colleges and Universities.

Villenas, Sofia A. 2019. "Pedagogies of Being With: Witnessing, *Testimonio*, and Critical Love in Everyday Social Movement." *International Journal of Qualitative Studies in Education* 32 (2): 151–66. https://doi.org/10.1080/09518398.2018.1533148.

Zambrana, Ruth E. 2018. *Toxic Ivory Towers: The Consequences of Work Stress on Underrepresented Minority Faculty*. New Brunswick, NJ: Rutgers University Press.

PART 3

Structural and Systemic Challenges Faced by Women Academics

The Great Gaslighting:
BIPOC Women in White Academia

AISHA AHMAD

I write this from a place of new power. As a Brown Muslim woman, I have long spoken from a subaltern position, pushing for justice from the low rungs of the academic hierarchy. Today, however, I am a tenured faculty member at a renowned university with a decorated professional record in the field of international security. I have multiple distinguished prizes in both research and teaching and have served as the chair of the board of *Women in International Security-Canada*. Today, I have an elite academic platform; however, with me comes nearly two decades of intimate knowledge of gendered racism in our universities.

This book can be a starting point for an urgently needed conversation about equality in Canadian academia, but that will require some hard talk and moral courage. It is insufficient, for example, to talk about how many women are deans without also looking at the racist hierarchy that exists in academia. For most scholars who are Black, Indigenous, and people of colour (BIPOC), universities are littered with discrimination and bias. Although nearly every departmental website now has a diversity statement, this performative allyship does not typically reflect any substantive changes in institutional policy or culture. Rather, I have witnessed shocking and inappropriate conduct toward many of my BIPOC colleagues, most especially toward Black women scholars. I have watched the tenure system protect both bigots and predators, and even allow them to acquire positions of power.

It is important to remember that perpetrators of discrimination against BIPOC scholars are not necessarily white men. I have personally observed multiple senior white women faculty members terrify and intimidate junior BIPOC women scholars, either luring them into closed door meetings or calling them at home to threaten them. The racist hierarchy in academia also gives some BIPOC scholars advantages over others, resulting in complex patterns of competition and discrimination. This hierarchy – upheld by white supremacy – thus undermines desperately needed solidarity among Black, Indigenous, Brown, Asian, Muslim, and LGBTQ2IA+ scholars. We therefore cannot speak of a singular experience among women in Canadian academia. Unless your gender analysis is intersectional, it is part of the problem.

While there is ample statistical evidence of these widespread biases in Canadian academia today, what is most remarkable about our universities is their culture of denial. In my nearly two decades in higher education, I have never seen a faculty member held personally accountable for biased or outright hostile conduct toward their BIPOC colleagues or students. On the contrary, I have evidence of atrocious conduct toward Black faculty members, including the use of racial slurs, exclusion from departmental opportunities, and erasure of notable accomplishments. I have seen some faculty silence Black colleagues in their own departments and then post performative support for Black Lives Matter on social media.

This behaviour reflects an institutional culture of gaslighting BIPOC scholars, especially racialized women, which is commonplace in higher education institutions across Canada. At the surface, the university will accept that gendered racism is systemic and ubiquitous ... but not here, not us. Rather, gendered racism is framed as an abstraction, a mythical beast that can be condemned and fixed with a diversity statement. But in any concrete case, it is almost always presented as a misunderstanding or isolated issue. If anyone dares say otherwise, they should prepare to face a wall of defensiveness, denial, and even vindictive retaliation.

This is institutional absurdity. The scatterplot shows an unmistakable pattern, yet somehow each data point is always treated as a mistake or an outlier. Even when there is an obvious gender and racial wage gap, supported with clear statistical evidence, it is hard to get an admission of institutional bias. When it comes to gendered racism, the burden of proof placed on BIPOC women is so high that it is often a waste of time to report each incident. (For those early in their careers: it is useful to keep a documented record of all inappropriate conduct on file with the lawyers at your faculty association so that you have a dated and cumulative record. I am not saying you have to sue anyone, but it is nice to know that you can.)

Time is the critical issue for BIPOC women scholars. Fighting gendered racist discrimination in academia is a full-time job and a huge distraction from research productivity and teaching excellence. Frankly, this work should be done by paid equity, diversity, and inclusion (EDI) experts, not by racialized women who are supposed to be spending their time doing biochemistry experiments or economic analyses. I should not have to explain this, but it is incredibly racist to dump EDI work on the nearest Black or Brown faculty members and ask them to do it for free. At minimum, if a university or department is not willing to pay for this EDI labour, then its leadership should stop their performative allyship and take down their empty diversity statements.

For BIPOC women scholars who are exhausted and fed up with the status quo, it is high time that we create a unified front. I, for one, would be happy to use my position as a tenured faculty member to shield new BIPOC scholars from this absurdity. It is time to say no to unpaid labour. Let us hand out the business cards of EDI expert consultants and then walk away. We have the right to focus on our own academic projects, receive equitable pay, and not have our energy wasted by low-impact service requests. Most importantly, it is not the job of BIPOC women to endlessly smile, explain, prove, forgive, coddle, and teach, as if our adult colleagues are fragile. Our job is to be brilliant, make groundbreaking research discoveries, inspire our students, and stay happy and healthy. The end.

7

Academic Gender Wage Gaps in Canada

CATHERINE BEAUDRY, LAURENCE SOLAR-PELLETIER,
and CARL ST-PIERRE

Despite their progressive reputation, Canadian universities are no exception to the gender wage gap evident in the rest of the world (Doucet et al. 2012; OECD 2018; Blevins et al. 2019). These gaps are most pronounced among the U15 research-intensive universities in Canada (Momani, Dreher, and Williams 2019; Catalyst 2020). Common explanations for these gaps include more significant career interruptions for women, primarily because of childbirth and childcare. Additionally, women move up the ranks more slowly or stagnate at lower ranks. In Canadian universities, only 27.6 percent of full professors are women, compared with almost 50 percent of assistant professors (see Table 7.1). Considering that salary grows with seniority, we would expect that women earn less on average at all senior ranks, but data on the wage gap rooted purely in salary is incomplete. One potentially major source of income is almost never mentioned in the academic literature – stipends and consulting incomes.

Although the wage gap is acknowledged and well-documented, less is known about the various stipends (e.g., additional remuneration for administrative, performance, chair holding, market-based work) and consulting income that

TABLE 7.1
Number and proportion of men and women academic staff at Canadian universities in 2016–17

Rank	N	Men (%)	Women (%)
Rank/level below assistant professor	3,561	46.2	53.8
Assistant professor	8,544	51.5	48.5
Associate professor	16,272	57.0	43.0
Full professor	16,239	72.3	27.6
Total	45,660	60.4	39.6

Source: Statistics Canada, Centre for Education Statistics, University and College Academic Staff System (UCASS) Table 37-10-0077-01.

contribute to maintaining, even widening, the gender wage gap in Canada. Our research attempts to fill this gap by questioning the relative importance of stipends and consulting income to the ongoing gender wage gap in academia by relating it to other, more common, explanations. To this end, we conducted a survey in five provinces (Nova Scotia, Quebec, Ontario, Alberta, and British Columbia). The data we gathered confirmed the persistent gender wage gap and also showed that consulting incomes tend to favour men academics in all fields, thereby widening the existing gap.[1] This chapter begins with a brief survey of the literature, detailing the various factors believed to affect salaries in general, and salaries in academia in particular. The next section presents the methodology for our study, followed by a discussion of the descriptive statistics of each of the variables we utilize. We then move into a summary of the regression results before concluding with a summary of our findings.

GENDER PAY INEQUALITY

The literature suggests that pay gaps in academia can be explained by academic rank, administrative positions, parenthood, and academic field. Other factors that contribute to the gender pay gap include the fact that women are discouraged from negotiating or expecting higher salaries (Babcock and Laschever 2009; Kulik and Olekalns 2012), that the labour market favours higher salaries for women in fields such as business, computer science, economics, law, and medicine (Barbezat and Hughes 2005), and that many women select out of academia or feel pushed out, a phenomenon called "the pipeline effect" (Momani, Dreher, and Williams 2019). Few studies in the literature on the gender gap in academia account for these factors, and even fewer examine the gendered nature of stipend allocations and consulting income acquisition, which also contribute to pay differences between men and women.

Age and Rank

Part of the gender pay gap in academia can be explained by the fact that women are underrepresented in senior positions. This gap can be partly explained by the fact that women in academia occupy fewer senior positions, but this is not a sufficient explanation onto itself because data from Statistics Canada shows that a consistent gender pay gap at the same rank keeps growing with every percentile (see Table 7.2). The gap is at its highest with full professors.

The economists Casey Warman, Frances Woolley, and Christopher Worswick (2010) showed that rank consistently explained the gender pay gap over the 1970–2001 period, underlining the fact that discriminatory promotion practices may be reflected in rank. Even when controlling for rank, however, the authors saw a gap in salaries between men and women, which was also observed by

TABLE 7.2

Number, median age, and salary of men and women academic staff at Canadian universities in 2016–17

		Men	Women	Total[a]
Assistant professor				
Number reporting salary		4,338	4,017	8,358
(proportion of total)		(51.9%)	(48.1%)	
Median age		39	40	39
Salary[b]	10th percentile	$81,750	$80,350	$81,075
	Median	$100,500	$98,300	$99,325
	90th percentile	$132,600	$127,000	$129,575
Associate professor				
Number reporting salary		9,129	6,846	15,978
(proportion of total)		(57.1%)	(42.8%)	
Median age		49	49	49
Salary[b]	10th percentile	$101,075	$99,625	$100,275
	Median	$126,925	$124,000	$125,650
	90th percentile	$162,625	$157,725	$160,825
Full professor				
Number reporting salary		11,637	4,422	16,059
(proportion of total)		(72.5%)	(27.5%)	
Median age		58	57	57
Salary[b]	10th percentile	$128,250	$125,475	$127,325
	Median	$160,850	$152,850	$158,750
	90th percentile	$211,800	$195,900	$207,400
Total[c]				
Number reporting salary		27,216	17,697	44,913
(proportion of total)		(60.6%)	(39.4%)	
Median age		52	49	51
Salary[b]	10th percentile	$91,150	$86,625	$89,125
	Median	$135,800	$120,900	$129,525
	90th percentile	$189,600	$169,850	$182,200

Source: Statistics Canada, UCASS Table 37-10-0077-01.
Notes: The number of individuals for which a salary is reported is slightly less than in Table 7.1.
a   Includes the category "Sex unknown/other," which is generally suppressed for confidentiality reasons.
b   Calculations of salary statistics are based on annual rate of salary plus administrative stipends.
c   The data also include information for "Rank/level below assistant professor" and "Other" categories of full-time teaching staff.

Jerome T. Bentley and Rebecca Adamson (2003) in their special report to the National Science Foundation. The fact that women are promoted less or take longer to be promoted has been well-documented (Ornstein et al. 1998; Ginther and Hayes 1999; Harper et al. 2001; Perna 2001; Nakhaie 2002; Ginther and Hayes 2003; Perna 2005; Nakhaie 2007; Ornstein, Stewart, and Drakich 2007). For example, women receive fewer promotions under the age of forty, are less likely to reach tenure, and are more likely to be in nontenure-track positions (Bentley and Adamson 2003).

Administrative Position and Productivity

A survey of Canadian academics showed that those who performed more administrative work were better rewarded in terms of reaching tenure (Wijesingha and Ramos 2017). This does not mean, however, that individuals in these ranks receive the same stipends. One study found that in Ontario, women deans earned 5.26 percent less than men deans and that "pay gaps increase as women faculty move up the echelons of the university system" (Momani et al. 2019, 3). In the US, the median salary of administrators in higher education maintained a consistent gap of about 20,000 USD between 2001 and 2016 (Bichsel and McChesney 2017), which is consistent with the higher estimated stipend for men occupying administrative position seen in a 2005 study (Barbezat and Hughes 2005).

Occupying an administrative position may also be detrimental to career promotion. Part of the literature shows that women faculty have heavier loads in teaching, community outreach, and administrative duties. These tasks are not highly valued for tenure and promotion and divert time that could be spent on research, publication, and writing grants (Bellas and Toutkoushian 1999; Nettles et al. 2000; Fairweather 2002).

Children and Career Interruption

Progress within the salary scales and promotion to higher academic ranks may be slowed by career interruptions. The economists Rob Euwals and Melanie E. Ward (2005) found that career breaks were associated with a pay penalty that could only be compensated by generating an extra four to five articles.

Having a child usually coincides with the pretenure years, a time when academics need to demonstrate progress by rapidly improving their academic productivity. In this crucial and extremely busy period, women are at a particular disadvantage (Bentley and Adamson 2003; Doucet, Smith, and Durand 2012; Bishu and Alkadry 2017). In their studies on women in the humanities (Ginther and Hayes 2003), economics (Ginther and Kahn 2004), and sciences, technologies, engineering, and mathematics (STEM) (Ginther 2001), the authors concluded that having a child had a positive influence on the promotion of men and a negative impact for women, even in cases where their productivity was similar, suggesting that lost productivity is not the only challenge women face as a result of childbearing and childrearing.

The sociologists and economist Christine Doucet, Michael R. Smith, and Claire Durand (2012) listed strategies adopted by women to counter the potential negative impact of having children on one's career: delaying the start of their career to have a first child and then waiting for tenure to have a second child, having children only after obtaining tenure, or simply not becoming a parent. Indeed, women are less likely to have children or to be married than men in academia (Harper et al. 2001; Ginther and Hayes 2003). Furthermore, it seems that men benefit more from having children and being married (Perna 2005).

Academic Field

A 2013 study found that the majority of women work in fields with lower salaries, and in lower ranks (Carlin et al. 2013), a suggestion that is confirmed by the University and College Academic Staff System (UCASS) of Statistics Canada's Centre for Education Statistics. This may explain some of the wage gap found in academia. For instance, engineers earn more on average than researchers in other fields (Ceci et al. 2014), but women in engineering are too few to raise the salary average for women in general. Table 7.3 illustrates this gap between three fields: STEM, health-related fields, and social sciences and humanities (SSH). Donna K. Ginther (2001), an economist specialized in gender-based wage inequalities, found a persistent gender pay gap for doctoral graduates in the sciences from 1973 to 1997 who chose a career in academia, but in the humanities, the gender salary differences were not statistically significant (Ginther and Hayes 2003).

DATA AND METHODOLOGY

With collaboration from the Canadian Association of University Teachers (CAUT), the Quebec Federation of University Teachers and Professors (FQPPU) provided us with a comprehensive list of academic email addresses from universities located in six provinces: Nova Scotia, Quebec, Ontario, Saskatchewan,[2] Alberta, and British Columbia. Of the 45,531 full-time teaching staff in Canadian universities and colleges that Statistics Canada counts in 2016–17, our sample of universities represents 34,419 individuals. Of those, 5,253 completed surveys (corresponding to a 15.3 percent response rate when compared with Statistics Canada data), 5,153 reported both basic salary and gender, of which 2,431 were women. Our sample therefore overrepresents women (47.1 percent) compared

TABLE 7.3
Number, average, median age, and salary of men and women academic staff at Canadian universities in 2016–17

	Group of fields			
	STEM	Health	SSH	Total
Number reporting salary				
Men	10,566	3,066	13,929	27,561
Women	2,886	3,555	11,658	18,099
Total[a]	13,458	6,621	25,581	45,660
Average[b] median age				
Men	51.6	53.5	51.8	51.8
Women	48.0	51.0	49.7	49.6
Total[a]	50.6	52.2	51.0	51.0
Average[b] median salary				
Men	$141,305	$136,285	$130,397	$135,065
Women	$128,439	$118,300	$120,399	$121,108
Total[a]	$138,730	$126,720	$125,820	$129,587

Source: Statistics Canada, UCASS Table 37-10-0077-01.
Notes:
a Includes the category "Sex unknown/other," which is generally suppressed for confidentiality reasons.
b Statistics Canada reports the median age and the median salary per field. For both variables, we have calculated the weighted average of these medians using the number of full-time university teachers per field and sex as weights. The figures reported are technically neither an average nor a median.

to Statistics Canada data. Such an overrepresentation of women provides us with enough observations of women in all fields, including those in which women are traditionally underrepresented, such as STEM, to perform regression analyses where the coefficients that highlight gender differences are likely to be significant.

The questionnaire asked individuals the amount of their gross annual salary for 2016, excluding stipends (*BasicSalary*). It then explored those stipends awarded to academics for different types of positions and activities (see Table 7.4 for the list of corresponding variables accounted for in this chapter).

Building on basic salary, we constructed two additional variables: *TotalSalaryNoConsult*, which includes basic salary and all additional income excluding consultation income, and *TotalSalary*, which includes consultation income. To build the regression model, fourteen other independent variables were constructed to account for gender, age, rank, number of children, number of dependents, number of months of career interruption, and disciplinary field. These are described in Table 7.5. To account for all factors and their interactions

TABLE 7.4
Description of the stipend and consulting income variables

Variable	Type	Description (year = 2016)
dAdminPos1	Dummy	The respondent held a tier 1 administrative position from head of department to university president (1), otherwise (0)
AdmStipend1	Continuous	Amount of the stipend associated with occupying an administrative position from head of department to university president (tier 1)
dAdminPos2	Dummy	The respondent held a tier 2 administrative position linked to directing a program, a research or studies centre (1), otherwise (0)
AdmStipend2	Continuous	Amount of the stipend associated with occupying an administrative position linked to directing a program, a research or studies centre (tier 2)
dMktStipend	Dummy	The respondent received a wage market stipend (1), otherwise (0)
MktStipend	Continuous	Amount of the wage market stipend received
dChair	Dummy	The respondent was a chair holder (1), otherwise (0)
ChairStipend	Continuous	Amount of the annual stipend received as chair holder
dPerfStipend	Dummy	The respondent received a performance stipend (1), otherwise (0)
PerfStipend	Continuous	Amount of the performance stipend received
dOtherStipend	Dummy	The respondent received any other type of stipend (1), otherwise (0)
OtherStipend	Continuous	Amount of the other types of stipend received
dConsultInc	Dummy	The respondent received any consulting income (1), otherwise (0)
ConsultInc	Continuous	Amount of the consulting income/fees received

with one another, we estimate simple Ordinary Least Squares (OLS) as well as Blinder-Oaxaca decomposition (BOD) regression models of the natural logarithm of *TotalSalary*.[3]

DESCRIPTIVE STATISTICS

As mentioned above, several factors affect the basic salary and the global remuneration of academics. This section will briefly explore the discrepancies in salaries and stipends found in our sample.[4]

Gender Effects

Men are more likely to occupy administrative positions, 32.5 percent compared to 29.7 percent for women, particularly tier 1 administrative positions (*dAdminPos1* – from head of department to university president), 10.3 percent compared to 6.9 percent for women. Equal proportions of men and women receive stipends once in these administrative positions; however, men receive on average $7,000 more than women. In contrast, both men and women occupy

TABLE 7.5
Description of the independent variables

Variable	Type	Description (year = 2016)
dWomen	Dummy	The respondent is a women (1), otherwise (0)
Age	Continuous	Age of the respondent in 2017
dAssistant	Dummy	The respondent occupies an assistant professor's position (1), otherwise (0)
dAssociate	Dummy	The respondent occupies an associate professor's position (1), otherwise (0)
dFullProf	Dummy	The respondent occupies a full professor's position (1), otherwise (0)
dChildren	Dummy	The respondent cares for children aged 0 to 18 whether they are his/her children or dependents (1), otherwise (0)
nbChildren	Continuous	Number of children aged 0 to 18 that the respondent cares for whether they are his/her children or dependents
dDepAdult	Dummy	The respondent cares for adult dependents (1), otherwise (0)
nbDepAdult	Continuous	Number of dependent adults under the responsibility of the respondent
MInterrupt	Continuous	Number of months of career interruptions. Reasons for interruptions include maternity and parental leave, accidents or illnesses, being appointed as a caregiver, etc.
dSabbLocal	Dummy	The respondent has taken sabbatical leave in a local organization (1), has not taken sabbatical leave (0)
dSabbNoLocal	Dummy	The respondent has taken sabbatical leave in a nonlocal organization (1), has not taken sabbatical leave (0)
dUniversity$_i$	Dummy	The respondent's university is University$_i$ (1), otherwise (0)
dDiscipline$_j$	Dummy	The respondent's discipline is Discipline$_j$ (1), otherwise (0)

tier 2 administrative positions (*dAdminPos2* – directing a program or a research or studies centre) in equal proportions, but more men (41.2 percent) are likely to receive a stipend than women (34 percent), and when they do, they get paid slightly more. For almost all categories, men perform better than women in terms of administrative stipends (see Figure 7.1). On average the stipend gap is 17 percent, but in the top decile the gap widens, reaching 40 percent (which translates to a difference in stipends of $10,000).

Our results paint a similar picture with regards to holding a chair. While 11.9 percent of men are chair holders compared to 8.8 percent of women, they are equally likely to receive a chair stipend, but the amount is larger for men (see Figure 7.2). Furthermore, the distribution is highly skewed, with the gender gap widening to 16.7 percent in the top decile (reaching $8,000). In contrast, more women than men receive performance stipends, but the amount received

FIGURE 7.1
Gender pay gap for administrative stipends

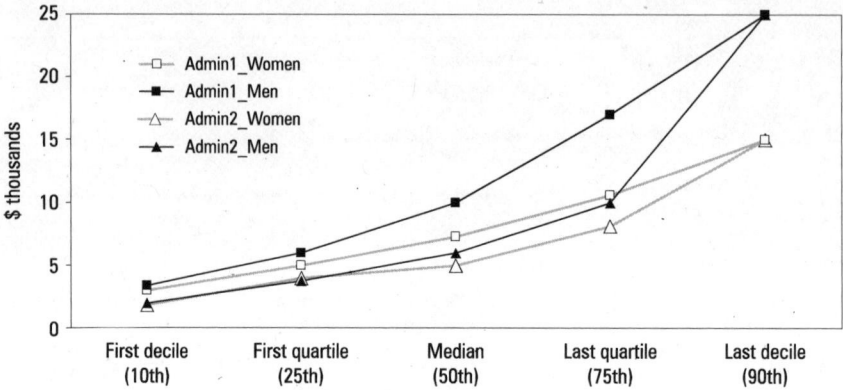

FIGURE 7.2
Gender pay gap for chair holding and performance stipends

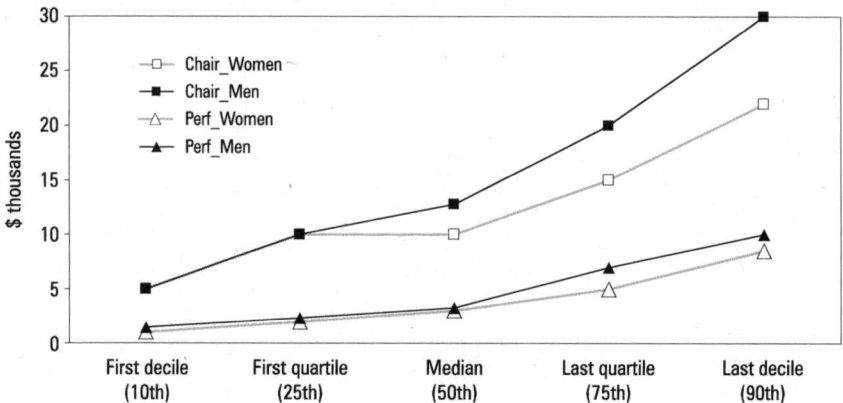

is almost equal for both genders, perhaps because the rules regarding such stipends are often made very clear within each institution.

Women are losing out in regard to wage market stipends and consulting activities (see Figure 7.3). Our results seem to give credence to the argument that women are notoriously bad at negotiating such stipends or that these types of stipends are either smaller or simply refused to them. In the top quartile and decile, the gap reaches 38–40 percent. Men venture into consulting activities in greater numbers (26 percent), and when they do, their earnings are much higher

FIGURE 7.3
Gender pay gap for various stipends and consulting income

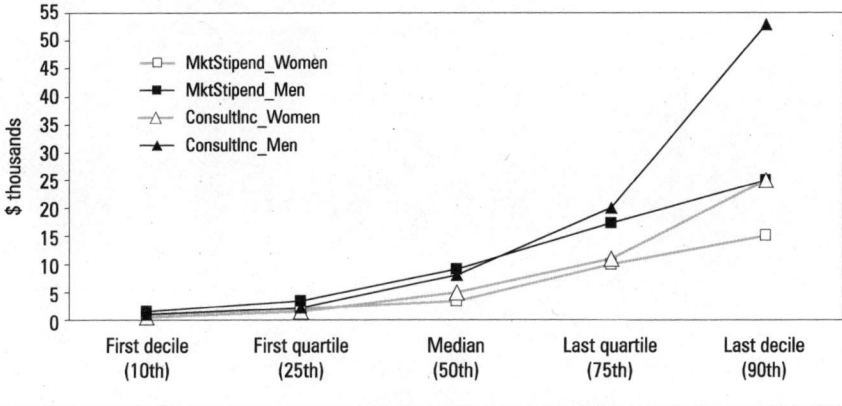

than those of women. Top women earners obtain a mere 47 percent of what men earn in consulting income. There are field biases underlying these results, which we will explore in the regressions analysis.

When we cumulate all these gender discrepancies, women earn on average 87.5 percent of what men earn compared to 91.1 percent when considering only basic salary. All types of stipends widen this gap, and consulting income further contributes to exacerbating the global pay differences. In the top twenty-fifth and tenth percentiles, the most striking differences are due to wage market stipends and consulting activities (Figure 7.4 shows the growing gap).

FIGURE 7.4
Overall gender pay gap (women/men ratio), including and excluding consulting

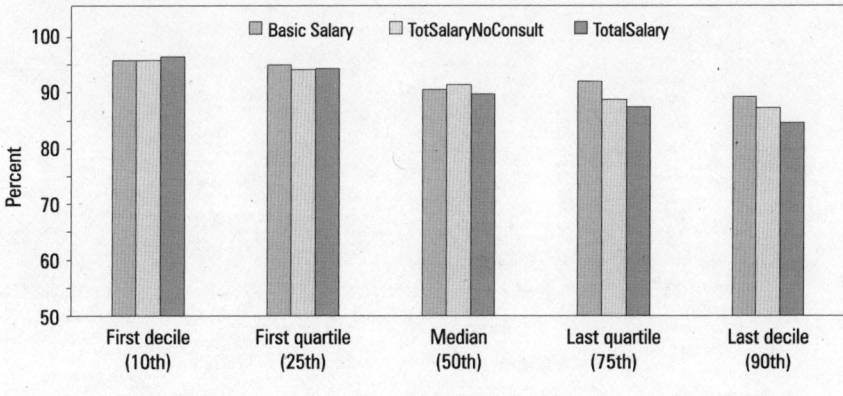

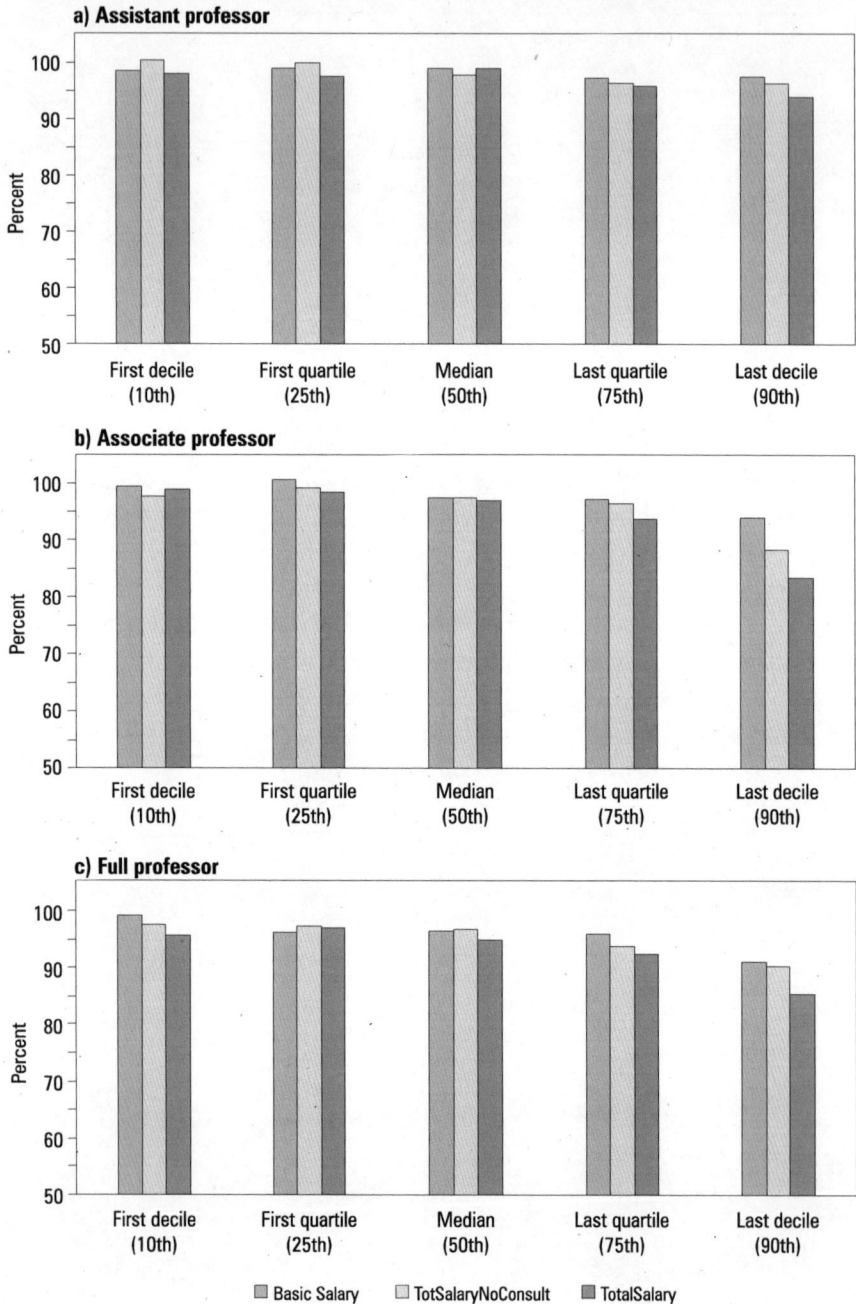

FIGURE 7.5

Gender pay gap (women/men ratio) for assistant, associate, and full professors

a) Assistant professor

Percent

First decile (10th) First quartile (25th) Median (50th) Last quartile (75th) Last decile (90th)

b) Associate professor

Percent

First decile (10th) First quartile (25th) Median (50th) Last quartile (75th) Last decile (90th)

c) Full professor

Percent

First decile (10th) First quartile (25th) Median (50th) Last quartile (75th) Last decile (90th)

Basic Salary   TotSalaryNoConsult   TotalSalary

Rank

Splitting our sample into three cohorts according to academic rank yields a similar story to that seen above; stipends and consulting income widen the global wage gap. As women climb the academic ladder, the gap worsens, not so much in terms of basic salary but because of consulting income and, to a lesser extent, stipends. All three salary measures are always significantly different for full professors, but not for the other ranks (see Figure 7.5), as the gender gaps are not always significantly different.

Exploring administrative and wage market stipends as well as consulting income, we find that women full professors in the top managing positions (*AdmStipend1*) earn 50.3 percent of the administrative stipends that their male counterparts obtain. For the tier 2 managing positions (*AdmStipend2*), women associate professors earn 63.8 percent of what their male colleagues do. Similar gaps are found for wage market stipends: women associate and full professors obtain 48.8 percent and 54.6 percent, respectively, of what men get. Finally, consulting incomes further deepen the global income gap as women associate and full professors raise 54.0 percent and 49.8 percent, respectively, of what men earn.

Parenthood

Our results do not contradict the literature on parenthood as an impediment in women's academic careers. Women who took care of children aged zero to eighteen at the time of the survey earned less than men in a similar situation. In fact, both genders earned less than their colleagues without children. Figure 7.6 shows the gender wage gap per decile for both categories. We must, however, caution the reader not to draw strong conclusions in this regard. First, these results may be attributable to age: more senior academics are very likely the parents of adults and very young academics may not have started families yet. The average age of academics caring for children is forty-five years, compared to fifty-five for those without such responsibilities.

We will explore this issue further in the regression analysis, which will account for all different types of additional income, age, and rank concurrently. Before we do, however, it is important to bear in mind that within each rank category, particularly at the associate and full professor levels, individuals that do not have children aged zero to eighteen at home are significantly older, 7.4 and 8 years older for associate professors, and 10.6 and 10 years older for full professors, respectively (see Table 7.6). Any salary differences found between academics who currently care for children aged zero to eighteen and those who do not will likely be due to age of the academic and not to child care. Our regression analysis accounts for both children and adult dependents.

FIGURE 7.6
Gender pay gap (women/men ratio) for professors without and with children

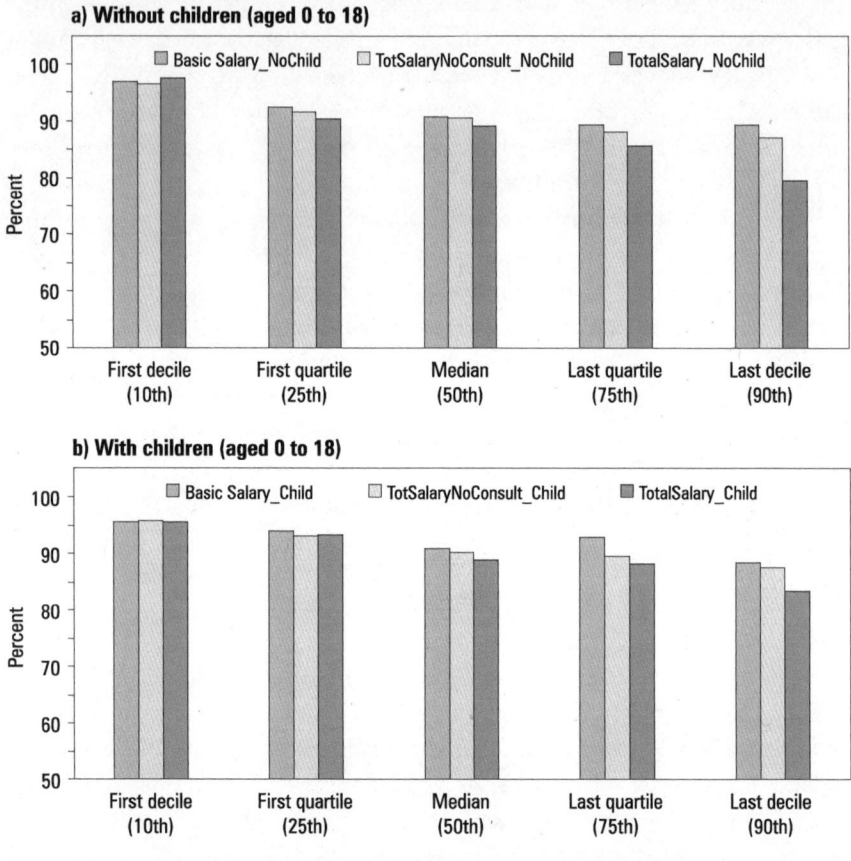

a) Without children (aged 0 to 18)

b) With children (aged 0 to 18)

Gender and Academic Field

Our data show a significant field effect on the average basic salary: SSH academics receive a lower income than their counterparts in other fields (see Table 7.7), for example, $11,400 and $14,000 less compared to the health and STEM fields respectively. The field differences further grow when including various stipends and consulting income.

Figure 7.7 highlights the gender pay gap in favour of men in every field and for most percentiles.[5] In all three figures, the widening gap toward the top percentiles is partly due to the fact that more women are at the beginning or in the middle of their career in comparison with men, and the salary is higher for full professors.

TABLE 7.6
Descriptive statistics for age by rank and parenthood

	Assistant professors			Associate professors			Full professors		
	No Kids	Kids	Δ	No Kids	Kids	Δ	No Kids	Kids	Δ
Women									
N	167	283		177	325		346	270	
Median	38	40		52	43		59	48	
Mean	41.9	40.6	1.3	51.3 ***	43.9	7.4	58.9 ***	48.3	10.6
Std. Dev.	(9.5)	(5.2)		(8.9)	(4.8)		(6.3)	(5.6)	
Men									
N	105	256		129	312		564	489	
Median	37	39		54	44		61	50	
Mean	41.2 **	40.0	1.2	52.6 ***	44.5	8.1	60.5 ***	50.5	10.0
Std. Dev.	(10.4)	(4.8)		(9.8)	(5.7)		(7.5)	(6.7)	

Note: ***, ** indicate that the Mann-Whitney two-tailed test finds a significant difference between both genders at the 1% and 5% level, respectively.

TABLE 7.7
Descriptive statistics for salaries by field

Variable		STEM	SSH	Health	SSH_STEM		SSH_Health		STEM_Health
BasicSalary	N	1,344	2,660	1,149					
	Mean	$131,362	$119,950	$134,115	***	91.3%	*** 89.4%	***	97.9%
	Std. Dev.	($39,863)	($43,907)	($76,331)					
TotSalary NoConsult	N	1,344	2,660	1,149					
	Mean	$135,717	$123,066	$139,804	***	90.7%	*** 88.0%	***	97.1%
	Std. Dev.	($43,045)	($47,576)	($82,892)					
TotalSalary	N	1,344	2,660	1,149					
	Mean	$138,778	$126,153	$149,270	***	90.9%	*** 84.5%	*	93.0%
	Std. Dev.	($48,614)	($50,759)	($95,241)					

Note: ***, * indicate that the Mann-Whitney two-tailed test finds a significant difference between both genders at the 1% and 10% level, respectively.

Women in STEM earn 96.5 percent of what men do for basic salary and 93.5 percent for total salary. Women are doubly penalized in the SSH fields: fewer get stipends or generate consulting income, and the amounts that are received are smaller. This leads to a cumulative gap of 9.3 percent in favour of men. Women in the field of health are the most disadvantaged. Their average basic

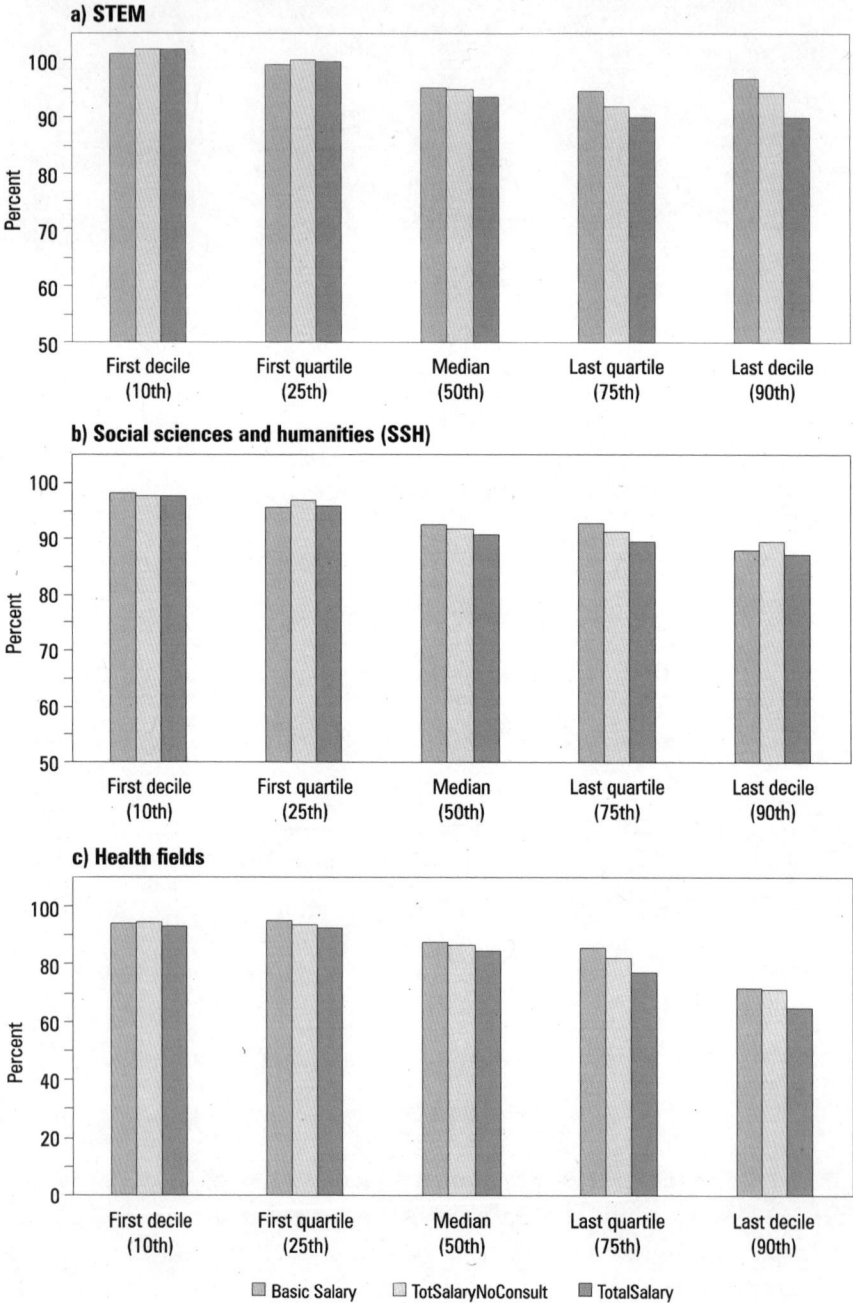

FIGURE 7.7
Gender pay gap (women/men ratio)

a) STEM

b) Social sciences and humanities (SSH)

c) Health fields

Basic Salary   TotSalaryNoConsult   TotalSalary

salary accounts for only 83.9 percent of what men earn in the same field, and the disparity reaches 78.3 percent for total salary. Administrative stipends and consulting income markedly contribute to increasing the gap. For example, women in tier 2 administrative positions earn less than half of what men earn. Furthermore, women are underrepresented as chair holders (9 percent compared to 17 percent of men). This result is worrisome because there are more women than men in the health fields. At the median, the gender pay gap amounts to 15.5 percent, and in the top decile the gap reaches as much as 35 percent.

REGRESSION ANALYSIS

When all variables at our disposal are accounted for in a multivariate regression, we expect some of the differences found in the descriptive statistics to disappear and the strong discrepancies to stand out, all things being equal. We estimated our models on basic salary (*BasicSalary*), basic salary plus all stipends (*TotSalarynoConsult*), and total salary including all stipends and consulting income (*TotalSalary*); only the latter will be discussed in this chapter. For the sake of brevity, the OLS and BOD regression results are provided as an online appendix (http://hdl.handle.net/2429/87285).

Depending on the independent variables used (dummy or continuous), the estimated BOD regression significantly explains about 94 to 97 percent of the 6.41 percent predicted gender wage gap in SSH, and about 94 to 100 percent of the 4.42 percent predicted gender gap in STEM.[6] Including information about stipends and consulting income therefore contributes to explaining almost all of the gender wage gap; because the overall unexplained part (treatment) is never significant, our results are in agreement with Laura K. Brown and Elizabeth Troutt (2017), specialists of economics of gender and pay equity, who observed the disappearance of the overall treatment effect in 2013.

Our OLS results for the relationship between age and salary clearly show the diminishing increments of academic salary scales, reaching a maximum value[7] around an age in the mid-sixties for the SSH fields and less than eighty for the STEM fields.[8] The explained wage gap, or endowment effect, between men and women due to age differences is significant and explains about 20 ($p < 0.01$)[9] to 26 percent ($p < 0.1$) of the 6.41 percent SSH and 4.42 percent STEM wage difference, respectively, in the BOD analysis.[10]

Academic rank obviously plays an important contributory role in explaining salary differences. The greatest proportion of the wage gap is explained by the full professor rank.[11] We consistently obtain a negative effect for associate professor in the BOD, which suggests that women remain in the associate professor rank longer (reach higher salary scales at that level) and have a lesser access to the upper echelon of academic ranks. When women reach full professorship, they earn about 1.5 to 2.3 percent less than their men colleagues, which corresponds to 35–37 percent of the 4.42 percent STEM and 6.41 percent SSH fields wage gap, respectively.

Because all stipends add up to make the total salary, all corresponding variables, except those related to performance, whether in dummy format or in dollar amounts, have a positive and significant impact on our dependent variable in the OLS regressions results. This is not the case for the BOD endowment results, as only tier 1 administrative and market stipends as well as consulting income explain a significant but small part of the SSH gender gap (4.2–4.7 percent, 2.6–4.7 percent, and 8.7–13.3 percent, respectively, of the 6.41 percent wage gap), and in the STEM fields, only consulting income contributes significantly to 12.4–17.9 percent of the 4.42 percent gender wage gap.[12] In the SSH fields, the BOD treatment results show that there remains a significantly higher penalty for being a woman with regard to tier 1 administrative positions and to generating consulting income. This is not the case in the STEM fields, where no treatment effects are noticeable. Either there are not enough observations to single out differences, ceteris paribus, or the voice of "women in science" has been heard.

Taking into consideration both gender and rank as interactive variables for each of the stipend types yields some interesting moderating effects. Men associate professors that occupy tier 1 administrative positions (*AdmStipend1*) in the SSH fields are paid significantly more, an additional $17,000 (OLS), than their women colleagues, all things being equal. In the BOD analysis, only at the full professor level do administrative stipends show a significant impact. They contribute to explaining 11.7 percent (tier 1) and 6.2 percent (tier 2) of the 6.41 percent gender wage gap in the SSH fields and 17.7 percent (tier 1) of the 4.42 percent STEM wage gap. Surprisingly, when the dollar amounts of these stipends are introduced in the regression analysis, their wide distribution causes too much noise to provide significant results.

At the top professorial rank, our results show gender gaps in favour of men full professors for negotiated wage market stipends (OLS): Men earn about $8,500 and $13,000 more than women full professors in the SSH and STEM fields, respectively.[13] Furthermore, the BOD endowment results suggest that market stipends contribute to explaining 13.9 percent of the 6.41 percent wage gap in the SSH fields but none in the STEM fields, probably because of the smaller sample.

Where both women associate and full professors clearly lose out is in terms of consulting income; according to our OLS results, SSH men earn nearly $7,000 to $9,000 more (for full and associate professors, respectively), and STEM men associate professors earn more than $17,000 in addition to their salaries and stipends. Moreover, the BOD results highlight that consulting income, when interacted with rank, contributes to explaining 0.55 percent of the wage gap for both fields, and it explains 34.8 percent and 24.6 percent of the full professor wage gap in the SSH and STEM fields, respectively.[14] The impact of the full professor wage gap therefore appears to be in a large part due to consulting income.

Turning now to the other control variables, the lack of a negative effect of children compared to the positive effect of dependent adults (only in the SSH fields) is in fact another age-related artifact. We saw in Table 7.6 that academics caring for kids aged between zero and eighteen were considerably younger than their counterparts without children (which includes those with adult dependents, e.g., their older children). Once we account for age and rank, however, the effect of children disappears, but not that of dependent adults. Additionally, we found that full professors with dependent adults are only three years older than other full professors, which suggest that at this stage, it is not an age-related effect. The BOD endowment effects show that dependent adults only contribute around 2 percent ($p < 0.1$) of the 6.41 percent wage difference in favour of men and only in the SSH fields. Disentangling the rank, age, gender, and children/ dependent adults' effects is outside the scope of this chapter, but clearly deserves further detailed investigation. Furthermore, during our investigation, we found that having children at any point in one's career does not explain a gender pay gap once all other factors have been accounted for.

In fact, interrupting one's career, for numerous reasons, is what really has a negative effect for STEM women and, to lesser extent, SSH women. Because such career interruptions are generally well-documented and accounted for in collective agreements, we would have expected to find mild effects, probably due to maternity leave, that would not be accounted for by having children. Our results show that a greater number of months of career interruptions contributes to about 10 percent ($p < 0.05$) of the SSH wage gap but 33.8–36.4 percent of the 4.42 percent wage gap in the STEM fields. STEM women are clearly extremely penalized for these career interruptions and for not being present in the lab during their maternity leave.

In sum, the greatest contributors to the gender wage gap in favour of men in the SSH fields are the full professor rank, age, career interruptions, and consulting income, which account for 76–79 percent of the explained (endowment) 6.41 percent gender wage gap. In the STEM field, professor rank, career interruptions, and consulting income account for 82–89 percent of the 4.42 percent wage gap. Adding all stipends and consulting income therefore appears to almost completely explain the gender pay gap, hence specifically pointing toward where potential discrimination (the BOD treatments) occurs.

CONCLUSION

Our results reveal a consistent gender wage gap that widens when all contributions to total earnings (including stipends and consulting income) are accounted for. To our knowledge, this is the first study that aims to disentangle all the different types of income additions that exacerbate the gender pay gap in academia. Our regression analysis shows that administrative positions held by professors had a significant, positive impact on their salary due to the stipends associated with such positions. Because men are more likely to rise in the academic hierarchy, they are more prone to receiving such stipends, whereas women perform more service work, which is generally not financially rewarded (Baker 2012; Guarino and Borden 2017). We also found that wage market stipends are still much more important for men than they are for women. These are very often negotiated on an ad hoc basis and not enshrined in collective agreements or standardized. In contrast, some chair-related and performance stipends (e.g., a stipend for a publication in a top tier journal) are more likely to be somewhat standardized, which helps explain why we do not find widespread gender discrepancies here.

In the chapter, we explored the most common explanation for the gender pay gap in academia. Women generally take more and longer career interruptions and are more likely than men to interrupt their careers to care for their children or to act as caregivers to adult dependents. Our results show that having children leads to lower take-home pay, but also suggest that these results are intertwined with rank and age and require a more in-depth analysis. Such career interruptions have a nonnegligible negative impact on total salary in SSH, but being absent from the lab in the STEM fields explains more than a third of the wage gap.

Our last finding concerns the huge discrepancies found in terms of consulting income. The sums generated by men are considerably larger than those of women. It is often argued that women do not make or have the time to perform consultancy work as they have more difficulty saying no to service requests and have thus less time for consulting (Baker 2012; Guarino and Borden 2017) or feel less competent (on the imposter syndrome, see, e.g., Dancy and Brown 2011). We wonder whether for some individuals, an expert is, de facto, a man. This (un)conscious bias could also contribute to explaining why women are less solicited as experts. Through this work, women academics know that the pay gap is partly the result of unconscious bias against their expertise and slightly less due to their caregiving and service contributions.

ACKNOWLEDGMENTS

We are grateful to Pauline Huet who helped create and manage the survey. We want to thank students for their research assistance: Hakim Belkouch, Yesmine Boukhili, Melika Jafari, and Pietro Cruciatta. We are indebted to Hans Poirier and Jean-Marie-Lafortune for their support throughout the project. Finally, we thank the participants of the 2017 Gender Summit, of the FQPPU AGM, and of the RRISIQ, where this research was presented. None of them are responsible for any mistakes or opinions that this text may contain.

NOTES

1 The survey asked respondent which gender they identify with: male, female, other (the respondent was asked to specify the gender). As very few "other" responses were received, this chapter focuses only on the self-identified men and women.

2 Saskatchewan was used for the pretest and is therefore not included in the analysis.

3 The exact transformation is: ln (TotalSalary/100,000 + 1).

4 All detailed descriptive and regression statistics tables can be downloaded at http://hdl.handle.net/2429/87285.

5 Comparative data by gender, rank, and field are available as an unpublished appendix upon request from the authors.

6 Using continuous variables rather than dummies always yields a proportionately larger endowment. The first number reported refers to the regression results that include dummy variables and the second, to those using dollar amounts.

7 The relationship between age and total salary follows an inverted U-shaped curve.

8 For the sake of brevity, we will include in this chapter the results for the SSH and STEM fields. There is too much variability within the health fields to reach robust conclusions.

9 Most of the p-values reported in the chapter respect $p \leq 0.05$. For the sake of brevity, only when this is not the case will the p-value be reported.

10 The BOD regressions account for a wage gap contribution of 13–14 percent explained by the business field disciplines of SSH, and 6–7 percent explained by engineering in the STEM fields.

11 We estimated the VIF to be 1.63 for the overall regressions and to be 2.4 for *Age* and 3.95 for *dFullProf*. When we drop *Age*, the VIF for *dFullProf* drops slightly to 3.4, which is a minimal drop. As a consequence, although there is correlation between the rank and age variables, there is no multicollinearity problem to discredit the regression analysis. Moreover, it is important to account for both variables as women may access to the higher echelons at an older age than men.

12 Because women may receive stipends in equal proportions to men (measured by dummy variables) but associate them with smaller dollar amounts, we report both sets of regressions. The analysis systematically shows that accounting only for receiving a stipend (dummy variable) explains less of the wage gap than when the dollar amounts are taken into consideration.

13 In the regressions using the dollar amounts, the estimated gender gaps for full professors in the SSH and the STEM fields are more than $6,500 and $7,600, respectively.
14 The large variability in the dollar amounts of consulting income in both SSH and STEM diminish the quality of the results for the second set of regressions.

WORKS CITED

Babcock, Linda, and Sara Laschever. 2009. *Women Don't Ask: Negotiation and the Gender Divide*. Princeton, NJ: Princeton University Press.

Baker, Maureen. 2012. *Academic Careers and the Gender Gap*. Vancouver: UBC Press.

Barbezat, Debra A., and James W. Hughes. 2005. "Salary Structure Effects and the Gender Pay Gap in Academia." *Research in Higher Education* 46 (6): 621–40.

Bellas, Marcia L., and Robert K. Toutkoushian. 1999. "Faculty Time Allocations and Research Productivity: Gender, Race, and Family Effects." *Review of Higher Education* 22 (4): 367–90.

Bentley, Jerome T., and Rebecca Adamson. 2003. *Gender Differences in the Careers of Academic Scientists and Engineers: A Literature Review*. Report by Mathtech Inc. Arlington, VA: National Science Foundation, Directorate for Social, Behavioural and Economic Sciences, Division of Science Resources Statistics.

Bichsel, Jacqueline, and Jasper McChesney. 2017. *The Gender Pay Gap and the Representation of Women in Higher Education Administrative Positions: The Century So Far*. Research report. College and University Professional Association for Human Resources. https://www.cupahr.org/wp-content/uploads/cupahr_research_brief_1.pdf.

Bishu, Sebawit G., and Mohamad G. Alkadry. 2017. "A Systematic Review of the Gender Pay Gap and Factors That Predict It." *Administration and Society* 49 (1): 65–104.

Blevins, Dane P., Steve Sauerwald, Jenny M. Hoobler, and Christopher J. Robertson. 2019. "Gender Differences in Pay Levels: An Examination of the Compensation of University Presidents." *Organization Science* 30 (3): 600–16.

Brown, Laura K., and Elizabeth Troutt. 2017. "Sex and Salaries at a Canadian University: The Song Remains the Same or the Times They Are a Changin'?" *Canadian Public Policy* 43 (3): 246–60.

Carlin, Paul S., Michael P. Kidd, Patrick M. Rooney, and Brian Denton. 2013. "Academic Wage Structure by Gender: The Roles of Peer Review, Performance, and Market Forces." *Southern Economic Journal* 80 (1): 127–46.

Catalyst. 2020. *Women in Acadamia: Quick Take*. https://www.catalyst.org/research/women-in-academia/.

Ceci, Stephen J., Donna K. Ginther, Shulamit Kahn, and Wendy M. Williams. 2014. "Women in Academic Science: A Changing Landscape." *Psychological Science in the Public Interest* 15 (3): 75–141.

Dancy, T. Elon, and M. Christopher Brown. 2011. "The Mentoring and Induction of Educators: Addressing the Impostor Syndrome in Academe." *Journal of School Leadership* 21 (4): 607–34.

Doucet, Christine, Michael R. Smith, and Claire Durand. 2012. "Pay Structure, Female Representation and the Gender Pay Gap among University Professors." *Relations industrielles/Industrial Relations* 67 (1): 51–77.

Euwals, Rob, and Melanie E. Ward. 2005. "What Matters Most: Teaching or Research? Empirical Evidence on the Remuneration of British Academics." *Applied Economics* 37 (14): 1655–72.

Fairweather, James S. 2002. "The Mythologies of Faculty Productivity." *The Journal of Higher Education* 73 (1): 26–48.

Ginther, Donna K. 2001. "Does Science Discriminate against Women? Evidence from Academia, 1973–1997." Working Paper 2001–02. Atlanta, GE: Federal Reserve Bank of Atlanta.

Ginther, Donna K., and Kathy J. Hayes. 1999. "Gender Differences in Salary and Promotion in the Humanities." *American Economic Review* 89 (2): 397–402.

–. 2003. "Gender Differences in Salary and Promotion for Faculty in the Humanities 1977–95." *Journal of Human Resources* 38 (1): 34–73.

Ginther, Donna K., and Shulamit Kahn. 2004. "Women in Economics: Moving Up or Falling Off the Academic Career Ladder?" *Journal of Economic Perspectives* 18 (3): 193–214.

Guarino, Cassandra M., and Victor M.H. Borden. 2017. "Faculty Service Loads and Gender: Are Women Taking Care of the Academic Family?" *Research in Higher Education* 58 (6): 672–94.

Harper, Elizabeth P., Roger G. Baldwin, Bruce G. Gansneder, and Jay L. Chronister. 2001. "Full-Time Women Faculty off the Tenure Track: Profile and Practice." *The Review of Higher Education* 24 (3): 237–57.

Kulik, Carol T., and Mara Olekalns. 2012. "Negotiating the Gender Divide: Lessons from the Negotiation and Organizational Behavior Literatures." *Journal of Management* 38 (4): 1387–1415.

Momani, Bessma, Emma Dreher, and Kira Williams. 2019. "More than a Pipeline Problem: Evaluating the Gender Pay Gap in Canadian Academia from 1996 to 2016." *Canadian Journal of Higher Education/Revue canadienne d'enseignement supérieur* 49 (1): 1–21.

Nakhaie, M. Reza. 2002. "Gender Differences in Publication among University Professors in Canada." *Canadian Review of Sociology/Revue canadienne de sociologie* 39 (2): 151–79.

–. 2007. "Universalism, Ascription and Academic Rank: Canadian Professors, 1987–2000." *Canadian Review of Sociology/Revue canadienne de sociologie* 44 (3): 361–86.

Nettles, Michael T., Laura W. Perna, and Ellen M. Bradburn. 2000. *Salary, Promotion, and Tenure Status of Minority and Women Faculty in U.S. Colleges and Universities.* National Center for Education Statistics.

Organisation for Economic Co-operation Development (OECD). 2018. *Gender Wage Gap.* https://data.oecd.org/earnwage/gender-wage-gap.htm.

Ornstein, Michael, Penni Stewart, and Janice Drakich. 1998. "The Status of Women in Canadian Universities 1957–95." *Education Quarterly Review* 5 (2): 29–47.

–. 2007. "Promotion at Canadian Universities: The Intersection of Gender, Discipline, and Institution." *Canadian Journal of Higher Education* 37 (3): 1–25.

Perna, Laura W. 2001. "Sex and Race Differences in Faculty Tenure and Promotion." *Research in Higher Education* 42 (5): 541–67.

–. 2005. "Sex Differences in Faculty Tenure and Promotion: The Contribution of Family Ties." *Research in Higher Education* 46 (3): 277–307.

Warman, Casey, Frances Woolley, and Christopher Worswick. 2010. "The Evolution of Male-Female Earnings Differentials in Canadian Universities, 1970–2001/ Evolution des différentiels de salaires entre hommes et femmes dans les universités canadiennes 1970–2001." *Canadian Journal of Economics/Revue canadienne d'économique* 43 (1): 347–72.

Wijesingha, Rochelle, and Howard Ramos. 2017. "Human Capital or Cultural Taxation: What Accounts for Differences in Tenure and Promotion of Racialized and Female Faculty?" *Canadian Journal of Higher Education/Revue canadienne d'enseignement supérieur* 47 (3): 54–75.

8

Representation of Women in STEM in Senior Administration

MELANIE A. MORRISON, JOSHUA W. KATZ, BIDUSHY SADIKA,
JESSICA M. McCUTCHEON, and TODD G. MORRISON

Women in STEM disciplines, broadly described as "hard" disciplines, occupy a unique position in society: they are members of a privileged group yet remain marginalized within it.[1] While they are less likely than men counterparts to assume leadership roles (Daldrup-Link 2017), there is evidence to suggest that women may generally benefit from pursuing education and careers in hard disciplines when compared to women who do not. Indeed, a series of recent studies that describe the demographic characteristics of various American academic and corporate leaders hint at the benefits that STEM expertise can provide for women (McCullough 2019; Stevenson and Orr 2017). In particular, Laura McCullough (2019), a professor in the Department of Chemistry and Physics at the University of Wisconsin-Stout, highlights how women with STEM educational backgrounds may be advantaged with regard to obtaining leadership positions within the academy (e.g., deans, provosts, and chancellors). No study, to date, has examined women academic leaders' disciplinary backgrounds within a Canadian context. The purpose of this chapter is to address this gap in the literature.

We begin by describing the current climate as it pertains to leadership and gender within the context of STEM and other hard disciplines. Then, we detail our methodology and key findings.

GENDER AND HARD DISCIPLINES

STEM is best described as a constellation of so-called hard disciplines of traditional scientific and technological fields, which also expanded to include business, health, and agriculture (for a discussion of why STEM should encompass more disciplines including the arts see Zollman 2011, 2012). Despite increases in the number of women obtaining bachelor's degrees in specific STEM fields such as biology, chemistry, and mathematics, men continue to dominate other traditional STEM disciplines including physics, computer science, and engineering (Cheryan et al. 2016; Heilbronner 2013; National

Science Foundation 2013, 2014; Piatek-Jimenez et al. 2018). Women are much less likely to have careers in STEM than are men; for example, there are significantly fewer women professors than men in these "hard" hard disciplines (Sussman and Yssaad 2005). This gender-based discrepancy may be attributed, in part, to the stereotyping of STEM and other hard disciplines as masculine (Carli et al. 2016; O'Brien et al. 2015). STEM fields are believed to be ill-suited to women, who stereotypically hold gendered norms that are believed to be less agentic, which is viewed as a necessary skill for scientists (Carli et al. 2016; Eagly and Karau 2002; Farrell and McHugh 2017). Another argument explaining the discrepancy of women in STEM is the inhospitable environment the disciplines create for women. Women in STEM-related fields often experience increased discrimination in the form of lower wages and workplace harassment when compared to their men counterparts (Carli et al. 2016; Daldrup-Link 2017; Michelmore and Sassler 2016; Piatek-Jimenez et al. 2018). In tandem, these factors create an environment that does not appear to welcome women into STEM education and academic careers.

Successful leaders are still often stereotyped as having masculine traits (Chamorro-Premuzic 2019; Kawakami et al. 2000; Prime, Carter, and Welbourne 2009; see Koenig et al. 2011 for a discussion of how these stereotypes may be changing and may be less accurate with respect to specific domains like education). Consequently, it is not surprising that a greater proportion of men are promoted to leadership positions – a trend that is exacerbated at the top of the leadership hierarchy (Simpson et al. 2004). To illustrate, men occupy 68.5 percent of all senior managerial positions across Canada (Statistics Canada 2020) and 94 percent of all CEOs at American Standard & Poor's 500 Index companies (Catalyst 2020). This gender imbalance has persisted in spite of the fact that more women are now pursuing higher education than are men (Northouse 2016).

Mindy Baumgartner and David Schneider (2010), researchers in communication studies, contend that the underrepresentation of women in leadership positions is attributable to the glass-ceiling effect, which is defined as "a set of impediments and/or barriers to career advancement for women" (Jackson and O'Callaghan 2009, 460). For example, women leaders face added performance expectations and often have their legitimacy as leaders questioned (Ridgeway 2001). This effect is evident across the globe and well-documented in countries such as the US, Norway, and Germany (Baker and Cangemi 2016; Bertrand et al. 2018; Collischon 2018).

To adapt to masculine leadership models, some women may attempt to adopt more so-called masculine traits. Researchers have demonstrated that women who display more of these traits can achieve greater career success in the form of access to a wider range of professions and higher wages (Drydakis et al. 2017; Ellemers et al. 2012). Similarly, Russell Kent and Sherry Moss (1994), researchers in organizational studies, observed that individuals displaying masculine or androgynous traits were more likely to become leaders than those displaying traditional feminine traits. Given these findings, it seems feasible that some women, desirous of leadership positions, may preemptively behave in a masculine manner or even pursue education in a traditional masculine field to achieve this objective. One obvious choice to facilitate a leadership objective would be to obtain a degree in STEM or one of the hard disciplines.

Myriad researchers articulate how women who enter STEM fields and other hard disciplines may experience increased levels of discrimination when compared to men in these same fields (see, e.g., Carli et al. 2016; Daldrup-Link 2017; Michelmore and Sassler 2016; Piatek-Jimenez, Cribbs, and Gill 2018). In addition, there are glass-ceiling effects, which prevent women from achieving top-ranking leadership positions (Baumgartner and Schneider 2010; Daldrup-Link 2017). Thus, a paradox is evident: women, desirous of leadership opportunities, may gravitate toward disciplines and institutions they believe will serve as conduits to becoming leaders; however, in actuality, these disciplines and institutions actively disfavour women and, thus, squelch their ability to rise to the top. It is unclear, at present, if these women's experiences differ from women in fields perceived stereotypically as "soft." While both groups of women are disadvantaged in attaining leadership positions, it is possible that fewer disadvantages are accrued by women working in hard disciplines compared to soft disciplines. A recent series of studies in the US suggest this is indeed the case (i.e., women who hold an educational background in one of the traditional STEM fields or business are more likely to become leaders than are women who hold other educational backgrounds) (see Stevenson and Orr 2017; Welch 2020). Similarly, and of direct relevance to this chapter, McCullough (2019) found that, within a US context, holding a STEM-based education helped women academics get promoted to senior administrative positions.

Unfortunately, to date, no researchers have examined the disciplinary backgrounds of women in senior administrative positions within Canadian postsecondary institutions. While Canada and the United States are similar in many ways, several notable differences with respect to postsecondary education exist between the two countries. For example, at Canadian institutions, tuition fees are markedly lower, especially for domestic students, and unlike at many of the prestigious colleges and universities in the US, acceptance rates tend to be higher, meaning that postsecondary education may be more accessible to a wider range of prospective students in Canada than in the United States (Hoffmann 2019). Our study examines whether a STEM discipline bias exists in Canadian research-intensive (U15) institutions regarding the attainment of women in senior administration by addressing several gaps in the literature on women and leadership in academia. First, most of the research on women leaders' background and experiences in educational institutions is situated in the United States (see, e.g., McCullough 2019). Second, few researchers have paid attention to the academic disciplines of women leaders in postsecondary institutions. Indeed, to our knowledge, this is one of the first studies to examine biases toward certain academic disciplines (i.e., STEM and other hard disciplines) among women leaders in universities, and the first study to do so within a Canadian context.

Based on the literature, we postulate that (1) a majority of women academic administrators will belong to hard rather than soft academic disciplines and (2) this discrepancy will be most pronounced at the highest rungs of the leadership hierarchy.

METHOD

We investigated the disciplinary background of 586 women holding academic administrative positions, including associate dean ($n = 184$; 31.2 percent), assistant dean ($n = 92$; 15.6 percent), vice-dean ($n = 84$; 14.2 percent), and dean ($n = 72$; 12.2 percent). As bios and photographs appeared inconsistently across the university websites we reviewed, no additional demographic details (e.g., age and ethnicity) were derived.

In 2018–19, we conducted a quantitative content analysis of the U15 institutions' websites. Quantitative content analysis is a systematic research technique to code manifest content (i.e., materials that are present and directly identifiable) and is a useful tool for researchers to study gender prevalence (Neuendorf 2011). We performed an extensive search on the governance and faculty webpages of the U15 institutions and created a database with the relevant information of academic leaders in senior administrative positions.

For each university included in our sample, we extracted the following information about every individual occupying a senior leadership position: name, position, gender (only women were included in the final sample), gender pronouns (where listed), and academic discipline. Of the U15 universities, twelve are English-based and three are French-based. We removed idiosyncratic positions (e.g., warden) because they did not appear consistently across all U15 institutions. Additionally, to get a more granular picture of gender representation in senior administration, we did not record information on whether individuals in certain positions were interim or acting because this added noise. Figure 8.1 outlines the hierarchy of the senior administrative academic positions that we analyzed in this study.

FIGURE 8.1
Academic hierarchy of senior leadership positions in U15 institutions

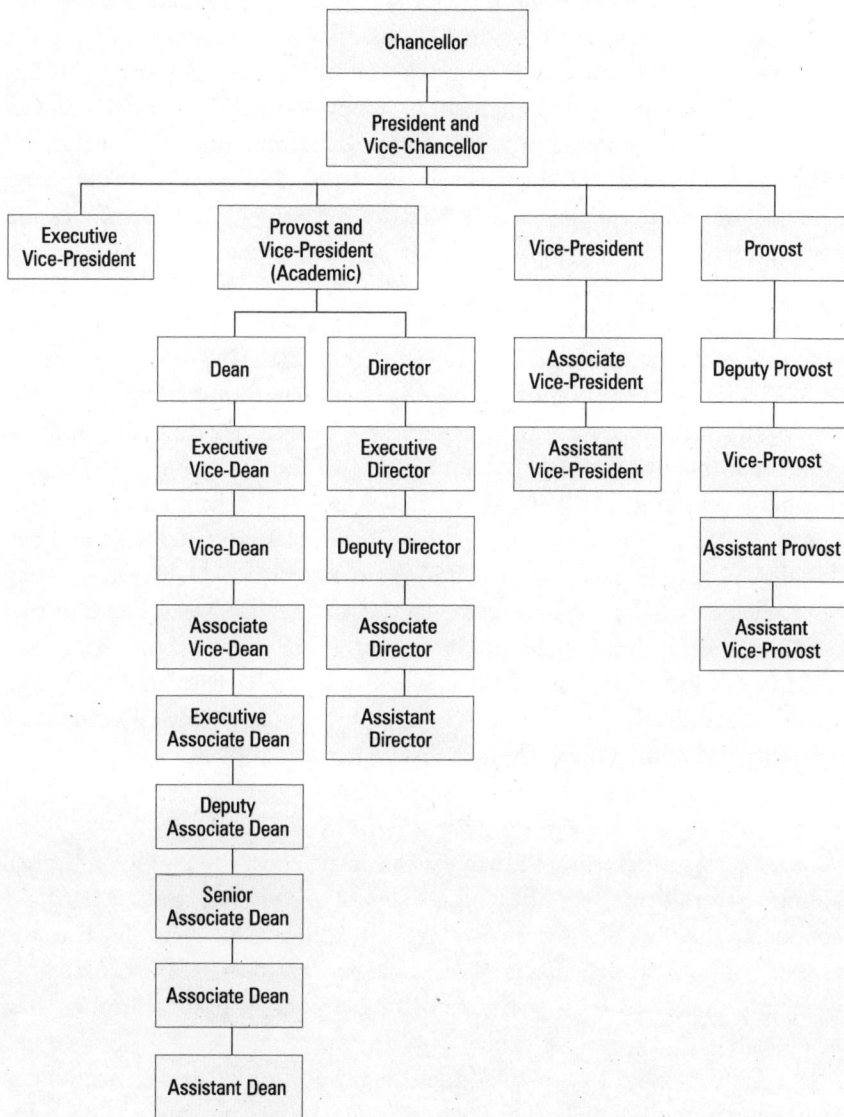

We should note that the directors and associate/assistant directors led the smaller faculties or departments that did not have deans. We also coded the academic positions in French-based universities (e.g., rectors and vice-rectors) to be consistent with definitions used by English-language institutions. For example, at the University of Laval, we coded the rector as a chancellor because the rector is at the top of the academic hierarchy.

We then coded every discipline on the spreadsheet using academic categories derived from the 2016 Canadian Census (Statistics Canada 2016). These categories are: (1) Science and Science Technology; (2) Engineering and Engineering Technology; (3) Mathematics, Computer and Information Sciences; (4) Business and Administration; (5) Arts and Humanities; (6) Social and Behavioural Sciences; (7) Legal Professions and Studies; (8) Health Care; (9) Education and Teaching; and (10) Trades, Services, Natural Resources and Conservation. These disciplines were further categorized as either hard (1, 2, 3, 4, and 8) or soft disciplines (5, 6, 7, 9, and 10; see Zollman 2011, 2012). While we wish to acknowledge how there is some degree of subjectivity with regard to which disciplines are hard or soft, we generally classified disciplines on the basis of traditional associations. It is worth noting, for example, that "Trades, Services, Natural Resources and Conservation" was categorized as a soft discipline on account of its catchall nature. Next, we coded every tenth academic discipline on the spreadsheet, using the categories determined by Statistics Canada (2016). Inter-rater reliability for all variables was calculated and was initially found to be relatively strong (Cohen's Kappa = .757). However, rating discrepancies between the coders emerged because certain backgrounds proved particularly difficult to classify (e.g., the third author coded "Aboriginal Rights and Dispute Resolution" as "Social and Behavioural Sciences," but the fourth author coded this background as "Legal Professions and Studies"). All rating discrepancies were resolved through discussion and mutual consent.

RESULTS

We used R statistics software to analyze the data. To test whether more women administrators come from disciplines stereotypically regarded as hard, we conducted a series of binomial tests. We also used a Mann-Whitney U test to ascertain if women administrators who hold backgrounds in STEM disciplines were more likely to hold positions of higher rank (e.g., dean rather than vice-dean).

Our first binomial test revealed that the proportion of women with backgrounds in hard disciplines ($n = 320$; see Table 8.2 for a summary of how many women at each academic tier come from hard and soft disciplines) was 54.6 percent, which is greater than half (i.e., 50 percent) the total number of women who held senior administrative positions ($n = 586$, $p = .014$). Our second binomial test investigated whether the number of women administrators with backgrounds in hard disciplines differed from the proportion of women with degrees in those same fields. According to the National Centre for Education

Statistics (2019; NCES), as of 2017, 42.4 percent of women majored in traditional STEM subjects, business, and health studies. Thus, we performed a binomial test to gauge whether the proportion of women with backgrounds in the STEM disciplines occupying senior administrative posts exceeded 42.4 percent. The test was statistically significant ($p < .001$), suggesting that women from STEM disciplines are overrepresented in administrative positions relative to the proportion of women actually obtaining degrees in these fields. In addition, to determine whether administrators were more likely to come from the hard disciplines in general, we performed a binomial test to see if the number of hard administrators ($n = 782$) was greater than half the number of total administrators ($n = 1,297$). Our results indicated that this was indeed the case ($p < .001$).

Finally, we converted different academic posts into an ordinal variable, with more senior positions assigned a higher rank (chancellor = 1, president and vice-chancellor = 2, etc.). We then conducted a Mann-Whitney U test to investigate if women with backgrounds in hard disciplines were disproportionately

TABLE 8.1
Number of women who come from hard and soft disciplines sorted by academic position

Academic Position	Number of women/men from hard discipline	Number of women/men from soft discipline	Total number of women/men
Chancellor	3 / 3	5 / 4	8 / 7
President and vice-chancellor	1 / 7	0 / 7	1 / 14
Provost and vice-president	18 / 31	18 / 9	36 / 40
Deputy vice-president and deputy provost	2 / 4	3 / 4	5 / 8
Vice-provost	12 / 14	13 / 13	25 / 27
Associate vice-president and associate provost	17 / 40	21 / 17	38 / 57
Assistant vice-president and assistant vice-provost	7 / 5	10 / 2	17 / 7
Dean and director	49 / 81	34 / 65	83 / 146
Executive director and executive vice-dean	3 / 4	0 / 2	3 / 6
Vice-dean	49 / 70	35 / 38	84 / 108
Associate director and associate vice-dean	4 / 2	1 / 3	5 / 5
Assistant director and executive associate dean	2 / 0	0 / 0	2 / 0
Deputy associate dean	1 / 7	0 / 1	1 / 8
Senior associate dean	2 / 7	3 / 1	5 / 8
Associate dean	98 / 150	86 / 73	184 / 223
Assistant dean	52 / 37	37 / 10	89 / 47

represented at the top of the administrative hierarchy. As the test was not statistically significant ($U = 44888, p = .244$), it appears that women from traditional STEM disciplines are evenly dispersed throughout this hierarchy.

DISCUSSION AND CONCLUSION

In the current study, we examined whether women in senior administrative positions in the U15 research-intensive universities in Canada were disproportionately likely to come from STEM and other hard disciplines; our finding revealed this to be the case. With this being said, it should be noted that the total proportion of administrators coming from the hard disciplines was greater than half. This might, in turn, explain why women academic administrators are more likely to come from hard disciplines. As well, the proportion of women administrators coming from hard disciplines exceeded the proportion of women obtaining degrees in those same fields. While there is no conclusive evidence with respect to why women from hard disciplines are overrepresented, one potential explanation regards beliefs surrounding the fundamental difference between hard and soft academic programs. Specifically, it may be that those women who excel in traditionally hard program streams are more likely to be noticed and are, accordingly, seen as prime candidates for academic administrative positions. In other words, because the hard disciplines tend to have fewer women students, it is easier to stand out in these programs. Contrary to our prediction, however, women from the hard disciplines were no more likely to be at the top of the administrative hierarchy when compared to women with backgrounds in the soft disciplines.

Our study is novel because it is the first one to examine this trend within the context of Canadian U15 institutions. Moreover, our findings underscore that certain disciplines (typically, those dominated by men) are accorded more value than other disciplines. Indeed, universities typically cut programs in the arts and humanities rather than in STEM (see, e.g., Johnson 2019) because the latter are often regarded as "core" components of university training. The implied message is clear: soft disciplines are extraneous; hard disciplines are essential.

Our findings also link with research on stereotypic beliefs about leaders. Because leaders are stereotyped as masculine (Chamorro-Premuzic 2019) and masculine people are viewed as more agentic (among other positive attributes; Carli et al. 2016; Eagly and Karau 2002; Farrell and McHugh 2017), women coming from hard (i.e., more masculine) disciplines may be allowed to progress through the academic hierarchy less encumbered than their soft counterparts. We find it disheartening that this bias exists within university settings – a milieu that prides itself on diversity and inclusion.

Limitations and Future Directions

Several limitations warrant mention. First, we did not conduct an in-depth analysis of the experiences of women occupying leadership positions in universities. The presumption that individuals occupying the same stratum within the academic hierarchy have similar experiences may be faulty. It is possible, for example, that a "soft" woman leader may be perceived as more maternal and less threatening than her "hard" counterpart. Indeed, the soft disciplines are considered feminine, and femininity is associated with being nurturing, sensitive, and emotional (Sussman and Yssaad 2005). Accordingly, Victoria Brescoll (2016), an expert in organizational behaviour, noted that gender stereotypes associated with emotion might create obstacles that women leaders have to navigate to be successful. Women leaders, for example, may be reprimanded for minor or moderate displays of emotion; yet, paradoxically, being emotionally inexpressive may result in penalties because unemotional women are seen as failing to fulfill their warm, communal role as women.

Another limitation is that designating a discipline as hard or soft operates from the assumption that disciplines are homogeneous (see, e.g., Zollman 2011, 2012). For example, social and behavioural sciences was coded as soft. However, taking the discipline of psychology as an example, some subfields are clearly perceived as more scientific (i.e., harder) than other subfields (e.g., neuroscience versus child development). These differences are issues to consider. In line with this observation, it has been noted that several humanities and social science disciplines such as psychology and anthropology employ quantitative data and hard methodologies (Seising and Sanz 2012). Likewise, hard disciplines often utilize qualitative methodologies, which are typically considered to be soft (Miller 2010). To address this limitation, researchers should attempt to recategorize certain disciplines so they are more in keeping with the skillset they actually entail (for example, neuroscience should be considered among the hard disciplines).

Finally, we did not examine other sites of marginalization such as ethnicity and race and the interplay between these intersectional identities and gender. In this regard, a theoretical framework based on intersectionality allows researchers to adopt "a critical analytic lens to interrogate racial, ethnic, class, ability, age, sexuality, and gender disparities and to contest existing ways of looking at these structures of inequality" (Crenshaw 1989; Thornton-Dill and Zambrana 2009, 1). Racialized and Indigenous women are underrepresented in senior administrative roles at Canadian postsecondary institutions (Campbell 2020). Unfortunately, we could not conduct an intersectional analysis because many of the individual academic profile pages we reviewed did not contain information about an academic's race or identity. Given our reliance on university webpages, we also were unable to gather data on sociodemographic variables such as age and sexual orientation.

Given that more than half of women who hold senior-level administrative positions in U15 universities come from STEM-related fields, it appears that the skills and training in STEM disciplines are viewed as more amenable to leadership than are the abilities developed in softer disciplines. In conclusion, researchers should delve more deeply into the attitudes surrounding hard versus soft disciplines vis-à-vis leadership in academia. Discounting a large swath of women because their academic background and training presumably render them less suitable to senior administrative posts is reactionary, hinders innovation, and is, ultimately, counterproductive.

NOTE

1 Quotation marks are used around the words "hard" and "soft" on first mention because, at their core, these terms are subjective and value-laden (for an example of the debate over what should be classified as STEM, see Zollman 2011, 2012).

WORKS CITED

Baker, John, and Joseph Cangemi. 2016. "Why Are There So Few Women CEOs and Senior Leaders in Corporate America?" *Organization Development Journal* 34 (2): 31–43.

Baumgartner, Mindy, and David Schneider. 2010. "Perceptions of Women in Management: A Thematic Analysis of Razing the Glass Ceiling." *Journal of Career Development* 37 (2): 559–76. https://doi.org/10.1177/089485309352242.

Bertrand, Marianne, Sandra Black, Sissel Jensen, and Adriana Lleras-Muney. 2018. "Breaking the Glass Ceiling? The Effect of Board Quotas on Female Labour Market Outcomes in Norway." *The Review of Economic Studies* 86 (1): 191–239. https://doi.org/10.1093/restud/rdy032.

Brescoll, Victoria. 2016. "Leading with Their Hearts? How Gender Stereotypes of Emotion Lead to Biased Evaluations of Female Leaders." *The Leadership Quarterly* 27 (3): 415–28. https://doi.org/10.1016/j.leaqua.2016.02.005.

Campbell, Kofi. 2020. "Why Don't Canadian Universities Hire More Racialized and Indigenous Senior Administrators?" *University Affairs*, May 8, 2020. https://www.universityaffairs.ca/opinion/.

Carli, Linda, Laila Alawa, YoonAh Lee, Bei Zhao, and Elaine Kim. 2016. "Stereotypes about Gender and Science: Women ≠ Scientists." *Psychology of Women Quarterly* 40 (2): 244–60. https://doi.org/10.1177/0361684315622645.

Catalyst. 2020. *List: Women CEOs of the S&P 500*. New York: Catalyst.

Chamorro-Premuzic, Tomas. 2019. *Why Do So Many Incompetent Men Become Leaders? (And How to Fix It)*. Boston: Harvard Business Review Press.

Cheryan, Sapna, Sianna Ziegler, Amanda Montoya, and Lily Jiang. 2016. "Why Are Some STEM Fields More Gender Balanced than Others?" *Psychological Bulletin* 143 (1): 1–35. https://doi.org/10.1037/bu10000052.

Collischon, Matthias. 2018. "Is There a Glass Ceiling over Germany?" *German Economic Review* 20 (4): e329–59. https://doi.org/10.1111/geer.12168.

Crenshaw, Kimberle. 1989. "Demarginalizing the Intersection of Race and Sex: A Black Feminist Critique of Antidiscrimination Doctrine, Feminist Theory and Antiracist Politics." *University of Chicago Legal Forum*, 139–67.

Daldrup-Link, Heike. 2017. "The Fermi Paradox in STEM – Where Are the Women Leaders?" *Molecular Imaging and Biology* 19 (6): 807–9. https://doi.org/10.1007/s11307 -017-1124-4.

Drydakis, Nick, Katerina Sidiropoulou, Vasiliki Bozani, Sandra Selmanovic, and Swetketu Patnaik. 2017. "Masculine vs Feminine Personality Traits and Women's Employment Outcomes in Britain." *International Journal of Manpower* 39 (4): 621–30. https://doi.org/10.1108/IJM-09-2017-0255.

Eagly, Alice, and Steven Karau. 2002. "Role Congruity Theory of Prejudice toward Female Leaders." *Psychological Review* 109 (3): 573–98. https://doi.org/10.1037//0033-295X. 109.3.573.

Ellemers, Noomi, Floor Rink, Belle Derks, and Michelle Ryan. 2012. "Women in High Places: When and Why Promoting Women into Top Positions Can Harm Them Individually or as a Group (and How to Prevent This)." *Research in Organizational Behavior* 32:163–87. http://dx.doi.org/10.1016/j.riob.2012.10.003.

Farrell, Lynn, and Louise McHugh. 2017. "Examining Gender-STEM Bias among STEM and Non-STEM Students using the Implicit Relational Assessment Procedure (IRAP)." *Journal of Contextual Behavioral Science* 6 (1): 80–90. https://doi.org/10. 1016/j.jcbs.2017.02.001.

Heilbronner, Nancy. 2013. "The STEM Pathway for Women: What Has Changed?" *Gifted Child Quarterly* 57 (1): 39–55. https://doi.org/10.1177/0016986212460085.

Hoffmann, William. 2019. *Are Canadian Universities a Better Choice than U.S. Schools for International Students.* Value Champion, November 15, 2019. https://www.value champion.sg/.

Jackson, Jerlando, and Elizabeth O'Callaghan. 2009. "What Do We Know about Glass Ceiling Effects? A Taxonomy and Critical Review to Inform Higher Education Research." *Research in Higher Education* 50 (5): 460–82. doi:10.1007/s11162-009-9128-9.

Johnson, Steven. 2019. "Colleges Lose a 'Stunning' 651 Foreign Language Programs in 3 Years." *Chronicle*, January 22, 2019. https://www.chronicle.com/.

Kawakami, Christine, Judith White, and Ellen Langer. 2000. "Mindful and Masculine: Freeing Women Leaders from the Constraints of Gender Roles." *Journal of Social Issues* 56 (1): 49–63. https://doi.org/10.1111/0022-4537.00151.

Kent, Russell, and Sherry Moss. 1994. "Effects of Sex and Gender Role on Leader Emergence." *The Academy of Management Journal* 37 (5): 1335–46.

Koenig, Anne, Alice Eagly, Abigail Mitchell, and Tiina Ristikari. 2011. "Are Leader Stereotypes Masculine? A Meta-Analysis of Three Research Paradigms." *Psychological Bulletin* 137 (4): 616–42. https://doi.org/10.1037/a0023557.

McCullough, Laura. 2019. "Proportions of Women in STEM Leadership in the Academy in the USA." *Education Sciences* 10 (1): 1–13. https://doi.org/10.3390/edusci10010001.

Michelmore, Katherine, and Sharon Sassler. 2016. "Explaining the Gender Wage Gap in STEM: Does Field Sex Composition Matter?" *RSF: The Russell Sage Foundation Journal of the Social Sciences* 2 (4): 194–215. https://doi.org/10.7758/rsf.2016.2.4.07.

Miller, Wendy. 2010. "Qualitative Research Findings as Evidence: Utility in Nursing Practice." *Clinical Nurse Specialist* 24 (4): 191–93. doi:10.1097/NUR.0b013e3181e36087.

National Center for Education Statistics. 2019. *Number of Persons 25 to 34 Years Old and Percentage with a Bachelor's or Higher Degree, by Undergraduate Field of Study, Sex, Race/Ethnicity, and U.S. Nativity and Citizenship Status: 2017*. U.S. Department of Education. https://nces.ed.gov/.

National Science Foundation. 2013. *Women, Minorities, and Persons with Disabilities in Science and Engineering: 2013*. US National Center for Science and Engineering Statistics, Directorate for Social, Behavioral and Economic Statistics. http://www.nsf.gov/.

–. 2014. *Earned Bachelor's Degrees, by Sex and Field: 2000–11*. https://www.nsf.gov/.

Neuendorf, Kimberly. 2011. "Content Analysis – A Methodological Primer for Gender Research." *Sex Roles* 64:276–89. https://doi.org/10.1007/s11199-010-9893-0.

Northouse, Peter. 2016. *Leadership: Theory and Practices*. Thousand Oaks, CA: Sage.

O'Brien, Laurie, Alison Blodorn, Glenn Adams, Donna Garcia, and Elliott Hammer. 2015. "Ethnic Variation in Gender-STEM Stereotypes and STEM Participation: An Intersectional Approach." *Cultural Diversity and Ethnic Minority Psychology* 21 (2): 169–80. http://dx.doi.org/10.1037/a0037944.

Piatek-Jimenez, Katrina, Jennifer Cribbs, and Nicole Gill. 2018. "College Students' Perceptions of Gender Stereotypes: Making Connections to the Underrepresentation of Women in STEM Fields." *International Journal of Science Education* 40 (12): 1432–54. https://doi.org/10.1080/09500693.3018.1482027.

Prime, Jeanine, Nancy Carter, and Theresa Welbourne. 2009. "Women 'Take Care,' Men 'Take Charge': Managers' Stereotypic Perceptions of Women and Men Leaders." *The Psychologist-Manager Journal* 12 (1): 25–49. https://doi.org/10.1080/108871 50802371799.

Ridgeway, Cecilia. 2001. "Gender, Status, and Leadership." *Journal of Social Issues* 57 (4): 637–55. https://doi.org/10.1111/0022-4537.00233.

Seising, Rudolf, and Veronica Sanz. 2012. "From Hard Science and Computing to Soft Science and Computing – An Introductory Survey." In *Soft Computing in Humanities and Social Sciences*, edited by Rudolf Seising and Veronica Gonzalez, 3–36. Berlin: Springer.

Simpson, Ruth, Jane Sturges, Adrian Woods, and Yochanan Altman. 2004. "Career Progress and Career Barriers: Women MBA Graduates in Canada and the UK." *Career Development International* 9 (5): 459–77. https://doi.org/10.1108/13620430410550736.

Statistics Canada. 2016. *Education Highlight Tables, 2016 Census: Major Field of Study Primary Groupings for Selected Age Groups 25 to 64, Both Sexes and Selected Highest Levels of Educational Attainment (Total – Highest Postsecondary Certificate, Diploma or Degree), Percent Distribution 2016, Canada, Provinces and Territories, 2016 Census – 25 Percent Sample Data*. https://www12.statcan.gc.ca/.

–. 2020. *Proportion of Women and Men Employed in Management, Annual.* https://www150.statcan.gc.ca/.

Stevenson, Jane, and Evelyn Orr. 2017. "We Interviewed 57 Female CEOs to Find Out How More Women Can Get to the Top." *Harvard Business Review,* November 2017.

Sussman, Deborah, and Lahouarua Yssaad. 2005. "The Rising Profile of Women Academics." *Perspectives: Statistics Canada* 6 (2): 6–19. https://www150.statcan.gc.ca/.

Thornton-Dill, Bonnie, and Ruth Zambrana. 2009. "Critical Thinking about Inequality: An Emerging Lens." In *Emerging Intersections: Race, Class, and Gender in Theory, Policy, and Practice,* edited by Bonnie Thornton-Dil and Ruth Zambrana, 1–21. New Brunswick, NJ: Rutgers University.

Welch, James. 2020. "Success beyond STEM: An Analysis of Educational Backgrounds of the Fortune 50 CEOs." *Higher Education, Skills and Work-Based Learning,* August 18, 2020. https://doi.org/10.1108/HESWBL-02-2020-0018.

Zollman, Alan. 2011. "Is STEM Misspelled?" *School Science and Mathematics* 111 (5) (May).

–. 2012. "Learning for STEM Literacy: STEM Literacy for Learning." *School Science and Mathematics* 112 (1): 12–19. https://doi.org/10.1111/j.1949-8594.1012.00101.x.

9

Women Faculty and Contrapower Harassment in the Canadian Academy

JENNIFER CHISHOLM, KASEY EGAN, and KRISTIN BURNETT

Gender remains a salient factor influencing women's participation, advancement, and overall satisfaction in their academic careers. While many universities have identified the recruitment and retention of women faculty as a priority, corresponding attention has not been paid to the ways these directives are operationalized within university spaces (CAUT 2018). Working conditions for many women in academe remain challenging and institutions have failed to effectively address the range and breadth of gender-based violence and harassment faced by women. In this chapter, we discuss the findings from a survey of women faculty at Canadian universities about their experiences with contrapower harassment (CPH). CPH occurs when a victim holds more formal institutional power than the perpetrator, for example, between a faculty member and a student (Benson 1984). In these instances, expectations regarding the direction in which power normally flows are inverted by the operation of patriarchy and gender. CPH can include intimidation, hostility, bullying, aggression, retaliation, sexual harassment, or physical violence (Lampman et al. 2009). The extent and persistence of CPH at postsecondary institutions ensures conditions of employment that allow, and encourage, a gender gap, particularly in relation to important career indicators such as job satisfaction, pay, promotion, and tenure. While more research is needed to make definitive links between CPH and faculty attrition, our findings suggest that women faculty undertook additional labour to manage the personal and professional impacts of CPH. Survey respondents described how the emotional work involved in coping with experiences of CPH functioned alongside institutional inaction, dismissal, or further harassment and bullying from colleagues or administrators. Participants indicated developing a range of coping or survival strategies that, in some cases, involved normalizing or downplaying the impacts of CPH on their personal and professional lives. We suggest that CPH is normalized at the institutional level and reflects social and cultural beliefs about gender and gender-based violence.

The data for this study were collected through an online survey directed at women teaching at Canadian postsecondary institutions. Of those surveyed, 90 percent indicated that they had experienced *more than one* instance of CPH. More than half of participants questioned whether their accounts met the basic standard of harassment, and the majority described these experiences as something women had to learn to live with to work in postsecondary institutions. These troubling responses point to the need to understand CPH as part of a continuum of gender-based violence that affects women in academia (Kelly 1987; Osborne 1995). Understanding CPH as part of a continuum of violence allows us to adopt a sexual and gender-based violence (SGBV) lens to analyze its impact. In particular, an SGBV analysis acknowledges the persistence of gender-based hierarchies and the relationship between subtle and overt forms of violence.

A useful example of applying an SGBV lens to a social problem can be found in the concept of rape culture. Scholars have argued there are clear connections between objectification, sexualization, domination, and sexual violence and refer to this practice as "rape culture" (Lorber 2012; Fraser 2015; Boyle 2019; McCabe 2020). Rape culture stems from patriarchal ideals of gender, sex roles and responsibility, and morality (Maxwell and Scott 2014; Suarez and Gadalla 2010; Lorber 2012; Burt 1980). High rates of victimization, low rates of reporting, and the persistence of victim blaming are all indicators of rape culture. Acknowledging this link shifts focus from the individual action (i.e., rape or sexual violence) to the culture that excuses, condones, and normalizes gender-based violence. This is not to say that an individual is not responsible for the harm they cause, but rather it acknowledges the social and cultural conditions that allow violence to take place. A focus on culture, rather than individual action, allows us to recognize the ways we all participate in the normalization of violence, in often subtle or unconscious ways, regardless of our gender. In other words, violence need not be enacted by men (only) against women (only) to be recognized as contributing to rape culture. Rather, rape culture relies on the maintenance and legitimization of existing power relations to enable harassment and violence. Thus, ending SGBV becomes a communal task that involves dismantling gender-based hierarchies and addressing systemic and institutional violence in concert with individual acts of aggression. Excusing and normalizing the continuum of gender-based violence and victim blaming constitute some of the markers of rape culture (Burt 1980). These markers were reflected in survey responses such that internalized excusal, normalization, and self-blame (victim blame) emerged as significant themes. Respondents described their experiences with CPH using words like stalk, threaten, yell, scream, bully, and sexually harass. However, they also frequently suggested that their experiences were "not that bad," were "just a normal part of the job," or did not meet the threshold of "real violence or harassment." We suggest that this normalization is consistent with, and indicative of, the pervasiveness of gender-based violence in Canadian postsecondary institutions and Canadian society more broadly. Thus, it is important we understand CPH as systemic and institutional rather than isolated or individualized.

CONTRAPOWER HARASSMENT
AND THE CONTINUUM OF VIOLENCE

To date, most research on contrapower harassment in higher education has reflected the US context. Studies by Rospenda, Richman, and Nawyn (1998), Juliano (2006), DeSouza (2011), DeSouza and Fansler (2003), and Lampman (2012) each identify CPH as in direct contradiction to Title IX, which bans sex-based discrimination in education. A 2012 study involving faculty at a number of US institutions reported that 91 percent of respondents had experienced at least one act of student harassment or bullying (Lampman 2012). Women, BIPOC, and junior faculty reported more instances than men and those with more seniority or tenure. These findings echoed previous studies, which cast CPH as a pervasive and systemic issue in postsecondary education (McKinney 1990, 1992; Rospenda, Richman, and Nawyn 1998; Juliano 2007; DeSouza 2011). A follow-up study by Claudia Lampman et al. in 2016 found that women faculty reported greater negative outcomes related to CPH including stress-related anxiety and job loss. Lampman and colleagues (2009, 334) expand their description of CPH to include bullying, disrespectful or rude behaviour, hostility, threats, sexual comments, and innuendo. Behaviours constitutive of CPH also involve online harassment and "zoombombing," a practice that entails disrupting online course sessions with harassing comments; pornographic drawings and images; or racist, sexist, and homophobic slurs. Such harassment is particularly concerning given the rapid move to online instruction following the COVID-19 global pandemic of 2020.

According to Rachel Osborne (1995, 637), university spaces are frequently "violent and dangerous" for women. Postsecondary institutions have been found to have high rates of SGBV and deeply ineffectual methods of addressing its impacts (CFSO 2015). Sociologist Liz Kelly (as cited in Osborne 1995, 638) argues that understanding SGBV as occurring along a continuum "enables a linking of the more common, everyday abuses women experience, such as leering, cat calls, and verbal assaults, with less common abuses such as rape and sexual assault." For both scholars, the link between these subtle and overt sexist behaviours is the desire for power and control. Osborne (1995, 638) suggests that within postsecondary institutions, men's privilege operates through "various forms of institutionalized violence" and that "when women refuse or resist their 'proper place' in the patriarchal, competitive, hierarchical structure of universities, they are met with a backlash." A woman's mere presence within the university can be taken as evidence of resistance to her "proper place" in the gendered social order – even when she is not explicitly challenging male dominance and privilege.

In their groundbreaking 1989 report, Constance Backhouse, Roma Harris, Gillian Michell, and Alison Wylie (99) observed that, in addition to SGBV, women faculty experience exclusion and isolation in a range of ways that "communicate a lack of confidence in women, a lack of recognition, or a devaluation of their capabilities and successes." Nicknamed the Chilly Collective, Backhouse et al. investigated the hostile environment (or "chilly climate") for women at Western University. The authors suggested that the beliefs, behaviours, and practices that produced the chilly climate for women were often informal and unconscious, such that they operate below the level of awareness. These beliefs, behaviours, and practices, whether intentional or not, communicated a "clear understanding that those who deviate from the norm, who depart from the characteristics of White, able-bodied, heterosexual, middle-class, gentile men, are still outsiders" (99). Positioning women as outsiders in the university left them more vulnerable to CPH and institutional inaction.

The Chilly Collective (Backhouse et al. 1989, 99–100) argued that because of the informal and often unconscious nature of the chilly climate, its "practices are particularly pernicious. Their effect is, predictably, that women's self-esteem is undermined, and their authority and credibility subverted in ways which ensure that they will not have an opportunity to realize their potential." Beliefs about gender roles and women's place in the public sphere, therefore, continue to limit their educational and professional attainments. This has also been described, by educational scholar Judith Bessant (1998), as "opaque violence." Bessant (1998, 50) suggests that opaque violence is "discriminatory in that it typically 'targets' women and it's firmly rooted in well-established practices ... it includes harassment, surveillance, bullying, interrogation, persecution, victimization, intimidation, and subjugation." The intent of such practices, whether conscious or unconscious, is to undermine, isolate, and alienate women faculty. It is important to note that anyone can participate in these practices, regardless of gender.

The underlying impacts of a chilly climate and opaque violence are compounded by the pervasiveness of sexual violence on university campuses. The ways that SGBV is tolerated, excused, and normalized in society is an example of rape culture. Rape culture is enacted in very specific ways at universities due to the complex nature of the social and professional hierarchies that exist within such institutions. When we understand SGBV as a continuum of violence, we connect the subtle or opaque violence underlying the hostility, bullying, and aggression enacted by perpetrators of CPH to more overt forms of violence such as sexual assault. In other words, the act need not be rape, or sexual assault, to be part of rape culture. It is important to note here that we are not drawing equivalencies between hostility, bullying, and harassment, and rape or sexual violence. Rather, our analysis suggests that each form of violence is interconnected and related to the other through underlying beliefs, assumptions, and dominant ideologies of gender and power that normalize and legitimize such behaviours as acceptable and "part of everyday life" for women.

The chilly climate is further compounded by the persistent and problematic concept of the "ideal victim." Within rape culture, the ideal victim is characterized as a well-behaved white woman who is attacked by a dangerous stranger in a public but deserted place is forcefully penetrated while resisting, and receives significant physical injuries due to the "heroic" nature of her resistance (Randall 2010; Delacollette et al. 2013). Within CPH, the narrative of the "ideal victim" calls into question the "legitimacy" of all harassment and violence that does not conform to that narrative. Our research indicates that this kind of questioning happens at both the individual and institutional levels, demonstrating the deeply complex ways problematic beliefs about SGBV and victimhood are embedded into our collective thinking. When an idealized threshold of violence is not met, victims internalize their experiences as "not that bad." The unrealistic and significant standards of victimization that must be met to constitute "real violence" are well-documented (Barnett, Maticka-Tyndale, and Kenya 2016; Maxwell and Scott 2014; Stoll, Lilley, and Pinter 2017; Suarez and Gadalla 2010). We contend that these standards are upheld by both individuals and institutions in ways that support the continuation of CPH in academe. Herein lies the necessity of utilizing an SGBV lens to understand the effects of CPH on women faculty at Canadian postsecondary institutions. Below we review the methods and results of our study, before discussing the findings in more detail.

SURVEYING WOMEN FACULTY ON CPH

The data for this study was collected through an online survey directed at women who teach or have taught at Canadian postsecondary institutions. The survey included both quantitative and open-ended qualitative questions about women's experiences with CPH as it broadly related to their teaching responsibilities. The only inclusion criteria were that respondents self-identify as women and that they were currently, or had previously, taught at a Canadian postsecondary institution. Participants were recruited through online listservs, on social media, and through social networks and word of mouth. We received forty-two responses from a wide range of disciplines, including social sciences and humanities, STEM, law, and health sciences. To protect participant anonymity, and encourage disclosure, we did not ask respondents to identify their current institution or location. Other demographic information was collected, including position, rank, length of time employed, age, and personal identifiers (such as gender and race). Participants were provided with a definition of contrapower harassment that specifically identified hostility, contempt, bullying, aggression, retaliation, sexual harassment, and violence as examples of behaviour constitutive of CPH. Additionally, participants were asked to indicate the number of times they had experienced CPH throughout their career. Qualitative questions asked respondents to describe experiences of CPH, how they dealt with these experiences, what supports were available, and whether they felt believed and supported by colleagues, superiors, and the institution more broadly. Respondents were asked if they had any experiences that would fit the definition of CPH, regardless of whether they recognized it as harassment in the moment or had reported the incident to anyone.

FINDINGS

All participants reported experiencing at least one incident of CPH in their role as instructor. Eighty-three percent of respondents indicated experiencing more than one incident of CPH, while 12.5 percent reported experiencing more than five instances of CPH during their career. More than half of the respondents (54 percent) were junior scholars, meaning the length of their employment was recorded as five years or less. The remaining 46 percent of respondents reported between six and twenty years of experience teaching at the postsecondary level. Eighty-three percent of respondents had completed doctoral degrees and 16 percent had a master's degree. The current academic rank of survey participants was split relatively evenly: 27 percent identified as sessional instructors or lecturers, 27 percent as assistant professors, 19 percent as associate professors, 19 percent as full professors, and the remaining 7 percent identified as graduate students. Forty-two percent of respondents were tenured, 23 percent were tenure-track, and the remaining 35 percent of respondents were employed in limited term, contract, or sessional positions.

"Part of the Job": Normalizing Contrapower Harassment

Overall, participants understood CPH to be a part of the job and inevitable. One participant stated succinctly what many others alluded to: "I guess I am just used to considering these instances as part of the job." Expecting to experience harassment as a condition of employment speaks to the underlying lack of safety women continue to experience in academe and society more broadly.

Downplaying the impacts of CPH, which occurs at both the institutional and personal level, serves to normalize gender-based violence and harassment. Signalling the extent to which CPH is normalized in academia, one respondent explained: "I am hesitant to call ongoing microaggressions and differential experiences harassment. Yes, they are ongoing and cause harm, based on my identity, but ought they reasonably be known to be unwelcome? I'm not convinced they pass the bar in our current society."

While the participant clearly identifies the "microaggressions" as causing ongoing harm, she hesitates to label them as harassment. In other words, the kinds of behaviours that fall under the umbrella of CPH are to be expected by women in the workplace; therefore, they do not necessarily register as harassment. Another respondent indicated that the situation she described "has me unsure as it doesn't seem as severe as sexual harassment." The term harassment seems to have been reserved for extreme and ill-defined behaviours that went beyond bullying, contempt, and aggression. Such a belief reflects the "ideal victim" narrative endemic of rape culture. Given the definition of CPH outlined at the beginning of this chapter, all of the behaviours identified by participants indeed constituted CPH.

The last question of the survey asked participants if they would be willing to participate in an interview about their experiences of CPH. Of those who declined, many cited the belief that their experiences did not reach the level of CPH or "weren't that bad" comparative to other women's experiences. Again, this kind of violence is normalized and placed on a hierarchy of severity that serves to silence those impacted. The conclusion here is that women faculty should expect to experience some degree of CPH as a condition of their employment.

However, in some of the reflections provided by participants, clear reference was made to experiences of overt violence. For example, one respondent detailed a campaign of harassment she endured at the hands of two students. She described:

> A year ago I had two student athletes stalk my office hours, threaten me, dismiss my feedback, and in their teaching evaluations, draw me naked and refer to me as having a low IQ and being a "Fat disgusting loser teacher." They would come to every office hour – together, report their marks to the dean and accuse me of being a "stupid teacher." They talked through my lectures, laughed at slides, and were all around abusive. It was the worst incident I've ever endured.

Clearly, this example describes a sustained pattern of overt sexual harassment. Minimizing and reducing the severity of this harassment is reflective of common institutional responses to SGBV (Ahmed 2019). Other respondents detailed similarly blatant experiences of sexual harassment by students:

I was sexually harassed during lecture this past year. A student made lewd sexual/ pornographic comments directed at me in response to an open question I posed using a polling app. The comments were visible to the class, projected on screen in real time [and] a white, male student in an Indigenous master's program added a sexually suggestive comment using my spirit name to his assignment.

These incidences of overt sexual harassment were described alongside countless examples of more subtle sexualization and innuendo. Most participants reported receiving comments about their appearance and clothing on student evaluations of teaching; being called by their first name or by "miss" instead of professor or doctor; or being addressed with degrading language such as "chick," "girl," or "bitch." Each of these examples serves to undermine women faculty and invalidate their education and expertise.

Women faculty members described being undermined in other ways as well. In particular, respondents suggested that they were frequently challenged and questioned by students, both in relation to their education and credentials as well as to their expertise and grasp of the material they were teaching. For instance, one participant shared:

In one example, a white male student (approximately my age or older) would ask questions in class about why I selected certain readings, assignments, etc. and on occasion came to class early and upload[ed] what he thought I should be teaching that day. It would be projected on the PowerPoint screen when I came to class, and he would explain to me why this is what should be taught. As a result, some students in the class would listen to his advice over mine on assignments etc. despite the fact that I was the one marking them.

The above example can be understood as a form of disrespectful behaviour or contempt on the part of the student toward his woman professor. His actions were meant to diminish her expertise and authority in the classroom and to assert his own. Participants cited many examples of contempt, or attempts to undermine, including eye rolling, demands for grade changes, and directly questioning competency and expertise.

Retaliation: Individual and Institutional Responses to Contrapower Harassment

Respondents indicated that their fear of, and experiences with, retaliation influenced how they handled CPH and remained the central factor for not coming forward or reporting their experiences. Women rarely report their experiences of violence, within both universities and society more broadly, with current statistics demonstrating that as little as 5 percent of sexual assaults having been reported to the police (Rotenberg 2017; Conroy and Cotter 2017). Many reasons are cited for not reporting to formal bodies, most notably the fear of not being believed, assuming personal blame or responsibility, fear of repercussions from their perpetrator, and a lack of faith in the system (Angelone, Mitchell, and Grossi 2015; Rotenberg 2017; Conroy and Cotter 2017; Randall 2010).

Explaining why they did not report or pursue formal disciplinary procedures in response to CPH, participants stated: "I was worried that the harassment would reflect poorly on me"; "I chose not to file an official grievance against this male student for fear of furthering the process. I just wanted him out of my life. I was scared to make things worse"; and "I know other professors are not believed and their complaints denigrated."

These responses demonstrate aspects of internalized victim blaming and a belief that they will not be believed or supported. Rather than viewing instances of CPH as the result of student behaviour and misconduct, women faculty are cast in the role of "bad managers" or incompetent employees for not preventing the harassment in the first place. This understanding ignores the responsibility of both the perpetrator and the institution. Indeed, within this context, the perpetrator becomes invisible and the onus is placed entirely on the instructor. Rather than a recourse or remedy, utilizing a formal complaints process is positioned as "making things worse" or too time onerous to pursue, especially for vulnerable and underemployed faculty.

Of those participants who sought support and pursued formal disciplinary procedures, many faced backlash. As one noted, "I had one student actively campaign with another sessional instructor against my conversion to tenure track." Another noted, "While they did believe what I said, they also made sure to write criticisms into my performance reviews at the time." Finally, one noted, "A coordinating professor sided with the students and decided to use his own lack of organization during my maternity leave to try and get me fired. Luckily he was not successful but I spent my whole maternity leave feeling stressed about whether I would have a job to come back to." Particularly troubling here is the collusion between students and opportunistic faculty members who attempt to gang up on and intimidate women faculty. Indeed, CPH and lateral or hierarchical forms of harassment are not distinct from one another; they exist alongside and compound the effects of CPH.

Beyond retaliation, participants described other professional consequences: stepping down from administrative roles (i.e., chair or program coordinator), stepping away from departments or disciplines, or transferring institutions. Perhaps less drastic, participants cited a range of coping mechanisms employed to offset the personal and professional effects of CPH. On a personal level, nearly all participants talked about the need to "develop a thick skin" to deal with student harassment. Other participants cited "crying" and "stress eating" as personal strategies for coping with ongoing CPH.

On a more formal level, participants drew on the support of colleagues, chairs, and deans and read up on institutional processes regarding SGBV, sexual harassment, and student conduct. Fewer reported the CPH to campus security or administration. Those who reached out to colleagues mostly did so with other women, which speaks to the unacknowledged emotional labour performed by women. Institutions are disproportionately downloading the costs and impacts of CPH onto women. Regardless of the steps taken, the overwhelming message was that, as women faculty, they were responsible for dealing with the impacts of CPH. This was true whether she was the person experiencing the harassment or the person providing support.

Unequal Impacts: Tenure, Precarity, and Contrapower Harassment

Tenure emerged as both a site of empowerment to deal proactively with students perpetrating CPH and a potential site of conflict. Participants described a sense of empowerment to ignore the things that were happening to them or to seek institutional supports to deal with CPH once they had received tenure. Respondents indicated, "Most times I ignore [CPH] but as of late I challenge the student. Having tenure helps with building my confidence." And, "I remember that I am much further in my career and have the education to support my knowledge and skills." Here, tenure serves as both a confidence boost and a safety net for retaliation. Tenure was framed by some respondents as a reward for enduring years of CPH: "I got tenure in a Liberal Arts college that is known for its high quality of teaching because I took shit from students and managed to get good SETs despite a series of toxic relationships with students who were hell bent on using me as a whipping post for their overwhelming anxiety and trauma." Here, the respondent equates her ability to endure CPH as a factor in her achievement of tenure. This suggests that because CPH is considered by many women a "normal" part of the job and an expected aspect of university teaching for women, receiving tenure in spite of CPH is taken to be a measure of "success."

Whatever sense of security or empowerment that may have been felt by respondents with tenure was counteracted by the vulnerability of experiencing CPH as a precarious employee. It should be noted that having tenure did not impact whether the respondent would experience CPH, but it shaped how incidences of CPH affected participants on a personal level and how vulnerable they felt. Numerous respondents described their sense of vulnerability and precarity:

> I did not have much of a voice to speak up since I am a sessional instructor and early in my career.
>
> Sessionals aren't offered much institutional support at my school.
>
> I was so scared about my future employment that I tried to downplay things.

An absence of tenure or full-time employment meant that the stakes were much higher in coming forward or seeking support. For instance, one respondent stated they hesitated to come forward because they didn't want the administration to perceive them "as a troublemaker."

Indeed, flipping the script on responsibility from perpetrator to victim is a common element of rape culture. In this case, it is the person reporting the harassment who is positioned as the troublemaker rather than the perpetrator. This sentiment was echoed by other respondents who suggested, "You want to be careful about making accusations ... try to fly below the radar as much as possible ... As a sessional, I was worried that the harassment would reflect poorly on me." Here, respondents demonstrate an awareness of their own precarity and the relationship between their precarity, believability, and the responsibility or willingness of the institution to protect them from harassment.

Although a few participants noted positive outcomes from seeking formal institutional disciplinary processes, an equal number felt ignored and dismissed, especially if they were precarious faculty. One participant noted, "When I reported the abuse, I was told that student athletes were 'different,' but that these things were not uncommon. My chair was supportive, but I was told that abusive teaching evaluations weren't something they'd consider because 'they really couldn't prove that it was the student' and that I should just let it go."

Again, the response this participant received reflects the excusal and normalization of CPH at a senior and institutional level and the "boys will be boys" attitude assigned to certain student populations. Overall responses suggested a distinction between feeling believed and supported on a personal level and having their reports taken seriously and acted upon in ways that were helpful and not harmful. Another participant shared:

> I was believed. But the university chose not to remove this student from this program because "being creepy isn't enough of a reason to do so." So instead, we changed classroom times, locations, I was dropped off at university and met by a security guard to walk me to class. Support staff attended my class so that I was not alone ... I do not believe this was handled effectively. I will never get back the lost time – meetings, emails, precautions.

This experience highlights the excusal and normalization of CPH, in particular, by the implementation of the lengthy and burdensome precautions for the identified victim of CPH. In the above case, these precautions were instituted only after an additional complaint was made by an Indigenous woman faculty member who reminded the university about the breadth of Missing and Murdered Indigenous Women and Girls (MMIWG). Apparently, the university believed implementing these costly and time-consuming safety measures was easier than removing or disciplining the perpetrator. The perpetrator is not required to learn from their behaviour and the cost of the situation is paid by the victim.

Responses to Contrapower Harassment: Gendered Care Work

When asked directly about coping strategies, participants described a range of emotional labour: ignoring the harassment, seeking support from colleagues, stress eating, navigating institutional policies and procedures and informal practices, developing new ways of teaching and delivering materials, never meeting with students alone, and requesting escorts to and from class as well as during class. All of this adds to the work undertaken by women faculty to remain in academia safely.

Participants largely did not experience effective support from university administrators or institutional processes. The vast majority of respondents indicated finding support and solace in other women colleagues, noting, "Luckily, I have female colleagues who had similar experiences (well, that part is not lucky for them) but they believed me and warned me about potential problem students." The onus is placed on women faculty to support and protect each other through advice and commiseration and, most importantly, an informal system of mutual protection through knowledge sharing about potential abusers. Such a system should not be required to protect women faculty from CPH. Other respondents echoed similar sentiments:

> The dean downplayed it. Her secretary at least said that she was sorry that it happened. The union did not respond. I spoke with colleagues for emotional support. And I have never filed a complaint. When instances like this happen, I find support in colleagues who face similar struggles. And I never sought out help from a superior. But I have confided in one colleague with whom I coteach this particular course. She's offered advice, but mostly it's nice to have a supportive ear.

While these responses indicate the power and value of the support and affirmation provided by other women faculty, they also highlight a "closed" and informal circle or system of gendered support. In other words: women doing women's work for other women. While these are powerful, beautiful acts of care that demonstrate the incredible resourcefulness and resilience of women, this is also gendered care work that has arisen in response to the white-hetero-capitalist-patriarchy (hooks 1984). This work accounts for additional unpaid labour by and for women faculty. It is labour that is, by and large, not expected of men faculty, and men are not evaluated or judged based on their lack of care work in the same ways as women faculty. Where men faculty are applauded and celebrated for undertaking any forms of care work, women are expected and required to do so.

It is essential that we acknowledge and examine CPH as existing along a continuum of violence to recognize how it contributes to the overall lack of safety for women in academe. Despite not rising to the level of physical violence, respondents described taking great lengths to develop safety protocols to deal with problem students, including having security escorts to and from class, changing classrooms, or not meeting with or being alone with students. Further, the extra work involved in navigating and managing emotional distress adds to the work of women faculty, on both a personal and professional level. Women faculty require, and deserve, a safe environment in which to work – one that is free of contrapower harassment and sexual and gender-based violence.

CONCLUSION

To understand CPH as functioning along a continuum of violence acknowledges how subtle behaviours or microaggressions relate and often lead to more overtly aggressive forms of violence. This view recognizes that incidences or behaviours that might appear minor, such as a student aggressively challenging a grade or constantly questioning and undermining their women professors, are analogous to rather than distinct from other more recognized forms of gender-based violence such as sexual harassment or physical assault. Thus, CPH happens alongside, or as a precursor to, more aggressive or violent and controlling behaviours (Osborne 1995). We cannot adequately address SGBV at Canadian postsecondary institutions without acknowledging and addressing women faculty members' experiences with CPH.

All the incidences and behaviours described by respondents fit the definition of CPH. Incidents ranged from interrupting lectures and questioning professional expertise to unwanted touching, stalking, and verbal threats. How respondents dealt with CPH shared common attributes. Several respondents described changing how they comported themselves in the classroom by adopting "more maternal and feminine behaviours." Others talked about dismissing the behaviours as "normal" or "not a big deal" and expressed how they were afraid people would find out and think they were unable to manage their classrooms. These latter coping strategies, which comprised by far the most common responses, involved internalized strategies of excusal and self-blame that served to shift responsibility from the perpetrators and institutions to those experiencing CPH. Participants indicated a range of tools and strategies they employed to deal with the additional fear, stress, and anxiety. Many of these "self-care" strategies involved extensive emotional labour from the individual and from their (largely women) colleagues. In fact, the support of women colleagues emerged as the most reliable and effective mechanism respondents used to deal with the impacts of CPH.

The community of support that women developed formed a critical component of their coping strategies. The value of supportive, compassionate friendship, and many women's skills in this regard, cannot be overlooked. Nevertheless, we argue that this labour is not work that should be absorbed by women faculty alone. Such emotional labour adds to what is already expected of women in academe, remains invisible and unrewarded, and enables the institution and its structures to persist unaffected. Instead, we need to develop social, cultural, and structural ways of addressing the full continuum of SGBV within institutions and in academia more broadly so that the labour for supporting those affected by CPH is not individualized. This includes how we recognize the existence of, and provide support for, those experiencing CPH. This is not (or should not be) women's work.

WORKS CITED

Ahmed, Sara. 2019. "Damage Limitation." *Feministkilljoys,* February 15, 2019. https://feministkilljoys.com/2019/02/15/damage-limitation/.

Angelone, D.J., Damon Mitchell, and Laura Grossi. 2015. "Men's Perceptions of an Acquaintance Rape: The Role of Relationship Length, Victim Resistance, and Gender Role Attitudes." *Journal of Interpersonal Violence* 30 (13): 2278–2303.

Backhouse, Constance, Roma Harris, Gillian Michell, and Alison Wylie. 1989. "The Chilly Climate for Women at UWO: Postscript to the Backhouse Report." Unpublished report.

Barnett, Jessica Penwell, Eleanor Maticka-Tyndale, and Trocaire Kenya. 2016. "Stigma as Social Control: Gender-Based Violence, Stigma, Life Chances and Moral Order in Kenya." *Social Problems* 63:447–62.

Benson, Katherine A. 1984. "Comment on Crocker's 'An Analysis of University Definitions of Sexual Harassment.'" *Signs* 9 (3): 516–19.

Bessant, Judith. 1998. "Women in Academia and Opaque Violence." *Melbourne Studies in Education* 39 (2): 41–68.

Boyle, Karen. 2019. "The Sex of Sexual Violence." In *Handbook on Gender and Violence,* edited by Laura J. Shepherd, 101–14. Cheltenham, UK: Edward Elgar Publishing.

Burt, Martha R. 1980. "Cultural Myths and Supports for Rape." *Journal of Personality and Social Psychology* 38 (2): 217–30.

Canadian Association of University Teachers (CAUT). 2018. "Underrepresented and Underpaid: Diversity and Equity among Canada's Postsecondary Education Teachers." *CAUT Equity Review*. https://www.caut.ca/sites/default/files/caut_equity_report_2018-04final.pdf.

Canadian Federation of Students–Ontario (CFSO). 2015. *Sexual Violence on Campus* (factsheet). https://cfsontario.ca/wp-content/uploads/2017/07/Factsheet-Sexual Assault.pdf.

Conroy, Shana, and Adam Cotter. 2017. "Self-Reported Sexual Assault in Canada, 2014." *Juristat*, Statistics Canada, catalogue no. 85-002-X. https://www150.statcan.gc.ca/n1/pub/85-002-x/2017001/article/14842-eng.htm.

Delacollette, Nathalie, Muriel Dumont, Marie Sarlet, and Benoit Dardenne. 2013. "Benevolent Sexism, Men's Advantages and the Prescription of Warmth to Women." *Sex Roles* 68 (5–6): 296–310.

DeSouza, Eros R. 2011. "Frequency Rates and Correlates of Contrapower Harassment in Higher Education." *Journal of Interpersonal Violence* 26 (1): 158–88.

DeSouza, Eros R., and A. Gigi Fansler. 2003. "Contrapower Harassment: A Survey of Students and Faculty Members." *Sex Roles* 48 (11–12): 529–42.

Fraser, Courtney. 2015. "Ladies First and 'Asking for It': Benevolent Sexism in the Maintenance of Rape Culture." *California Law Review* 103:141.

hooks, bell. 1984. *Feminist Theory: From Margin to Centre*. Boston: South End Press.

Juliano, Ann Carey. 2007. "Harassing Women with Power: The Case for Including Contrapower Harassment within Title VII." *Boston University Law Review* 87 (3): 491–550.

Kelly, Liz. 1987. "The Continuum of Sexual Violence." In *Women, Violence and Social Control: Explorations in Sociology*, edited by Jalna Hanmer and Mary Maynard, 46–60. London: Palgrave Macmillan.

Lampman, Claudia. 2012. "Women Faculty at Risk: US Professors Report on Their Experiences with Student Incivility, Bullying, Aggression, and Sexual Attention." *NASPA Journal About Women in Higher Education* 5:184–208.

Lampman, Claudia, Earl C. Crew, Shea D. Lowery, and Kelley Tompkins. 2016. "Women Faculty Distressed: Descriptions and Consequences of Academic Contrapower Harassment." *NASPA Journal About Women in Higher Education* 9 (2): 169–89.

Lampman, Claudia, Alissa Phelps, Samantha Bancroft, and Melissa Beneke. 2009. "Contrapower Harassment in Academia: A Survey of Faculty Experience with Student Incivility, Bullying, and Sexual Attention." *Sex Roles* 60 (5–6): 331–46.

Lorber, Judith. 2012. *Gender Inequality*. Oxford: Oxford University Press.

Maxwell, Louise, and Graham Scott. 2014. "A Review of the Role of Radical Feminist Theories in the Understanding of Rape Myth Acceptance." *Journal of Sexual Aggression* 20 (1): 40–54.

McCabe, Megan. 2020. "Discipline Is Not Prevention: Transforming the Cultural Foundations of Campus Rape Culture." *Journal of Moral Theology* 9 (2): 49–71.

McKinney, Kathleen. 1990. "Sexual Harassment of University Faculty by Colleagues and Students." *Sex Roles* 23 (7): 421–38.

–. 1992. "Contrapower Sexual Harassment: The Effects of Student Sex and Type of Behaviour on Faculty Perceptions." *Sex Roles* 27 (11): 627–43.

Osborne, Rachel L. 1995. "The Continuum of Violence against Women in Canadian Universities: Toward a New Understanding of the Chilly Campus Climate." *Women's Studies International Forum* 18 (5–6): 637–46.

Randall, Melanie. 2010. "Sexual Assault Law, Credibility, and 'Ideal Victims': Consent, Resistance, and Victim Blaming." *Canadian Journal of Women and the Law* 22 (2): 397–433.

Rospenda, Kathleen M., Judith A. Richman, and Stephanie J. Nawyn. 1998. "Doing Power: The Confluence of Gender, Race, and Class in Contrapower Sexual Harassment." *Gender and Society* 12 (1): 40–60.

Rotenberg, Christine. 2017. "Police-Reported Sexual Assaults in Canada, 2009 to 2014: A Statistical Profile." *Juristat,* Statistics Canada, catalogue no. 85-002-X. https://www150.statcan.gc.ca/n1/pub/85-002-x/2017001/article/54866-eng.htm.

Stoll, Laurie Cooper, Terry Glenn Lilley, and Kelly Pinter. 2017. "Gender-Blind Sexism and Rape Myth Acceptance." *Violence Against Women* 23 (1): 28–45.

Suarez, Eliana, and Tahany M. Gadalla. 2010. "Stop Blaming the Victim: A Meta-Analysis on Rape Myths." *Journal of Interpersonal Violence* 25 (11): 2010–35.

10

Challenging Systemic Discrimination in the Canada Research Chairs Program

LOUISE FORSYTH

This chapter is an account of my own experiences and those of seven other senior academic women who joined around the turn of the century to challenge the inequitable practices woven into the structural and epistemological fabric of Canadian universities.[1] Specifically, we sought to reform the newly created and highly prestigious Canada Research Chairs Program (CRCP). Under the CRCP, which was created in 2000 and continues to function today, two thousand new research positions were created and made available to universities on a pre-determined distribution basis for all academic disciplines across Canada's post-secondary system (see Side and Robbins 2007). Unfortunately, omissions and weaknesses in its design, including ineffective monitoring and regulation, facilitated practices of unjust discrimination and exclusion within the program. For example, in the first year of the CRCP, the twenty-eight universities that competed successfully for awards did not nominate a single woman. To address these shortcomings, we launched two formal complaints with the Canadian Human Rights Commission (CHRC), one in 2003 and a second in 2016.

Our first complaint in 2003 was directed at Industry Canada (now called Innovation, Science and Economic Development Canada), at that time the administrative home of the CRCP. In our complaint, we claimed that both statistics and anecdotal accounts brought to light a serious absence of equitable results or progress toward such results in the CRCP's implementation. One indication of this lack of oversight was the percentage of women CRCP chairholders, which had remained in the low twenties with little change since the beginning of the program, despite the much larger percentage of women in the general population and the growing percentage of women undergraduate and graduate students.

Although our first challenge was successful, the mediation did not bring an end to the problem of systemic discrimination within the CHRP. Little thought and less oversight was put into revising the procedures and criteria used in advertising positions or the selection of nominees and research projects by universities and the government agency responsible for the program. We had the impression that those who designed the CRCP had little knowledge or appreciation of either established practices for tenure-track appointments or the place of research activity in the operations of Canadian universities. Indeed, it seemed that the underlying assumption at the time CRCP was conceived was that *excellence* – easily, unproblematically (and even infallibly) recognized as such – would emerge, without oversight, as the determining factor for appointments. Information distributed by the Ottawa office about the CRCP provided no indication of their awareness that the very notion of *excellence* could be, and almost always is, biased. It also seemed that the designers of the CRCP did not anticipate it having any secondary effects on campus affairs across the country.

Our second complaint in 2016 went to the Tri-Agency Institutional Programs Secretariat (TIPS),[2] which had been created for the purpose of assuming administrative responsibility for the CRCP. This time, we took steps to have the first settlement agreement declared a Federal Court Order. Rather than undergo a formal court process, the TIPS "entered into a collaborative mediation process" with us "to come to an agreement on changes to the settlement agreement that would address the inequities within the Program in a systemic, structural and sustainable way" (Hewitt and Bérubé 2019). The settlement agreement arising from this mediation was declared Federal Court Order in 2019 and the first settlement agreement, from 2006, was added as an addendum.

As part of our agreement, the chairs of the CRCP Steering and Management Committees sent an open letter to Canadian university presidents and vice-presidents on July 31, 2019, informing them of the enhanced status for matters of equality in the CRCP and the changes that would be coming in the program "in a systemic, structural and sustainable way," thereby facilitating actions intended to address "the underrepresentation of individuals from the four designated groups."[3] In the letter, the CRCP committee chairs acknowledged and stressed their concern about the evidence of tenacious underrepresentation of the designated groups among CRCP chairholders. They saw this underrepresentation as unacceptable and requiring urgent and decisive action both from within the CRCP and in participating universities.

After many years, revised procedures and accompanying documents began to show a way toward a discrimination-free research enterprise. We were delighted to know that the results of our own research, our years-long commitment to equality, and our mediations with Industry Canada and TIPS before the CHRC encouraged the transformation of the management and functioning of the CRCP, with no loss of academic excellence, in such a way that requirements for equity, diversity, and inclusion (EDI) in Canadian university research now characterize every aspect of the program. These changes have had a significant impact on most campuses across the country beyond just the CRCP. Policies, principles, and procedures that are in place for CRCP awards are now seen, within and beyond the program, as relevant throughout the academy. In this chapter, I use autoethnographic details of our multiyear challenge against discriminatory elements of the CRCP to highlight the value of collective action to effect systemic change.

INITIAL 2003 COMPLAINT TO THE CANADIAN HUMAN RIGHTS COMMISSION

We are scholars in a range of academic disciplines at Canadian universities coast to coast. All of us saw very early on our own campuses the serious flaws in the conception, administration, and implementation of the CRCP.[4] These flaws were such that they made it possible for a disproportionate percentage of the awards to go without challenge and with minimal oversight to able-bodied and already privileged white men, to the disadvantage of many others. We shared our concerns immediately with each other regarding the program's damaging effects. Despite the difficulty in obtaining good data early in the program's existence, we came together, moved and inspired by the determination of our colleague Wendy Robbins.

It was the infectious engagement, outrage, and determination of Wendy Robbins, activist and brilliant academic, who brought us together as a committed group in our awareness of the injustices occurring from the start in the implementation of the CRCP (see Robbins 2012; Robbins and Simpson 2009). She convinced us of the need to take concerted action. Robbins had already built extensive connections across the country as a result of her activism, engagement, and research. She was the first woman to become full professor of English at the University of New Brunswick, where she cofounded the Women's Studies Program. She was cocreator of the very successful listserv PAR-L, which was a forum for women interested in promoting equality. She also brought her expertise in women's and gender studies and postcolonial studies to multiple other organizations (Alberta College of Social Workers, Humanities and Social Sciences Federation of Canada, Canadian Association of University Teachers) and received the Governor General's Award in Commemoration of the Persons Case in 2007, which recognizes outstanding contributions in the advancement of equality for women in Canada. In the year we lodged our complaint against the CRCP with the CHRC (2003), Robbins was named Visiting Scholar at the Canadian Association of University Teachers (CAUT). She was also chair of the CAUT Women's Committee. Robbins died suddenly and unexpectedly of an aneurysm in 2017. We miss her terribly.

Our first collective action in the early years of the twenty-first century was to work with Robbins in the preparation and distribution of the "Ivory Towers,

Feminist Audits," which we simply called the Equity Audits. The Equity Audits contained statistical data that revealed to us, and to many others, the ongoing glaring inequities in the granting of CRCP awards. We prepared these audits annually starting in 2001 with the legal, statistical, and financial support of CAUT. We continued to prepare and distribute them widely through to the time of the mediation in 2006 – our first complaint to the CHRC. The Equity Audits had considerable impact at the annual Congress of the Federation for the Humanities and Social Sciences. They were printed on handy cards that lent themselves to easy sharing among colleagues and with all those having the same concerns regarding inequities occurring on our campuses and across the country.

While the CRCP was designed by the Government of Canada specifically to provide bold new support to university-based research, the creation and implementation of the program had an immediate negative impact on the teaching and learning function of universities, even on research that was not supported through the CRCP. This happened for several reasons, including the fact that expectations for CRCP chairholders to participate in administrative and teaching functions, particularly at the undergraduate level, were minimal. This served to increase the teaching and administrative workload of other faculty members, who found themselves facing more challenges completing their own research projects. Universities were also expected to increase internal fiscal allocations to academic units housing Canada Research Chair (CRC) award holders, to the detriment of units without CRCs. Additionally, faculty members with appointments outside the foundational academic disciplines: sciences, arts, humanities, and the social sciences, found themselves disadvantaged when applying for a CRCP award because the national distribution of funding support in their fields was comparatively low. This reality was the product of the program design, which sought to attract funding, often international, from external private sources, who were less interested in funding these fields. These detriments persisted, even though members of the four designated groups are disproportionately represented in these fields.

We learned through Robbins that the CRCP was not preparing and administering the forms needed for self-identification by members of the four designated groups. It appeared to us that there was little will in program management to learn about discrimination in practices associated with research activities in participating universities and in the CRCP. Advertisements, applications, and nominations of candidates for positions had few formal requirements to follow. Program structures were unclear. Ad hoc research teams – arising from existing old boys' networks – were being formed for the sole purpose of opportunistically taking advantage of the new and generous CRCP. Nominations were going from universities to the CRCP Secretariat and awards were being approved by that Ottawa office with very little transparency. Little or no attention was being paid to the need for the respect of procedures contained in collective agreements. Open advertising and decisions from collegially elected appointment committees for positions to be filled were not required and rarely happened. Those who already had the ear of power were in a position to influence institutional decision making to such an extent that their candidate and that candidate's field of research enjoyed insurmountable advantages. They were able to position themselves in ways that made them seem to be the ideal choice for a CRCP award within the frame of the university's priorities. As we became aware of these practices, we grew ever more convinced of the need for our formal complaint to shed light on the secrecy, unfairness, irregularities, and lack of transparency in the process. We kept these shoddy procedures in mind as we prepared our brief for the mediation, which occurred in October 2006.

When the mediation concluded, we were initially pleased with the settlement agreement. The document we signed contained statements of principle that mattered, such as the clear and unambiguous affirmation that goals of equality do not run counter to goals of excellence in research. On the contrary, the agreement states that the CRCP agrees to "inform universities in Program documents and on the Program website that the goals of excellence and equity are not mutually exclusive, and that equity ensures that the largest pool of qualified candidates is accessed without affecting the integrity of the selection process." Indeed, the agreement insisted on the vital importance of diversity and stressed the advantage of accessing the largest possible pool of candidates in a national and international context. It also drew attention to the fact that prioritizing traditional types of research risks excluding innovative research. Even further, it stressed that such innovative research might well not be published in the most established journals where norms observed by reviewers continue to use established and possibly biased criteria.

Other clauses in the agreement contained specific actions to be taken by those responsible for CRCP administration and management. These appeared to us to augur well for positive change in the program. The following are some of the items with which we agreed (and with which we were led to believe the respondents agreed) during the 2006 mediation. We assumed, naïvely, that they were not just idle phrases. The CRCP agreed:

- to collect and retain information on the status of chair nominees in the protected groups and to monitor adherence and progress in terms of established targets;

- to require universities to develop targets for the representation of members of the four designated groups and to monitor adherence and progress;[5]
- to conduct and complete a gender-based and a diversity-based analysis of the chairs program;
- to ensure that all CRC recruitment processes are transparent, open, and equitable, consistent with the principles and safeguards embodied in the universities' existing tenure-track hiring practices and containing features such as open advertising with a statement of commitment to equity in the nomination and appointment process;
- to require that universities confirm that all nominations were submitted in accordance with the university's official nomination and recruitment processes;
- to undertake a review of systemic barriers faced by people in the four designated groups;
- to monitor the reasons individuals decline or resign from chair appointments and renewals;
- to ensure that all employees and management personnel responsible for developing, implementing, and monitoring the CRCP receive gender-based and diversity-based analysis training, as well as training on systemic discrimination;
- to post on the CRC website full contact information on a person to whom complaints about equity issues could be addressed.

We left the 2006 mediation feeling that we had reached quite a good agreement with those negotiating on behalf of the CRCP, recognizing, of course, that compromises had been made and that there was still much work to be done. However, as information soon began to come to us on what was actually happening in the program, we were more than discouraged to realize that almost nothing had changed in its management and functioning. Those with management responsibilities demonstrated little will to implement measures that would produce real equity, diversity, and inclusion. As was clear through the following years and, finally, at the time of the 2016 mediation, there were glaring breaches and almost no evidence of compliance with the settlement agreement. We could see no apparent impact from the agreement on the way the program was functioning. And we watched for over a decade as the statistics continued to show us that abuses remained. Distribution of awards remained unchanged, inequalities unaddressed. Indeed, for some universities, these inequalities grew even more grievous.

We came to realize that the settlement agreement was not proving effective. It was not sufficiently explicit in requiring strong and unambiguous measures for the monitoring of compliance and the implementation of rigorous penalties for universities' noncompliance. The settlement agreement was in place, but without the force of a Federal Court Order, the CRCP management chose to ignore it. The CRCP management continued along the path it had carved for itself at the turn of the century, with serious and sustained discrimination evident in every part of the program. As a result, we did not hear of even a single case where failure to comply with the terms of the settlement agreement meant CRCP management's refusal to make an award. We believe that no penalties further to the 2006 settlement agreement were imposed.

SECOND 2016 COMPLAINT TO THE CANADIAN HUMAN RIGHTS COMMISSION

In 2015, Goss Gilroy Inc. completed a thorough external evaluation of the CRCP, which acted as the catalyst for an impressive new direction for the CRCP, insofar as the many facets of equity, diversity, and inclusion are concerned. The evaluation repeatedly mentions that "the majority of institutions do not meet targets set for women, visible minorities, Aboriginal Persons, and persons with disabilities." Thus, although their evaluation of the CRCP was generally positive, they recommended that the term *guidelines* be replaced by *requirements* in the CRCP guidelines and requirements. Their recommendation said: "Management should require institutions to adopt greater transparency in their processes for allocation of Chair positions and selection and renewal of chairholders in order to ensure institutions have greater accountability in terms of meeting their equity targets." This was the only recommendation in their evaluation ranked as requiring urgent action.

This evaluation led to a range of effective actions on the part of CRCP management, including a proactive look back at the 2006 settlement agreement. CRCP management sent open letters to university presidents (2016, 2017, 2018, 2019) and published a detailed and specific response to address the underrepresentation of individuals from the four designated groups (see CRC 2022) as well as an "Update on CRC Equity and Diversity Concerns," a "Commitment to Equity, Diversity and Inclusion," and "Equity, Diversity and Inclusion: Best Practices for Recruitment, Hiring, and Retention."[6] The CRCP also created its own "Equity, Diversity and Inclusion Action Plan" and required that all participating universities prepare their own equity action plans and post them in full visibility on their websites. These documents, along with several other policy statements regarding target-setting, compliance, remedies, and penalties for violations, thoughtfully address the weakness of the 2006 settlement while showing the way forward through newly developed best practices. Overall, we felt that the path toward equality in the program was well laid out by CRCP management in the interim period between the fifteenth-year evaluation in 2015 and our second mediation in 2018.

In 2017, the 2006 mediation agreement was finally declared an Order of the Federal Court. This meant it was legally enforceable. Around the same time, we lodged our second complaint against the CRCP with the CHRC. Position papers prepared for the 2018 mediation recognized that equality issues with the CRCP were still unresolved as of 2017, including issues of target-setting, methodology, compliance, and enforcement. Mediation between us and TIPS, the body currently responsible for the management of the CRCP, took place in November 2018 in the presence of representatives of the CHRC and the Canadian Department of Justice. The 2018 mediation settlement agreement became the addendum and an integral part to the 2006 settlement agreement. This new settlement agreement document, which brought negotiations in every aspect of the agreement up to date, was declared a Federal Court Order in 2019. This time we got it right by making sure the requirements for compliance by every participating university were clear, rigorous, and enforceable.

The settlement expressed the enormous wish that its implementation would result in a real transformation of academia in pursuit of the broader goals of EDI through the implementation of critical structural changes in universities. The agreement begins with the clear and unambiguous affirmation that the Canadian research enterprise will be at its best if it reflects the diversity of the entire Canadian population, abandoning current patterns favouring certain groups. The agreement states that "the Respondent and the Complainants recognize that achieving a more equitable, diverse and inclusive (EDI) Canadian research enterprise is essential to creating excellent, innovative and impactful research. As such, the Respondent recognizes that it would be a best practice to consider representation within the Chairs Program as reflecting the level of diversity within the Canadian population." The settlement agreement also contains the clear affirmation that there is no contradiction between equality and excellence in research.

In the wake of this official acknowledgment, statistics showed the need to take serious and sustained action in the implementation of measures to ensure equal opportunity in the CRCP. Data discrepancies within the program also demonstrated the need for credible processes of data-gathering, target-setting, and analysis, as well as a coherent and consistent approach for monitoring and compliance. Despite these ongoing concerns, available data had already begun to show positive gains for underrepresented groups. Whereas nominations of women for new awards and renewals submitted by universities in the pre-EDI action plan cycle in April 2017 were 30.2 percent of the total (Bérubé 2018), in October 2018, following adoption of the EDI action plan, nominations of women were 50.3 percent. Nominations for racialized persons rose over the same period from 17.7 percent to 22.2 percent (Government of Canada 2022). Reliable statistics for persons with disabilities and for Indigenous peoples were unavailable for the same period because they had never been collected using sound methodologies. Categories of LGBTQ2IA+ persons were added to the designated groups and so became legally protected from bias and discrimination in all matters covered under the agreement regarding the CRCP by the Federal Court Order. There was also agreement by the CRCP management of the need to investigate and address systemic barriers faced by chairholders from the designated groups on entry, retention, and promotion.

DISCUSSION AND CONCLUSION

Despite the often tense exchange of views and arguments during the mediations, the terms of our initial settlement agreement with Industry Canada appeared quite promising to us in that it brought our claims out in the open and lent them legitimacy. The agreement also enlarged the scope of what could be seen as discrimination in Canadian universities. In response to our demands, the 2006 settlement agreement included explicit recognition of the systemic discrimination endured by members of the four designated groups, an explicit statement that equality and excellence in research are not mutually exclusive, the requirement for firm targets based on recent census statistics, and the obligation for advertising and adherence to tenure-track appointment procedures as contained in the collective agreements in effect at all participating universities. We marked the conclusion of our mediations with a press release to inform colleagues across the country of the major changes officially requiring equitable procedures in the functioning of the chairs program. It was our very reasonable hope that our actions and the consequent documents and policy statements would serve as precedents and strategies for the transition toward equality for all throughout the Canadian university system. We believed that our agreements with managers of the CRCP foresaw the creation of a solid infrastructure underpinning the research establishment of Canadian universities.

Unfortunately, our initial optimism in 2006 was seriously misplaced. While the terms of the mediation agreement had at first appeared promising in addressing and removing the systemic sources of inequities, as time passed, we quickly came to realize that no real change was occurring in the actual functioning of the program. Transparency was not achieved, although the data showing systemic discrimination were clear and disturbing. We had been led to believe that chairs program administrators would assume responsibility for implementing the new policies and procedures agreed upon in our mediation. Unfortunately, managers of the CRCP in Ottawa and in universities across the country demonstrated little will to move away from the program's original flawed basis. It seemed that a desire not to know was being systemically normalized and widely shared; apathy, wilful blindness, and complacency were the norm. A certain self-interested way of seeing the values protected by *academic freedom* came to work in support of complacency. The status quo suited those who were served by the terms of the program as they had been written, allowing the institutionalization of power and privilege for some while marginalizing others. And so, the chairs program continued on its way largely unchanged and formally unchallenged for more than a decade. As was clear through these years and finally at the time of the 2018 mediation, there were glaring breaches and little evidence of compliance with the settlement agreement. We watched for over a decade as the statistics kept coming in showing us that distribution of CRCP awards remained unchanged, inequities unaddressed. Indeed, for some years and for some universities, inequities grew even more grievous.

It was with considerable frustration that we realized that the settlement agreement had an insurmountable weakness. This weakness flowed from the absence of power and voice among those victimized and marginalized by systemic discrimination. As a result, there was a lack of strong and unambiguous enforcement measures available to monitor compliance and implementation of rigorous penalties. We did not hear of even one case where failure to comply with the terms of the settlement meant chairs program managers refused to make awards for university-nominated persons. We believe that no penalties further to the 2006 mediation agreement were imposed. It was only in 2017, eleven years after our first mediation settlement agreement, that TIPS, the body now with responsibility for administration of the chairs program, took the necessary steps to have the settlement agreement declared a Federal Court Order.

As our case wound its way through the systemic labyrinth of research in Canadian postsecondary systems, it became increasingly clear to us that the most promising approach to producing change leading to genuine equality for all and an end to systemic discrimination is through collective action, with the help of reliable data.[7] Statements of principle and laws are not enough. It was our experience that for actions to be effective, they must have an immediate and concrete impact within the workings of systems. Statements favouring fairness for all can be formulated and even consensually received and abstract policies can be announced without stirring too much controversy; however, when the time comes for real social, cultural, and institutional change involving transformation of practices, discourse, ideologies, definitions, implementation, enforcement, and penalties, powerful differences of opinion come out in the open, too often in the form of insults, ridicule, and violence.

We believe that our years-long challenge to the functioning of the CRCP produced real change for the better in Canadian universities. It is now our hope that this step toward equity, diversity, and inclusion in research areas, in combination with many initiatives that went before us, will help to dismantle the systems of inequity and discrimination that have not yet disappeared in the universities, systems that continue to disadvantage those who are unjustly excluded from access to the many resources available in postsecondary education and research.

NOTES

1 Members of our group who jointly lodged the complaint in 2003 to the Canadian Human Rights Commission regarding the Canada Research Chairs Program were Marjorie Cohen (Economics, SFU), Glenis Joyce (Distance Education, USask), Audrey Kobayashi (Geography, Queen'sU), Shree Mulay (Community Health and Humanities, MemorialU), Michèle Ollivier (Sociology, UOttawa), Susan Prentice (Sociology, UManitoba), Wendy Robbins (English and Women's Studies, UNB), and Louise Forsyth (French and Women's Studies, USask). The number in the group fell to six for the second complaint and to four for the 2018 mediation as a result of the death of two members, Michèle Ollivier and Wendy Robbins.

2 The Tri-Agency Institutional Programs Secretariat (TIPS), through the Social Sciences and Humanities Research Council (SSHRC), manages tri-agency programs that provide grants to institutions in support of institutional capacity for research excellence.

3 The four designated groups are as follows: women, Indigenous peoples, persons with disabilities, and members of visible minorities.

4 For an account of our experiences during the period after we lodged a complaint with the CHRC and the subsequent mediation (2003–6), see Forsyth (2011, 173–93).

5 There was not agreement regarding the basis to be used in establishing targets for each of the FDGs. The CRCP representatives described the availability pool as "active university researchers," as opposed to our position, which was that targets must reflect the diversity of the Canadian population. The targets for the program had, therefore, in our view, to be determined by representation of the specific group in the general population. We believed that anything less was to accept and therefore condone the historic and persistent disadvantages facing Indigenous and other equity-seeking groups. In addition, there was not agreement on the methodology to be used for the analysis of data regarding targets.

6 See the CRC main webpage for these archived documents at: https://www.chairs-chaires. gc.ca/program-programme/updates-mises_a_jour-eng.aspx.

7 "Institutions that are found to not meet public accountability and transparency requirements or EDI Action Plan requirements shall be subject to measures to enforce compliance and shall have their peer review withheld for all nominations other than those that help meet targets" (2018 Mediation Agreement #37).

WORKS CITED

Bérubé, Dominique. 2018. "Open Letter from the Canada Research Chairs Program Management to Institutional Presidents." September 10, 2018. https://www.chairs -chaires.gc.ca/whats_new-quoi_de_neuf/2018/letter_to_presidents-lettre_aux_ presidents-eng.aspx?pedisable=true.

Canada Research Chairs (CRC). 2022. "Management Response to the Canada Research Chairs Program 15th-Year Evaluation." https://www.chairs-chaires.gc.ca/about_us-a_ notre_sujet/publications/evaluations/chairs_response-chaires_reponse-eng.aspx.

Forsyth, Louise. 2011. "Desperately Seeking Equity: Systemic Discrimination and the Canada Research Chairs Program." In *Not Drowning but Waving: Women, Feminism, and the Liberal Arts*, edited by Susan Brown, Jeanne Perreault, Jo-Anne Wallace, and Heather Zwicker, 173–93. Edmonton: University of Alberta Press.

Government of Canada. 2022. "Program Representation Statistics." https://www.chairs -chaires.gc.ca/about_us-a_notre_sujet/statistics-statistiques-eng.aspx.

Hewitt, Ted, and Dominique Bérubé. 2019. "Open Letter to University Presidents and Vice-Presidents from the Canada Research Chairs Program: 2019 Addendum to the 2006 Canadian Human Rights Settlement Agreement." July 31, 2019. https: //www. chairs-chaires.gc.ca/program-programme/2019_open_letter=eng.aspx.

Robbins, Wendy. 2012. "Critiquing Canada's Research Culture: Social, Cultural, and Political Restraints on Women's University Careers." *Forum on Public Policy: A Journal of the Oxford Round Table* 2012 (2).

Robbins, Wendy, and Vicky Simpson. 2009. "Pyramids of Power: A Statistical Snapshot of Women in Postsecondary Education in Canada and Some Ideas for Making Change." *Atlantis: Critical Studies in Gender, Culture and Social Justice* 33 (2): 6–18.

Side, Katherine, and Wendy Robbins. 2007. "Institutionalizing Inequalities in Canadian Universities: The Canada Research Chairs Program." *NWSA Journal* 19 (3): 163–81.

PART 4

Approaches to Practical and Institutional Change

Institutional Culture
and Implications for EDI Practice

MICHAEL F. CHARLES

In collaboration with great colleagues across the country, I had the privilege of contributing to the benchmark 2019 Universities Canada national Equity, Diversity, and Inclusion (EDI) report as part of its Advisory Group. The findings from our survey revealed several dynamics in tension. On the one hand, we saw progress in women's representation and greater attention to the broader concept of EDI in institutional planning. On the other hand, we saw structural and cultural impediments continuing to serve as drags on future success. By structure, I mean the organizational architecture, dedicated resources, policies, plans, processes, programs, and procedures that frame the operations and support the governance of the university, while culture refers to the implicit, explicit, and generally self-perpetuating values, beliefs, and behaviours shared by members of a group and sustained over long periods of time. As an EDI practitioner supporting academic and nonacademic institutions, I am interested in the interplay of culture with structure. Specifically, I am preoccupied by the way culture can frustrate, defeat, or drive the stated goals of universities. In my daily work, I attempt to embolden efforts to harness culture as a means of enlivening structure.

In academia, institutional culture often determines how structures are both expressed and experienced. As Boris Groysberg et al. (2018, 4) write, "Cultural norms define what is encouraged, discouraged, accepted, or rejected within a group. When properly aligned with personal values, drives, and needs, culture can unleash tremendous amounts of energy toward a shared purpose and foster an organization's capacity to thrive."[1] But when culture and structure conflict, it becomes difficult to enact institutional change. I have often witnessed this challenge in universities. Consider the preeminent value of individual excellence in the culture of academic institutions. We now find it untenable that such excellence resides in only half the population, but based on current data on recruitment in institutions, this is a relatively new belief. To the extent there has been progress for gender representation in the academy, it is in part because the cultural value of individual excellence has been increasingly reconciled with equality and equity processes and structures. Had those structures, by themselves, been determinative, we would have seen transformational change with the arrival of formal legal equality from the 1960s through to the 1980s. Instead, we continue to see women's underrepresentation in the professoriate relative to men, a pattern that is even more dramatic for women along various intersectional dimensions.[2]

Of course, a quantitative assessment of recruitment outcomes is only one perspective from which to assess the efficacy of such structural efforts. What happens from the standpoint of retention and promotion also matters. Over the years, I have been involved in and reviewed representation-based program effectiveness assessments in various academic and nonacademic organizations and continue to be taken aback by the reflections and experiences of equity-seeking members. In the specific context of institutional efforts to improve the proportion of women, racialized persons, Indigenous peoples, and persons with disabilities in the academy, many describe as commonplace the perception among colleagues of EDI as inconsistent with candidate "excellence." Equity-seeking individuals regularly report being asked whether their appointments were facilitated by "affirmative action" as a proxy for challenging the excellence of their scholarship. Others express reluctance to self-declare their identity to avoid stigma and bias in cases where their identities cannot be readily inferred by names or understandings of the ways they culturally present. Still other equity-seeking group members refer to experiences of isolation relative to colleagues who do not so identify. For all the work of EDI, it is shocking that this continues. As this work continues, university leaders should double-down on support for gender equity with particular attention to outcomes for racialized and disabled women in ways that further manifest substantive rather than merely rhetorical intersectional feminist advocacy.

After more than thirty years of employment equity policies, procedures, training, employee resource group formation, and other structural interventions, representation outcomes, particularly for women who are racialized and/or disabled, demonstrate the significance of institutional culture to the enactment of successful structural change. Of course, this should not be understood as a general argument against the use of structural propositions to affect change – well-conceived programs are a bedrock to transformation – but my sense is that these programs must be enacted with cultural considerations at the fore. To this end, I offer five interconnected approaches to consider (as a preliminary and nonexhaustive list).

First, universities need to assess their institutional culture(s) and improve channels of communication. Deploying mixed methods approaches including interviews, focus groups, and surveys, university leaders need to assess the relationship between their institutional culture(s) and the strategic objectives they want EDI to drive. Doing so may well reveal gaps between the intentions behind institutional structures and processes and how those efforts are experienced. From there, shifts in culture necessary for successful EDI action may be identified and appropriate and targeted interventions imagined. University leaders can then use their elevated platforms to organize community conversations and communicate those desired shifts, interventions, and related rationales with reference to tangible evidence-based goals.

Second, structural proposals for improved EDI policies and procedures must use cultural levers and connect to comprehensive, whole-of-institution planning rather than focusing on a few targeted interventions. For example, there is a growing recognition that decolonized and EDI-informed pedagogy and curriculum is related to student success. This may well lead to further implications for gender diversification within the professoriate as well as the composition of graduate student cohorts by extension. In this way, the objective of addressing EDI in pedagogy and curriculum extends beyond social justice concerns and connects to other strategic objectives.[3]

Third, universities need more employee education and professional development. While cynicism appropriately abounds the latest trend toward two-hour asynchronous instruction on unconscious bias training, not all interventions are the same. Indeed, I suggest we reject the concept of training, which implies the delivery of a set of rules and formulas that may be directly apprehended and converted to behaviour, and move toward an orientation of longitudinal education and professional development, which implies practices and processes of learning and behavioural transformation that may not be immediate or linear. With this type of transformation in mind, there are more longitudinal forms of unconscious bias education that show more promise. Interactive workshops that last two to three days over a period of

months with "take-home" reflection exercises connecting the facilitated
sessions, practical applications to work, and supported by pre- and post-
psychometric assessments, have been shown to move the needle.

Fourth, universities need to better support mentorship and sponsorship.
Social and professional networks within and across universities are critical
to research collaborations, conference participation, relationships within the
university and broader society, and retention and promotion. They also contribute to a sense of belonging and other generative benefits. Too often we find
that faculty members from equity-seeking groups express concern about
impediments to the development of social and professional networks that tend
to accrue more organically for their nonequity group colleagues. Informal
mentorship and sponsorship play a big role in the development of these networks, especially for faculty at early stages in their careers. Mentor relationships take many forms but generally provide a forum for the ad hoc sharing
of information. Sponsorships are much more expansive and structured,
pairing a leader or a more senior faculty member with someone at an early
stage in their career to provide professional development, career advancement advice, and advocacy. In either case, universities' formalizing both
mentorship and sponsorship using EDI-based designs would ensure that
no faculty is excluded from these crucial social and professional assets.

Finally, universities need to be more transparent in their planning and
policy formation. Transparency makes the values and beliefs that inform our
actions explicit. Apart from being viewed through an EDI lens, the criteria
and principles used to determine opportunities and eligibilities should be
published, clear, and consistent across comparable posts. In recruitment,
tenure, promotion, and confirmation processes, this means a movement away
from obtuse criteria such as candidate "excellence" – and other terms so
broad they operate as codifications of bias – and toward a clearer rationale
for decisions. This would also apply to the conferral of awards and other
recognition as well as recruitment for leadership in special projects.

Universities are culturally complex institutions. Members are fiercely
individualistic in their defence of both academic freedom and freedom of

thought, yet they also aspire to concepts of community bounded by service to a common purpose. They value dynamism and innovation but often reproduce systems characterized by allegiance to sometimes antiquated processes. I believe that the success of present and future EDI strategies depends on our ability to shift organizational culture where possible and align EDI goals where we cannot.

NOTES

1 To accelerate and sustain such change, comprehensive planning should be accompanied by multiple and varied incentives to shift values, beliefs, and behaviours. There are examples of such comprehensive EDI planning at institutions in the United States; however, at the time of writing, Canadian universities are at earlier stages of adopting these approaches, and time is required to evaluate their efficacy.

2 I am reminded of the work of Howard Ramos and Peter S. Li (2017), who examined, among other indicators, the representation of women and racialized professors in the academy. Using Canadian census data of the professoriate undifferentiated by ranking from 1991 to 2006, they found professors who were women remained underrepresented relative to the proportion of women in the general population, although the gap certainly closed over the course of the study period. By undifferentiated ranking, I highlight that the analysis does not distinguish between tenured and nontenured faculty. Following this aggregated view of the professoriate, the proportion of professors who were women was roughly equal to the proportion of those with earned doctorates who were women. This relationship held between 1991 (18 percent vs. 20 percent) and 2006 (32 percent vs. 32 percent). During that same period however, the proportion of professors who were racialized fell when measured against the proportion of those with doctorates who were racialized. Specifically, in 1991, those ratios were 13 percent and 18 percent for a five-point underrepresentation. By 2006, the gap had almost doubled to nine points (16 percent vs. 25 percent). Changes to the census in 2011 preclude a more current assessment, but the recent self-identification disclosures by senior leaders in the Universities Canada survey seem to echo these diverging demographic patterns.

3 I have not recommended the expulsion of all discretion in the way criteria may be applied in deference to the fact that decisions are as much art as science, but to the extent that unbridled discretion tends to perpetuate status quo biases, some restraint remains appropriate.

WORKS CITED

Groysberg, Boris, Jeremiah Lee, Jesse Price, and J. Yo-Jud Cheng. 2018. "The Leader's Guide to Corporate Culture." *Harvard Business Review* January–February 2018: 4.

Ramos, Howard, and Peter S. Li. 2017. "Differences in Representation and Employment Income of Racialized University Professors in Canada." In *The Equity Myth: Racialization and Indigeneity at Canadian Universities,* edited by Frances Henry, Enkashi Dua, Carl E. James, Audrey Kobayashi, Peter Li, Howard Ramos, and Malinda S. Smith, 46–64. Vancouver: UBC Press.

11

Reclaiming Kindness and Compassionate Pedagogy

JANICE NIEMANN

Despite actual and alleged efforts to create gender-equitable academic work environments (Abramson, Rippeyoung, and Price 2015, 239; Wallin and Wallace 2016, 372), women academics, although often inhabiting positions of privilege, remain disadvantaged in the academy due to patriarchal power structures (Abramson, Rippeyoung, and Price 2015, 226; Dengate, Farenhorst, and Peter 2019, 2). Students consistently rate women professors lower than men professors on teaching evaluations, a gender gap demonstrated by scholarship in gender studies, the scholarship of teaching and learning (SoTL), and higher education studies. Recently, scholarship has shown the nuances of this disparity: although women tend to score lower than men on overall teaching effectiveness, there are some distinct traits on which they score higher. Unsurprisingly, given the patriarchal structures of most higher education institutions, the qualities associated with women are markedly undervalued despite myriad evidence that points to kindness, compassion, and community-building as beneficial to student learning.

This chapter first reviews current scholarship on gender disparities in student evaluations of teaching (SETs), focusing on areas in which women's and men's SET results differ in discernable ways and critiquing the underlying, often unspoken, implications of scholars' discussions about this gender disparity. Most scholarship on gender differences in SETs maintains a gender binary and does not explicitly include the experiences of Two-Spirit, nonbinary, and gender-diverse academics; this chapter reflects the current, and notably incomplete, state of scholarship on the topic (for an exception that includes nonbinary respondents, see Lakeman et al. 2021). I use terms such as "women-coded qualities" to refer to characteristics stereotypically associated with women and women instructors, but that is not to say that these qualities occur only in women or that they prescribe any sort of inherent womanhood or preclude other genders. Many academics also face discrimination based on factors other than gender, especially academics who are Black, Indigenous, and people of colour (BIPOC), so, while this chapter focuses primarily on gender, it addresses intersections with race throughout. By commenting on race, my intention is not to discount the experiences of other marginalized women academics, such as disabled women, queer women, fat women, poor women, or women who speak English as an additional language; rather, in light of worldwide protests against anti-Black police violence in the wake of Minneapolis police officer Derek Chauvin murdering George Floyd, race seems particularly important to foreground at this moment in time. By participating in ongoing scholarship about antiracist work, I hope to avoid "tiptoeing around whiteness in feminist spaces" (Eddo-Lodge 2017, 154), including the space of this chapter. This chapter offers a new analysis of the patriarchal premises behind research on gender disparities in SETs, demonstrating the degree to which much scholarship on SETs reinforces the gender disparities it seeks to interrogate, which is why an extended literature review is important – the implicit (and likely unintentional) bias against women-coded qualities is pervasive throughout most of the research cited in this chapter.

Second, this chapter makes the case for compassionate pedagogy – teaching with active kindness – as an evidence-based pedagogical method that prioritizes the creation of learner-centred environments. Recent years have seen a compassionate turn in SoTL, accompanied by a surge of scholarship on compassionate pedagogy. This section frames compassionate pedagogy as a feminist response to scholarly concerns about gender disparities in SETs. Third, this chapter proposes that higher education institutions in Canada embrace compassionate pedagogy in the classroom and write it into policy, in part because compassionate pedagogy is one potential way to decentre whiteness in Canadian higher education institutions and practice antiracist pedagogy; vitally, significant increases in federal funding to higher education institutions would enable the implementation of compassionate pedagogy on a larger scale than any one person could in their classroom. This work is not the first of its kind, nor is this argument the first to advocate for kindness as feminist. Reknowned activist, educator, and intersectional feminist bell hooks (2003, 90), for instance, posits that in imperialist white-supremacist capitalist patriarchal culture, caring for and "serving students well is an act of critical resistance." Similarly, gender studies scholars Shoshana Magnet, Corinne Lysandra Mason, and Kathryn Levenen (2014, 8) propose "kindness as a feminist tool for radically reshaping feminism within the academy." Building on this body of research, this chapter proposes compassionate pedagogy as an evidence-based strategy to combat this gender discrimination, ultimately addressing a gap at the intersection of SoTL and gender studies.

GENDER DISPARITIES IN STUDENT EVALUATIONS OF TEACHING

SETs are widely used in higher education to inform hiring, tenure, and promotion decisions, despite there being little evidence of their validity when it comes to measuring teaching skill. In addition to gender disparities, learning-analytics researchers Leah P. Macfadyen and colleagues (2016, 821) point out other problems with SETs, including low student response rates, the potential for students to exhibit biases beyond gender biases when completing them, and students' lack of qualifications to objectively evaluate teaching strategies (see also Chapter 1 in this volume). These factors prompt many academics to advocate for alternative methods of teaching assessment or the abolishment of SETs altogether. SETs can have monumental impacts on the careers of precarious academics such as graduate students, early-career researchers, and sessional or adjunct instructors (Smith, Gamarro, and Toor 2017, 287), and these people are often the ones without the institutional clout to prompt policy changes around SETs. Within this context of bias and shaky validity, this chapter focuses specifically on differences in ratings that students give women and men instructors – and how SETs maintain traditional gender stereotypes – as well as the critical implications of gender disparity and how the scholarship that discusses it continues to perpetuate some of these biases.

Historically, scholars have acknowledged the existence of gender disparities in SETs, although the consensus seemed to grant that, although there were gender differences, they were ultimately insignificant (see, e.g., Centra and Gaubatz 2000; Basow, Codos, and Martin 2013). In the latter half of the 2010s, a new wave of SET research on gender shifted away from examining general scores of overall effectiveness and toward the specific areas in which different genders score differently (see, e.g., Punyanunt-Carter and Carter 2015). At a large public North American medical school, researcher in medicine and medical education Helen K. Morgan and colleagues (2016) found that women instructors scored lower in "overall quality of teaching" in four different rotations in fields traditionally dominated by both women and men. Susan A. Basow, Stephanie Codos, and Julie L. Martin (2013, 354), experts in psychology, found that students scored women higher on faculty-student interactions, and, troublingly, that there seemed to be a correlation on SET scores between instructor attractiveness and other instructor qualities (361). Kristina M.W. Mitchell, educational director and political science instructor, and Jonathan Martin (2018), professor of government, analyzed content from course evaluations and the website Rate My Professors, where students post anonymous reviews of their higher education instructors; they found that, in identical online course sections, men received higher average scores than women in all categories except administrative categories unrelated to the instructor, where women and men scored similarly (these categories include "university-level procedures such as registration and advising" [651]). This finding about administrative categories suggests that students do not indiscriminately give women lower scores, but that students score women lower on teaching specifically (651). Mitchell and Martin also note that women are likely to be called "teachers," whereas men are likely to be called "professors," no matter their actual positions (649; see also Smith, Gamarro, and Toor 2017, 268). Aligning closely with traditionally women-coded qualities, and what Sandra Acker and Michelle Webber (2016, 237), scholars of social justice education and sociology, call "the popular image of women academics as committed teachers, good citizens and dedicated institutional housekeepers," Mitchell and Martin (2018, 649) also found that students are more likely to evaluate women instructors' personalities in SETs than they are men's, with common comments addressing women instructors' warmth, supportiveness, and nurturance.

Rate My Professors has also encouraged students to comment on instructors' appearances, with the protection of anonymity offered by the internet and the website's now-defunct "hotness" rating for instructors denoted by a hot pepper icon, a practice that further entrenched harmful gender stereotypes in SETs. Although Heather E. Campbell, Karen Gerdes, and Sue Steiner (2005), researchers in public affairs and social work, conducted a study that did not find a significant causal relationship between instructor attractiveness and SET scores, many other studies, such as economic sociologist Tobias Wolbring and sociology researcher Patrick Riordan's (2016) study on instructor beauty, have found that students do tend to give higher SET ratings to attractive instructors. Comments on instructor appearance, one type of what mental health nurse and scholar Richard Lakeman and colleagues (2021) call "non-constructive" feedback, are common occurrences for women instructors (see also Leong 2020), especially on anonymous online platforms. Of the 791 respondents in Lakeman and colleagues' Australian study, 723 reported receiving nonconstructive feedback through anonymous online SET platforms, with women reporting more instances than men of nonconstructive feedback, such as comments on their appearance, attire, and accents. Although some of these comments seemed to be intended as compliments, "most of the examples related to appearance and attire were clearly intended to be insulting," with some constituting "sexual harassment" (Lakeman et al. 2021, 1251). Due to the anonymity of posters on Rate My Professors, this platform has immense potential to contribute to further gendered discrimination in SETs and cyber violence against women academics beyond SETs through student comments on women instructors' appearances, fashion choices, sizes, and perceived attractiveness.

Much in the same way that women score higher in stereotypically women-coded qualities, men score higher in stereotypically men-coded qualities, such as "scholarship/knowledge" and "dynamism/enthusiasm" (Basow, Codos, and Martin 2013, 353). In her study on online course evaluations at a French university, Anne Boring (2017), expert in economics and gender studies, found that students rated men instructors higher than women instructors on knowledge, authoritativeness, and content delivery, despite there being no discernable difference in teaching effectiveness as measured by comparable results on students' final exam scores. Boring found that men and women scored similarly on warmth and nurturance. The most notable place where Boring found that students rate women instructors higher than men was in terms of encouraging group work, but, even then, it was only the women students who showed this rating pattern. Significantly, Boring notes that "students sometimes reward (or at least do not penalize) women on stereotypically female criteria, while systematically rewarding men on stereotypically male criteria" (35), speaking to one possible reason these disparities continue to persist: role congruity theory. Boring posits that "students may expect women to behave according to female gender stereotypes and men according to male gender stereotypes, while also evaluating overall teaching competence according to the characteristics of the stereotypical male professor" (28). These studies represent the field's general findings: SETs maintain traditional gender stereotypes for instructors, undervaluing women-coded qualities. Furthermore, implicit in these finding is that students expect women instructors to behave like stereotypically white women. As Boring suggests, there are three important aspects to these perpetuations of stereotypes: one, that students expect women to be kind, nurturing, helpful, and community-minded; two, that students expect men to be knowledgeable, authoritative, and organized and to hold a strong classroom presence; and three, that students expect good instructors to share these stereotypically masculine qualities. Thus, if an instructor, however effective, demonstrates stereotypically women-coded qualities, or qualities consistent with racial stereotypes, such as the so-called angry Black woman, role congruity theory would dictate that students view that instructor as less than ideal because women-coded qualities do not align with their ideal of a white man professor. Although students might respond to men transgressing gender and instructor stereotypes by giving lower scores to men who display women-coded qualities, current research does not demonstrate this phenomenon.

Several interwoven factors contribute to the persistence of these gender disparities and their prevalence in SETs. Extending role congruity theory beyond teaching to all of academia, sociologist Jennifer Dengate, environmental scientist Annemieke Farenhorst, and sociologist Tracey Peter (2019, 4) suggest that "academic success assumes an ideal masculine worker," again presumably white, who need not take on family or caregiving responsibilities, while SoTL scholars Dawn C. Wallin and Janice Wallace (2016, 363) position the "gendered organizational structures" within the academy as obstacles to women's work and as potential opportunities to enact change for the better in regard to dismantling gender norms. Returning to teaching, experts in cultural diversity Anish Bavishi, Juan M. Madera, and Michelle R. Hebl (2010, 246) suggest that "occupational stereotyping," similar to role congruity theory, might cause disparities in SETs. Laura J. Weinkle, Jennifer M. Stratford, and Lisa M.J. Lee (2020), researchers in technology, neuroscience, and biology, found that low student ratings were linked to perceptions of instructors as nonnormative or nonstereotypical, despite finding no significant differences in Likert ratings across the four instructor voices in their study (old woman, young woman, old man, young man). Again, though, current research does not suggest that men are penalized for failing to conform to this "ideal masculine worker" script. This dearth of evidence does not mean that men who transgress gender stereotypes are not punished in some way, only that, if they are, it is not well documented.

While this chapter focuses on gender, and this book focuses largely on the experiences of women, it is important to acknowledge that SETs discriminate beyond gender. SETs work unfairly against BIPOC instructors; instructors in fine arts, arts, and humanities; and instructors in other marginalized groups. Bavishi, Madera, and Hebl (2010, 252) discuss the "double stigma" experienced by, among others, Black women, women who teach in the humanities, and Asian American women, with the bias against BIPOC women rooted in racism, and the bias against humanities instructors resulting from a privileging of STEM fields (science, technology, engineering, and mathematics, which are notably all disciplines dominated by men) in higher education. Acker and Webber (2016, 237) note that in Ontario, BIPOC academics "frequently find themselves taking on extra responsibilities as students turn to them for mentoring and departments ask them to take on diversity-related service responsibilities," adding extra labour, and extra emotional labour, to already adverse working conditions. Elsewhere, Acker and Webber (2017, 544) comment on the "chronic disadvantages for women and minorities" experienced by early-career academics in the US, meaning that while these problems exist in Canada, they do not exist in Canada alone. Political scientists Malinda S. Smith, Kimberly Gamarro, and Mansham Toor (2017, 289) discuss the specifics of student evaluations and "unconscious biases about subject matter content and role expectations," noting that BIPOC instructors teaching English literature or women teaching in traditionally men-dominated fields such as business, STEM, and political science will likely face additional challenges in the classroom. In addition to dealing with harmful racist stereotypes, BIPOC women instructors must also contend with not meeting the idealized white man stereotype; as Reni Eddo-Lodge (2017, 185), journalist, feminist, and antiracist activist, succinctly articulates, the "angry black woman stereotype wields misogyny as a stick to beat black women over the head with." This context is not to suggest that white women are being rewarded in SETs for being women (they are not), but that BIPOC women are even further from the image of an ideal white man professor (see also Collins 2000) and that distance is often reflected in their SET scores and comments. Here, too, it is important to note that there are disproportionately fewer BIPOC women in Canadian academia than there are white women, a disparity that speaks to the broader white-supremist foundations of many Canadian higher education institutions.

Scholarship on gender disparities in SETs explicitly positions this disparity as a problem for two main reasons: first, the patriarchal structure of higher education institutions is persistent, and second, institutions make hiring, tenure, and promotion decisions based on inherently discriminatory documents. The first of these two problems remains present in research on gender disparities and gender inequities in higher education, and Canadian research often frames it as a problem despite institutional efforts to combat it since at least the 1980s (Abramson, Rippeyoung, and Price 2015, 239; Wallin and Wallace 2016, 372). One of the most obvious signs that the patriarchy persists in academia is research that consistently shows "that men progress through the ranks more quickly than women, especially to full professor" (Abramson, Rippeyoung, and Price 2015, 228), and this progress may be due in part to their comparatively stronger teaching evaluations than those of their women and gender-queer colleagues. In terms of institutional pragmatism and policy implications, this SET gender disparity is a problem because SETs are discriminatory, and they are being used to inform hiring, tenure, and promotion decisions (see Macfadyen et al. 2016, 822–23). By continuing to use SETs in their current form, Canadian higher education institutions remain complicit in perpetuating gender-based discrimination.

Consistently implied throughout the literature, though, is the idea that gender disparities in SETs are a problem because women are linked to women-coded qualities and are, therefore, portrayed as lesser teachers than men. This implication, though not articulated outright, is a serious problem because the premise is flawed. One goal of this chapter is to demonstrate the extent to which much SET research unintentionally reinforces aspects of the gender disparities that it aims to interrogate. This scholarship rightly raises the issue of gender disparity but, in the process, unwittingly conflates women-coded qualities with being a lesser teacher. In actuality, I argue that educators who exhibit or embody women-coded qualities, such as kindness, compassion, and community-building, are not lesser instructors at all. As the next section demonstrates, these characteristics are often the foundation of compassionate pedagogy, an effective and evidence-based teaching method. Scholarship on SETs has thoroughly and responsibly documented gender disparities in SET results, and the next step must be reflecting on and interrogating these metanarratives of gender and teaching. By allowing the hierarchy of gender-coded qualities to remain unquestioned, and, indeed, remain a hierarchy at all, scholars may end up undermining their own missions for gender equity in higher education. A critical question emerges from the research: Why are women not being given adequate credit for their knowledge and leadership? Another equally critical question, however, emerges as well: Why are higher education institutions not placing more value on the kindness and community-mindedness for which so many women instructors are regularly lauded, and which undergird so much effective, learner-centred teaching? One way to validate these women-coded qualities is by turning to compassionate pedagogy.

THE CASE FOR COMPASSIONATE PEDAGOGY

Recent years have seen a compassionate turn in pedagogy studies. In the United Kingdom, Caroline Walker-Gleaves (2019, 94), expert in education theory, notes that "the documentation of excellent and exceptional teaching, especially through the increasing publicity given to teaching awards ... together with the growth in awareness of movements such as the Scholarship of Teaching and Learning, suggests that a key attribute of such academics is the ability to care and enact their practice of a caring pedagogy." Similarly, Saloshna Vandeyar and Ronel Swart (2016), experts in education and diversity, and Yusef Waghid (2019), philosopher of education, both discuss ways to incorporate care into postapartheid classrooms in South Africa. Much of this new scholarship on compassionate pedagogy focuses on its benefits for marginalized groups in the academy, such as BIPOC students and first-generation students. Again, kindness in the classroom is not a new idea, but compassionate pedagogy as a formal method of teaching is relatively new. Twenty-five years ago, Sandra Acker and SoTL scholar Grace Feuerverger (1996, 403) lamented that "a discourse of teaching as caring is not the dominant one" in faculties and departments in Canadian higher education institutions. In what follows, I argue that compassion *should* be one of the dominant teaching discourses in higher education institutions in Canada because it offers a tangible and implementable means of combatting some of the gender disparities in SETs.

Compassion comprises "two key components: observing suffering and taking action" (Hancock 2018, 67). Paul Gibbs (2017, 3), director of education research at the University of Middlesex, reiterates, "while empathy refers more generally to our ability to take the perspective of, imagine and feel the emotions of another person, compassion is when those feelings and thoughts include the desire to help those who are vulnerable or in distress." This distinction is important because the practice of compassion, actually doing things for your students and yourself, differentiates this method from merely recognizing students' struggles or offering a generic kindness for kindness's sake, what renowned feminist and educator Nel Noddings (2013) would call "caring-about," instead of the relationship-based "caring-for" that most closely aligns with compassionate pedagogy.

In other words, compassionate pedagogy is teaching with active kindness. This concept sounds simple but is seldom foregrounded in Canadian higher education institutions because, in the era of neoliberal universities and colleges, "compassion does not feature in business models of profit maximization" (Gibbs 2017, 9). Compassionate pedagogy requires compassion for learners and compassion for educators, which can, occasionally, come at the expense of on-paper productivity. Kathryn Waddington (2017, 49), psychologist and expert in creating compassionate institutions, starts with the self, positing three "interacting components" of self-compassion: "self-kindness," "a sense of common humanity," and "mindfulness." Self-compassion should be emphasized first because it can be easy to lose oneself amid compassion for others, especially if teaching large first-year courses with hundreds of students. Without cultivating this self-kindness, sense of common humanity, and mindfulness, instructors might not have the emotional resources to practice compassionate pedagogy, nor will they be modelling compassion for their students because "self-compassion lays the foundation for the ability to engage genuinely and sustainably compassionately with others" (Waddington 2017, 51; see also Russell 2014). Practically, self-compassion might look like taking weekends off, forgiving oneself for missing a deadline, designing learning opportunities for students that do not need to be marked, or maintaining firm assignment deadlines in large classes to respect self-set marking schedules. It might also look like BIPOC instructors seeking out or creating BIPOC-only spaces within their institutions for research or teaching support. White instructors can practice compassion by respecting BIPOC spaces and using their white privilege to ensure that higher education institutions allow and support the existence of these BIPOC spaces. In terms of supporting students, compassionate pedagogy overlaps with many tenets of universal design in that it aims to create a learning environment that helps students thrive, whatever thriving might look like for them. Here, compassionate pedagogy could look like polling students regularly to check their understanding of course concepts and reviewing topics that remain confusing, granting students extensions without a doctor's note (often more easily done in small classes than large ones, although a possible option in large classes would be granting extensions with the caveat that late assignments will not receive full written feedback) (see Wood 2017), or giving assignment options so that students who dislike public speaking or write most clearly in colloquial English have the opportunity to showcase their learning on their own terms. Because the primary task of higher education institutions should be meeting the needs of its students as caregiving organizations (Waddington 2017, 58), compassionate instructors do not aim to churn out adequate test scores but, rather, work sincerely to support and facilitate student learning.

Compassionate pedagogy embodies the women-coded qualities that higher education institutions and SoTL scholarship have discounted as less valued and less valuable than men-coded qualities. Noddings (2013, chap. 3) distinguishes a teacher from merely "a textbook-like source" by looking at the care they provide for their students. Walker-Gleaves (2019, 101) lists the following instructor qualities among those that exemplify the creation of "effective and impactful pedagogical relationships": "listen to students," "show empathy for students," "[be] active in the processes of learning in class," and "show an active concern in students' personal lives," although this concern for students' personal lives might be possible only in small classes or one-on-one during office hours. hooks (2003) argues that community-building and compassion are components of antiracist pedagogy, which makes compassionate pedagogy particularly important for white instructors: she writes that "teachers are often among that group most reluctant to acknowledge the extent to which white-supremacist thinking informs every aspect of our culture including the way we learn, the content of what we learn, and the manner in which we are taught" (25). Note the explicit overlap here with stereotypically women-coded qualities – instructors who practice compassionate pedagogy are kind, nurturing, focused on creating a sense of community in the classroom, and committed to individual faculty-student relationships. Magnet, Mason, and Levenen (2014) explore the history of the academy's double emotional standard for women, where women academics are expected to perform all tasks based in caring, but not any other emotions, such as frustration or anger. This chapter does not advocate for compulsory compassion. Rather, it advocates for higher education institutions to recognize compassion as an effective, evidence-based, and valuable method of instruction while also acknowledging that compassionate pedagogy will likely manifest differently depending on the size of a course or an instructor's teaching load. In their study of women faculty in Canada, Acker and Feuerverger (1996, 413) interviewed a woman who "noted laconically 'Students crying in your office don't count for a damn on your CV.'" Sitting with a crying student, as so many women instructors have done (and many nonwomen instructors too), becomes compassionate pedagogy when the instructor offers to help, offers to connect the student with on-campus support resources, offers to review an assignment draft (although this feedback may be possible only for instructors with lighter marking loads or if students book appointments during office hours), offers to extend a deadline, offers anything to help the student achieve their learning goals, or even just helps the student regain some emotional equilibrium. This work is important, and this work is often the mark of a valued and effective instructor.

Compassionate pedagogy creates a learner-centred environment where the instructor facilitates students' learning on their own terms. A foundational method for creating learner-centred classrooms is giving students control over their own learning and offering individual support, all of which play a part in compassionate pedagogy. As hooks (2003, 92) explains, the

> teacher who can ask of students, "What do you need in order to learn?" or "how can I serve?" brings to the work of educating a spirit of service that honors the students' will to learn. Committed acts of caring let all students know that the purpose of education is not to dominate, or prepare them to be dominators, but rather to create the conditions for freedom. Caring educators open the mind, allowing students to embrace a world of knowing that is always subject to change and challenge.

Students learn better when they feel they belong to a classroom community because they are comfortable expressing new and potentially vulnerable ideas (Ludvik 2017, 158; Waghid 2019, 22; Walker-Gleaves 2019, 98–100). Caring about students and students' ideas also helps to create excitement for the topics covered in class, as well as the students' own research interests (Magnet, Mason, and Levenen 2014, 14–15; Noddings 2013, chap. 8). This buy-in from students, as most educators know at least anecdotally, is vital to long-term student engagement and sustained learning. It is much easier to foster this student excitement by listening to individual learners than it is by authoritatively delivering knowledge in a one-way transmission. Although one-on-one conversations with students can be impossible in large lectures, there are many other methods of centring student voices in the learning process; for instance, one might allot a portion of lecture time to small group discussions, with representatives from two or three groups quickly reporting back to the whole class. Interactive participation and engagement activities for students that receive either no mark or a completion mark can also build classroom community without adding to the labour of already overworked instructors, incorporating both compassion for students and self-compassion. Practising compassion with students also models for students the importance of care and empathy (Boyd and Grant 2019, 73). Although it is difficult to measure, one result of a humanities education is often the cultivation of empathy in students because many humanities disciplines ask students to critically consider multiple subjective perspectives on a given topic: a historical event, a literary work, a philosophical concept, a translation, a cultural context. However, the humanities are certainly not the only discipline where compassion is important. In other disciplines, it might seem harder to incorporate this compassionate education into courses, but adopting a practice of compassionate pedagogy could help achieve that aim without drastically altering course content. The adoption of compassionate pedagogy, remembering that it begins with self-compassion, might also encourage Canadian academics to find a balance between work and rest that so often remains elusive in our capitalist culture of expecting, encouraging, and rewarding overwork and, especially in the case of precariously employed academics, unpaid labour.

By moving away from compulsory compassion and, instead, reclaiming kindness as an active instructional choice, compassionate pedagogy becomes feminist pedagogy. If we take gender equity as the basis of feminism, then recognizing women-coded qualities as at least as valuable as men-coded ones, especially when there is ample evidence to demonstrate that these qualities make effective educators, is a feminist act. Opting to practice intentional compassion in the classroom and write compassion into higher education policy then becomes feminist praxis. I am indebted to scholars before me who have named variations of compassion, such as community (hooks 2003), care (Noddings 2013), and kindness (Magnet, Mason, and Levenen 2014), as opportunities for feminist empowerment for laying the foundation for this cornerstone of my argument. Returning once again to SETs, higher education institutions in Canada should focus not on finding ways to give women instructors the currently unacknowledged credit they deserve for exhibiting men-coded qualities; rather, these institutions should strive to shift their underlying pedagogical values to make hiring, tenure, and promotion decisions based on the evidence-based methods that many women instructors are already performing successfully. The problem here is not women; neither is it misrepresentations of women. Despite SETs having been proven to show and (presumably) perpetuate gender stereotypes, the real issue is rooted in the patriarchal value frameworks of higher education institutions.

To address gender disparities in SETs, in addition to dismantling harmful patriarchal structures, Canadian higher education institutions should actively value compassionate pedagogy in their classrooms and actively write compassion into their policies. If colleges and universities want their instructors' teaching assessed, then providing funding (including funding for hiring qualified individuals and training in pedagogy) to have peers or staff from learning and teaching centres perform the assessments could be one alternative to SETs. If SETs remain the same, then higher education institutions should make explicit that compassionate pedagogical qualities will be weighted at least equally with conventional pedagogical qualities in hiring, tenure, and promotion decisions. Although SETs should perhaps be abolished altogether, that simple shift will not address the underlying gender disparity in instructor expectations and appreciation. Even though there seems to be a contemporary discourse about Canada being advanced in its gender equity, there still exist in Canadian universities "structural obstacles differentially affecting women, which are informed by stereotypes of femininity (e.g., women are more compassionate and nurturing)" (Dengate, Farenhorst, and Peter 2019, 11), which is why this specific pedagogical method is so apt: it addresses and embraces the qualities that most scholarship seems to assume are limiting the advancement of women academics. Magnet, Mason, and Levenen (2014, 8) advocate for the mobilization of kindness as a political act, reiterating "the importance of micropolitical tactics in the classroom," and aiming to simultaneously "address the importance of curricular reform and larger institutional reflections on kindness" and "argue that kindness is valuable and should be cultivated at the micro level." This chapter, then, adds to a lively discussion about how academics, particularly women academics, can legitimize kindness as a method on multiple levels – practical, theoretical, and bureaucratic.

Starting with individual pedagogical choices, compassion in the classroom works best when instructors actively create a community of practice with themselves and their students, a learning relationship based in what hooks (2003) calls "mutuality." Inspired by Noddings, for instance, Waghid (2019, 21) posits that "when students and teachers engage with one another in an atmosphere of mutual trust, they act respectfully and admirably towards one another thereby confirming and recognising one another's satisfying achievements. In such a way, caring becomes a pedagogical possibility," ultimately framing caring pedagogy as inclusive (2) and interrelational (5). Similarly, Magnet, Mason, and Levenen (2014, 3) "advocate for a form of kindness in the classroom that can bear the vulnerability of others and that bothers to do the labor of being compassionate while not giving in to forms of leniency that make appraisal impossible." Such pedagogy promotes working together, learning together, and mutual support in the classroom. It would be impossible to foster the vulnerability that Magnet, Mason, and Levenen name as vital to this project without the reciprocal respect that Waghid (2019) repeatedly emphasizes. In Canada, most academics have the freedom to dictate, at least to an extent, how they run their classrooms, so space exists in the academy for compassionate pedagogy to flourish, or, at the very least, for educators to experiment with aspects of it as a new method. Something as simple as peer review activities for student assignments reinforces communal learning, asks students to be vulnerable in sharing their work with peers, and creates space for students to celebrate each other's achievements and ideas. These peer review activities do not necessarily need to be graded, either, making them one option for incorporating compassionate pedagogy into large classes. Granting students extensions without demanding formal documentation explicitly demonstrates compassion for the student's situation, but it also implicitly demonstrates compassion by showing that the instructor trusts the student and by not forcing the student to disclose personal or medical details. This level of instructor respect for the student experience is not necessarily a commonplace occurrence, and it could be a relatively simple way to begin facilitating a compassionate environment. Although this chapter has twice mentioned granting extensions as an example of compassionate pedagogy (see also Wood 2017), it is possible to be too flexible for students; granting extensions is undoubtedly compassionate toward students, but it might not foster the resilience that most students need to be successful in higher education. It also might not be compassionate for a sessional instructor teaching four sections of academic writing or for instructors teaching large first-year lectures with hundreds, or possibly thousands, of students – in that case, compassionate pedagogy would likely mean reminding students that deadlines are firm and explaining why they are. Part of compassionate pedagogy is asking for compassion from students because compassionate classrooms are mutually supportive communities, and sharing knowledge, as hooks (2003) explains, helps to dismantle oppressive systems within education institutions, even when that knowledge is as basic as the logic behind course policies.

Compassion, though, needs to be implemented beyond the classroom and written into institutional policy. This call for action is amplified by other scholars' similar calls for policy reform – calls "for institutions to recognize and valorize this important care work, especially as it is mostly performed by women" (Magnet, Mason, and Levenen 2014, 4); recognition that "it is what the university stands for, and what it rewards and what it ignores, that is at issue. The disadvantage women encounter is more systemic than it is intentional – though no less problematic for all that" (Acker and Feuerverger 1996, 417–18). It is a desire for universities to aspire to compassionate practice (Gibbs 2017, 8), and a call to action because "to intervene in dominator culture, to live consciously, we must be willing to share with anyone knowledge about how to make the transition from a dominator model to a partnership model. If we want change, we must be willing to teach" (hooks 2003, 75–76). The time for change is now, and Gibbs (2017) suggests a number of ways that higher education institutions can show their compassion for students (many of which would require significant funding increases, as this chapter has emphasized): time should be built into instructors' schedules for student support; compassion should be embedded in the substance, context, and application of curricula; and higher education institutions should recognize, in some way, compassionate acts of others. Additionally, this list should include an amendment to hiring, tenure, and promotion guidelines that values instructor compassion as much as instructor knowledge. Following geography professor Bill Boyd and SoTL scholar Airdre Grant (2019, 72), this notion of compassionate pedagogy should be extended to include mentorship of graduate students and early-career researchers, as well as mid-career researchers for whom there exist few mentorship opportunities. Of course, institutional policy reform takes more than changing a late submission policy on a course syllabus, and, as Acker and Webber (2016, 234) point out, "Provincial higher education policy efforts in Ontario tend to focus on the institutional level, requiring various forms of compliance from each university. Expansion of these policy initiatives is relatively recent. Thus far, they have not reached deep down into the everyday lives of academics." Thus, compassion-based changes need to happen simultaneously from the top down and from the bottom up. Implementing compassion only in institutional policy or only in the classroom may be just enough to address gender disparities in SETs, but our goals for gender equity, antiracism, and compassionate teaching should extend beyond the bare minimum to create lasting change for women in academia and the students they teach. Because social relationships form the foundation for compassion (Gibbs 2017), the entire social context of the institution needs to change to support compassionate pedagogy.

CONCLUSION

So, how should we go about implementing compassion and reclaiming kindness as feminist pedagogy? Wallin and Wallace (2016, 366) "found strong evidence that the women of [their] study successfully challenged the structural discourses of the academy in ways that (re) shaped and transformed the higher education milieu of Educational Administration in Canada," and if that level of change is achievable in one field, then it seems possible that we could also achieve it at an institutional and a national level. Nancy Billias (2017, 147), philosopher and educator, shares US examples of successful compassionate policy at Western Connecticut State University, the University of St. Joseph, and Central Connecticut State University, with compassion defined at the latter "in terms of action: not merely feeling for victims of violence or trauma, but actively working to alleviate suffering, wherever possible." In other words, this compassion does not need to focus on extreme cases of suffering, but, rather, policy should include compassion for every student who might need it. The timeliness of this chapter, written during the COVID-19 pandemic, is not lost on me. In this moment of global crisis, more than ever, the value of compassionate pedagogy is apparent – creating space for learning (and inevitable mistakes) as we collectively shifted to online teaching; accommodating students' absences; asking for support when we need it, as instructors, and, thus, strengthening communities of practice; and forgiving ourselves and each other if the impacts of our actions do not align with our intentions. Canadian academia is currently undergoing a monumental shift, and, if we embrace compassionate pedagogy as so many higher education institutions have done in the short-term, we could make substantial long-term changes.

An important future project would involve a study of these policies themselves and drafts of compassionate policies for Canadian higher education institutions. Gibbs (2017, 9) posits that "compassion does not feature in business models of profit maximization," but that might not be true for compassionate pedagogy. The marketability of compassionate pedagogy is beyond the scope of this chapter but well worth considering as a potential marketing or recruitment option for universities and colleges looking to promote teaching and positive student experience, as many liberal arts colleges do in the United States. Our aims going forward should be to practice compassionate pedagogy ourselves, role modelling for students, colleagues, and administrators the benefits of kindness and compassion. They should be to push for policy change based on the premise that higher education institutions have an obligation to show compassion to students and employees. They should be to demand dramatically increased federal funding to support pedagogy training, more academic staff and faculty hires, and smaller classes. They should advocate for a value shift when interpreting SETs for all hiring, tenure, and promotion decisions. This chapter highlighted an implicit gender bias underlying scholarship on gender disparities in SETs and proposed compassionate pedagogy as a solution to that problem and as a way to practice feminist pedagogy in patriarchal higher education institutions.

To close this chapter, consider an observation about making lasting change by Eddo-Lodge (2017, 184–85), who explains that "equality is fine as a transitional demand, but it's dishonest not to recognize it for what it is – the easy route. There is a difference between saying 'we want to be included' and saying 'we want to reconstruct your exclusive system.' The former is more readily accepted into the mainstream." Now is the time for Canadian academics and higher education institutions to take the difficult route, look to compassionate pedagogy, and reconstruct entire systems.

WORKS CITED

Abramson, Zelda, Phyllis L.H.F. Rippeyoung, and E. Lisa Price. 2015. "Collective Insecurity: An Exploration of the Experiences of Women Faculty in Atlantic Canada." In *Solitudes of the Workplace: Women in Universities*, edited by Elvi Whittaker, 224–41. Montreal: McGill-Queen's University Press.

Acker, Sandra, and Grace Feuerverger. 1996. "Doing Good and Feeling Bad: The Work of Women University Teachers." *Cambridge Journal of Education* 26 (3): 401–22. doi:10.1080/0305764960260309.

Acker, Sandra, and Michelle Webber. 2016. "Discipline and Punish: The Tenure Review Process in Ontario Universities." In *Assembling and Governing the Higher Education Institution: Democracy, Social Justice and Leadership in Global Higher Education*, edited by Lynette Shultz and Melody Viczko, 233–55. London: Palgrave Macmillan. doi: 10.1057/978-1-137-52261-0_13.

–. 2017. "Made to Measure: Early Career Academics in the Canadian University Workplace." *Higher Education Research and Development* 36 (3): 541–54. doi:10.1080/07294360.2017.1288704.

Basow, Susan A., Stephanie Codos, and Julie L. Martin. 2013. "The Effects of Professors' Race and Gender on Student Evaluations and Performance." *College Student Journal* 47 (2): 352–63. EBSCOhost.

Bavishi, Anish, Juan M. Madera, and Michelle R. Hebl. 2010. "The Effect of Professor Ethnicity and Gender on Student Evaluations: Judged before Met." *Journal of Diversity in Higher Education* 3 (4): 245–56. doi:10.1037/a0020763.

Billias, Nancy. 2017. "On Becoming a Campus of Compassion." In *The Pedagogy of Compassion at the Heart of Higher Education*, edited by Paul Gibbs, 141–53. Cham, Switzerland: Springer.

Boring, Anne. 2017. "Gender Biases in Student Evaluations of Teaching." *Journal of Public Economics* 145: 27–41. doi:10.1016/j.jpubeco.2016.11.006.

Boyd, Bill, and Airdre Grant. 2019. "Unveiling Opportunities for Hope: Is It Too Much to Ask for a Compassionate University?" *Australian Universities' Review* 61 (1): 71–75.

Campbell, Heather E., Karen Gerdes, and Sue Steiner. 2005. "What's Looks Got to Do with It? Instructor Appearance and Student Evaluations of Teaching." *Journal of Policy Analysis and Management* 24 (3): 611–20. doi:10.1002/pam.20122.

Centra, John A., and Noreen B. Gaubatz. 2000. "Is There Gender Bias in Student Evaluations of Teaching?" *Journal of Higher Education* 71 (1): 17–33. doi:10.1080/00221546.2000.11780814.

Collins, Patricia Hill. 2000. *Black Feminist Thought: Knowledge, Consciousness, and the Politics of Empowerment*. 2nd ed. New York: Routledge.

Dengate, Jennifer, Annemieke Farenhorst, and Tracey Peter. 2019. "Sensible or Outdated? Gender and Opinions of Tenure Criteria in Canada." *The Canadian Journal of Higher Education* 49 (2): 1–16. doi:10.7202/1063776ar.

Eddo-Lodge, Reni. 2017. *Why I'm No Longer Talking to White People about Race*. London: Bloomsbury Circus.

Gibbs, Paul. 2017. "Introduction." In *The Pedagogy of Compassion at the Heart of Higher Education*, 1–16. Cham, Switzerland: Springer.

Hancock, Jessica Clare. 2018. "Engaging with Liminalities and Combatting Toxicity: A Compassionate Approach to Developing Professional Identities for PhD Students Who Teach." *Journal of Perspectives of Applied Academic Practice* 6 (3): 66–74. doi: 10.14297/jpaap.v6i3.380.

hooks, bell. 2003. *Teaching Community: A Pedagogy of Hope.* New York: Routledge.

Lakeman, Richard, Rosanne Coutts, Marie Hutchinson, Megan Lee, Debbie Massey, Dima Nasrawi, and Jann Fielden. 2021. "Appearance, Insults, Allegations, Blame and Threats: An Analysis of Non-Constructive Student Evaluation of Teaching in Australia." *Assessment and Evaluation in Higher Education* 47 (8): 1245–58. doi:10.1 080/02602938.2021.2012643.

Leong, Pamela. 2020. *Rating Professors Online: How Culture, Technology, and Consumer Expectations Shape Modern Student Evaluations.* London: Palgrave Macmillan.

Ludvik, Marilee Bresciani. 2017. "Learning about Consequences, Community, Creativity and Courage: Cultivating Compassion in Higher Education Leadership." In *The Pedagogy of Compassion at the Heart of Higher Education,* edited by Paul Gibbs, 155–72. Cham, Switzerland: Springer.

Macfadyen, Leah P., Shane Dawson, Stewart Prest, and Dragan Gašević. 2016. "Whose Feedback? A Multilevel Analysis of Student Completion of End-of-Term Teaching Evaluations." *Assessment and Evaluation in Higher Education* 41 (6): 821–39. doi:10. 1080/02602938.2015.1044421.

Magnet, Shoshana, Corinne Lysandra Mason, and Kathryn Levenen. 2014. "Feminism, Pedagogy, and the Politics of Kindness." *Feminist Teacher* 25 (1): 1–22. https://www. jstor.org/stable/10.5406/femteacher.25.1.0001.

Mitchell, Kristina M.W., and Jonathan Martin. 2018. "Gender Bias in Student Evaluations." *Political Science and Politics* 51 (3): 648–52. doi:10.1017/S104909651800001X.

Morgan, Helen K., Joel A. Purkiss, Annie C. Porter, Monica L. Lypson, Sally A. Santen, Jennifer G. Christner, Cyril M. Grum, and Maya M. Hammond. 2016. "Student Evaluation of Faculty Physicians: Gender Difference in Teaching Evaluations." *Journal of Women's Health* 25 (5): 453–56. doi:10.1089/jwh.2015.5475.

Noddings, Nel. 2013. *Caring: A Relational Approach to Ethics and Moral Education.* 2nd ed. Berkeley: University of California Press. *ProQuest.*

Punyanunt-Carter, Narissa, and Stacy L. Carter. 2015. "Students' Gender Bias in Teaching Evaluations." *Higher Learning Research Communications* 5 (3): 28–37. doi:10.18870/ hlrc.v5i3.234.

Russell, Tamara. 2014. "Mindfulness and Compassion – From a Neuroscience Point of View." *Royal College of Psychiatrists.* https://www.rcpsych.ac.uk/docs/default-source/ members/sigs/spirituality-spsig/tamara-russell-mindfulness-and-compassion.pdf.

Smith, Malinda S., Kimberly Gamarro, and Mansham Toor. 2017. "A Dirty Dozen: Unconscious Race and Gender Biases in the Academy." In *The Equity Myth: Racialization and Indigeneity at Canadian Universities,* edited by Frances Henry, Enakshi Dua, Carl E. James, Audrey Kobayahsi, Peter Li, Howard Ramos, and Malinda S. Smith, 263–96. Vancouver: UBC Press.

Vandeyar, Saloshna, and Ronel Swart. 2016. "Educational Change: A Case for a 'Pedagogy of Compassion.'" *Education as Change* 20 (3): 141–59. doi:10.17159/1947-9417/ 2016/1362.

Waddington, Kathryn. 2017. "Creating Conditions for Compassion." In *The Pedagogy of Compassion at the Heart of Higher Education*, edited by Paul Gibbs, 49–70. Cham, Switzerland: Springer.

Waghid, Yusef. 2019. *Towards a Philosophy of Caring in Higher Education: Pedagogy and Nuances of Care*. London: Palgrave Macmillan.

Walker-Gleaves, Caroline. 2019. "Is Caring Pedagogy Really So Progressive? Exploring the Conceptual and Practical Impediments to Operationalizing Care in Higher Education." In *Higher Education and Hope: Institutional, Pedagogical and Personal Possibilities*, edited by Paul Gibbs and Andrew Peterson, 93–112. London: Palgrave Macmillan.

Wallin, Dawn C., and Janice Wallace. 2016. "From Foxy Loxy to Grit and Moxie: Women Academic Challenging the Orthodoxy in Higher Education." In *Assembling and Governing the Higher Education Institution: Democracy, Social Justice and Leadership in Global Higher Education*, edited by Lynette Shultz and Melody Viczko, 361–83. London: Palgrave Macmillan. doi:10.1057/978-1-137-52261-0_20.

Weinkle, Laura J., Jennifer M. Stratford, and Lisa M. J. Lee. 2020. "Voice in Digital Education: The Impact of Instructors' Perceived Age and Gender on Student Learning and Evaluation." *Anatomical Sciences Education* 13 (1): 59–70. doi:10.1002/ase.1865.

Wolbring, Tobias, and Patrick Riordan. 2016. "How Beauty Works: Theoretical Mechanisms and Two Empirical Applications on Students' Evaluations of Teaching." *Social Science Research* 57: 253–72. doi:10.1016/j.ssresearch.2015.12.009.

Wood, Tara. 2017. "Cripping Time in the College Composition Classroom." *College Composition and Communication* 69 (2): 260–86. https://www.jstor.org/stable/44783615.

12

Social Media for Women in Academia

AUDREY E. BRENNAN and KATHERINE V.R. SULLIVAN

The glass ceiling in the academic ivory tower remains firmly intact, as evidenced by persistent vertical gender segregation (Bertrand and Hallock 2001), with women underrepresented at the highest rungs. The origins of this disparity are varied but include the unequal distribution of nonpromotable work – that is, unpaid or volunteer tasks (Vesterlund 2015) – and the misrecognition of women academics' work and its value. In addition, contemporary sexism exacerbates these roadblocks, which can be insidious and enabled by subtle insults or dismissals (Bennett 2016), sexual harassment, and in more common – and often less obvious – ways, such as mansplaining and manterrupting. The latter terms refer to the realities of women feeling interrupted and talked down to by men (Bridges 2017, 95), a form of sexism that is often compounded by men's obliviousness to the sexist nature of the act due, at least in part, to an inflated sense of entitlement (Manne 2020). Collectively, these barriers lead to a cycle of silence and invisibility for women in academia. With the advent of the internet and social media, however, there are outlets that women can and do use to voice their successes and misgivings (Norris 2001). With these outlets in mind, this chapter aims to answer the following questions: How is Twitter used to discuss the day-to-day professional life of women in academia? What topics and themes emerge? And what do these digital conversations tell us about the state of higher education?

In this chapter, we argue that social media, and most specifically the use of academic-oriented hashtags on Twitter,[1] can act as an alternative space for women to voice their opinions and professional struggles and create a sense of community (Rocheleau and Millette 2015), a space that many lack in the hallowed halls of academia. If women are unheard, their successes go unrecognized in the workplace. We explore whether women academics use alternative outlets to create online communities where they can be heard. Consequently, we ask whether women are also using the online echo chambers dedicated to academia-related discussions to engage, mobilize, and encourage other women.

There is evidence that digital activities, such as being active on social media platforms like Twitter, can be a helpful tool to build online and offline networks (Li et al. 2019). Social media platforms are beneficial when current offline networks include people from similar backgrounds. Unfortunately, there is a dearth of research providing a gendered analysis of Twitter to date, but the existing literature does warn that the digital world can also be a hostile environment for women and marginalized users (Banet-Weiser and Miltner 2016).

We collected a sample of the academic discursive context using key Twitter hashtags, such as #WomenInAcademia and #WomenAlsoKnowStuff. These keywords were collected using an application programming interface (API).[2] Keywords were selected because they address two topics: 1) the struggles faced by women in general and 2) the struggles related to life in academia. This approach allows us to determine how these topics intersect. In doing so, we look at how Twitter is used by women to talk about academia. First, we look at the struggles individuals face as women in academia. Second, we hypothesize that Twitter can be used as an alternative space to discuss women's issues in academia. The crucial reason women look for alternative spaces to exercise their voices, as outlined in the introduction of this book, is that there seems to be a lack of space to do so within the university. We call this the "Ursula effect," whereby the cost of entry into academia for women is their silence on some key issues. However, this silence can also be seen as women's resilience within a world not meant for them. Just as in Disney's telling of *The Little Mermaid* (Clement and Musker 1989), Ursula asks Ariel to give up her voice so she can become human and gain the love of Prince Eric, we believe Twitter is a stepping-stone to breaking the enchanted nautilus shell that holds Ariel's voice, thereby returning it to her so women can likewise reclaim their voices in the academy.

Using a sentiment analysis, we find that academic Twitter and tweets related to the struggles of women are mainly positive. In short, the sentiment analysis we conducted on the tweets demonstrates that Twitter is used primarily as a place of support and encouragement on matters related to academia and to the broader struggles of women. Hence, Twitter can – and is – used as an alternative space for women in academia.

THE WHITE MAN TEMPLATE

Like many other things in the modern world, the academy was built on the white man template (Thomas 2017). A pertinent analogy is the ever-present gender data gap in analyzing many everyday items, such as automobile safety features. Automobile companies use crash-test dummies based on the average man, leading to higher injury and death tolls for women drivers (Perez 2019). This white man template analogy highlights the concept of gender bias. For example, Peter Gronn and Kathy Lacey's (2006) gender bias theory asserts that the lens through which a dominant group – in this case white men – view the world is based on their own biases and, thus, excludes all other perspectives, including those of women. This is the case because, in being dominant, there is no motivation to do otherwise; dominant groups delineate the premises and significance of action conducted via the cloning of their perspectives and priorities to minimize risk for themselves. Hence, women can find that many "little" things, such as the temperature in the office or even the size of smartphones, are othering (Perez 2019). In academia, women leaders often feel othered and that they must minimize their gender differences to be successful (Probert 2005). In this sense, masculinity dominates academia – for example, where men dominate STEM fields and hiring panels that ostensibly hire on merit also rely on masculinist norms for assessment (Knights and Richards 2003).

It is also well established that there is a glass ceiling – a range of informal and invisible barriers – for women in the workplace. Social scientist Belinda Probert (2005) argues that vertical gender segregation in academia – the under-representation of women at senior levels within universities – can be explained by two frameworks: 1) the unequal treatment of employees according to gender and 2) work outcomes resulting from gendered choices (e.g., parenting, family obligations). The gendered allocation of nonpromotable tasks exacerbates this vertical gender segregation (Vesterlund 2015). Part of the explanation may stem from the fact that women, more than men, value the civic nature of their role as professors (Vesterlund 2015) and are more likely to offer their time to actively mentor students. Additionally, academic mothers must navigate two workloads and often build their careers later than their men colleagues (Bagilhole and White 2011). Their caring responsibilities at home have been linked, in an Australian study, to slower career progressions, often equating to a five-year difference between men and women in academia (Ledwith and Manfredi 2000). Nonetheless, Catherine Beaudry and colleagues (Chapter 7 in this volume) find that although women take more time to care for their families, their caring responsibilities have only a weak negative impact.

Another factor that helps to explain vertical gender segregation is misrecognition, "bropropriation,"[3] or the inaccurate reading of the value of specific groups of individuals. For example, in 2019, there was a backlash from misogynist commentators, more commonly known as trolls, about Dr. Katie Bouman's achievement of capturing the first ever image of a black hole. These attacks included fake social media accounts impersonating Bouman and questioning her contribution to the project. Similarly, Professor Dag W. Aksnes and colleagues (2011) found that women researchers are cited less than men researchers; also Michał Krawczyk (2017), professor at the University of Warsaw, screened academic literature for cases of misattribution of cited author's gender and found that women scholars are cited with the presumption that they are men more than ten times more often than men scholars are cited presumed to be women. Amber E. Budden and colleagues (2008) show that, following the introduction of double-blind peer review by the journal *Behavioural Ecology* in 2001, there was a significant increase in women first-authored papers.

This ivory ceiling – and the social and cultural norms behind it – are highly problematic, contributing to a cycle of invisibility or career stagnation for women academics. For example, if women spend more time teaching and, consequently, less time writing and publishing, there will be a gap between their publishing record and the publishing record of their male colleagues. These dynamics lead to men being more highly valued by academia's publish or perish model and therefore invited to more panels due to their scientific contributions. Additionally, motherhood, which can hinder one's academic career, is often used to explain the gender pay gap within academia, further perpetuating the cycle (for more on the gender wage gap, see Johnstone and Momani, Chapter 5, and Beaudry et al., Chapter 7, in this volume).

Indeed, in terms of the gender gap in academia, what is at issue is not so much women's lack of leadership but that institutions have inadequately addressed the insidious sexism and sexual harassment among faculty in the workplace. However, contemporary sexism can be challenging to identify and is often best described as a "death by a thousand cuts" because it can be "insidious, casual, politically correct, even friendly" (Bennett 2016, 5) and masked by subtle insults or dismissals through unnecessary interruptions (manterruptions) and condescending explanations (mansplaining). While these may not seem important individually, they can have an important impact collectively.

Journalist Rebecca Solnit coined the term "mansplaining" in her 2012 essay critiquing men's conversational arrogance. This habit of explaining something to someone in a manner regarded as condescending or patronizing trains women in "self-doubt and self-limitation just as it exercises men's unsupported over-confidence" (5). This disruptive discourse has been analyzed by sociology major Anna Grace Kidd (2017, 3), who argues that institutionalized socialization has led to a society in which a man's voice is seen as having greater value than the voice of a woman: "As long as men continue to dominate the public sphere, women will continue to be interrupted, valued as less than men, and violently silenced." Studies focusing on conversational differences between men and women show very different behaviours. For example, Charlyn M. Laserna, Yi-Tai Seih, and James W. Pennebaker (2014), researchers in psychology, analyzed filler words from transcripts recorded[4] over several days showed that while men and women used filled pauses (uh, um) at almost the same rate, the latter were more likely to use discourse markers (e.g., "I mean," "you know," "like") to show that they were listening or to create a more inclusive conversation. Similarly, Adrienne Hancock and Benjamin Rubin (2015), voice and communication resrearchers, found that women were more likely to be interrupted during a conversation than men, even by other women, and a study by Brigham Young and Princeton University researchers in 2012 shows that women spoke 25 percent less than men in professional meetings (Karpowitz, Mendelberg, and Shaker 2012). Similar occurrences are also found online, where gender inequality can also be measured by the perception of knowledge (Koc-Michalska et al. 2021). For example, a study on the gender dynamics of political discussion online shows that, in general, when commenting online, women are more likely to receive explanations than men (Koc-Michalska et al. 2021). Additionally, more than half of the women in the study's sample experienced digital mansplaining; posting about politics on Twitter increases those odds.

In addition to the lack of verbal space, women have difficulty securing safe physical space. Sexual harassment is a significant threat to women in academia. Sexual harassment has both direct and indirect health effects, including nausea and sleeplessness, loss of self-esteem, fear and anger, feelings of helplessness and isolation, and nervousness and depression (van Roosmalen and McDaniel 1999). According to a 2015 survey conducted by the Association of American Universities (Cantor et al. 2017), one in ten women graduate students report being sexually harassed by a faculty member. In Canada, all fourteen schools with student unions that have signed on to the Our Turn Action Plan (Student Society McGill University 2018), a national, student-led action plan to address campus sexual violence, received a letter grade reflecting rates of sexual harassment on campus. Concordia University in Montreal received the score of D-, whereas Toronto Metropolitan University (formerly known as Ryerson University) received an A-. Unfortunately, very little data are available about sexual harassment among faculty members. According to a 2018 Angus Reid Institute poll, half of women, and one in five men, face sexual harassment in the workplace. Wanda Hurren (2018), a faculty member who has worked in higher education at several Canadian institutions, published an op-ed in *University Affairs* explaining that she has always been subordinate to someone, usually a man, and believes that most situations of sexual harassment among faculty in higher education are not reported for many reasons, including, for example, the secret code or code of silence, coercion, consent, and structural aspects of higher education that enable a secrets code. Caroline Fredrickson (2017), president of the American Constitution Society, talks about the lack of consequences affecting harassers and the fear that speaking out would result in loss of funding, career advancement, and reputation. The 500 Women Scientists Leadership

(2018) add that racialized women and people who are marginalized along sexual and gender minority axes experience higher rates of harassment in academia.

TWITTER AND ACADEMIA

Although there remains a tradition of keeping such experiences quiet, social media platforms such as Twitter have acted as rallying points for social movements such as #MeToo, a digital social movement advocating for survivors of sexual harassment or violence to speak out about their experiences. For example, in 2015, amid the #MeToo movement, the former head of the University of British Columbia's Creative Writing program was accused of sexual assault by a former student on Twitter. The former professor filed a defamation suit against the former student, as well as other professors of the department who publicly supported the claim online (see Quan 2021). Although Twitter has the potential of offering individuals the freedom to act and develop a sense of agency (Singh 2020b), women continue to lack legislative protection when turning to social media to voice issues they must otherwise keep quiet. In 2019, the province of British Columbia passed the Protection of Public Participation Act, which protects free expression by preventing wealthy individuals and large companies from using their resources to sue anyone, such as journalists and activists, with the intention of silencing them.

People need the required technical skills and knowledge of relevant issues to reap any benefits from their use of social media (Singh 2020b). Having such skills influences whether academics choose to use Twitter for professional reasons (Kapidzic 2020; Schneider and Carpenter 2020). Lacking those skills makes it challenging to locate an online network, let alone communicate with it. Interviews with academics about their Twitter use suggest that users tweeting within a given subject field tend to represent the community they target with their tweets (Jordan 2019). A study of Italian academics shows that Twitter is used to discuss topics of interest and academic professional development (Manca and Ranieri 2017, see also Singh 2020a). "Particularly among PhD students and early career scholars, the norms of open online participation helped minimize academia's hierarchies for participants" (Stewart 2015, 305). For these reasons, we hypothesize that PhD students and early-career scholars will be the highest academic users of Twitter.

In a study of German academics, social scientist Sanja Kapidzic (2020) found that Twitter is used for managing professional relationships and academic networking, even if study participants did not add information to their profile that suggested they were using it as a professional rather than personal communication tool. However, it is challenging to separate the personal from the professional on Twitter (Veletsianos, Johnson, and Belikov 2019), and many use Twitter to bridge the personal and the professional. One drawback to this is that tweeting a personal opinion that is not widely shared within relevant disciplines can have professional consequences. Homero Gil de Zúñiga, Matthew Barnidge, and Andrés Scherman (2017), communication researchers, also note that while an online network can benefit a person offline, an offline network does not benefit a person online. But for those who possess the necessary skills, Twitter can be beneficial (Jordan and Weller 2018). While Twitter does not create democratic interactions between scholars, PhD students and early-career scholars can use their online networks as alternate spheres of influence. Studies (see, e.g., Sullivan and Bélanger 2016) have pointed to the potential of social media to offer a more accessible, alternative space for citizens, journalists, and political actors.

LACK OF SPACE: OUR HYPOTHESIS

We argue that there is a lack of "space" for women in academia, primarily because they work under masculine norms and tend to be othered and silenced for breaking these norms.[5] This lack of space, which may look like departments that have not achieved gender parity or few allies in the professional space, can make it unsafe for women to express their struggles. Consequently, we believe that women in academia can use and are using alternative avenues to voice their professional struggles to create a sense of community. We argue that social media platforms offer women academics much-needed online "space," particularly Twitter, which until recently was used as a platform to advocate for the recognition of professional achievement (Waters 2018) but can be used as an alternative space for sharing both successes and grievances to get support from their digital community.

Twitter does not offer defined meeting points, such as those found on Facebook groups or other social media pages. Instead, we argue, hashtags are the glue that holds women in academia together. A hashtag is a keyword that Twitter users include in their tweets to organize information: "Hashtag use can imply a sense of collectiveness, a sense of an audience who, even if its contours are blurred, shares the same interest" (Rocheleau and Millette 2015, 245). Using a hashtag is a good way to share ideas about something (Baker and Lowenthal 2019) and can lead to community formation. Understanding how to use hashtags is one of the necessary skills of social media, and tech-savvy women academics are more likely to use them correctly, helping them locate the social media communities congruent with their views.

Looking at the #MeToo hashtag, sociologists Kaitlynn Mendes, Jessalynn Keller, and Jessica Ringrose (2019) explain that using a hashtag reduces the amount of heavy lifting the person writing the tweet must do. When hashtags are well developed, their use makes implicit reference to an existing discourse. They argue that "although these tweets are on the surface unconnected, when read together, they build a powerful picture of the structural and systemic nature of sexual violence via repetition and accumulation of similarities of experience offered through the hashtag and its sheer volume of usage" (1302). The use of the hashtag also allows others to search for and take part in the community they create (Schneider and Carpenter 2020). Interstingly, however, sociologist Shelley Boulianne (2019) argued that such hashtags tend to mobilize only when they relate to revolutions or social movements. As with Twitter, hashtags can bring both supportive *and* hateful responses (Mendes, Keller, and Ringrose 2019), but the relative safety of using #MeToo denunciations on social media, as opposed to doing it in person, might create space to call out gendered injustices on Twitter.[6]

Academics and PhD students mainly use academic and HigherEd Twitter communities to create their brand image, follow community hashtags, stay in the loop with conferences, and create a support community. Though, as Singh (2020a) has argued, this community is an echo chamber. For example, a Twitter network often begins with an exchange of tweets during a conference (Quan-Haase, Martin, and McCay-Peet 2015). These professional tweets about similar experiences eventually evolve into a social network connection between scholars. However, only about one-third of these new "relationships" transition offline (Greenhow, Li, and Mai 2019).

The creation of *new* hashtags is varied: some emerge organically from the community or another hashtag, eventually gaining recognition by a broader network, while others emerge as a response to a social movement or the media (Antonakis-Nashif 2015, 102). For example, #Mansplaining emerged as a way for women to highlight specific gendered problems, but it is also used by men to contradict and challenge the term and, therefore, the stereotype (Bridges 2017). The latter might be a hateful response to the hashtag in question. However, this study seeks to shed light on women's use of Twitter to discuss their shared experiences of the trials and tribulations of academic life in a safe(r) space.

METHODS AND DATA ANALYSIS

We collected tweets that contained specific hashtags associated with academia, feminism, and gendered injustices using Twitter's rest API. We also considered the co-occurrence of specific hashtags using bigrams – two words that occur next to each other in a given text, in this case, tweets. By selecting a series of hashtags used to talk about academia and gender biases, we isolate specific tweets published by users who speak to these issues within the hashtag publics. However, because not everyone uses hashtags, and when they do, they do not necessarily

TABLE 12.1
Collected hashtags

Hashtag	Speaking to
#AcademicTwitter	*All* academics on Twitter
#WomensReality	Struggles related to gender
#WomenInHigherEd	Women in higher education
#AcademiaIsBroken	Those who think the academic system generally needs fixing
#PhdLife	All PhD students
#EverydaySexism	Those who face sexism
#Manterruptions	Those who are constantly interrupted by men
#Mansplaining	Those who have been interrupted and corrected by men

do it well, we searched Twitter for the *word* instead of just the hashtag. This means that Twitter users did not need to use the "#" symbol to be collected by the API; words relating to the topics were also isolated and collected. Using the term, even without the "#" symbol, still allows a Twitter user to speak to a specific community, and following the threads of that term allowed us to zero in on particular echo chambers (communities), thereby determining the links between the hashtag publics and the theme of relevant discussions.

Data collection began on April 12, 2019. We collected the data over one year. While data collection ranged from April 12, 2019, to April 14, 2020, the analyses were run on tweets published from April 1, 2019, to April 14, 2020, since the April 12, 2019, collection caught tweets dating back to April 1, 2019. All tweets containing the hashtags listed in Table 12.1 were collected using an eighteen thousand a week per hashtag net for each word. While it was possible to get eighteen thousand tweets containing the target hashtags every week, the selection of tweets was random; we had no control over what we would capture in our sample. Casting the net every week for a year allowed us to capture a diverse sample and to isolate trends in how academics use Twitter. We did collect some doubles, which we removed when we cleaned the data. We also limited our data collection to English-language tweets because we were looking for a community (e.g., the echo chamber), and because English is the predominant academic language. This is a limitation of this research since some hashtags cross languages barriers.

Because of the anarchic and sometimes anonymous nature of Twitter, we did not set any restrictions on the geographic location of tweets or their authors.[7] Indeed, the location Twitter users list on their profile often is not a city or a country. Nonetheless, many of the English-language academic tweeters in Canada came from Toronto, Vancouver, Ottawa, and Saskatoon. Consequently,

FIGURE 12.1
Descriptors used in user profiles in the dataset

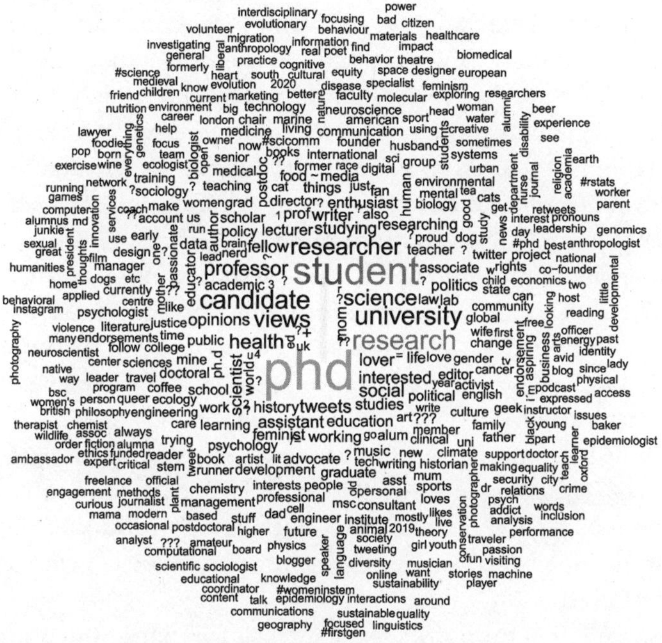

despite not knowing where most of our dataset tweets originate from or reside, we have key Canadian metropolises. In addition, again, due to the anonymous nature of Twitter, it is challenging to isolate women or individuals who identify as women. Nonetheless, given the hashtags that we used to frame the data collection, we assumed that the dataset would be composed chiefly of women, individuals identifying as women, or allies. To validate this, we ran a text analysis of the profile descriptions of the individual profiles listed in our dataset, and the results confirmed our assumption. Figure 12.1 shows that among the 250 most used descriptors in the Twitter profiles are *feminist, feminism, women, pronouns, mom, women, gender, womeninstem,* and *wife.* While we cannot claim that we have mostly women in our dataset, the dataset represents users who are more likely to tweet about academia and issues related to the struggle of working women.

DATA ANALYSIS

The collected tweets were organized into a data frame using the R packages Tidyverse[8] and Quanteda (see Benoit et al. 2018).[9] Finally, the hashtags and the tweet texts were prepared for analysis through formatting and cleaning with the tm package (see Feinerer, Hornik, and Meyer 2008).

First, we ran a network analysis on *all* hashtags present in the dataset. This allowed us to see whether there are links between the echo chambers destined for academia and those destined to discuss the daily struggles women face. Second, we looked at the most frequent hashtags present in the tweets. This allowed us to determine which subjects were most prominent in our data. Third, we ran a sentiment analysis on all tweets to determine whether the words used had positive or negative connotations over time. We also looked at which words contribute to the overall tone of tweets related to academia and gendered struggles while monitoring monthly trends. We used both a Bing sentiment dictionary and an AFINN sentiment dictionary to determine the tone. Hence, the software determines which words are positive and which are negative. We chose the Bing dictionary for the descriptive analyses to get an idea of the tone of the words in the dataset and the AFINN to determine whether hashtags are used to convey positive or negative meanings, with the degrees of tone of given words ranging from −5 (really negative) to +5 (really positive) (see Silge and Robinson 2017). Finally, we took a selection of hashtags, including those selected for the data collection, and looked at whether they tend to be associated with positive or negative sentiments.

Because we feared the possibility of "hashtag hijacking," when a hashtag is used for a different purpose than the one initially intended (Xanthopoulos et al. 2016, 353), we did not look at whether specific tweets were retweeted (shared). The following section discusses the results of these analyses.

First, Figure 12.2 shows that, of the most frequently used hashtags in the dataset, those related to #AcademicTwitter, #AcademicChatter, #PhdChat, #PhdLife, #Mansplaining, and #EverydaySexism are the most prominent. Consequently, our first assumption that early-career scholars might be the primary users of Twitter is confirmed, suggesting that Twitter is used mainly to talk about issues related to graduate studies. Of all possible frequent hashtags within our dataset, #Mansplaining and #EverydaySexism are the most prominent among gender-issue hashtags. Consequently, it is difficult to bring the gendered struggles in academia together with the struggles faced by women more generally.

To see how the two echo chambers intersect, we ran a network analysis of the relationship between hashtags illustrated in Figure 12.3. We looked at hashtags used in the same tweet to determine how the academic and gendered struggle echo chambers intersect. The interpretation of Figure 12.3 is twofold. First, the darker the line, the greater the connection between the hashtags. Second, the closer the words are to each other, the closer they are within the

FIGURE 12.2
Most frequent hashtags

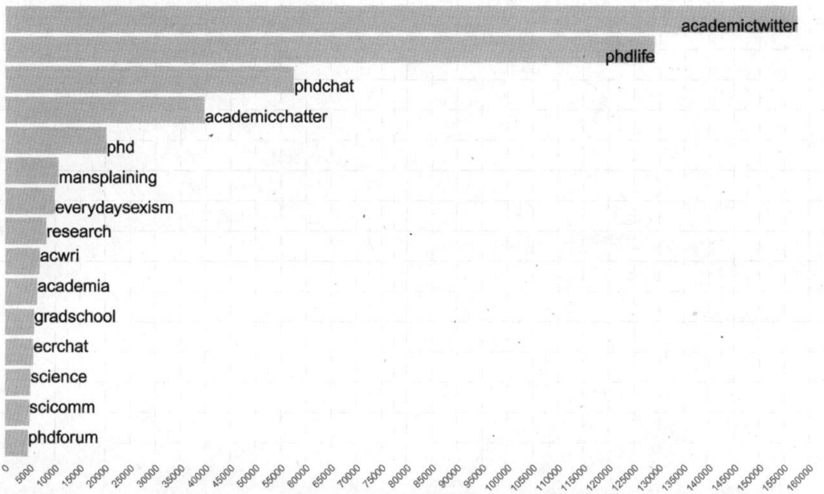

academictwitter
phdlife
phdchat
academicchatter
phd
mansplaining
everydaysexism
research
acwri
academia
gradschool
ecrchat
science
scicomm
phdforum

0 5000 10000 15000 20000 25000 30000 35000 40000 45000 50000 55000 80000 65000 70000 75000 80000 85000 90000 95000 100000 105000 110000 115000 120000 125000 130000 135000 140000 145000 150000 155000 160000

FIGURE 12.3
Network analysis on hashtags

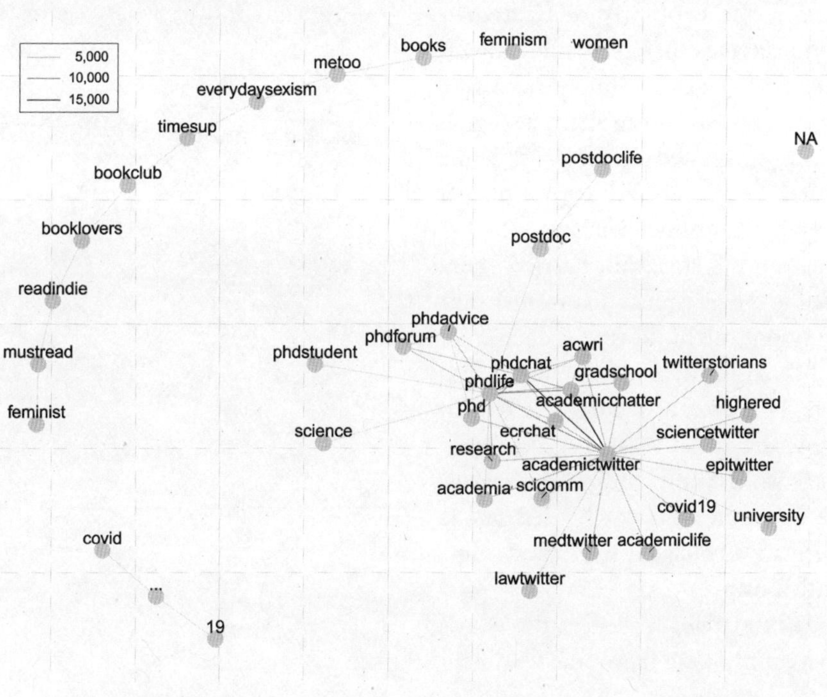

5,000
10,000
15,000

books feminism women
metoo
everydaysexism
timesup
bookclub

postdoclife

NA

booklovers
postdoc
readindie

mustread phdstudent phdforum phdadvice acwri
phdchat gradschool twitterstorians
phdlife
feminist phd academicchatter highered
science ecrchat sciencetwitter
research academictwitter epitwitter
academia scicomm covid19 university
covid medtwitter academiclife
... lawtwitter
19

Twittersphere. For example, there is a distinction between academic tweets and sexual assault and feminism tweets. If we were to run an analysis of hashtag pairs that occur at least once, we could illustrate a sort of "six degrees" of separation between the two echo chambers. However, it would not tell us much about this sample.

The #AcademicTwitter cluster is dominated by #PhdLife hashtags: #PhdChat and #PhdAdvice, for example. We also see that the feminist hashtags are more closely connected to the sexual assault tweets. However, no lines connect the feminist hashtag cluster to the academic hashtag cluster. Based on this analysis, that academic hashtags are not used with other hashtags leads us to conclude that an alternate space explicitly dedicated to gender issues that academic women face does not exist. Simply put, while there is evidence of an alternate digital space, it is limited to general academic issues. Given this finding, we turned then to a sentiment analysis.

Given the struggles, barriers, hurdles, and harassment that women face daily, one might expect the dataset we collected to be predominantly negative. However, as Figure 12.4, which shows the negative words, and Figure 12.5, which shows the positive words, demonstrate, the words used in the tweets we collected were predominantly positive.

Taking a closer look at the words that contribute to the overall sentiment

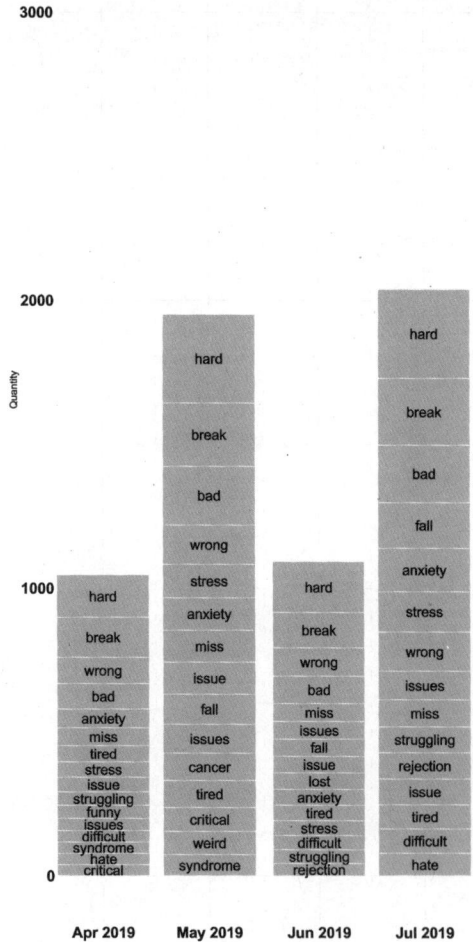

FIGURE 12.4
Negative words over time (Bing dictionary)

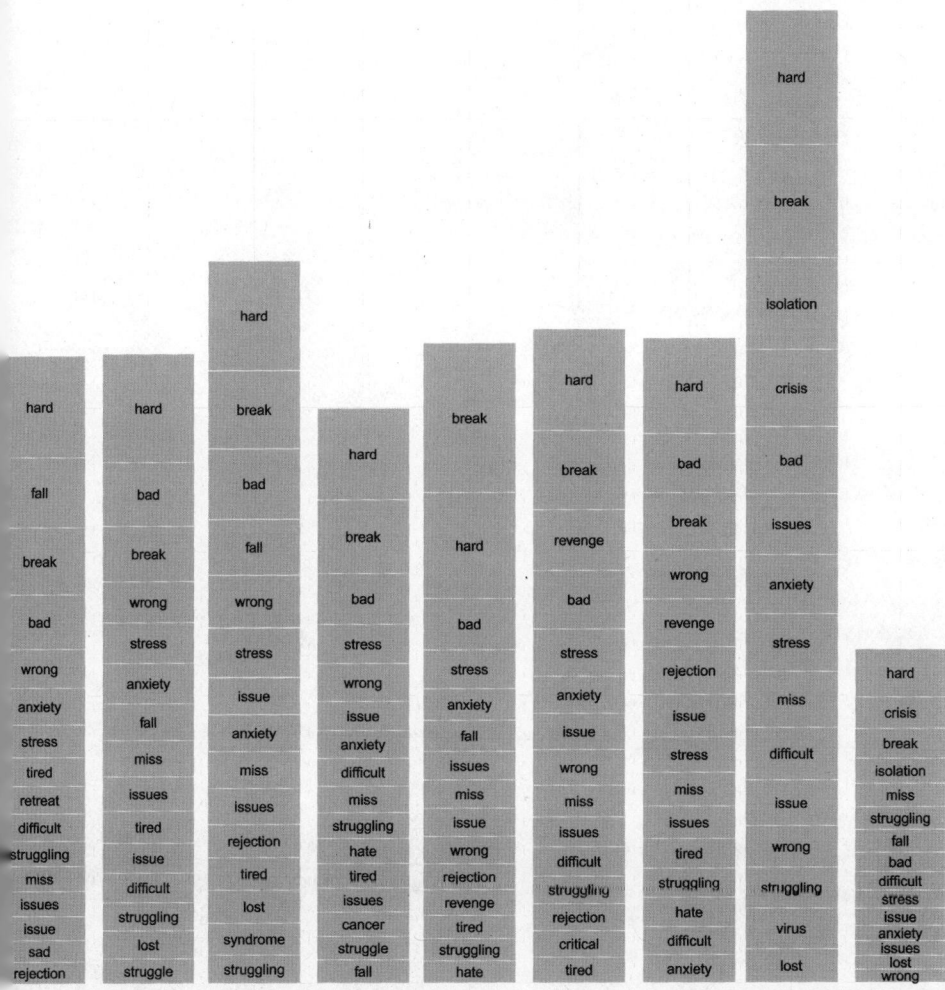

Aug 2019	Sep 2019	Oct 2019	Nov 2019	Dec 2019	Jan 2020	Feb 2020	Mar 2020	Apr 2020
hard	hard	hard					hard	
		break	hard	break	hard	hard	break	
fall	bad	bad			break	bad	isolation	
		fall	break	hard	revenge	break	crisis	hard
break	break	wrong	bad	bad	bad	wrong	bad	crisis
bad	wrong	stress	stress	stress	stress	revenge	issues	break
wrong	stress	issue	wrong	anxiety	anxiety	rejection	anxiety	isolation
anxiety	anxiety	anxiety	issue	fall	issue	issue	stress	miss
stress	fall	miss	anxiety	issues	wrong	stress	miss	struggling
tired	miss	issues	difficult	miss	miss	miss	difficult	fall
retreat	issues	rejection	miss	issue	issues	issues	issue	bad
difficult	tired	tired	struggling	wrong	difficult	tired	wrong	difficult
struggling	issue	lost	hate	rejection	struggling	struggling	struggling	stress
miss	difficult	syndrome	tired	revenge	rejection	hate	virus	issue
issues	struggling	struggling	issues	tired	critical	difficult	lost	anxiety
issue	lost		cancer	struggling	tired	anxiety		issues
sad	struggle		struggle	hate				lost
rejection			fall					wrong

Date

each month, we see that the most frequent negative words, except for procrastination, are related to mental health (see Figure 12.4): racism, stress, anxiety, cancer, exhausted, and tired (although the software also categorized "badass" as a negative word, we believe it to be positive). The same is also true for positive words (Figure 12.5). The dataset reflects that the positive tweets were intended to encourage members of the echo chamber (e.g., congratulations, happy, support, exited, and amazing). Consequently, while we thought Twitter would be used as an alternate space for women to voice their struggles, we instead find that it is principally used as an alternate space to find support and encouragement. It is important to note that part of the data collection occurred during the early stages of the COVID-19 pandemic. Consequently, in March 2020, COVID-19 made its way into the data, likely explaining the higher proportion of negative words for that month, notably relating to the virus (e.g., isolation, stress, and difficult).

Finally, we brought our analysis back to the hashtags of interest to this particular project: #AcademicChatter, #AcademicTwitter, #EverydaySexism, #Harassment, #Mansplaining, #Manterruptions, #MeToo, #PhdLife, #WomenInAcademia, and #WomenInStem. We looked at which words contributed to the overall sentiment of the hashtags we collected. The results

FIGURE 12.5
Positive words over time (Bing dictionary)

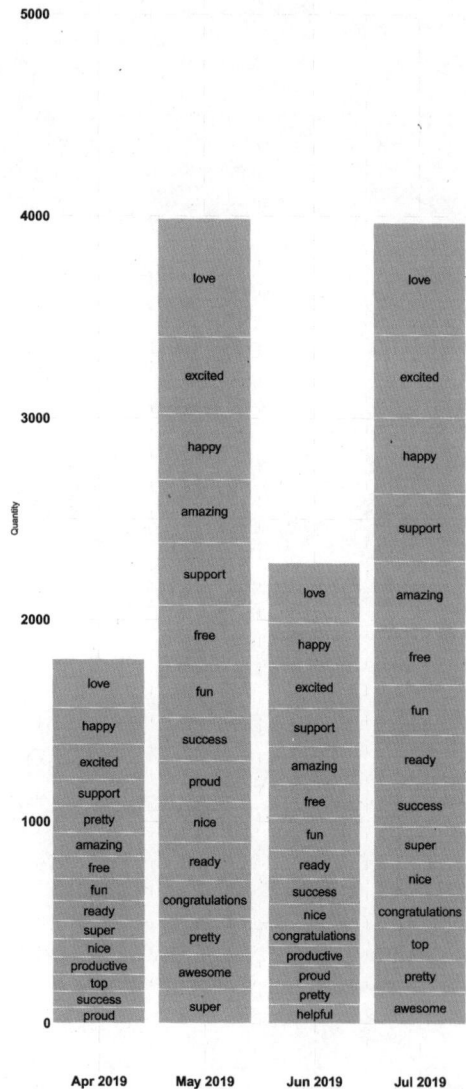

Aug 2019	Sep 2019	Oct 2019	Nov 2019	Dec 2019	Jan 2020	Feb 2020	Mar 2020	Apr 2020
love	love	love	love	love	love	love	love	free
excited	excited	happy	happy	happy	happy	happy	support	support
free	happy	support	amazing	support	excited	excited	happy	happy
support	support	excited	support	amazing	free	amazing	amazing	love
happy	free	amazing	excited	free	support	support	excited	productive
amazing	amazing	free	free	excited	amazing	free	productive	amazing
fun	fun	fun	fun	fun	fine	fun	fun	excited
ready	ready	success	proud	success	fun	success	nice	nice
success	success	ready	nice	ready	ready	fine	helpful	proud
pretty	proud	pretty	ready	proud	success	super	grateful	success
super	nice	proud	success	nice	nice	ready	ready	grateful
awesome	pretty	awesome	grateful	congratulations	favorite	nice	excellent	fun
top	top	nice	awesome	top	top	proud	success	helpful
favorite	super	top	super	favorite	proud	congratulations	pretty	recommend
helpful	cool	favorite	excellent	grateful	pretty	pretty		excellent
								congratulations

Date

depicted in Figure 12.6 show two things: the first is that the academic hashtags are mostly positive, which aligns with the previous analyses. For example, the #WomenInAcademia hashtag is entirely positive, with high frequencies of words such as support, award, and success. However, while "support" was defined as a positive by the dictionary, it might be negative. For example, someone might tweet "I need help" or "I don't have enough help," in which case the word "help" is used to communicate a struggle.

Interestingly, the #WomenInStem is the most negative of the academic hashtags. Indeed, strictly based on our tweet sample, we can conclude that women in STEM disciplines struggle more than women in academia generally. Considering the words used in these hashtags, women's struggle in these fields are largely the result of racism. This should be studied further, as our tweet sample is not representative of women in STEM, but only of those who tweeted using the selected keywords. Hence, if we looked at hashtags related to professional fields whose barriers of entry might be higher for women, we would find negative echo chambers. Finally, #Mansplaining is – unsurprisingly – the second most negative of the hashtags. Women use this hashtag to take back their voice when a man attempts to shut them down or act condescendingly. We analogously related this to the experience of Ariel in the *Little Mermaid*, when

FIGURE 12.6
Hashtag sentiment (AFFINN dictionary)

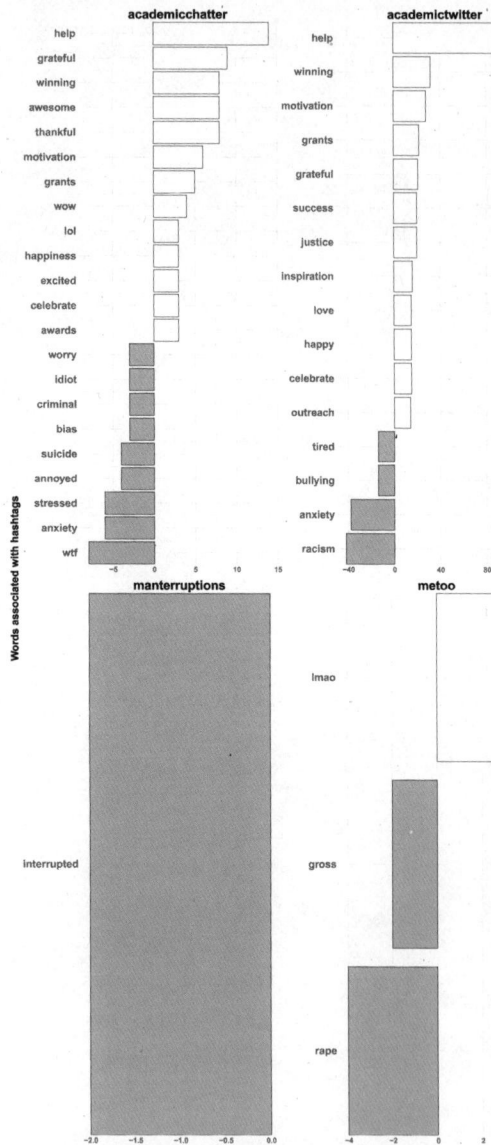

everydaysexism

solidarity
fearless
consent
wrong
weird
unprofessional
unfair
tragic
sigh
shame
scary
retard
rage
intimidation
infuriating
ignored
fuming
fail
depressing
bullying
biased
anxiety
hysteria
disgusting
boring
abuse
rapist
rape
bullshit
stereotype
disappointed
bias
tired
racism
wtf

−25 −20 −15 −10 −5 0

harassment

consent

bullying

−2 −1 0 1 2

mansplaining

fun
god
winning
marvel
love
humor
hilarious
comedy
treason
humiliation
greed
evil
douche
sigh
pathetic
nonsense
clueless
annoying
irony
bullshit
asshole
bullying
idiot
shameful
racist
fail
wtf
racism

−20 −10 0 10

phdlife

grateful
winning
help
outreach
fun
motivation
happy
excited
proud
progress
happiness
love
inspiration
exhausted
anxiety
tired

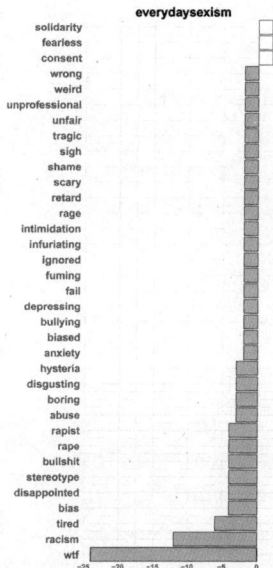

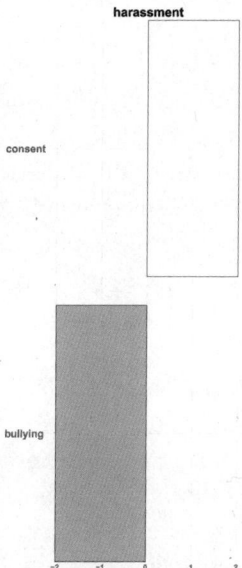

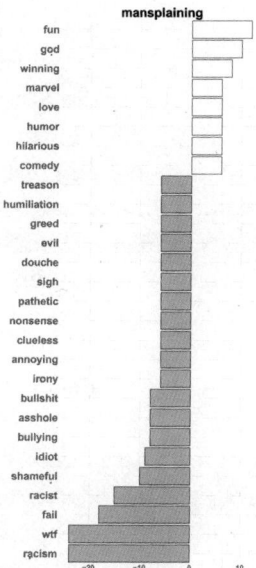

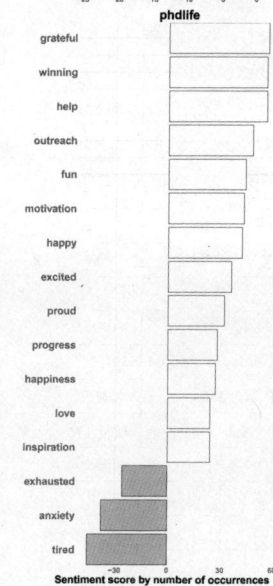

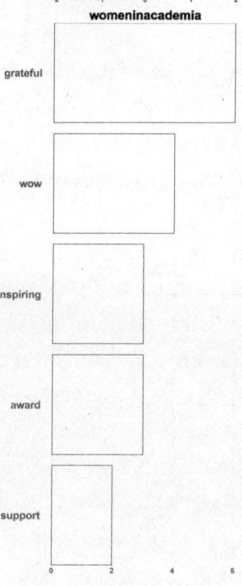

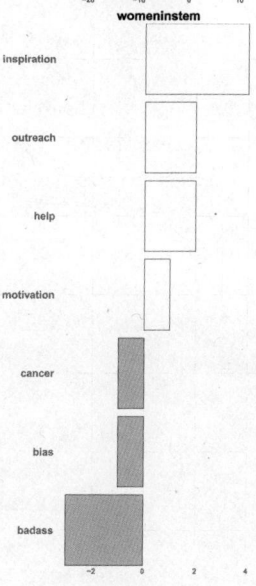

−30 0 30 60
Sentiment score by number of occurrences

womeninacademia

grateful
wow
inspiring
award
support

0 2 4 6

womeninstem

inspiration
outreach
help
motivation
cancer
bias
badass

−2 0 2 4

Ursula takes her voice in exchange for the privilege of enjoying a new experience. Arguably, this hashtag is actually entirely negative, with the positive words most likely sarcasm.

CONCLUSION

We began this chapter by discussing the white male template, the attempt to silence women, notably through mansplaining, and the lack of space for women in academia. We hypothesized that Twitter could be used as a proxy – instead of a real-life community – to talk about the struggles women face daily in their professional lives. While it would be bold to suggest that the digital communications analyzed herein are exclusively shared for and by women, we believe that we have convincingly shown that Twitter is used as an alternative space for women in academia.

After analyzing two distinct echo chambers, academia and the gendered struggle, we can confirm our original hypothesis. There were noticeably more tweets within the academic echo chamber, supporting our earlier claim that those more likely to use Twitter are tech-savvy and will also know which hashtags to mobilize, which is probably the case for early-career scholars. Because our dataset was primarily positive, we conclude that Twitter can be a positive alternative space. While we showed that some hashtags are often associated with negative words, such as those tied to gendered struggles more generally, hashtags specifically related to women in academia are more positive: #WomenInStem and #WomenInAcademia. Furthermore, we believe the echo chamber's general positivity is due to supportive responses to tweets containing a grievance or a milestone.

This leads us to our second argument: the academic Twittersphere is more encouraging and validating because women are inadequately recognized or valued in the "real world." Indeed, women take on more unpaid work within their respective university departments; they are also interrupted, manterrupted, and mansplained to, even by women. These struggles do not exist in the same form on Twitter, though this does not mean that women are not interrupted or discriminated against on Twitter. The example we offered at the beginning of the chapter of the violence that followed a #MeToo confession regarding a UBC creative writing professor shows that too well. Indeed, the World Health Organization has estimated that "*one in ten women* have already experienced a form of cyber violence since the age of fifteen."[10] Hence, women are no less prone to being trolled for expressing themselves in what can otherwise be a positive space for them – if they locate the proper echo chamber.

The beauty of social media is, in some regard, its anonymity. While this chapter looks at how women's issues are discussed on Twitter, there is no way of knowing how much of that echo chamber is occupied by women. Indeed, world-renowned political scientist Pippa Norris (2001) postulates that the internet emphasizes already existing gaps, suggesting that men are the primary users of the internet. However, she also argues that the internet allows citizens to choose where they spend their time or get their information. Hence, if one seeks cat videos or political information, the constraints that exist in the physical realm do not apply.

Consequently, if a woman is looking for a space to voice her struggles or seek comfort and encouragement from her peers, she will likely have fewer obstacles to finding such an online space. Thus, while we cannot confirm whether our dataset contains more women, we are hopeful that it is constituted chiefly of our target audience. Finally, while this book strictly considers the Canadian experience, we cannot confirm whether our Twitter users are from or work in Canada. However, we are comfortable with this limitation as it assures us that users' privacy is protected.

We know that not all women in academia use Twitter or hashtags to discuss their work life. For example, a study of Italian academics' use of different social media platforms showed that 90 percent of respondents did not use Twitter and that the most widely used platform (35 percent of respondents) was Academia. edu-ResearchGate (Manca and Ranieri 2017). However, as no other research has been done in this field, we believe our results shed light on the potential of social media platforms like Twitter. Although this study focuses on women in academia, this is only the tip of the iceberg, especially regarding intersectional women. We also believe that we, in part, opened the discussion for a subsequent chapter on #MeToo.

Finally, to answer the third question asked at the outset: What does the use of Twitter to talk about academia mean for the field of higher education? Although there are alternative spaces for women to overcome the Ursula effect and reclaim their voice, Twitter in no way compensates for the fact that their voices may otherwise go unheard in the academy. The fact that the hashtags on women in academia were positive leads us to hypothesize that women may not be getting the recognition they deserve. More generally, despite recognition and validation from our peers IRL,[11] it may just be common practice to seek the more external validation social media provides. Moreover, the frequent use of #PhdLife and #PhdChat raises questions about how academia is tailored to doctoral students, particularly because these hashtags were linked to mental health and exchanging encouragements. While it does fall outside the scope of this book, we think that, since women represent 57.1 percent of all Canadian university graduates, they tend to complete more unpaid work at university and at home. The strain faced by graduate students is of concern for the future of academia, and, more specifically, for women in universities. We fear that relying too much on social media will strengthen the Ursula effect, which would be detrimental to any academic environment. Just like Ariel, who had to give up her voice, we fear that to be accepted into the academy, women feel they must be silent. This may be partly why we are optimistic that Twitter is a positive space for expression. Provided that they do not filter themselves for fear of violence.[12]

NOTES

1 The study was conducted on Twitter, which has since been renamed "X." The term Twitter is used throughout this chapter to reflect the name at the time of study.

2 In a nutshell, it allows one to write, or in our case, read Twitter data through software that is not an internet platform. We like to think of it as a robot we ask to locate specific types of words in the Twittersphere.

3 "Bropropriation" is when a man takes credit for a woman's idea.

4 Conversations were recorded using the Electronically Activated Recorder (EAR).

5 Although this paper focuses on women in academia, these issues affect many people, such as first-generation, racialized, LGBTQ2IA+, disabled, and Indigenous academics.

6 This safety is relative because many women face retaliation following a #MeToo denunciation, as indicated by the creative writing professor addressed earlier in this chapter.

7 Here, we mean anonymous because some users may use aliases, enabling them to hide behind their screens and do as they please. Furthermore, due to the sheer size of the tweet database we created for this chapter, it became difficult to identify specific users.

8 See https://github.com/tidyverse/tidyverse.

9 See https://quanteda.io.

10 See https://eige.europa.eu/gender-based-violence/cyber-violence-against-women.

11 In real life.

12 See the European Commission's (2021) statement on stopping violence against women.

WORKS CITED

Aksnes, Dag W., Kristoffer Rorstad, Fredrik Piro, and Gunnar Sivertsen. 2011. "Are Female Researchers Less Cited? A Large-Scale Study of Norwegian Scientists." *Journal of the American Society for Information Science and Technology* 62 (4): 628–36.

Angus Reid Institute. 2018. "#Metoo: Moment or Movement?" http://angusreid.org/me-too/.

Antonakis-Nashif, Anna. 2015. "Hashtagging the Invisible: Bringing Private Experiences into Public Debate." In *Hashtag Publics: The Power and Politics of Discursive Networks*, edited by Nathan Rambukkana, 101–13. Digital Formations no. 103. New York: Peter Lang.

Bagilhole, Barbara, and Kate White, eds. 2011. *Gender, Power and Management: A Cross-Cultural Analysis of Higher Education*. Houndmills, UK: Palgrave Macmillan.

Baker, Fredrick W., III, and Patrick R. Lowenthal. 2019. "Analysing Professional Discourse on Twitter: A Mixed Methods Analysis of the #openeducation Hashtag." *International Journal of Social Media and Interactive Learning Environments* 6 (2): 107–21.

Banet-Weiser, Sarah, and Kate M. Miltner. 2016. "#MasculinitySoFragile: Culture, Structure, and Networked Misogyny." *Feminist Media Studies* 16 (1): 171–74.

Bennett, Jessica. 2016. "Workplace a Bit Sexist? Welcome to Feminist Fight Club." *The Guardian,* September 3, 2016. https://www.theguardian.com/lifeandstyle/2016/sep/03/workplace-sexist-feminist-fight-club.

Benoit, Kenneth, Kohei Watanabe, Haiyan Wang, Paul Nulty, Adam Obeng, Stefan Müller, and Akitaka Matsuo. 2018. "Quanteda: An R Package for the Quantitative Analysis of Textual Data." *Journal of Open Source Software* 3 (30): 774.

Bertrand, Marianne, and Kevin F. Hallock. 2001. "The Gender Gap in Top Corporate Jobs." *ILR Review* 55 (1): 3–21.

Boulianne, Shelley. 2019. "Revolution in the Making? Social Media Effects across the Globe." *Information, Communication and Society* 22 (1): 39–54.

Bridges, Judith. 2017. "Gendering Metapragmatics in Online Discourse: 'Mansplaining Man Gonna Mansplain ...'" *Discourse, Context and Media* 20: 94–102.

Budden, Amber E., Tom Tregenza, Lonnie W. Aarssen, Julia Koricheva, Roosa Leimu, and Christopher J. Lortie. 2008. "Double-Blind Review Favours Increased Representation of Female Authors." *Trends in Ecology and Evolution* 23 (1): 4–6.

Cantor, David, Bonnie Fisher, Susan Helen Chibnall, Reanne Townsend, Hyunshik Lee, Carol Bruce, and Gail Thomas. 2017. *Report on the AAU Campus Climate Survey on Sexual Assault and Sexual Misconduct.* Westat Inc. Revised October 20, 2017. https://www.aau.edu/sites/default/files/AAU-Files/Key-Issues/Campus-Safety/AAU-Campus-Climate-Survey-FINAL-10-20-17.pdf.

Clements, Ron, and John Musker. 1989. *The Little Mermaid.* United States: Buena Vista Pictures.

European Commission. 2021. "Stop Violence Against Women: Statement by the European Commission and the High Representative," November 24, 2021. https://neighbourhood-enlargement.ec.europa.eu/news/stop-violence-against-women-statement-european-commission-and-high-representative-2021-11-24_en.

Feinerer, Ingo, Kurt Hornik, and David Meyer. 2008. "Text Mining Infrastructure in R." *Journal of Statistical Software* 25: 1–54.

Fredrickson, Caroline. 2017. "When Will the 'Harvey Effect' Reach Academia?" *The Atlantic,* October 30, 2017. https://www.theatlantic.com/education/archive/2017/10/when-will-the-harvey-effect-reach-academia/544388/.

Gil de Zúñiga, Homero, Matthew Barnidge, and Andrés Scherman. 2017. "Social Media Social Capital, Offline Social Capital, and Citizenship: Exploring Asymmetrical Social Capital Effects." *Political Communication* 34 (1): 44–68.

Greenhow, Christine, Jiahang Li, and Minhtuyen Mai. 2019. "From Tweeting to Meeting: Expansive Professional Learning and the Academic Conference Backchannel." *British Journal of Educational Technology* 50 (4): 1656–72.

Gronn, Peter, and Kathy Lacey. 2006. "Cloning Their Own: Aspirant Principals and the School-Based Selection Game." *Australian Journal of Education* 50 (2): 102–21.

Hancock, Adrienne B., and Benjamin A. Rubin. 2015. "Influence of Communication Partner's Gender on Language." *Journal of Language and Social Psychology* 34 (1): 46–64.

Hurren, Wanda. 2018. "Breaking the Code of Silence on Sexual Harassment within the Faculty." *University Affairs*, July 10, 2018. https://www.universityaffairs.ca/opinion/in -my-opinion/breaking-the-code-of-silence-on-sexual-harassment-within-the-faculty/.

Jordan, Katy. 2019. "From Finding a Niche to Circumventing Institutional Constraints: Examining the Links Between Academics' Online Networking, Institutional Roles, and Identity-Trajectory." *International Review of Research in Open and Distributed Learning* 20 (2).

Jordan, Katy, and Martin Weller. 2018. "Academics and Social Networking Sites: Benefits, Problems and Tensions in Professional Engagement with Online Networking." *Journal of Interactive Media in Education* 2018 (1).

Kapidzic, Sanja. 2020. "The Social Academic: A Social Capital Approach to Academic Relationship Management on Social Media." *Information, Communication and Society* 23 (11): 1–16.

Karpowitz, Christopher F., Tali Mendelberg, and Lee Shaker. 2012. "Gender Inequality in Deliberative Participation." American Political Science Review 106 (3): 533–47.

Kidd, Anna Grace. 2017. "Mansplaining: The Systematic Sociocultural Silencer." Presented at the 22nd UNG Annual Research Conference, Dahlonega, GA, United States, March 24, 2017.

Knights, David, and Wendy Richards. 2003. "Sex Discrimination in UK Academia." *Gender, Work and Organization* 10 (2): 213–38.

Koc-Michalska, Karolina, Anya Schiffrin, Anamaria Lopez, Shelley Boulianne, and Bruce Bimber. 2021. "From Online Political Posting to Mansplaining: The Gender Gap and Social Media in Political Discussion." *Social Science Computer Review* 39 (2): 197–210.

Krawczyk, Michał. 2017. "Are All Researchers Male? Gender Misattributions in Citations." *Scientometrics* 110 (3): 1397–1402.

Laserna, Charlyn M., Yi-Tai Seih, and James W. Pennebaker. 2014. "Um ... Who Like Says You Know: Filler Word Use as a Function of Age, Gender, and Personality." *Journal of Language and Social Psychology* 33 (3): 328–38.

Ledwith, Sue, and Simonetta Manfredi. 2000. "Balancing Gender in Higher Education: A Study of the Experience of Senior Women in a 'New' UK University." *European Journal of Women's Studies* 7 (1): 7–33.

Li, Xiaoqian, Wenhong Chen, Yoonmo Sang, and Na Yeon Lee. 2019. "Structure and Returns: Toward a Refined Understanding of Internet Use and Social Capital." *Information, Communication and Society* 22 (10): 1479–96.

Manca, Stefania, and Maria Ranieri. 2017. "Exploring Digital Scholarship: A Study on Use of Social Media for Scholarly Communication among Italian Academics." In *Research 2.0 and the Impact of Digital Technologies on Scholarly Inquiry*, 117–42. Hershey, PA: IGI Global.

Manne, Kate. 2020. *Entitled: How Male Privilege Hurts Women*. New York: Crown Publishing.

Mendes, Kaitlynn, Jessalynn Keller, and Jessica Ringrose. 2019. "Digitized Narratives of Sexual Violence: Making Sexual Violence Felt and Known through Digital Disclosures." *New Media and Society* 21 (6): 1290–310.

Norris, Pippa. 2001. *Digital Divide: Civic Engagement, Information Poverty, and the Internet Worldwide*. Cambridge: Cambridge University Press.

Perez, Caroline Criado. 2019. *Invisible Women: Data Bias in a World Designed for Men*. New York: Abrams Press.

Probert, Belinda. 2005. "'I Just Couldn't Fit In': Gender and Unequal Outcomes in Academic Careers." *Gender, Work and Organization* 12 (1): 50–72.

Quan, Douglas. 2021. "She Accused a University Prof of Sexual Assault. Now He's Suing for Defamation. Some Fear the 'Landmark' Case Could Have a Chilling Effect." *Toronto Star*, April 8, 2021. https://www.thestar.com/news/canada/2021/04/08/she-accused -a-university-prof-of-sexual-assault-now-hes-suing-for-defamation-some-fear-the -landmark-case-could-have-a-chilling-effect.html?rf.

Quan-Haase, Anabel, Kim Martin, and Lori McCay-Peet. 2015. "Networks of Digital Humanities Scholars: The Informational and Social Uses and Gratifications of Twitter." *Big Data and Society* 2 (1): 2053951715589417.

Rocheleau, Sylvain, and Mélanie Millette. 2015. "Meta-Hashtag and Tag Co-Occurrence: From Organization to Politics in the French-Canadian Twittersphere." In *Hashtag Publics: The Power and Politics of Discursive Networks*, edited by Nathan Rambukkana, 243–54. Digital Formations no. 103. New York: Peter Lang.

Schneider, Kimberly T., and Nathan J. Carpenter. 2020. "Sharing# MeToo on Twitter: Incidents, Coping Responses, and Social Reactions." *Equality, Diversity and Inclusion: An International Journal* 39 (1): 87–100.

Silge, Julia and David Robinson. 2017. *Text Mining with R: A Tidy Approach*. 1st ed. Sebastopol, CA: O'Reilly Media. https://www.tidytextmining.com.

Singh, Lenandlar. 2020a. "A Systematic Review of Higher Education Academics' Use of Microblogging for Professional Development: Case of Twitter." *Open Education Studies* 2 (1): 66–81.

–. 2020b. "Cultural Affordances of Twitter in Higher Education Professional Development: A Literature Review." *Asian Journal of Distance Education* 15 (1): 127–43.

Solnit, Rebecca. 2012. "Men Explain Things to Me." *Guernica*, August 20, 2012. https:// www.guernicamag.com/rebecca-solnit-men-explain-things-to-me/.

Stewart, Bonnie. 2015. "Open to Influence: What Counts as Academic Influence in Scholarly Networked Twitter Participation." *Learning, Media and Technology* 40 (3): 287–309.

Student Society McGill University. 2018. "Our Turn Action Plan." http://s3.document-cloud.org/documents/4106721/Our-Turn-Action-Plan-Final-English-2.pdf.

Sullivan, Katherine V.R., and Pierre C. Bélanger. 2016. "La cyberdémocratie québécoise: Twitter bashing, #VoteCampus et selfies." *Politique et sociétés* 35 (2–3): 239–58.

The 500 Women Scientists Leadership. 2018. "When It Comes to Sexual Harassment, Academia Is Fundamentally Broken." *Scientific American*, August 9, 2018. https:// blogs.scientificamerican.com/voices/when-it-comes-to-sexual-harassment -academia-is-fundamentally-broken/.

Thomas, Paul L. 2017. "Power, Responsibility, and the White Men of Academia." *Huffpost*, May 30, 2017. https://www.huffpost.com/entry/power-responsibility-and-the-white -men-of-academia_b_592d58bce4b08861ed0ccbce.

van Roosmalen, Erica, and Susan A. McDaniel. 1999. "Sexual Harassment in Academia: A Hazard to Women's Health." *Women and Health* 28 (2): 33–54.

Veletsianos, George, Nicole Johnson, and Olga Belikov. 2019. "Academics' Social Media Use Over Time Is Associated with Individual, Relational, Cultural and Political Factors." *British Journal of Educational Technology* 50 (4): 1713–28.

Vesterlund, Lise. 2015. "Breaking the Glass Ceiling with 'No': Gender Differences in Accepting and Receiving Requests for Non-Promotable Tasks." Working Paper 5663, Department of Economics, University of Pittsburgh.

Waters, Lowenna. 2018. "Women Are Adding 'Dr' to Their Twitter Names to Make a Point and the Results Are Awesome." *Indy 100*, June 15, 2018. https://www.indy100. com/article/women-immodest-women-twitter-dr-phd-academic-fern-riddell -8400206.

Xanthopoulos, Petros, Orestis Panos Panagopoulos, Georgios A. Bakamitsos, and Elizabeth Freudmann. 2016. "Hashtag Hijacking: What It Is, Why It Happens and How to Avoid It." *Journal of Digital and Social Media Marketing* 3 (4): 353–62.

13

The Public Face of
Gender Inequality and Allyship

CHERYL N. COLLIER

In 2017, Universities Canada established seven equity, diversity, and inclusion (EDI) "excellence" principles after two years of consultations with university leaders across the country. All universities publicly committed to these principles over a five-year period, which began with principle number one in the primary agreement: to "make our personal commitment to diversity and inclusion evident," even while recognizing that universities vary in "identity and thought, with room for a variety of ideas, geographies, cultures and views" (1). In 2019, Universities Canada released a self-reporting survey summary document that served as a benchmark of institutional progress with respect to the seven EDI principles and as a means to identify ongoing challenges and barriers. While this survey indicated that gender parity had essentially been reached at the "senior leadership levels"[1] at a 49 percent rate when averaged across participating institutions, it also noted that executive head/president and vice-president positions were stubbornly men dominated: women were only 25 percent of university presidents, 39 percent of provosts/vice-presidents academic, and 30 percent of vice-presidents research.[2]

Systemic gender bias and institutional path dependency are two core challenges that persist inside the university sector and make progress on improving equality for gender and BIPOC (Black, Indigenous, and people of colour) members in various institutional areas of leadership particularly difficult, despite verbal commitments to do better. In its most recent report, Universities Canada (2019, 5) highlights "institutional systems, policies, structures and cultures that can hinder progress" as one key common challenge noted by survey respondents. Related challenges identified by the report included 1) insufficient resources to commit to EDI strategies, 2) an overarching problem of "attracting and retaining diverse talent," 3) an inability to collect sufficient "data on institutional challenges," and 4) "insufficient information on best practices for EDI" in general.

One strategy that has been suggested to combat systemic institutional resistance – and one that is not mentioned at any length in the Universities Canada

2019 document[3] – is embracing men's allyship models to pivot institutional cultures away from intersectional gender biases and toward a broader embrace of equity goals across the institution (Drury and Kaiser 2014; Sherf, Tangirala, and Weber 2017). Allyship can be defined simply as the active support and equity-seeking engagement of members of dominant, powerful groups inside an organization. For the purposes of this chapter, men's allyship occurs when men (especially white, heterosexual men) become active allies by confronting sexism, alongside racism and other forms of discrimination, by "recognizing the need for further progress in the fight for equal rights ... [and working] alongside a disadvantaged group in the search for justice" (Drury and Kaiser 2014, 637).

Men's allyship modelling has recently been adopted by some postsecondary institutions in the mid-western United States as an effective approach to advancing gender equity[4] (Bilen-Green and Carpenter 2015), but it is not clear whether Canadian universities have followed suit. This chapter examines the level of institutional commitment to allyship and gender equality in general to establish if any Canadian universities are attempting to deal with institutional biases via equity-focused or men's allyship models and, importantly, whether or not they are transparently communicating these approaches via their publicly available websites. I employ a rhetorical and content analysis model to assess the public commitment levels of Canadian institutions to these core equity strategies. Arguably, an absence of this public commitment represents a lack of systemic attention to these issues and signals the same implicit message to community partners and current and prospective students of the university. I argue that while the presence or absence of these programs on websites does not say everything about an institution's commitment to equity, diversity, and inclusion, it likely helps explain institutional depth of commitment (or lack thereof) to the problem of gender diversity and underrepresentation in the highest levels of university leadership. This is true notwithstanding Universities Canada's self-report survey conclusion that gender parity has ostensibly been reached in "senior leadership." The reality of slow progress and stubborn resistance to change that appears in the Canadian university sector is perhaps not surprising when we examine the lack of commitment to EDI and men's allyship modelling on central university webpages and inside their core mission statements and strategic planning documents.

This chapter begins with a brief overview of the men's allyship model and how it can assist institutions in tackling persistent and stubborn sexism embedded in historical institutional practices. It then outlines the rhetorical and content analysis approach used, noting that the way an institution frames and then communicates a problem to stakeholders tells us a lot about their policy responses and how likely those responses are to address the real issues underpinning those problems. The chapter will then outline the specific rhetorical and content analysis method used to examine Canadian universities' approaches to EDI and men's allyship and the persistent lack of evidence of gender awareness and allyship as a strategy writ large in most cases under examination. It concludes by suggesting pathways to more promising institutional approaches to expedite an EDI progress that appears to have stalled.

MEN'S ALLYSHIP IN INSTITUTIONS

The persistently thorny problem of women's lack of representation in the highest levels of leadership in a variety of sectors, including business, politics, and academia, is well-documented in the literature (see, e.g., Madsen, Townsend, and Scribner 2019; Sawyer and Valerio 2018). Often the first instinct for organizations that have recognized this as an inhibitor to growth and overall organizational success is to cast this as a problem that women themselves should solve through leadership development programs and training aimed to help them crack the glass ceiling. This focus on women's agency alone as a solution leads organizations to "unintentionally alienat[e] men while creating a dynamic that fails to acknowledge and change the very 'organizational practices that maintain the status quo'" (Prime and Moss-Racusin in Madsen, Townsend, and Scribner 2019, 2).

According to organizational behaviour experts Elad Sherf, Subrahmaniam Tangirala, and Katy Connealy Weber (2017, 193), achieving gender parity is a significant challenge for most organizations, and progress, while initially evident, has essentially stalled because "gender-parity initiatives are failing in achieving their prescribed goals." This ineffectiveness has been linked to a lack of involvement by men. Men's agency is crucial to combat organizational sexism for several reasons. Men have been and continue to be the dominant actors inside existing leadership circles, and even though many of these men may endorse gender equity as essential for business growth, they "lack effective strategies they can use in workplace settings to advance women" (Madsen, Townsend, and Scribner 2019, 2). Additionally, research shows that men, particularly white men, who challenge sexism in the workplace are less likely to suffer backlash from colleagues for their interventions. When men initiate such interventions, these efforts are seen as more legitimate and men face far fewer social capital losses compared to women advancing similar challenges (Madsen, Townsend, and Scribner 2019, 4).

As a model, allyship used to combat organizational gender inequality is not organic. According to Benjamin Drury and Cheryl Kaiser (2014), psychology researchers from the Social Identity Lab at the University of Washington, legal and psychological research studies consistently show that men generally have more difficulty recognizing sexism and sexual harassment in the workplace than women, and if men do not see the sexism, they are unlikely to become or act as an ally. Even though men-led allyship offers legitimacy, men themselves are often reticent to get involved because they "don't see it as their place or responsibility" and have "low psychological standing on the issue"[5] (Sherf, Tangirala, and Weber 2017, 194). Yet, Sherf, Tangirala, and Weber (2017, 193–94) argue that unless employees of all genders are involved, change is less likely "because participation in change processes reduces employees' resistance to change, enhances their commitment to it, and improves the quality of enacted change ... When men remain outside observers, their ideas cannot be leveraged to improve gender-parity initiatives and they become less likely to promote implementation of those initiatives." This involvement needs to be encouraged from the top down and the bottom up and requires specific training to give men colleagues the latitude and the perceived legitimacy to intervene when necessary and to become allies in the fight against workplace inequality. It is also important to ensure that this involvement does not marginalize women but serves as a call to motivate allies and to allow the entire organization to be part of the solution instead of passive bystanders.

Efforts to encourage men's allyship in organizations, including inside academia, are presently scant beyond broader social movement efforts, including the United Nations HeForShe campaign and Lean In Together, which grew out of Sheryl Sandberg's leadership call for women to lean in to their significant potential to be successful. One fairly recent exception is in the United States where North Dakota State University created the Advocates and Allies program as a key component of its broader efforts to improve gender equity in STEM programs under a project begun in 2008 titled ADVANCE FORWARD. Advocates and Allies builds off the theory that to effect positive change, we must address the central role of "masculinities and male culture ... in shaping men's behaviour and institutional climate" (Bilen-Green and Carpenter 2015, 2). Advocates and Allies does this by:

1 Educat[ing] men faculty about gender inequity in academia;
2 Introduc[ing] men faculty to strategies for bringing about positive change in their departments and colleges;
3 Build[ing] a supportive network of men to act as Advocates and Allies for all faculty. (Bilen-Green and Carpenter 2015, 2)

The program has since been expanded to eight other US postsecondary institutions. It has been shown to be effective in not only improving women's representation in leadership positions but also in improving the overall institutional climate, with "positive changes in terms of increased understanding, greater awareness of women faculty's perspectives, and appreciation of the impact of climate" overall (Bilen-Green and Carpenter 2015, 5).

The promise of men's allyship programming in institutions is strong and thus worthwhile to track, alongside the general commitment of postsecondary institutions toward EDI goals. This is particularly the case in light of Universities Canada's (2019, 5) efforts to improve EDI practices under its five-year plan and its recent recognition that existing "institutional systems, policies, structures and cultures" have been highlighted as hindering these goals in universities across the country. In the next section, I discuss the theory and methodology that guides this examination, before turning to the findings and discussion.

THEORY AND METHOD

One premise of this chapter is that rhetoric, the framing of policies and institutional missions, the crafting of strategic plans, and the implementation of vision matter. It is well-documented in political theory that rhetoric and language are intentional and inform a great deal about an institution's or actor's approach to a problem (see, e.g., Rein and Schön 1996; Phillips and Hardy 2002; Finlayson 2007). Feminist political scientist Carol Bacchi (2009) argues that contested policy problems have competing frames and that the ways an institution characterizes the problem helps justify and frame the scope of potential solutions to that problem. She argues that this exercise, known as the "what's the problem represented to be?" approach, is deeply gendered and helps researchers understand limitations in policy responses, particularly ones that fail to take a gendered approach to problem definition because it "draws attention to the ways in which particular issues are given a shape, which in turn affects what will be done, or not be done" (2).

I employed this framework in my analysis of Canadian university websites and their publicly posted central mission statements/strategic mandates.[6] Exploring the websites of twenty-five universities across Canada, I first established whether the rhetoric and language of EDI, or equity, diversity, inclusion, and Indigeneity (EDI-I)[7] – including more recent references to anti-Black racism and men's allyship – is present on the main outward facing webpages or the president's main webpage.[8] I then followed relevant links on these pages to mission statements or strategic planning documents, paying particular attention to the documents that are publicly available. I was interested in establishing how each university a) recognizes and communicates the goal(s) and ongoing problem(s) of reaching EDI/EDI-I, particularly with respect to gender equity; b) frames the issue; and c) attends to gender parity and EDI in their core mission statements and to what depth. This type of analysis is not common in the education sector. Marie-Pierre Moreau, Jayne Osgood, and Anna Halsall (2008), from the Institute for Policy Studies in Education at London Metropolitan University, conducted a similar analysis of equal opportunity policy statements for British public schools, examining the extent to which the institutions addressed gender and assessing the impact of this dearth of language on gender parity in those schools. Using this precedent as a reference point, this chapter shines a light on postsecondary institutional commitment levels to EDI-I and gender parity in Canada.

Central webpages and their content are core aspects of a university's branding to incoming students, community partners, and on-campus as well as off-campus stakeholders. According to communications experts Consuelo Vásquez, Viviane Sergi, and Benoit Cordelier (2013, 136), "Corporate branding is therefore one of the core mechanisms through which organizational members make sense of who they are, individually and collectively, and develop as subjects in relation to the brand." Branding for universities is an understudied field, but current research examines the important transformation of the university into "an industry" where universities can reflect and project "what defines them and how they are viewed" (137).

I have chosen to focus on twenty-five universities in Canada, including all U15 universities plus ten smaller institutions (below 10,000 students) that are as geographically representative of universities across Canada as possible (not all provinces include a U15 school). Universities in the smaller size category were selected to ensure that all provinces were included in the analysis. I included both small and large institutions to assess any trends related to institutional capacity, if applicable. I avoided federated universities but included specialized and comprehensive universities to ensure each province (with the exception of PEI and Newfoundland and Labrador) had at least two universities included in this study.

I included rhetorical and content analysis of the most recent EDI-specific studies or documents produced by the universities to evaluate the presence or absence of gender and allyship content/concepts. I also assessed how easy or difficult it was to locate these documents. Although the inclusion of EDI-specific documents in the analysis does not speak to core branding and how the university takes up the concepts of EDI/EDI-I, allyship, and gender equity, they were included in the study to provide more insight into how specific EDI-focused initiatives that may or may not have been enacted are framed and whether they are easy to access. I discuss the findings of this rhetorical/content analysis in the next section.

RHETORICAL/CONTENT ANALYSIS FINDINGS

As we can see in Table 13.1, there was some interesting variation in use of rhetoric/content related to EDI and EDI-I across the twenty-five universities under review, with the term "Indigenous" appearing the most on both the main webpages and the presidents' pages for a total of forty-nine mentions. This likely reflects the commitment of all universities to the Truth and Reconciliation Commission's (TRC) 2015 Calls to Action and a wide embrace of the need to address Indigenous research, teaching, and community outreach as a core mandate in line with TRC recommendations. Those ninety-four TRC recommendations include a general call to improve educational opportunities for Indigenous peoples at all levels, including in the postsecondary education sector, alongside specific calls to better educate the educators themselves on Indigenous history, colonization, and its contemporary legacies (Truth and Reconciliation Commission 2015). According to a 2018 report in *Maclean's* magazine, over 65 percent of universities had made strides in improving Indigenous knowledge, methods, and protocols inside their teaching and research practices. Another 71 percent had improved Indigenous representation in administration (Treleaven 2018). Websites at a few universities also referenced land acknowledgments, particularly on president's home pages.

While the acronym "EDI" was only used four times (all at the same university – McMaster), separately, the terms appeared quite frequently – equity (twenty-two times), diversity (twenty-seven times), and inclusion (twenty-nine times). The acronym EDI-I[9] was not found in the analysis of these specific universities. When looking at terms associated with gender parity, equity, and equality, there was much less evidence of this focus on these webpages. Gender appears only three times across all universities, equality only once, and equity goals and equity targets were not mentioned at all on either the main university interface pages or the president's main page.

The concept of allyship, or the incorporation of men allies/allyship, was almost entirely absent across the cases reviewed. However, the University of Waterloo's presidential page makes several mentions (four). Former president Feridun Hamdullahpur highlighted his commitment as a signatory to the UN's HeForShe Impact 10×10×10 initiative to increase gender parity across the institution.[10] He was the only U15 president to sign on to this commitment and Waterloo was the only university to have made efforts to incorporate some form of allyship modelling to address gender inequity at its institution. The analysis shows no mention of "visible minorities," "minorities," or "ability/disability," although it noted one mention of "multiculturalism."

More recent attention to anti-Black racism in the wake of George Floyd's murder in the United States in 2020 did appear in the content of eleven institutions,

TABLE 13.1

Content analysis of main university and presidential webpages

University	Type	EDI	EDI-I	Equity	Gender	Diversity	Inclusion	Allyship/male allyship	Equity goals/targets	Minorities/visible minorities	Disability	Equality	Indigenous/Indigeneity	ABR/anti-Black racism	Total
University of Toronto	U15	0	0	0	0	0	0	0	0	0	0	0	0	8	8
University of British Columbia	U15	0	0	1	0	0	1	0	0	0	0	0	1	0	3
Université de Montréal	U15	0	0	1	0	1	0	0	0	0	0	0	2	0	4
University of Ottawa	U15	0	0	0	0	0	0	0	0	0	0	0	0	95	95
Université Laval	U15	0	0	0	0	0	0	0	0	0	0	0	0	0	0
University of Waterloo	U15	0	0	2	1	0	0	0	0	0	0	0	1	10	14
University of Alberta	U15	0	0	0	0	0	0	0	0	0	0	0	2	0	2
McGill University	U15	0	0	0	0	0	0	0	0	0	0	0	0	0	0
McMaster University	U15	4	0	7	0	8	12	0	0	0	0	0	0	0	31
University of Calgary	U15	0	0	0	0	1	1	0	0	0	0	0	3	1	6
Western University (excludes colleges)	U15	0	0	0	0	1	0	0	0	0	0	0	0	3	4
Queen's University	U15	0	0	2	0	2	5	0	0	0	0	0	0	50	59
University of Manitoba	U15	0	0	0	0	1	0	0	0	0	0	0	2	0	3
University of Saskatchewan	U15	0	0	0	0	2	4	0	0	0	0	1	10	17	34
Dalhousie University	U15	0	0	0	0	1	0	0	0	0	0	0	1	24	26
Thompson Rivers University		0	0	1	0	3	1	0	0	0	0	0	2	9	16
University of New Brunswick		0	0	5	0	2	2	0	0	0	0	0	4	0	13
Lakehead University		0	0	0	0	0	0	0	0	0	0	0	10	0	10
University of Prince Edward Island		0	0	0	0	0	0	0	0	0	0	0	0	0	0
Mount Saint Vincent University		0	0	3	2	2	3	0	0	0	0	0	1	0	11
Brandon University		0	0	0	0	2	0	0	0	0	0	0	0	1	3
Bishop's University		0	0	0	0	1	0	0	0	0	0	0	0	0	1
Emily Carr University of Art + Design		0	0	0	0	0	0	0	0	0	0	0	1	3	4
Algoma University		0	0	0	0	0	0	0	0	0	0	0	1	0	1
First Nations University of Canada		0	0	0	0	0	0	0	0	0	0	0	8	0	8

with most attention coming from the U15 schools. Notably, the University of Ottawa had the highest tally of anti-Black racism-related terms, representing the entirety of its EDI mentions on its main and presidential webpages. This is perhaps not surprising since Ottawa drew national media scrutiny in 2020 after one of its professors used a racial slur in the classroom.

The rhetorical/content analysis also showed that other than the anti-Black racism file, size/U15 status did not impact the number of times specific institutions used EDI/EDI-I/gender/allyship terms. Of the twenty-five universities reviewed, only five mentioned these other terms ten or more times. Indigeneity was mentioned the most at Saskatchewan and Lakehead (ten times each), but not mentioned at all on McMaster's pages where equity (seven), diversity (eight), and inclusion (twelve) made up the bulk of their EDI content.

The analysis also shows three institutions had no mentions of any EDI content in their main or presidential webpages. These include both U15 – Laval and McGill – and non-U15 – University of Prince Edward Island – schools. While this does not mean those schools have ignored EDI/EDI-I, it does mean they did not feel it worthwhile to mention their commitment to EDI on either of these core webpages.

Table 13.2 shows the results of content analyses for the twenty-five universities' webpage statements of core missions, values, and visions. While there is a significant variety in how this is reported in each case (for example, some institutions had a specific mission page, whereas others had mission statements embedded in their long-term strategic planning documents), I did locate comparable webpage references to the core institutional mission of each university. Interestingly, eight of the twenty-five universities in the study did not incorporate any EDI/EDI-I/gender/allyship terms in these statements. Five of these were U15 schools and three were not, so again, no discernible pattern was shown vis-à-vis institutional capacity and the willingness of the institution to identify with this terminology.

There was also variation with the top four universities regarding number of references to these terms: two were non-U15; two were U15. First Nations University of Canada recorded the largest number of these terms in its mission statement with nineteen; not surprisingly, all of these included either Indigenous or First Nations references. Algoma was the other non-U15 university with a fairly high number of EDI/EDI-I terms with seven in total, five of which were in reference to Indigeneity. The University of Saskatchewan and the University of Toronto were the U15 schools that scored high with nine and six terms, respectively, inside their mission statements. These relied less on Indigenous identity and more on the use of terms "equity," "diversity," "inclusion," and "equality."

TABLE 13.2
Content analysis of university mission, vision, values webpages

University	Type	EDI	EDI-I	Equity	Gender	Diversity	Inclusion	Allyship/male allyship	Equity goals/targets	Minorities/visible minorities	Disability	Equality	Indigenous/Indigeneity	Total
University of Toronto	U15	0	0	2	0	2	1	0	0	0	0	1	0	6
University of British Columbia	U15	0	0	0	0	0	0	0	0	0	0	0	0	0
Université de Montréal	U15	0	0	0	0	0	0	0	0	0	0	0	0	0
University of Ottawa	U15	0	0	0	0	1	0	0	0	0	0	1	0	2
Université Laval	U15	0	0	0	0	1	1	0	0	0	0	0	0	2
University of Waterloo	U15	0	0	0	0	0	0	0	0	0	0	0	0	0
University of Alberta	U15	0	0	1	0	1	1	0	0	0	0	1	0	4
McGill University	U15	0	0	1	0	0	1	0	0	0	0	0	0	2
McMaster University	U15	0	0	0	0	0	2	0	0	0	0	0	0	2
University of Calgary	U15	0	0	0	0	1	1	0	0	0	0	0	0	2
Western University (excludes colleges)	U15	0	0	0	0	0	0	0	0	0	0	0	0	0
Queen's University	U15	0	0	0	0	0	0	0	0	0	0	0	0	0
University of Manitoba	U15	0	0	0	0	0	1	0	0	0	0	1	1	3
University of Saskatchewan	U15	0	0	1	0	3	3	0	0	0	0	1	1	9
Dalhousie University	U15	0	0	0	0	1	2	0	0	0	0	0	0	3
Thompson Rivers University		0	0	0	0	1	1	0	0	0	0	0	0	2
University of New Brunswick		0	0	0	0	0	0	0	0	0	0	0	0	0
Lakehead University		0	0	0	0	1	0	0	0	0	0	0	0	1
University of Prince Edward Island		0	0	0	0	0	0	0	0	0	0	0	0	0
Mount Saint Vincent University		0	0	0	0	0	0	0	0	0	0	0	0	0
Brandon University		0	0	0	0	2	0	0	0	0	0	0	1	3
Bishop's University		0	0	0	0	0	1	0	0	0	0	0	0	1
Emily Carr University of Art + Design		0	0	1	0	3	0	0	0	0	0	0	0	4
Algoma University		0	0	0	0	0	2	0	0	0	0	0	5	7
First Nations University of Canada		0	0	0	0	0	0	0	0	0	0	0	19	19

Again, this content analysis revealed no usage of the terms "allyship" or "men/male allies" in the mission statements reviewed. The University of Waterloo and Mount Saint Vincent University were the only two institutions that referenced "gender" in their mission statements.

Table 13.3 illustrates the results of the content analysis for the universities' most recent long-term strategic priority/planning documents. These documents were lengthier than the webpages analyzed above, and the analysis tracks higher numbers of terms as a result. Notably, all twenty-five universities included at least a few of the EDI/EDI-I terms in their strategic university documents, but as is evident in Table 13.3, the numbers vary substantially.

In the more general strategic planning document for the institutions overall, we see that four institutions – all U15 schools – contained over one hundred references to these EDI/EDI-I terms: Queen's (137), University of British Columbia (132), the University of Toronto (130), and the University of Manitoba (113). Yet the use of terms varied in the range of ten to sixty, with Lakehead being the highest scoring non-U15 university at fifty-seven. Two schools on the other end of the scale had less than ten references to EDI/EDI-I terms. These included one U15 school (Dalhousie) and one non-U15 (Algoma University).

Again, the analysis showed zero references to "allies," "allyship," or "men's allyship" modelling. When we look specifically at the use of the term "gender" in these documents, only eight universities included a reference to gender in their long-term strategic planning/priority documentation. These included Queen's, with four mentions; Mount Saint Vincent University and McGill at three; Universities of Montreal, Alberta, and British Columbia at two; and the University of Toronto and the University of Waterloo with one reference to gender.

I then conducted an analysis of the most recent EDI/EDI-I documents produced by each university.[11] I conduct a similar rhetoric/content analysis as above but paid close attention to any inclusion of allyship, men's allyship, and gender in these documents. Because these documents speak directly to institutional commitments to EDI/EDI-I, they show us how terms are used to frame and give shape to EDI conceptualizations and institutional EDI goals.

Table 13.4 shows that it was not easy to locate EDI-specific documents on the websites of four of the twenty-five institutions under review, the University of Montreal, Bishop's, Algoma, and First Nations University. I cannot say definitively that those documents do not exist, only that I could not locate them as part of this research project. It is possible these documents exist only in hard copy form.[12] Additionally, the analysis only located EDI Action Plans specific to the Canada Research Chair programs at four institutions – Saskatchewan, Thompson Rivers University, the University of Prince Edward Island, and

TABLE 13.3
Content analysis of university long-term strategic plan documents

University	Type	EDI/EDI-I	EDI-I	Equity	Gender	Diversity	Inclusion	Allyship/male allyship	Equity goals/targets	Minorities/	Visible minorities	Disability	Equality	Indigenous/Indigeneity	ABR	Total
University of Toronto	U15	0	0	19	1	29	18	0	0	1	0	3	5	27	27	130
University of British Columbia	U15	0	0	10	2	29	29	0	0	0	1	1	0	45	16	132
Université de Montréal	U15	0	0	8	2	21	2	0	0	1	1	1	1	3	0	40
University of Ottawa	U15	1	0	0	0	3	1	0	0	0	0	0	0	5	4	14
Université Laval	U15	0	0	4	0	4	5	0	0	0	0	0	1	0	0	14
University of Waterloo	U15	0	0	4	1	23	7	0	0	0	0	0	1	5	2	42
University of Alberta*	U15	0	0	5	2	21	6	0	0	4	2	2	1	11	0	54
McGill University	U15	7	0	6	3	23	5	0	0	0	0	0	0	8	2	54
McMaster University*	U15	0	0	0	0	3	2	0	0	0	0	1	0	19	4	29
University of Calgary	U15	0	0	0	0	6	6	0	0	0	0	0	0	1	0	13
Western University (excludes colleges)	U15	0	0	2	0	8	1	0	0	1	1	1	0	8	0	22
Queen's University	U15	0	0	18	4	36	19	0	2	2	2	3	2	36	13	137
University of Manitoba	U15	0	0	1	2	12	7	0	0	2	0	3	0	81	5	113
University of Saskatchewan	U15	0	0	0	0	22	1	0	0	2	0	0	0	24	5	52
Dalhousie University	U15	0	0	0	0	5	3	0	0	0	0	0	0	0	2	10
Thompson Rivers University		0	0	0	0	3	4	0	0	0	0	0	0	1	4	12
University of New Brunswick		0	0	3	0	1	5	0	0	0	0	0	0	2	1	12
Lakehead University		0	0	5	0	13	4	0	0	0	0	0	0	31	4	57
University of Prince Edward Island		0	0	2	0	4	7	0	0	0	0	1	0	9	1	24
Mount Saint Vincent University		0	0	2	3	10	4	0	0	0	0	2	0	0	1	22
Brandon University		0	0	0	0	9	8	0	0	0	0	0	0	2	5	24
Bishop's University		0	0	0	0	6	3	0	0	0	0	0	0	4	0	13
Emily Carr University Art + Design		0	0	3	0	12	5	0	0	0	0	0	0	8	15	43
Algoma University		0	0	0	0	2	0	0	0	0	0	0	0	0	0	2
First Nations University of Canada		0	0	0	0	1	0	0	0	0	0	0	0	39	0	40

* Both Alberta and McMaster have specific EDI Strategic Plan documents.

TABLE 13.4
Content analysis of university EDI-specific documents

University	Type	EDI	EDI-I	Equity	Gender	Diversity	Inclusion	Allyship	Equity goals/targets	Minorities/	Visible minorities	Disability	Equality	Indigenous	Total
University of Toronto	U15	36	0	178	43	116	89	0	0	0	0	14	2	35	513
University of British Columbia	U15	0	0	67	2	74	6	0	3	0	3	8	0	6	169
Université de Montréal	U15	N/A	N/A	N/A	N/A	N/A	N/A	N/A	N/A	N/A	N/A	N/A	N/A	N/A	N/A
University of Ottawa	U15	0	0	70	23	177	182	0	3	24	16	35	2	21	553
Université Laval	U15	183	0	69	24	78	40	0	0	7	20	5	26	0	452
University of Waterloo	U15	33	0	247	25	74	75	2	6	12	11	25	2	28	540
University of Alberta	U15	78	0	52	5	41	41	0	3	2	2	7	7	8	246
McGill University	U15	49	0	53	1	28	26	0	0	0	0	9	1	31	198
McMaster University	U15	73	0	43	3	29	64	0	0	1	1	1	2	5	222
University of Calgary	U15	28	0	37	8	62	30	0	0	0	0	4	0	12	181
Western University (excludes colleges)	U15	0	0	24	1	32	9	0	0	1	1	2	0	0	70
Queen's University	U15	4	0	97	17	74	83	0	0	4	7	11	0	68	365
University of Manitoba	U15	11	0	48	6	62	52	0	0	0	0	8	0	8	195
University of Saskatchewan	U15	7	0	95	3	77	61	0	4	3	3	15	1	22	291
Dalhousie University	U15	12	0	43	5	102	87	1	4	1	0	1	0	17	273
Thompson Rivers University		63	0	37	5	34	26	0	0	3	0	0	0	10	178
University of New Brunswick		90	0	89	4	26	21	0	3	8	7	8	0	4	260
Lakehead University		124	0	95	4	65	58	0	3	1	0	5	0	30	382
University of Prince Edward Island		21	0	214	5	181	195	0	8	9	8	14	1	15	671
Mount Saint Vincent University		0	0	0	2	20	13	0	0	0	0	1	0	0	49
Brandon University		30	0	48	0	49	30	0	1	6	6	7	0	7	184
Bishop's University		N/A	N/A	N/A	N/A	N/A	N/A	N/A	N/A	N/A	N/A	N/A	N/A	N/A	N/A
Emily Carr University of Art + Design		9	0	2	1	4	11	0	0	0	0	0	0	7	34
Algoma University		N/A	N/A	N/A	N/A	N/A	N/A	N/A	N/A	N/A	N/A	N/A	N/A	N/A	N/A
First Nations University of Canada		N/A	N/A	N/A	N/A	N/A	N/A	N/A	N/A	N/A	N/A	N/A	N/A	N/A	N/A

Brandon. The EDI document found for Laval was in French, so the analysis in Table 13.4 reflects equivalent French content and not exact word matches. The most recent EDI document I found for Western was for a "Diversity and Inclusion Plan" for 2011–15; this was used for the analysis below, even though it is not very recent. Finally, the only EDI document that was easily located for Mount Saint Vincent University was an EDI brochure, which was shorter than other documents reviewed in this section.

A few universities were in the process of updating or formulating EDI-specific documents at time of writing. For example, Emily Carr University's EDI webpage includes an Action Plan that is framed as a "living document" and thus could very well have changed by the time this chapter is published. Despite this, there are some interesting trends that continue from the earlier analysis of more central university webpages and strategic planning and mission statements. The first is the stark absence of reference to "allyship" or "men's allyship" programs in EDI-specific plans and web-based summaries. Only two universities mentioned allyship in EDI-specific documents – Waterloo with two mentions and Dalhousie with one. For the latter, allyship is mentioned among a long list of initiatives for student-focused curricular and cocurricular approaches to EDI. There is no elaboration on what "allyship" means or how it would be implemented. For the former, the reference reflects Waterloo's president's commitment to the HeForShe initiative. Allyship as a concept was completely absent from all the other EDI documents reviewed.

While there was no uptake of the term EDI-I, Indigenous references were mixed in these documents. While UBC, Western, and Mount Saint Vincent's EDI literature made no Indigenous references at all, others had quite high numbers: Queen's, sixty-eight mentions; Toronto, thirty-five; and Lakehead, thirty-four. As with the previous terms discussed, there is no distinction between small and large universities in their EDI approaches. References to "gender" also varied significantly, with Brandon (zero), McGill and Western (one), British Columbia and Mount Saint Vincent (two), and McMaster and Saskatchewan (three) at the lowest end and Toronto (forty-three), Waterloo (twenty-five), Laval (twenty-four), and Ottawa (twenty-three) at the highest. The terms "equity," "diversity," and "inclusion" were used the most (and more than "gender" in all of these cases), but it appears that the interpretation of what those words mean and how to approach EDI goals was defined quite differently across the cases under review.

CONCLUSION

This content analysis study has shown a number of key trends that may help explain the stalling of progress with respect to gender parity goals inside Canadian universities, particularly at the highest levels of leadership (vice-presidents and presidents). It also raises questions about institutional culture beyond a simple tallying of representational leadership numbers by assessing to what extent institutional cultures in Canada openly commit to stemming sexism and/ or sexual harassment at work. It is beyond the scope of this study to speak directly to the culture inside each of these institutions, but the evidence suggests that public affirmations of EDI/EDI-I commitments have been mixed to nonexistent in many of the main branding/core documents and webpages reviewed in this project, which arguably does not bode well for gender-inclusive culture. Additionally, a review of EDI-specific plans and documents did not show gender or male allyship to be a core aspect of how EDI was conceptualized. The fact that these documents were often hard to find, if they could be found at all, was also troubling.

Indigeneity and recognition of TRC-mandated calls to action were the most prevalent and visible aspects of institutional website branding, particularly on main university and presidential webpages. Not surprisingly, these were also dominant at universities with larger Indigenous student populations including First Nations University of Canada, Algoma University, and the University of Saskatchewan. Recent attention to anti-Black racism was also dominant in a few of the U15 schools, particularly one that was recently in the news for the use of racist language in the classroom. References to gender, gender equity, and equity targets and goals were not highly prevalent in any of the content studies included here. Gender was only mentioned a total of three times across all main university webpages and presidential webpages. Only two universities of twenty-five included the term gender in their mission statement pages. A higher number of universities – eight – included gender in their longer-term strategic planning documents, but no more than four times at the higher end of that range, and at only one institution.

The lack of attention to gender in these documents indicates that either gender was not a priority or it was not a priority in communications with the public. I did see more references to the terms "equity," "diversity," and "inclusion," but there were many instances where institutions avoided these terms as well, again signalling a lack of attention to these concepts in their publicly available websites and mission statements. The study did note that when longer-term strategic planning documents were reviewed, some – particularly U15 schools – were more willing to include EDI terms in their long-term plans. But again, the level of inclusion of these terms was mixed across institutions, arguably showing a mixed level of commitment.

The most striking finding in the content analysis was the complete absence of references to allyship modelling in any of the webpages or strategic documents reviewed – including in the majority of EDI-specific plans/documents. The only reference found on the central webpages was the University of Waterloo's presidential page. The only other university to mention allyship at all was Dalhousie, but it was mentioned very briefly without any context or elaboration.

Taking all of this into consideration, the chapter infers that the twenty-five Canadian universities under review (including all U15 schools) had not defined the problem or the goal of gender parity or allyship as core to their institutional mandates. While EDI terms may indeed have been referenced, at least in longer-term strategic priority documents, gender was not prevalent in these documents and was absent in most of them (seventeen/twenty-five). Even Waterloo, which included some reference to men's allyship through its president's commitment to the HeForShe Impact 10×10×10 initiative, did not use allyship or gender parity goals on its main webpage advertising; nor were these terms included widely in their long-term planning documents (gender appeared only once in this document). Referring to Bacchi's "what's the problem represented to be" framework, it appears that gender parity had not been identified as a goal or a problem with respect to EDI commitments at the time of this review. According to Moreau, Osgood, and Halsall (2008), who found a similar lack of commitment to gender parity in British public schools, this unwillingness to include gender in strategic documents can mean that gender parity is essentially "a token article commitment, available for display on ceremonial occasions or in moments of crisis" (Jewson and Mason, cited in Moreau, Osgood, and Halsall 2008, 574).

This study is only the first to try to tackle the issue of institutional commitment levels to EDI, EDI-I, allyship, and gender parity by examining rhetoric and content included in publicly available main university webpages, mission statements, long-term strategic planning documents, and recent EDI-specific plans and statements. It is incomplete in several areas, not the least of which is that it only covers twenty-five of Canada's ninety-six universities.[13] However, the study does seem to indicate that the lack of attention to these issues has been widespread, even in U15 schools, who arguably have the most capacity in the country to include programs and plans to deal with systemic inequity. Additionally, allyship and men's ally modelling has not been widely or even minimally embraced at the Canadian postsecondary institutions included in this study. If, as Universities Canada's most recent survey seems to suggest, the country's universities are perplexed by the lack of progress in EDI/EDI-I and require more information on best practices, they might want to consider adopting men's allyship models to encourage wider buy-in among employees and students alike, to embrace EDI/EDI-I more fulsomely, and to ensure progress is not stalled and is sustained into the future. It is my hope that further research into the levels of commitment to EDI/EDI-I at Canadian universities will illuminate useful practices that all institutions can model for effective progress now and into the future.

ACKNOWLEDGMENTS

Thanks to Justin Grainger for his impeccable research assistance with this project. Also, thanks to Lynn Arner, the anonymous reviewers, and the editors of this volume for helpful comments and suggestions.

NOTES

1 Note that the response rate for this larger category, which included deans, associate and assistant vice-presidents, as well as "other decision-makers reporting directly to the president," presidents, provosts, and other vice-presidents, was only 28.7 percent.

2 Note there were various response rates to this self-reporting data collection: presidents, 64.5 percent; provosts, 47.6 percent; vice-presidents research, 39 percent.

3 The foreword written by Universities Canada president Paul Davidson briefly mentions the United Nations HeForShe men leadership allyship campaign (3), and being an "ally" is mentioned in a list of promising practices at the end of the document under the heading "Recruit and retain and support advancement of diverse senior leaders" (35).

4 This is not to suggest that men's allyship programs alone can solve persistent gender inequities in organizations. Additionally, critiques of men's allyship programs (as well as white allyship) warn that they do not fully challenge patriarchy or racism and can create a "pedestal" effect where men benefit from credit/praise out of proportion to their actual efforts (see Peretz 2020, 450).

5 Low psychological standing occurs when someone's "self-perceived legitimacy" is not high enough for them to act in relation to "a cause or an issue" (Miller et al. 2009 in Sherf, Tangirala, and Weber 2017, 195).

6 University webpages can and do change over time. My research is based on the university website pages and strategic documents available primarily between May 11–29, 2020, and January 15–28, 2021.

7 The content analysis looked for specific words including EDI, EDI-I, equity, diversity, inclusion, gender, allyship, male allyship, equity goals, equity targets, minorities, visible minorities, disability, Indigeneity, equality, Indigenous. Additionally, I include a tally of anti-Black racism (ABR)-related terms including anti-Black racism, racism, racialization, racialized, anti-oppression, Black Lives Matter, critical race theory, BIPOC, people of colour, and white privilege.

8 I examine content on this page, including all direct links (only direct links) listed on the webpage menu.

9 EDI-I/EDII was adopted in some instances by some universities (for example, Queen's, Waterloo, and Wilfrid Laurier) in and around 2020 to highlight progress toward Indigeneity in EDI initiatives. The shift in usage of this term has not been fully embraced,

as the current content analysis demonstrates, but I included it to track its adoption at the time of study, nonetheless.

10 For more on the United Nation's HeForShe 10×10×10 initiative see: https://www. heforshe.org/en/impact.

11 See note 6 above regarding the time of data collection.

12 When I could not locate a specific long-term strategic plan document, I referenced either a long-term academic or research planning document. I could not locate a specific strategic plan document for two universities – McGill and Brandon. Only one document was used per university – the most recent that was located. In some instances, no EDI-specific documents were located on university websites. These are noted in Table 13.4 and discussed.

13 There were ninety-seven institutional members of Universities Canada but at time of writing, Brescia was merging with Western University.

WORKS CITED

Bacchi, Carol. 2009. *Analysing Policy*. Frenchs Forest, Australia: Pearson Higher Education AU.

Bilen-Green, Canan, and J.P. Carpenter. 2015. "Implementation of Advocates and Allies Programs to Support and Promote Gender Equity in Academia." Paper presented at American Society for Engineering Education Annual Conference, Seattle, WA, June 14–17, 2015.

Drury, Benjamin J., and C.R. Kaiser. 2014. "Allies against Sexism: The Role of Men in Confronting Sexism." *Journal of Social Issues* 70 (4): 637–52.

Finlayson, Alan. 2007. "From Beliefs to Arguments: Interpretive Methodology and Rhetorical Political Analysis." *British Journal of Politics and International Relations* 9:545–63.

Madsen, Susan R., A. Townsend, and R.T. Scribner. 2019. "Strategies That Male Allies Use to Advance Women in the Workplace." *Journal of Men's Studies*: 1–21. doi: 101177/1060826519883239.

Moreau, Marie-Pierre, J. Osgood, and A. Halsall. 2008. "Equal Opportunities Policies in English Schools: Towards Greater Gender Equality in the Teaching Workforce." *Gender, Work and Organization* 15 (6): 553–78.

Peretz, Tal. 2020. "Seeing the Invisible Knapsack: Feminist Men's Strategic Responses to the Continuation of Male Privilege in Feminist Spaces." *Men and Masculinities* 23 (3–4): 447–75.

Phillips, N., and C. Hardy. 2002. *Discourse Analysis: Investigating Processes of Social Construction*. SAGE Publications.

Rein, M., and D. Schön. 1996. "Frame-Critical Policy Analysis and Frame-Reflective Policy Practice." *Knowledge and Policy* 9 (1): 85.

Sawyer K., and A.M. Valerio. 2018. "Making the Case for Male Champions for Gender Inclusiveness at Work." *Organizational Dynamics* 47 (1): 1–7.

Sherf, Elad N., S. Tangirala, and K. Connealy Weber. 2017. "It Is Not My Place! Psychological Standing and Men's Voice and Participations in Gender-Parity Initiatives." *Organizational Science* 28 (2): 193–210.

Treleaven, Sarah. 2018. "How Canadian Universities are Responding to the TRC's Calls to Action." *Maclean's*, December 7, 2018. https://www.macleans.ca/education/how -canadian-universities-are-responding-to-the-trcs-calls-to-action/.

Truth and Reconciliation Commission of Canada. 2015. "Calls to Action." Winnipeg, MB. http://trc.ca/assets/pdf/Calls_to_Action_English2.pdf.

Universities Canada. 2017. "Universities Canada Principles on Equity, Diversity and Inclusion." https://www.univcan.ca/media-room/media-releases/universities-canada -principles-equity-diversity-inclusion/.

–. 2019. "Equity, Diversity and Inclusion at Canadian Universities." https://www.univcan. ca/media-room/publications/equity-diversity-and-inclusion-at-canadian-universities -report-on-the-2019-survey/.

Vásquez, Consuelo, Viviane Sergi, and Benoit Cordelier. 2013. "From Being Branded to Doing Branding: Studying Representation Practices from a Communication-Centred Approach." *Scandinavian Journal of Management* 29:135–46.

Reconciliation in the Research Ecosystem:
It's about Relationships

SARA ANDERSON

I work in the Office of Research at one of the U15 research-intensive institutions in the land we now call Canada. According to our Human Resources Department, I constitute the 0.7 percent of Indigenous self-identified staff in my unit. In this particular dataset, I am not even a full percentage point. I know this is just a numbers game and that it does not really mean that I am less than one full human being; at the same time, my situation is indicative of the challenge in postsecondary education when it comes to enacting Truth and Reconciliation.

But first, I have been taught to introduce myself so that you understand who I am and my context in writing this piece. I come from a mixed background. I was born and raised in Kitchener-Waterloo, on the Haldimand Tract, land granted to the Six Nations of the Grand River. This is also territory under the Dish With One Spoon wampum belt, an agreement between the Haudensaunee, the Anishinaabe, and now newcomers, to share the lands and the resources of the Great Lakes region. My mother is of German descent, from the Mennonite community; her father's family was one of the first settler families to come to this area in the early 1800s and "buy" parts of Blocks 2 and 3 of the Haldimand Tract. My father was part of the 60s scoop, taken from his family and community when he was four years old and later adopted by a settler family who attended a Mennonite church. Although I know where he was taken from, since I have not been claimed by that community officially, the most truthful thing I can say is that I am on a lifelong journey of learning and unlearning how to walk in both these worlds. After pursuing higher education away from my hometown, it now seems that I have come full circle, returning to work in the land in which I was raised, in a role dedicated to bridging the gaps of understanding between Indigenous and non-Indigenous academics, particularly within the context of university-based research.

Over the past five years, every postsecondary institution in Canada has adopted statements to the effect that they are committed to implementing the 94 Calls to Action released by the Truth and Reconciliation Commission (TRC) in 2015. Some institutions have walked further on this journey, setting up programs and initiatives that track their progress on various calls to action; others have barely begun hiring Indigenous leadership into either faculty or staff roles; still others are struggling to do even that. My institution is mere steps on its journey of reconciliation work, and while this is the case for the university as a whole, I believe this challenge is further amplified in the research ecosystem.

So, how does research relate to Truth and Reconciliation? Interestingly, the calls to action only mention the word "research" four times throughout the entire summary report: twice in the context of the development of a National Action Plan for Reconciliation, once concerning a SSHRC-based research program with multiyear funding to advance understanding of reconciliation, and once in the context of funding for Indigenous communities to conduct research to produce histories of their own experiences with residential schools (Calls to Action 53, 65, 78; TRC 2015, 328, 331, 334). It does not specifically reference the research context within educational institutions. But what the TRC report does fundamentally rely on, and indeed understands to be the "framework for reconciliation" (TRC 2015, 21), is the United Nations Declaration on the Rights of Indigenous Peoples (UNDRIP). The summary report states that "we remain convinced that the *United Nations Declaration* provides the necessary principles, norms, and standards for reconciliation to flourish in twenty-first-century Canada" (TRC 2015, 21). Even though Canada has only recently committed to implementing the Declaration, a cornerstone of UNDRIP is the right of "Free, Prior, and Informed Consent" (FPIC) – and I believe this is where Truth and Reconciliation intersects with research in academic institutions.

If FPIC is a right of Indigenous peoples, it follows that to obtain robust, free, prior, and informed consent, anyone wishing to work with Indigenous peoples and communities must have some kind of engagement with these peoples and communities before their work begins. Although this order of operations seems obvious, this understanding has not always been the case. In the past, university-based research has been considered anathema by many Indigenous communities. As Linda Tuhiwai Smith (Ngāti Awa, Ngāti Porou, Tūhourangi), professor of Māori and Indigenous Studies in New Zealand, noted in her seminal work *Decolonizing Methodologies*:

The word itself, "research," is probably one of the dirtiest words in the Indigenous world's vocabulary ... it stirs up silence, it conjures up bad memories, it raises a smile that is knowing and distrustful ... The ways in which scientific research is implicated in the worst excesses of colonialism remains a powerful remembered history for many of the world's colonized peoples. (1999, 1)

So, what does this mean for those wishing to do research with Indigenous communities today? How can researchers, particularly non-Indigenous people, stop perpetuating the harms of the past? I do not believe the answer lies in legal frameworks and justifications, which are important but continue to operate on assumptions of colonial worldviews; rather, a path forward can be found in Indigenous ways of knowing and being. That is to say: relationships must be at the heart of research.

This is not a new concept for Indigenous scholars. In 1991, Verna J. Kirkness and Ray Barnhardt, both Indigenous scholars and educators, conceptualized and published what has become widely known as the "4 R's" in Indigenous methodologies: respect, relevance, reciprocity, and responsibility. Grounded by the later addition of a fifth R, relationships, these deceptively simple concepts provide a principled approach for scholars engaging with Indigenous communities in research partnerships. Beyond a simple "consultation as engagement" framework, the purpose of this principled approach is to forefront community relevance and participation, promote mutual capacity building, and ensure that the research will benefit Indigenous communities.

Over the past year and a half, I have seen a rise in interest from non-Indigenous faculty in doing research with Indigenous communities, particularly since some granting agencies and funding calls now require engagement with Indigenous communities as an element of research proposals. I get many questions from faculty about what is actually meant by relationship-building. They are nervous, and often completely unfamiliar with what it is like to work with an Indigenous community. This anxiety translates into how the research ecosystem is administered in my institution: there seem to be many good intentions but no sense of how to even begin identifying barriers, let alone dismantling them in a way that would produce positive impacts on Indigenous faculty members, staff, students, and the broader community who work with university-led research projects.

I have also seen reluctance to let go of colonial ways of research. Although I would like to think of these harmful practices as existing in the past, I can share that in my second week working in the Office of Research I was asked by a non-Indigenous researcher to be introduced to an Indigenous community (it did not even matter which one) so they could conduct testing of a new medical device. Apparently, it was significant to their funders that they received consultation from Indigenous peoples. It is sometimes hard to believe that these types of requests stem from a genuine lack of understanding, rather than something more sinister; but I must approach my work as if they do, for my own mental health and sanity.

Ultimately, I believe we must begin to address these challenges to university research by building relationships. But how do we begin building relationships when our academic institutions do not make true relationship-building, supported with commitments to both time and finances, a priority? This brings me back full circle to the fact that I comprise the 0.7 percent of Indigenous self-identified staff in the Office of Research. With so few Indigenous people within the institution, how can we even begin to identify the barriers and harmful ways of operating that are preventing us from building true relationships? The Truth and Reconciliation Commission's summary report lays out our ongoing challenge: "Together, Canadians must do more than just talk about reconciliation; we must learn how to practice reconciliation in our everyday lives – within ourselves and our families, and in our communities, governments, places of worship, schools, and workplaces. To do so constructively, Canadians must remain committed to the ongoing work of establishing and maintaining respectful relationships" (TRC 2015, 21). If we truly want to continue on our journey of Truth and Reconciliation, universities can, and must, do better.

WORKS CITED

Kirkness, Verna J., and Ray Barnhardt. 1991. "First Nations and Higher Education: The Four R's – Respect, Relevance, Reciprocity, Responsibility." *Journal of American Indian Education* 30 (3): 1–15.

Smith, Linda Tuhiwai. 1999. *Decolonizing Methodologies*. London: Zed Books.

Truth and Reconciliation Commission of Canada (TRC). 2015. *Honouring the Truth, Reconciling for the Future: Summary of the Final Report of the Truth and Reconciliation Commission of Canada*. https://irsi.ubc.ca/sites/default/files/inline-files/Executive_ Summary_English_Web.pdf.

Conclusion
Silence Is *Not* Golden

LORNA A. TURNBULL

It is both a privilege and a challenge to write the conclusion for a collection such as this, created by diverse authors on such a broad range of topics.[1] The coherence and connection between the chapters gives life to the editors' over-arching goal of launching a national interdisciplinary conversation to better understand, and more effectively address, the persistent gender inequality in Canadian universities. Taken collectively, the chapters tell a compelling story of structural inequality that runs counter to Canadians' self-understanding of being fair and tolerant people. More importantly, the story they tell runs counter to the commitments Canadians made to ourselves in the adoption of the Charter of Rights and Freedoms and in the various provincial and federal humans rights codes. As the saga of the quest for equality in the Canada Research Chairs program in Chapter 10 has illustrated, the law in Canada prohibits systemic discrimination and upholds a vision of substantive equality that, while clearly and regularly affirmed by the courts, is still quite distant from our daily lives.

To draw this impressive collection to a close, I wish to outline three important ideas that I see emerging from the authors' work. First, I situate inequality in the academy within a larger social context. The coronavirus pandemic and the global antiracism movement spurred by police violence in the US, Canada, and around the world in 2020 have exposed societies' greatest inequalities to deeper scrutiny. Next, I highlight key crosscutting themes that emerge from the chapters in this book, reviewing them in light of the larger social context. Third, I situate these themes as elements of the necessary strategies to confront, disrupt, and replace the current structures that maintain the disadvantaged position of women in the academy, especially those marginalized on the basis of their race, ability, gender identity, or social class. Before presenting these three points of analysis, I begin by situating myself and my own connection to this wonderful and ambitious project.

I am a feminist legal scholar, a first-generation Canadian of Scottish origin. I live, research, and teach in Winnipeg, Manitoba, on the land covered by Treaty

One, where I am growing in my understanding of my own privilege and learning to listen and make space for marginalized voices. I began my law studies in 1986, a year after the equality provision of the Charter (s. 15) came into force. I was inspired by the appointment of the first woman, Bertha Wilson, to the Supreme Court of Canada (Turnbull 2009). The first Supreme Court decision under s. 15 was issued in my final year of law school, and I graduated filled with a great sense of hope given how the court interpreted equality in Canada (*Andrews* 1989; Turnbull 2006). But all was not rosy. In 1987, Mary Jane Mossman, a leading feminist scholar who was also well known for her work on access to justice, was passed over in the appointment of an external candidate as dean of Osgoode Hall Law School. A protest movement was launched, as graduates wearing buttons reading "Dare to Dream of a Feminist Dean" dropped pink carnations in her lap at convocation that year. A human rights complaint followed, launched not by Professor Mossman, but by a group of outraged students, lawyers, and fellow academics (Mossman 2021). Women in law schools in the 1980s were struggling to find their place and were often the objects of blatant discrimination and harassment (McIntyre 1986; Mossman 1985). Around the same time, Bruce Feldthusen (1990), a law professor at Western Faculty of Law, named and described the privilege of the men who enjoyed a "right not to know" about inequality and the discrimination women were facing in classrooms, offices, and faculty lounges.

My work as a feminist legal scholar has focused on inequality flowing from the gendered work of care, and in particular the work of mothering. Starting with the *Andrews* and *Brooks* decisions in 1989, I imagined that the Charter would provide the tools to create the equal society I dreamed of as a young woman. The thirty years that have elapsed since then have taught me that the fight for equality is very much one step forward and two steps back (Brodsky and Day 1989). The law has yet to live up to the potential that I believed it held when I was a starry-eyed student. My time in academic leadership at the University of Manitoba showed me how entrenched inequality is, even under the leadership of a "feminist dean."

In 2016, after finishing six years as dean myself, and five years before that as associate dean, of the Faculty of Law, I began to reconstruct my research program and, through serendipity, connected with a brilliant team of data scientists. Through this work, in which we used population data to document the adverse impacts of the child welfare system on children, I began thinking about the "evidence" that is needed to make a claim of systemic discrimination (Nickel et al. 2020). This need for evidence is a particularly relevant concern as I endeavour to offer a conclusion to the expansive work contained in this volume.

Of course, if you are a hammer, then everything looks like a nail, and so I am bound, by training and by a deep innate sense of justice, to look for a resolution, a remedy, for the wrongs that are so vividly illustrated by the research in this collection. I do not suggest that "law" is the answer, certainly not law alone, but it is part of the answer, and it is relevant because it is part of the larger social frame within which the inequality experienced by women in the academy is created and by which it could begin to be resolved.[2]

INEQUALITY IN SOCIAL CONTEXT

Law is one of the social systems that creates and maintains inequality. It is also a mechanism by which inequality can be addressed, as the story of the equality challenge to the Canada Research Chairs program so clearly illustrates. In confirming the settlement agreements as an order, the Federal Court made the agreed upon remedies enforceable. As Louise Forsyth noted, this gives the agreements the real power of law. This means that the universities receiving CRC funds must have EDI action plans in place, and that there will be penalties for noncompliance. The Federal Court also endorsed a target-setting process and laid out what data must be collected for those targets to ensure accountability. This allows enforcement of the targets and provides that the claimants can go back to court if the universities are not following the terms of the agreements. These are powerful remedies, but going back to court takes time, energy, and money, resources that women have in smaller supply than individual men, and the institutions still dominated by men, that oppose them. In this sense, the ongoing burden on those who are oppressed represents a form of cultural tax, as demonstrated by the fact that the claimants had to go back to court after the failure of universities and the federal government to respect the results of the original 2006 settlement. In this way, the law is both a means to gain access to equality and means to ensure the preservation of the status quo.

Laws set out our rights. Courts can uphold them and provide remedies. We need both. A declaration of rights provides visibility; it counters the right not to know and encourages those silenced to speak. Remedies can require that structures be changed, as did the remedies in the CRC case. Remedies need not just be monetary awards to individual claimants to make them "go away"; they can also be collective and structural. But remedies require claimants to demonstrate harm. The significant contribution of the chapters in this book is that they illustrate the harms experienced by women in the academy both collectively and individually.

Courts do not always understand or properly apply the law of systemic discrimination. Indeed, the civic conversations underway since the resurgence of

Black Lives Matter, following the killing of George Floyd in May 2020, show that many people, even political leaders, do not understand what systemic racism and systemic discrimination are (Turnbull 2020). In my area of research on gender equality, I have found that the Federal Court of Appeal consistently fails to recognize the disadvantage experienced by women seeking to access parental benefits and fails to understand the systemic nature of discrimination faced by mothers over the past decades, discounting women's claims as either unreasonable or too expensive (Turnbull 2006; Hansen and Turnbull 2013).

Despite these implementation issues, substantive equality *is* the Canadian model of equality. The equality guarantees in the Charter and in the federal and provincial human rights codes are for substantive, not formal, equality. Under this model, an intention to discriminate does not need to be established if the effect of a law, practice, or policy is to disadvantage the individuals and groups who are protected by those instruments (*Action Travail des Femmes* 1987; *Moore* 2012; *Kokopenace* 2015; *Fraser* 2020). Canada even has a protection for laws and policies that are implemented to remedy discrimination under s. 15(2) of the Charter. These institutional protections mean that language from other jurisdictions (such as the United States) about reverse discrimination should have no purchase in the Canadian discussion. We can, and should, expect our institutions, especially our universities, to take proactive steps to address inequality. Still, Mossman (2021) urges that we do not overestimate the power of law and reminds us we need "intrepid complainants" to overcome "herculean obstacles" to be able to advance claims of equality through the legal system.

CROSSCUTTING THEMES

Three themes, among the many, stand out for me in the work of the researchers in this volume. The first is that many women academics do work that is different from the work done by many of their male colleagues. Some of that work is care work, both at home and in the workplace. When they engage in typical care work, carrying heavier service burdens than some of their male peers, they may find that that work is not accounted for in the tenure and promotion processes. And when women do not behave in stereotypical caring ways, they may find themselves the victims of contrapower harassment. The different approaches taken by women in the classroom, especially racialized women, are not valued and adversely affect SETs with consequences for career progression and pay. Contract instructors find themselves even more vulnerable to the destructive feedback that SETs generate. Women also work differently when caregiving responsibilities outside of the academy affect their availability for research. The coronavirus pandemic has affected women's scholarly work given their heavier burden of family responsibilities, creating "cumulative advantages for men" (Squazzoni et al. 2020).

A second theme is that the data underlying much of the research undertaken here were difficult for the researchers to access. Canada has done a poor job of collecting disaggregated data, especially data disaggregated by race, gender identity, sexuality, or disability (Willsie 2020). As well, many of the processes that generate data that might be examined to reveal structural biases, such as hiring or promotion processes, are considered to be individual and private, meaning that the data they generate are not available for study. These data, taken together, could reveal structural constraints that disproportionately disadvantage women.

Data and research studies, like those in this volume, provide the evidence that courts need to make findings of inequality and systemic discrimination. It is not enough for one woman dean to point out how she has a lower salary than a male dean, because her complaint risks being dismissed as a failure to negotiate or as simply demonstrating that she does not meet the same threshold of "merit" as the male dean. A successful claim requires evidence that women, as a group, are ending up with lower salaries and fewer opportunities for advancement than are men, as a group. A pattern of shared experiences by many individual women is required to establish that the root of women's inequality is built into the structures and unconscious biases of the academy as an institution.

In *Fraser v. Canada (Attorney General)* (2020), the Supreme Court told us that two types of evidence can establish that a law or policy has a disproportionate impact on members of a protected group: evidence about the situation of the claimant group, and evidence about the results or impact of the law or policy (para. 56). First, evidence about the physical, social, cultural, or other barriers that illustrate the "full context of the claimant group's situation" can show that group membership is associated with certain characteristics that create disadvantage for group members. It may become possible to see that seemingly neutral policies are "designed well for some and not for others." The Supreme Court also notes that "issues which predominantly affect certain populations may be under-documented. These claimants may have to rely more heavily on their own evidence or evidence from other members of their group, rather than on government reports, academic studies or expert testimony" (para. 57).

Second, evidence about the outcomes that a law or policy has produced in practice may provide concrete proof that members of protected groups are being disproportionately impacted. This evidence may include statistics (para. 58) but "there is no universal measure for what level of statistical disparity is necessary to demonstrate that there is a disproportionate impact," and the court is wary of creating overly rigid guidelines (para. 59). When "clear and consistent statistical disparities" show a disproportionate impact on members of protected groups, "even if the precise reason for that impact is unknown" (para. 62), there is no requirement for the "claimant to bear the additional burden of explaining *why* the law [or policy] has such an effect. In such cases, the statistical evidence is itself a compelling sign that the law has not been structured in a way that takes into account the protected group's circumstances" (para. 66).

Although the research in this volume tells us what we already know, because we have lived it, and we have seen our older colleagues before us, and our younger ones after us, live it, it provides the evidence of "clear and consistent statistical disparities" that establishes the disparate impact on women in the academy. To make a change, we must prove that systemic inequality exists. It is work like the research in this volume that will allow us to do that.

Finally, many of the chapters, and certainly those in the fourth section of this volume, imagine changes that will completely disrupt the way the academy functions, making space for new ways of including and valuing diverse perspectives, talents, and concerns. For the work of women academics to be visible and valued, we need a radical transformation of the academy. Radical change, meaning from the root, will inevitably be disruptive, and we need it to be. We want changes not only in our day-to-day experiences, but in the places we occupy, the spaces where we have lived those oppressive experiences: in our classrooms, in our labs and research ethics boards, in our status within the university. Research that scrutinizes the websites and collective agreements of many universities across Canada allows us to see the patterns and, with that evidence, to begin to hold our universities accountable.

BUILDING A MORE INCLUSIVE AND DIVERSE ACADEMY

The work of the scholars in this book also gives us direction for finding the necessary strategies to confront, disrupt, and replace the current structures. First, we must value what we bring to the academy, raise it up, and have it count. Compassionate pedagogy is good pedagogy; collaboration and emotional intelligence are good for research leadership, mentoring, and supporting students; and engaging in service that benefits the university as a whole, or the communities beyond the university, is part of the mission of most Canadian universities. Such work is of value, and it should be recognized and rewarded. We are not entitled to equality only to the extent we teach, conduct research, and provide service the way men do. We are entitled to equality as matter of justice and dignity, and as a matter of belonging (Greschner 2002).

Second, we must build alliances with others who are seeking equality, as well as with those who have power and are willing to share it. As Robin DiAngelo

(2018) asserted in *White Fragility,* those of us with privilege assume that our experience is the norm and feel threatened when we begin to see that others experience disadvantage. As she suggests, issues of racism and discrimination are systemic and go far beyond individual moral culpability. The data, and evidence, collected in studies such as those in this volume create the space to build alliances. They can help those with power and privilege see that they too are caught within the structures that discriminate. We must also build alliances with our students as our population becomes increasingly diverse (Statistics Canada 2018). Those who are from marginalized communities rely on our presence to help create a path for them in their quest for a place of equality in Canadian society.

Third, building on our alliances, we also need solidarity across our diversity. Many of the remedies that will move us toward substantive equality must disrupt existing processes and values, and they must be pursued collectively, not individually. In addition to building relations with allies, we must sustain relationships among ourselves. The process of creating this book, from call for papers, to online authors' workshops, to shared manuscript reviews, provides an example. Social media spaces created for sharing experiences, finding support, and claiming authority are another.

Finally, we must speak up and insist that the inequality and discrimination that we experience are acknowledged so that those with power in the academy can no longer deny it. We must raise our voices and we must make space for those voices even more marginalized than our own. We must stop trying to squeeze ourselves into the space created by the hegemonic masculinity of university administration (Thornton 1989). We must insist that it is the responsibility of everyone to create an inclusive academy.

The editors of this collection set out to identify the issues that women face in the academy and create a conversation about best practices to address them. It is clear to me that they have succeeded. The breadth of research and the compelling documentation of the ways that women's experience in the academy is one of marginalization and silencing make it impossible for institutions to deny that universities still privilege white able-bodied men. They do so at the expense of many others who have an equal claim to be a part of the institutions that generate the knowledge and educate the young people who are building our shared future. As Chapter 13, which looks at U15 websites, illustrated by the relative absence of gender as an issue in diversity and inclusion, universities seem to think that gender inequality is resolved. As I have argued elsewhere, gender inequality is a wicked problem that needs the diverse participants to keep working together on a broad range of possible solutions (Turnbull 2010). This volume helps to define the problem, from the perspectives of the diverse women who are living it and who have gathered the evidence to prove it. Possible solutions and best practices flow directly from how we characterize the problem. The problem is systemic and structural, it includes white supremacy and patriarchy, and the time to address it is already past. The volume gives us the tools to roll up our sleeves and get to work ... again, and neither we nor our allies should remain silent.

NOTES

1 A note on this conclusion's title: "Silence is golden" is one part of an ancient proverb that suggests either that saying nothing is preferable to speaking or that saying nothing will allow one to properly formulate one's thoughts in order to speak with wisdom. The often forgotten part of the proverb is "speech is silvern," conveying the idea that speech also has value (Wasserstein 1999).
2 By way of example, in October of 2020, finding that female members of the Royal Canadian Mounted Police (RCMP) who job shared to manage childcare responsibilities were discriminated against in their access to pension benefits, the Supreme Court of Canada again reaffirmed that the equality guarantee in the Charter provides a means to remedy the harms of systemic discrimination (*Fraser* 2020).

WORKS CITED

Brodsky, Gwen, and Shelagh Day. 1989. "Canadian Charter Equality Rights for Women: One Step Forward or Two Steps Back." Ottawa: Canadian Advisory Council on the Status of Women.

DiAngelo, Robin. 2018. *White Fragility: Why It's So Hard for White People to Talk about Racism*. Boston: Beacon Press.

Feldthusen, Bruce. 1990. "The Gender Wars: Where the Boys Are." *Canadian Journal of Women and the Law* 4:66.

Greschner, Donna. 2002. "The Purpose of Canadian Equality Rights." *Review of Constitutional Studies* 6 (2): 291–323.

Hansen, N., and L.A. Turnbull. 2013. "Disability and Care: Still Not 'Getting It.'" *Canadian Journal of Women and the Law* 25 (1): 11–27.

McIntyre, Sheila. 1986. "Gender Bias within the Law School: The Memo and Its Impact." *Canadian Journal of Women and the Law* 2:362.

Mossman, Mary Jane. 1985. "'Otherness' and the Law School: A Comment on Teaching Gender Equality." *Canadian Journal of Women and the Law* 1:213.

–. 2021. "'Herculean Obstacles and Intrepid Complainants': The Sex Discrimination Complaint at Osgoode Hall Law School, 1987–1994." In *Gender and Careers in the Legal Academy,* edited by Ulrike Schultz, 898q–899c. Oxford: Hart Publishing.

Nickel, Nathan C., Lorna Turnbull, Elizabeth Wall-Wieler, Wendy Au, Okechukwu Ekuma, Leonard MacWilliam, Jennifer Emily Enns, Janelle Boram Lee, Scott McCulloch, Charles Burchill, and Marni Brownell. 2020. "Overlap between Child Protection Services and the Youth Justice System: Protocol for a Retrospective

Population-Based Cohort Study Using Linked Administrative Data in Manitoba, Canada." *BMJ Open.* doi:10.1136/bmjopen-2019-034895.

Squazzoni, Flaminio, Giangiacomo Bravo, Francisco Grimaldo, Daniel Garcıa-Costa, Mike Farjam, and Bahar Mehmani. 2020. "No Tickets for Women in the COVID-19 Race? A Study on Manuscript Submissions and Reviews in 2347 Elsevier Journals during the Pandemic." *PLoS ONE* 16 (10): e0257919. doi:10.2139/ssrn.3712813.

Statistics Canada. 2018. "Immigration and Ethnocultural Diversity in Canada." Catalogue no. 99-010-X. https://www12.statcan.gc.ca/nhs-enm/2011/as-sa/99-010-x/99-010-x2011001-eng.cfm.

Thornton, Margaret. 1989. "Hegemonic Masculinity and the Academy." *International Journal of Sociology of Law* 17:115.

Turnbull, L.A. 2006. "The Promise of Brooks v. Safeway Ltd.: Those Who Bear Children Should Not Be Disadvantaged." *Canadian Journal of Women and the Law* 17:161.

–. 2009. "A Way of Being in the World." *Justice Bertha Wilson: One Woman's Difference,* edited by Kim Brooks, 246–61. Vancouver: UBC Press.

–. 2010. "The Wicked Problem of Women's Economic Inequality." *Canadian Journal of Women and the Law* 23:271.

–. 2020. "Systemic Racism More than 'a Few Bad Apples.'" *Winnipeg Free Press,* July 14, 2020, A7.

Wasserstein, David J. 1999. "A West-East Puzzle: On the History of the Proverb 'Speech in Silver, Silence in Golden.'" *Israel Oriental Studies* 19:239.

Willsie, Janoah. 2020. "When It's Measured, It Matters: Disaggregated Race Data in Canada." *Policy Magazine,* June 17, 2020. https://policymagazine.ca/when-its-measured-it-matters-disaggregated-race-data-in-canada/.

CASE LAW

Andrews v Law Society of British Columbia [1989] 1 SCR 43

Brooks v Canada Safeway Inc [1989] 1 SCR 1219

Canadian National Railway Co v Canada (Action Travail des Femmes) [1987] 1 SCR 1114

Fraser v Canada (AG) 2020 SCC 28

Moore v British Columbia (Education) 2012 SCC 61

R v Kokopenace 2015 SCC 28

Balancing It All as a Contract Professor

MELISSA FINN

I spent years working as a contract professor while also tirelessly pursuing tenure-track appointments that eluded me. When I reflect on these experiences, I am astounded by the breadth of the sacrifices I made for my contract teaching roles and how little recognition and career advancement I received from them. As a woman, mother, and Muslim (among many other spiritual affiliations), my faith in the academy as a venue for intellectual innovation, a hub to teach methods of social transformation, and a place of work built on meritocracy is irretrievably broken. I can't speak for the sciences, but the social sciences and humanities are, in many respects, the opposite of these ideals; they are self-referential, wary of dynamism, out of touch with the reality of the real world and what is going on in the private sector (and suspicious of the private sector on principle), and hierarchically ordered in a near-military fashion, and they hire based on arbitrary and shifting markers of status rather than meritocratic logic.

I have many stories about challenges and visceral disappointments, but will share just one. Six months before I graduated with my PhD in 2011, I met with a department chair at a university in my hometown to introduce myself, pitch my teaching philosophy, and inquire about possible teaching jobs. Seeing potential in my enthusiasm, I was offered several sessional positions. I let the administrators know that I was pregnant and would have my baby at the end of the fall term. Very excited to finally get an academic work opportunity close to home and to be able to contribute financially to my family, I accepted a three-course load for the winter term. Five weeks after my second son was born in November of that year, I began teaching several courses for the first time. I distinctly remember holding my baby and trying to breastfeed him while also awkwardly trying to photocopy books for course readings, straining in two different directions, and feeling that I was reaching my physical limits. Still, I tarried on and delivered all forty-eight classes of that term. Long hours were spent typing emails and reading course materials while perpetually breastfeeding to keep my baby content and, to be frank, docile, so that I could get the work done. I would go to sleep at midnight and force myself to wake up at 3 a.m. to prepare for class at 9:30 a.m. It was bone-aching work that demanded mental and physical commitments from both me and my partner. Those profound and life-changing four months left me with a permanent stress line on my forehead. I did all of this to prove to myself and to my colleagues that I had what it takes to be employed in a permanent position. I now see that lack of self-care is based on a limiting belief that success demands self-effacement.

When my baby was three months old, I was invited to attend a fancy dinner with faculty colleagues and alumni after my class. A head administrator told me that I had "presence," and I thought this would be a great opportunity to gain important connections at this stage of my career. When my partner picked me up to take me to the restaurant, my baby was asleep in the car. We decided to let him keep sleeping. In retrospect, this was a very bad decision. In our family pre-mobile phone era, I spent most of the meal shuffling back and forth to the restaurant's front window to check on them in the parking lot. When the dinner was served, my son woke up and began screaming in the car. My partner tried to drive around the block to calm him down, but to no avail. I had to run from the gathering in haste with my food in take-out containers. The administrator who had invited me never looked at me the same way after that event. When I explained the situation to all in attendance before making my exit, he made me feel that I had embarrassed myself and him in front of the invited alumni and higher administrators. I did not feel very much empathy or understanding. When the term finally ended, I told a friend that I am hard to break but that this term had broken me. I was beyond burnt out.

In the years that followed, I continued to strive for a motherhood-work-life balance as a contract professor. I innovated in my teaching, built camaraderie in my department, tried to publish my work, and applied to a host of job positions. It was around this time that my situation turned around. I was offered a post-doctoral fellowship at the other big institution in my town. In this position, without the pressures of teaching, I was able to publish prolifically. But, even after the first year of my postdoc and after having published several academic articles, not one of the sixty tenure-track applications that I submitted bore the fruit of an interview. Neither did more applications to universities that knew me locally. Despite these disappointments, I continued to build my research profile.

After returning from fieldwork in Nairobi, where I examined Kenyan youth evaluations of counterterrorism policy, I attended a terrorism studies conference in Ottawa. I cannot even put into words how much of a watershed this event was for my life trajectory. I came to appreciate in a tangible way that being a Muslim woman in academia, especially one in hijab, can be a very lonely experience. During that conference, I watched a group of mainly white researchers go on and on about coding the speech acts of brown people for possible extremist language. The hairs on the back of my neck were going up. Challenging terrorism specialists at that time to see beyond the brown terrorist trope, to accept a woman academic in this field, and to accept that a Muslim woman academic might have a unique point of view worthy of consideration was a tremendous task. I left that workshop disillusioned by the white-centrism of terrorism studies specialists and angry about the ways that Islam is co-opted by fanatics. Drawing on my decade of experience studying terrorism, I started penning a letter-poem, which later became a seven-minute spoken-word track backed by music challenging the worldview of jihadis. I tried to convince my faculty coworkers and the dean of arts that spoken word and rap artforms and performances based on academic research were not only legitimate forms of research output and possibly forms of scholarly activism, but also pedagogical tools to enliven student interest in course material. Having performed poetry in my classes at least four times, I knew that it did enliven students, make them excited to come to class, and encourage them to see topics from new angles. Aside from friendly smiles, very few of my colleagues validated this idea or took it seriously. Academia's stodginess has driven me away from university teaching.

Today, I operate on the margins of academia in mind, body, and spirit, and in research practice. I am no longer invested in garnering interest and approval for what I do, and I have no interest in producing traditional academic outputs to satisfy hiring committees. The upside, and this may be surprising, is that after all of this struggle, I have found the deep inner courage to chart a professional career that is truly fulfilling because it's on my own terms.

Contributors

Sandra Acker is a professor emerita in the Department of Social Justice Education at the Ontario Institute for Studies in Education, University of Toronto.

Aisha Ahmad is an associate professor of political science at the University of Toronto.

Sara Anderson is the senior manager, Indigenous Research, at the University of Waterloo.

Tanya Bandula-Irwin is a PhD candidate at the University of Toronto whose research focuses on armed group taxation, rebel governance, and civil wars.

Catherine Beaudry is a professor and holder of the Canada Research Chair in Management and Economics of Innovation at Polytechnique Montréal.

Audrey E. Brennan is a PhD candidate and FNRS Research Fellow at Université Libre de Bruxelles (Cevipol) and Université Laval.

Kristin Burnett is a professor in the Department of Indigenous Studies at Lakehead University.

Michael F. Charles is the associate vice-president, Innovation, Inclusion, Reconciliation, and Healing, at Centennial College.

El Chenier is a professor in the Department of History at Simon Fraser University.

Jennifer Chisholm is an associate professor of Gender and Women's Studies at Lakehead University.

Cheryl N. Collier is dean of the Faculty of Arts, Humanities and Social Sciences, and a professor of political science at the University of Windsor.

Andrea M. Collins is an associate professor in the School of Environment, Resources and Sustainability and the Balsillie School of International Affairs at the University of Waterloo.

Kasey Egan is a PhD candidate at the University of Western Ontario in the Department of Gender, Sexuality, and Women's Studies.

Melissa Finn is a research associate in the Department of Political Science at the University of Waterloo specializing in the study of immigrant women, feminist economics, citizenship, transnationalism, youth studies, and cultural analysis.

Louise Forsyth is a professor emerita in the Department of Women's and Gender Studies at the University of Saskatchewan.

Genevieve Fuji Johnson (she/her) is a professor of political science at Simon Fraser University, which is on the traditional and unceded territories of the Musqueam, Squamish, Tsleil-Waututh, and Kwikwetlem Nations. She is a Yonsei settler of Japanese and Irish ancestry.

Elena Ignatovich is a professional programs manager at the UBC School of Population and Public Health. She recently graduated with a PhD in Educational Studies from the University of British Columbia.

Rachael Johnstone is an assistant professor of political science at Dalhousie University.

Joshua W. Katz is a PhD candidate in psychology at the University of Saskatchewan.

Jessica M. McCutcheon is an applied social psychology graduate from the University of Saskatchewan whose research focuses on gay and lesbian topics, gender roles, and mothering.

Bessma Momani is a professor of political science and associate vice-president, international, at the University of Waterloo. She is also a senior fellow at the Centre for International Governance Innovation and a non-resident fellow at the Arab Gulf States Institute in Washington, DC.

Melanie A. Morrison is a social psychologist and full professor in the Department of Psychology and Health Studies in the College of Arts and Science at the University of Saskatchewan.

Todd G. Morrison is a professor in the Department of Psychology and Health Studies at the University of Saskatchewan.

Maryam Nabavi is director of the Academic Leadership Development Program and an academic leadership coach at the University of British Columbia.

Janice Niemann is a PhD candidate in the Department of English at the University of Victoria and a faculty member in the English Department at Camosun College.

Andrea Quinlan is an associate professor in the Department of Sociology and Legal Studies at the University of Waterloo.

Bidushy Sadika is a PhD candidate in social psychology, specializing in migration and ethnic relations, at Western University, with research areas including intersectionality and feminist theories, gender roles, and the experiences of immigrants and newcomers in Canada.

Amorell Saunders N'Daw is a partner in the research firm KBRS and the lead for EDI.

Özlem Sensoy is a professor and the director of the Cassidy Centre for Educational Justice in the Faculty of Education at Simon Fraser University. She is of settler Middle Eastern ancestry, aspiring toward living and working respectfully on occupied Coast Salish territories.

Sandra Smele is a researcher with interests in care, intersectionality, and social gerontology.

Laurence Solar-Pelletier holds a PhD in management from HEC Montreal and is working in innovation management.

Carl St-Pierre is a research professional in statistics at Polytechnique Montréal.

Katherine V.R. Sullivan is a PhD candidate in the Department of Political Science at the University of Montreal.

Lorna A. Turnbull is a professor in the Faculty of Law and an adjunct scientist in the Manitoba Centre for Health Policy, Rady Faculty of Health Sciences, at the University of Manitoba.

Anne Wagner is a retired associate professor in the School of Social Work at Nipissing University.

Jude Walker is an associate professor in Adult Learning and Education at the University of British Columbia.

Index

Note: "(f)" after a page number indicates a figure; "(t)" after a page number indicates a table. BIPOC stands for Black, Indigenous, and people of colour; CRCP, for Canada Research Chairs Program; EDI, for equity, diversity, and inclusion; REB, for research ethics board; SET, for student evaluation of teaching; SSH, for social sciences and humanities; STEM, for science, technology, engineering, and mathematics; and TRC, for Truth and Reconciliation Commission. Subentries of the entry "equity, diversity, and inclusion (EDI), strategies to advance, at university leadership level" are arranged as presented in the text rather than alphabetically, with subentries indicated by parenthetical roman numerals.

Printed and bound in Canada

Set in Zurich Condensed, Sero, and Minion
by Artegraphica Design Co.

Copyeditor: Candida Hadley

Proofreader: Kristy Lynn Hankewitz

Indexer: Cheryl Lemmens

Cover designer: Setareh Ashrafologhalai